MacArthur and West Point

MacArthur
AND
WEST POINT

How the General and the Academy Shaped Each Other

Sherman L. Fleek

Texas A&M University Press
College Station

Copyright © 2024 by Sherman L. Fleek
All rights reserved

First edition

This paper meets the requirements of ANSI/NISO Z39.48-1992 (Permanence of Paper). Binding materials have been chosen for durability.

Library of Congress Cataloging-in-Publication Data

Names: Fleek, Sherman L., author.
Title: MacArthur and West Point: how the General and the Academy shaped each other / Sherman L. Fleek.
Other titles: Williams-Ford Texas A&M University military history series.
Description: First edition. | College Station: Texas A&M University Press, [2024] | Series: Williams-Ford Texas A&M University military history series | Includes bibliographical references and index.
Identifiers: LCCN 2023053068 (print) | LCCN 2023053069 (ebook) | ISBN 9781648431890 (cloth) | ISBN 9781648431906 (ebook)
Subjects: LCSH: MacArthur, Douglas, 1880–1964—Military leadership. | United States. Army—Officers—Biography. | United States Military Academy—History—20th century. | United States Military Academy—Influence. | Generals—United States—Biography. | Military education—New York (State)—West Point—History—20th century. | United States—History, Military—20th century. | LCGFT: Biographies.
Classification: LCC E745.M3 F57 2024 (print) | LCC E745.M3 (ebook) | DDC 973.9/4—dc23/eng/20231204
LC record available at https://lccn.loc.gov/2023053068
LC ebook record available at https://lccn.loc.gov/2023053069

CONTENTS

Preface: Discovering an Enigma vii

Introduction: *The Academy and the General* 1

1 The School above the Hudson 9
2 A Military Family 21
3 Facing the Beast: *New Cadet MacArthur* 36
4 The Corps 53
5 Classmates, Connections, and Careers .73
6 Fighting in France 88
7 Chaos on the Hudson 103
8 King of West Point: *Superintendent MacArthur* 115
9 Reforming the Monastery 139
10 Mentoring the Long Gray Line in Peace 163
11 Chief of Staff: Saving the Army 175
12 The Field Marshal Prepares for War 194
13 More War and Victory 211

14	American Shogun	237
15	The Fall	254
16	Home at Last	273
	Epilogue: *MacArthur and Memory at the Academy*	295

Notes 305
Bibliography 337
Index 345

PREFACE

Discovering an Enigma

History is a journey of discovery at times. It was for me. Prior to assuming the position as the command historian of the US Military Academy in May 2009, I had formed my own opinion about Douglas MacArthur. I look back now and realize how uninformed I was, being basically neutral regarding MacArthur's legacy. As most military historians I viewed General MacArthur as a great and significant historical figure, a central actor in the Pacific war against the Japanese, who was also a dazzling and vainglorious individual. I had read some books that dealt with him in a larger context of military history. I knew scarcely little about him as a man or a historical character and his contributions. My knowledge of Douglas MacArthur was like that of Winston Churchill, a towering giant in world history, but what made him so?

Then, some twenty years ago I read William Manchester's *American Caesar* and felt it was a quality telling of a complicated and controversial man who was wrapped and hidden in historical mystery—an enigma. I accepted this well-written and researched biography as the gospel; now I see it as the gospel according to Manchester. I read more in other books and soon perceived that Douglas MacArthur was accomplished, intelligent, even brilliant, and courageous to the point of recklessness, juxtaposed to his scheming and deliberate plotting to rise to greatness and glory. He was one of the greatest strategists ever, demonstrated at Inchon, the powerful American shogun of Japan, which few American soldiers could have equaled.

Over the years I had learned that many of my fellow military historians and even comrades in arms in the US Army had a low opinion of General MacArthur—to the point of contempt. I was often surprised by the venomous attacks by others against the hero of the Great War with his dozens of decorations for gallantry. The criticism of "Dugout Doug" rose time and time again, as did his blatant contempt for official policy resulting in his relief in 1951 during the Korean War by President Harry Truman. The first is untrue and unwarranted; the second stands, as Truman was justified to remove MacArthur as commander in the Far East and Korea. In a way I felt sorry for Douglas MacArthur without having really explored his life and character thoroughly. Still, I saw him as a great general and perhaps a misunderstood historical character, but I was not interested in pursuing any serious investigation into this very controversial American soldier. MacArthur was not my favorite general and combat leader, but I could not deny his accomplishments. I would not have liked to serve with or under MacArthur as a soldier.

Then I became the command historian at West Point in 2009. As a nongraduate of the US Military Academy, I was overwhelmed with the grandeur, traditions, and complexity of my stewardship over an amazing American institution that had just seven years earlier commemorated its bicentennial anniversary in 2002. I commenced a deep dive into the files, records, archives, books, and articles published to learn the history of this amazing place. I soon learned the stories, myths, and shining reputation of this military college that trained and educated Grant, Sheridan, Sherman, Pershing, and in modern times Omar Bradley and Dwight Eisenhower—and also Douglas MacArthur.

As I dived into the maze of history, the name and shadow, yes, the very image of Douglas MacArthur rose again and again. I had attempted to be neutral about him for years, but I did know that I had no interest to investigate him further. But, as I dug deeper and deeper into West Point's past, MacArthur was always there. His influence and contribution were so immense, so present, and so long-lasting; it was impossible to deny. I struggled with all the information and evidence I learned about MacArthur's accomplishments not only as a cadet but especially as the superintendent. I then realized that throughout his entire life he was absolutely devoted to the academy and the corps of cadets. The academy was his beacon in life. West Point was his home.

I recall a few years ago conducting a tour of the academy for a visiting retired four-star general of the US Air Force. As we approached the statue of General MacArthur at the corner of MacArthur Barracks, I began my standard MacArthur presentation, when the general interrupted me, "Sherman, I am no fan of Douglas MacArthur, not at all." He paused, then continued: "Yet, if one considers his life and service with personal integrity, one cannot help but realize and admit that MacArthur's accomplishments were significant, even astounding." I recorded these comments that evening in my personal journal.

On occasion I was asked as the West Point historian, Who was the most distinguished person associated with the school? Who contributed the most? Or, who influenced the academy above all else? The answer is, of course, Sylvanus Thayer, the Father of West Point, class of 1808. His influence as superintendent for sixteen years is unmatched and unsurpassed by anyone, especially in the early years and the nineteenth century. Following behind Thayer, but still next in line in influencing and shaping the academy in the twentieth century, is Douglas MacArthur. In the modern era his reforms, his vision, his guidance, and his leadership cemented West Point as one of the great institutions of higher learning in the land.

In nearly every aspect of the modern academy, Douglas MacArthur's hand is there: from academics to intercollegiate sports, from military training to a vision of the future campus and the school's mission, from governance to creating the honor system, all of which are hallmarks of West Point today. General MacArthur's fingerprints are on every facet of the academy. As a graduate pronounced, "If Sylvanus Thayer was the Father of the Military Academy, then MacArthur was its savior," meaning Superintendent MacArthur rescued West Point from oblivion after its near devastation during the Great War, where five classes graduated in less than two years.[1]

This knowledge led me to research and reconsider MacArthur's entire life and career. Here again, I was soon impressed by his enormous service and accomplishments in both war and peace. In fact, as army chief of staff he basically saved the officer corps from a severe reduction at the hands of President Franklin Roosevelt and his advisors during the Great Depression. His cooperation with New Deal advisors saved the officer corps from a severe reduction when they served as a cadre for training the new Civilian Conservation Corps beginning in 1933.

• • •

I never really considered writing a book about General MacArthur, even though I eventually recognized his tremendous achievements. I also knew of his baggage, a long train of unseemly behavior, radical impulses, vanity, poor decisions, and sometimes just plain pettiness. Thus, the human and frail side of a great soldier.

In the spring of 2014 I was invited to participate at a MacArthur Week Conference in Milwaukee, Wisconsin, the MacArthur family ancestral home. I was honored to speak at several venues about MacArthur's connection to West Point as a cadet and later as superintendent. Two results from this week became an amazing epiphany for me. First, I realized something I never understood as an American about the general. Second, I saw the opportunity to tell a story about Douglas MacArthur that has not been previously presented in a thorough way.

The week was so enlightening for me, meeting hundreds of people who respected and praised Douglas MacArthur the man and his legacy, and a few who did not. In fact, I encountered several speakers and presenters on the program who had great contempt for MacArthur. It was in small-group discussions that these people readily shared this very negative attitude. This proves that MacArthur was indeed a great historical figure, for there is both immense admiration and condemnation of the man.

The Saturday-morning agenda at Marquette University Law School inspired me as never before about MacArthur the soldier and the statesman. As an American I walked away with a new understanding that I had never fully realized. On the program were four guest speakers from four different nations, including one from a former enemy nation in World War II—Japan. I heard four consul generals—diplomats, not historians—declare the great respect and honor that they had for Douglas MacArthur. I sat amazed to hear these comments from foreign guests. I also recalled discussions earlier that week by a few fellow historians and their disdain for the general. Now I was hearing four accomplished representatives of foreign nations sing MacArthur's praises: to the Australian people he was the friend and protector; to the Filipinos he was the great liberator; to South Koreans he was the defending shield from Communist aggression; then ironically, to the Japanese he was first the vile, cursed enemy but later became the great law-giver, like Moses, who wrote and ordained Japan's first democratic constitution. I listened to these words of praise, admiration, honor, and even a feeling of reverence for this American. I had not understood this quality before, how foreign peoples

Statue of Douglas MacArthur, relocated and dedicated during MacArthur Week, Milwaukee, Wisconsin, May 2014. *Author's collection.*

and their representatives felt seventy years later, praise for MacArthur that I saw that afternoon that some Americans denied. More was to come.

That evening at the grand banquet in the Milwaukee Art Museum, the keynote speaker was the former Australian minister of defense and now the ambassador to the United States, Kim Beazley. For nearly an hour Ambassador Beazley spoke of how it was the United States, not Great Britain, that Australia turned to for the defense of its island nation. This American support came in the form of General MacArthur. Ambassador Beazley explained how Australian prime minister John Curtin and MacArthur, though polar opposites politically, drew together as allies against their common enemy, the Empire of Japan. They eventually became close friends, and it was the United States and Australia who were the major players in most of the great and bloody campaigns in the Southwest Pacific Area, which MacArthur commanded. I knew this factually, but not internally and personally.

The "MacArthur week" inspired me in another way. The several presentations and panels I participated in, and the research I made in preparation, convinced me that no one has completed a thorough study of MacArthur's connection with, influence over, and contribution to West Point. Also, how he looked upon the academy as his home, and relished any time or association with the school. This inspired me. As the historian and one of the foremost experts of the history of the academy, I was in the best position and had the resources and great opportunity to write a book about MacArthur and West Point.

It was about three years later, in 2017, that I began to outline and research some of the material on hand. As with most research projects, the more I looked, the more I found, and the more I relished the chance to do so. It was a great gift, even a calling or duty to write about a great American institution, the US Military Academy, and a remarkable, distinguished, but imperfect, graduate: Douglas MacArthur.

Finally, I state that I have always loved the William Shakespeare quote from his play, *Twelfth Night* which is very fitting here:

Some are born great, some achieve greatness,
and some have greatness thrown upon them.

If one considers the life and career of General Douglas MacArthur, he actually fits all three categories of greatness: he was born in a military family; his father, Arthur MacArthur Jr., was a hero and commander in the American Civil War; and he was also a recipient of the Medal of Honor, the highest decoration in the US military. MacArthur achieved greatness because of his amazing abilities, intelligence, talents, dedication, and his sense of honor and service, and his incredible courage on the battlefield. Lastly, MacArthur, like many world historical figures, lived during some of the great events of world history, and thus he was thrust into the midst of these major historical epics—the two world wars, the Great Depression, and then the early Cold War and later the Korean War.

Douglas MacArthur's incredible success is a credit to the US Military Academy that he adored. Yet, in America, even among historians and even some US military officers, General MacArthur is not well regarded. His personality, leadership style, and failures have been highlighted and often exaggerated. Here I say: no world historical figure, leader, and especially general, is perfect in all things and every decision. MacArthur certainly had his faults and shortcomings.

• • •

Soldiers are always a part of a team, and as a veteran of the US Army for some twenty-five years, I therefore acknowledge the assistance, guidance, and inspiration that friends, colleagues, and supporters provided. This book would not have materialized without two events in my life: first, serving as command historian at West Point for fourteen years; secondly, in May 2014 I attended MacArthur Week in Milwaukee, Wisconsin, where I realized this important story. After all, Milwaukee was the MacArthur family ancestral homeland. The agents behind my invitation to Milwaukee were two great Americans: Chas Mulchay, a community leader and a participant in the 1979 MacArthur Week when a statue of the General MacArthur was dedicated, and Maj. Gen. Paul Lima, retired, USMA class of 1967, who arranged for my visit and served as a sponsor for me. I will always appreciate Milwaukee's hospitality.

I greatly appreciate and thank several friends and colleagues who read, advised, and made recommendations on the manuscript. Lt. Col. Joseph Whitehorne, US Army retired, PhD and retired college professor, who has read every book manuscript I have published; I greatly thank him. West Point faculty members Brig. Gen. Lance Betros, class of 1977 and former head of the Department of History and later dean at the US Army War College, provided a thorough review, especially with his expertise on the history of the academy; and Col. Bryan Gibby, class of 1990, and deputy head of the academy's history department, is no great fan of General MacArthur, but he made many helpful recommendations and insights, especially concerning the Korea War period.

No quality scholarly book dealing with Douglas MacArthur can possibly succeed without the assistance of the MacArthur Memorial in Norfolk, Virginia. There towers James Zobel, the memorial archivist, the leading world authority on the collections, documents, and story of the general. I spent many days with Jim among the stacks, books, files, and documents mining and drilling for any and all evidence relative to my story.

MacArthur and West Point

INTRODUCTION

★ ★ ★ ★ ★

THE ACADEMY AND THE GENERAL

The evening waned across Manila Bay as ripples of water slapped against the plywood hulls of four small watercraft. Tied to a dock on Corregidor Island, the quartet of US Navy torpedo patrol boats was urgently awaiting the arrival of eighteen passengers. These passengers were military officers, and one small family: a father, a mother, a young boy, and a Chinese family housekeeper. The father, Gen. Douglas MacArthur, commanded the US Army Forces in the Far East, a command created in July 1941. He had been ordered to Australia by President Franklin Roosevelt because that more than a hundred thousand Japanese soldiers had invaded the Philippines and would soon reach Corregidor, the last bastion of Allied defense. Roosevelt would not allow a commander of MacArthur's rank, prestige, and ability to waste away for years in Japanese prison camp. He was needed for the war effort. General MacArthur himself was infuriated by the order to abandon Corregidor and avoided acting on it for weeks. Finally, he relented and prepared to leave. Strong emotions and shame engulfed him.

Looking up at Topside, a hill mass of Corregidor, MacArthur knew that Col. Paul Bunker, his US Military Academy classmate, was there, commanding his coast artillery regiments that were protecting Corregidor. He recorded this memory: "Forty years had passed since [Paul] Bunker had been twice selected by Walter Camp for the All-American team. I could shut my eyes and see again that blond head racing, tearing, plunging—210 pounds of irresistible power. I could almost hear Quarterback Charley Daly's shrill voice barking, 'Bunker back.' He and many others up there were old, old friends, bound by ties of deepest comradeship."[1]

The Paul Bunker story is one of the great West Point tragedies of the war. He would die two years later in a Japanese prisoner-of-war camp. The unity and ties MacArthur mentioned were strong and tangible among the graduates of the US Military Academy—especially for him. As MacArthur readied to leave seventy thousand of his soldiers behind and millions of Filipinos at the mercy of the brutal Japanese army, his thoughts turned to a classmate from West Point.

• • •

General of the Army Douglas MacArthur is one of the great historical figures in American and military history. Both loathed and revered, with some scholars and laypeople finding a middle ground between these two polar opposites, Douglas MacArthur remains one of the most extraordinary and controversial American soldiers ever. He continues to be an enigma: full of greatness, but with contradictions and foibles. Dozens of books about MacArthur praise his enormous triumphs and contributions, and nearly the same number condemn his outrageous character, failures, and personal flaws. One contemporary of MacArther, Benjamin Foulois, chief of the Army Air Corps in the 1930s when MacArthur was army chief of staff, keenly observed: "Aloof, yet understanding, military to the core, yet warmly human when you were alone with him, MacArthur was the kind of man you either deeply respected or hated with a passion. I not only respected him, I believed him to be possessed of almost godlike qualities."[2]

The subject of this book is the reciprocal influence between the US Military Academy and General MacArthur. More than a narration of his time at the academy as a cadet and then returning as superintendent, these pages focus on MacArthur *and* West Point, not merely MacArthur "at" West Point. Not only did this institution shape him, but he also shaped it—and many of those contributions remain today in some form, or at least in spirit. He is considered one of the few reformers and visionaries who guided and changed the direction of the academy. Also, in letters, speeches, official documents, and his personal contacts, he continually referred to West Point and its influence over time. Another important story, explained later, was that of his classmates and their close ties and relationships—born of their cadet days together.

Unlike most people, Douglas MacArthur never really had a home. The son of a career army officer, he moved frequently and never experienced the stability of hometown and common surroundings. Yet during his life, when asked about a home, he would usually say that West Point was home. The military academy became bookends to his professional career. He arrived on the storied Plain high above the Hudson River in 1899 at the age of nineteen to begin his profound career. More than sixty years later, he returned to the academy in 1962 to receive the annual Sylvanus Thayer Award, the highest award presented by the academy to an individual. At age eighty-two the still spry general delivered his enduring "Duty, Honor, Country" speech, the most legendary and popular speech given at West Point about the academy's legacy. This was the bookend of his public life. He died two years later.

There is little doubt that the US Military Academy had a tremendous impact on MacArthur in his young adult years and through his entire life. The education he received there, the leadership lessons, and the comradeship of his classmates were bulwarks in his life. Not only did the institution shape and influence him, but he in turn made lasting and valuable contributions to guide and direct this military college through a century of significant change and evolution. He looked upon West Point as one of the great beacons of America, an institution as significant as other governmental entities. MacArthur's regard for the academy is expressed by D. Clayton James, whose masterful three-volume biography remains the most detailed and comprehensive study yet: "Although most of its alumni felt a strong attachment to the school, MacArthur's loyalty and affection for his alma mater were unusually deep and seemed to grow with the years."[3]

Returning from World War I to become one of the youngest superintendents of West Point, MacArthur immersed himself in the world of the academy, bringing a zest of ideas and a new vision to challenge the entrenched faculty, who, like granite monuments, were sentinels of tradition and for decades guarded the sacred shrines of the status quo. MacArthur and West Point were akin to friends who challenged and taught each other, maintaining the closest

Cadet Douglas MacArthur was also First Captain of the class of 1903. *Courtesy MacArthur Memorial.*

of ties for decades. His regard for this institution was further strengthened by the friendship and soldierly comradery of the ninety-three graduates from his class of 1903. For decades, these graduates served together, corresponded to each other, and grew old together. A vast body of wonderful letters and memorials remain today—a testament of the college-aged young men who as soldiers endured a difficult and formative experience through the crucible of two world wars, the Great Depression, and the challenges of post-war modernity. They became men and remained friends throughout their lives regardless of rank, position, wealth, and status. Their missives are another legacy of MacArthur and West Point: the binding ties of a class of cadets who survived a rigid ordeal and then learned to value each other as friends and comrades.

Yet, it appears that General MacArthur did not judge fellow officers and especially subordinates by whether they wore a West Point graduate's ring. He probably expected more from academy graduates, but he never showed any prejudice or favoritism based on an officer's commissioning source. One of his heroes, fellow West Pointer of the class of 1843, General and President U. S. Grant, based much of his regard for combat leaders on whether an officer was an academy graduate. Lt. Col. Adam Badeau, Grant's military secretary, wrote in 1887, "He [Grant] preferred West Point men as soldiers, he loved them as friends.... He thought higher of Sherman and Sheridan because they were graduates of the Academy."[4] This was not true of MacArthur, because some of his closest and most cherished comrades were either not academy graduates or were from the US Navy, US Marine Corps, and US Army Air Forces—and, after 1947, the US Air Force. Judging them on their ability, leadership, and performance, MacArthur did not care what tribe they belonged to. MacArthur had both friends and detractors among the other services—again not by plan but by circumstance. He did demonstrate some prejudice against foreign officers and would not allow US troops to serve under Australian or British officers during World War II.

The book in your hands is more than a study of MacArthur's time at West Point—four years as a cadet and three years as its superintendent. Instead, it will explore and explain how the relationship of Douglas MacArthur and the US Military Academy shaped each other and informed their legendary stature. The influence that General MacArthur and West Point had on each other is significant and has not been pursued adequately. The chapters that follow will demonstrate and establish the unusual relationship between a significant historical figure and a storied American institution.

This association is staggered and carries a presumption. The US Military Academy was nearly a hundred years old when young Douglas arrived in 1899; in fact, as a cadet he would participate in the Centennial Commemoration ceremony in 1902. Cadet MacArthur left a unique and inspiring record in both leadership and scholarship and was also a bold example of suffering from a long-held cadet practice—hazing. He led the Corps of Cadets as cadet First Captain and graduated top of his class academically. MacArthur today is considered by many as having the highest cadet academic record ever, which is not true and is impossible to determine. Though these achievements as a cadet did not change or cause any reforms or evolution of the school directly, MacArthur's cadet years prepared him for a brilliant and controversial career as an agent of change later for the academy. The monastery, as he called it, was stagnant and entombed in tradition and paternalism when the young superintendent unleashed a whirlwind of reforms during his brief three years (1919–22) as superintendent.

General MacArthur's professional thoughts, dreams, and aspirations were based on his cadet years from the values and lessons he learned at the academy. Any success he achieved later, he attributed to his foundational experience at West Point. MacArthur enshrined his love and influence for this bastion of military training, character development, and educational excellence in all he did. A major theme is how he followed and lived the academy's motto, "Duty, Honor, Country," that was established in 1898, one year before he arrived and took the oath of allegiance on the famous Plain. The question to ask is: Did Douglas MacArthur remain true to the values and virtues of Duty, Honor, Country during his career and life? This can only be answered by following his life chronologically. Although this book is not a biography of the general, it traces his life path and highlights his relationships with other graduates, his emphasis and influence on the academy, and his adherence to West Point's foundational principles.

As you read along, you will encounter many statements and reminiscences of individuals associated with MacArthur, especially many of his academy classmates. They shed light on the fellowship and bond that West Point engrained in these men for all their lives. They corresponded tenderly and often, using their first names in salutations, regardless of rank and position. There are many others who commented on MacArthur's regard and loyalty to the academy, many of whom were not graduates. Historians have often examined and written about MacArthur's time and experience at West Point. But the real story is more than just seven years of his more than fifty years of service. It is, rather, what Douglas MacArthur himself felt, expressed, and recorded;

and how the military academy was changed, reformed, or evolved due to his influence, whether at the academy or apart from it. Although not an in-depth study of his life, the book follows MacArthur's passage through time, providing enough background to base the connections that he made or attained as a member of the "Long Gray Line," as alumni call their fellow graduates.

The closeness and comradery of West Pointers of all classes and eras are legendary, because of their common experience and tradition. For MacArthur and most members of the Long Gray Line, their friends and classmates joined together as a family in love and respect. There remain the rivalries, the pettiness, and attitudes of human frailty throughout, however. Douglas MacArthur was not Douglas MacArthur without West Point: it is impossible to separate the two. Most graduates feel the same. But, though MacArthur loved and respected his fellow West Pointers, his loyalty lay more strongly with the US Army and the nation, regardless of source of commission. Despite his great love for the academy, he never condemned or cast off officers because they hadn't worn cadet gray.

Besides the published works about MacArthur, I have read through some of the vast collections of primary sources in libraries, depositories, and other sources that explain and analyze the general, his life, his decisions, and his personality. As well, I have researched hundreds of letters and other documents at the MacArthur Memorial in Norfolk, Virginia, from his classmates and others who served with the general during his career. Another fascinating segment of this study is how military and American history and culture and the media have popularized MacArthur's connection to West Point, which I weave into the story. Finally, I have also made use of the academy's archives of rare source material and a collection of MacArthur's documents.

Anyone who has read or written anything about General MacArthur knows that West Point was more than just a school or a college experience for him. The academy to Douglas MacArthur was a shrine, a warrior's Valhalla, and a Greek temple for soldiers; it was his dream as young boy and a romantic remembrance all his life. When asked during his long life where his home was, he often answered in two ways: the Philippines because of his many years stationed there, but more often (as noted earlier), West Point. In his final great public address at the academy in May 1962, he said to the assembled Corps of Cadets: "In the evening of my memory, always I come back to West Point.

Always there echoes and reechoes in my ears—Duty-Honor-Country.... I want you to know that when I cross the river my last conscious thoughts will be of the Corps—and the Corps—and the Corps."[5]

Douglas MacArthur's adoration of the academy was based on the fact that his father, Arthur MacArthur Jr., career officer and Medal of Honor recipient, did not attend West Point but was a volunteer officer during the Civil War. Arthur MacArthur felt his sons had an obligation to serve their country.[6] Arthur MacArthur III, the oldest son, graduated from the US Naval Academy in 1896 and had a splendid career that was cut short after twenty years by a premature death from natural causes.

Then came Douglas, four years younger, who chose the US Military Academy. As you will read in the pages that follow, he and West Point shaped and molded each other as no other graduate of the US Military Academy has done before or since.

CHAPTER 1

★ ★ ★ ★ ★

THE SCHOOL ABOVE THE HUDSON

Before there was the United States Military Academy, there was West Point, the military garrison. For more than two hundred years, the two terms have been interchangeable. But it was not always that way. The story of West Point begins in the early colonial times when the Europeans first trespassed on the native soil of the New World. The Lenni Lenape, who were Delaware Indians, inhabited this rich and verdant land along a majestic river for centuries, long before the Europeans arrived. In their dialect known as Munsee, the Lenni Lenape called this river *Muhheakantuck*, "the river that flows two ways." The river did in fact flow two ways, with its normal current south to coast waters and then the daily tides ebbing northward against the current.

In September 1609 a European carrack sailed slowly north up the majestic river with the green-blue waves washing against the small ship. Channeling the river were a range of hills, like the Highlands of Scotland, beautiful, green with deep forests and scraggy granite ledges and cliff faces. The ship, christened the *Halve Maen*, or *Half Moon*, was owned by the Dutch East India Company (de Vereenigde Oost-Indische Compagnie). The hired captain, an Englishman, was an experienced navigator and sailing master who had sought the infamous Northwest Passage: Henry Hudson.[1]

Arriving at what is now New York harbor, the crew saw the mouth of the "North River," as other Europeans had named it. Hudson and his sixteen-man crew, half Dutch and half English, sailed north along the palisades on the western shore. Continuing up the river past Verplanck's Point, the river narrowed as the land rose into a range of hills that stood several hundred feet above, at Anthony's Nose and Bear Mountain, future names of significant landmarks.

Eventually, the *Half Moon* reached a prominent point jutting out from the west bank, where the river made a hard left turn below cliffs and a mesa-like tabletop of land, clear of trees and foliage. Looking up at the steep cliff-like ridge, Hudson and crew saw the Storm King Mountain. Where Hudson anchored the ship on the night of September 14, 1609, is not precisely known, but it was probably a little north of the flat mesa. This land—the highland hills and especially the promontory—are now enshrined in the history, lore, and memory of an American institution; a military academy that two centuries later would be founded on the famous Plain above the Hudson River named after the English sailing master who served the Dutch East India Company.[2]

In 1674 the English gained permanent control over New Netherland, which included much of eastern New York, with New Amsterdam (New York City) and Fort Orange (Albany) remaining the chief towns. Under English and later the rule of Great Britain, the colony of New York and its great future city prospered.[3] Influential and wealthy colonists gained land grants from the British monarchs and also Parliament. In 1723 the mesa, surrounding hills, and shore land adjacent to "The West Point" were granted to Charles Congreve. His royal grant of 1,463 acres occupied much of the future academy land. A smaller grant of 332 acres was awarded to John Moore in 1747. The area around the Plain was sparsely occupied; a few families lived on or near these larger tracts of lands. The West Point because of its flat plain was an ideal place for ranging cattle and sheep. Across the river was Martalear's Rock, with marshland that connected the east bank to the massive hill and stony outcroppings that ran nearly due west–east for about a mile.[4]

West Point and the Revolution

The American revolutionary cause was a roller-coaster ride of impressive victories and devastating defeats, a war of exhaustion that the British people and

King George III could not endure. Weeks after the battles of Lexington and Concord in April 1775, the patriots developed a poorly devised defensive plan for the Hudson Highlands; unfortunately, not using the full potential of the terrain and surrounding land, the amateur soldiers built a simple blockhouse on the north side of the Hudson on Martalear's Rock, later renamed Constitution Island. As the war progressed, the importance of the Hudson River as a waterway for armies and supplies became more apparent to both sides. In 1781 Gen. George Washington called West Point, the fortress garrison, "the most important Post in America."[5] Of course this reality was not apparent until much later in the war, but the geography and situation dictated future events at West Point.

From the initial and poorly conceived efforts to guard and control the river, eventually West Point became a Gibraltar for the patriot cause. However, in October 1777 the Americans lost a small but significant battle fought five miles to the south at Forts Montgomery and Clinton, at the foot of Bear Mountain. The British under Gen. Sir Henry Clinton advanced north from New York City to support two other British armies converging on Albany. The major British campaign failed when the British army from Canada was defeated and surrendered at Saratoga in October and General Clinton returned to New York.[6]

Taking advantage of their significant victory, Continental forces returned to the Hudson Highlands and in January 1778 established a stronger, permanent garrison at West Point and the surrounding hills. A regiment of Brig. Gen. Samuel Parsons's Connecticut Brigade crossed the ice-bound Hudson River from Constitution Island in late January 1778 and bivouacked on the famous Plain of West Point.[7]

The Continental Line regulars set out to construct a new fortress using the turns of the river and steep cliffs and emplaced two iron 1,700-foot-long chains across the river to block any ship sailing up the Hudson. Eight shore batteries, four on each side of the river, with some four guns each covered the river against British ships trying to force their way north. The fortress complex was completed by Washington's Polish staff engineer, Tadeusz Kosciusko, who fought for the new American republic. The fortifications at West Point were the patriots' most effective and comprehensive bastion made during the American Revolution. The garrison had two belts of chain, the thinner boom and the larger chain that spanned the 1,700-foot-wide river. Above the shore batteries on the flat Plain was Fort Arnold (later Clinton), which guarded the approaches and rear of the shore batteries. There were smaller forts and redoubts on both sides of the river that protected the shore batteries. The garrison troops were quartered on the Plain, and they manned the forts and redoubts. These defenses in the eighteenth century were very formidable.[8]

The British never attempted an armed attack against fortress West Point, but they nearly gained this crucial garrison through conspiracy and intrigue. Maj. Gen. Benedict Arnold was one of the great American combat leaders during the Revolutionary War, and he assumed command of West Point in August 1780. Previously, Arnold had helped take Fort Ticonderoga in 1775 with its large arsenal of siege guns and artillery. In December 1775, during the American invasion of British Canada, he was wounded at the battle of Quebec, which was a factor in the American defeat. He stopped the British in their attempt to dominate Lake Champlain in 1776. There he and his Continental soldiers constructed small gunboats and neutralized the British flotilla. In 1777 at Saratoga, Arnold led major forces and eventually defeated the British in two major engagements—being wounded again in the process—and causing British Gen. John Burgoyne's surrender. Arnold's combat finesse and valor were beyond question, but his ambition for promotions and his perception of enemies eroded his loyalty to the patriot cause. He faced a court-martial for misusing public property and funds in Philadelphia in 1779.[9]

Arnold's serious combat wounds allowed him to request command of West Point in order to accomplish a conspiracy he had entered into with the British. His attempt to turn over the garrison to the British failed. He escaped and later fought for the British in the Southern colonies. Benedict Arnold remains one of the most hated and notorious villains in American history—the legendary traitor.[10]

After the American victories at Saratoga and other battles in 1777, the French entered the war and supported the American cause. The final triumph at Yorktown, Virginia, in October 1781 ended the fighting against Great Britain. The final peace was achieved in 1783 with the Treaty of Paris. The American colonies were no longer politically bound to the United Kingdom of Great Britain.

Peace Comes to West Point

The end of war nearly brought the end of the American military establishment, officially the Continental Line, predecessor of the United States Army. By the end of 1783, Congress was grappling with the reduction of the Continental army, having no clear authority to maintain a standing army under the weak and impotent Articles of Confederation. Eventually, only eighty soldiers—artillerymen, with a few officers—were ordered to guard the artillery captured from the British that was kept at Fort Pitt (future Pittsburgh) and West Point.[11] This collection of field artillery, heavy siege guns, and smaller howitzers later became the basis for the Ordnance Corps, the Department of Ordnance, and the Ordnance Museum that became the West Point Museum.

There were dozens of Revolutionary War buildings remaining on and near the Plain above the river, and chief among these was the Long Barracks, which later became the cadet barracks. In 1793 the Washington administration struggled to piece together a government and federal authority over the separate thirteen states. Among the many issues great and small, the idea of establishing a military academy surfaced. Secretary of War Henry Knox, Treasury Secretary Alexander Hamilton, and even President Washington himself deplored the general lack of professionalism and expertise of the officer corps during the war. There were many aggressive patriot combat leaders, but they were unschooled in logistics and the administration of armed forces. Knox, Hamilton, and Washington felt it was necessary to improve the level of professionalism among the officers of the new army. As discussions continued, Thomas Jefferson, then secretary of state, was against the notion. He stated that the Constitution did not authorize an academy, and so the concept was tabled, except that the next year Congress approved the authorization of the rank of cadet, officer trainees, in the new Corps of Artillerists and Engineers.[12]

About this same time the United States became embroiled in a political and economic conflict with revolutionary France and Great Britain, who were at war. President Washington steered the young republic away from open war with either entity, but tensions mounted through the presidency of John Adams, his successor. The need for a trained and professional officer corps became evermore apparent. The army had no established education or development program except unit training, so the cadets assigned to the Corps of Artillerists and Engineers received only basic military training and some fundamental academics as apprentice officers.[13]

Thomas Jefferson became president in 1801, and as the first Democratic-Republican he was opposed to the policies and actions of his Federalist Party predecessors. He soon made his military policy known based on his personal bias against a large standing army—indeed, against any type of professional military class as was so common in Europe. The small officer corps he inherited was full of Federalists, whom Jefferson was determined to purge from the army.

An American Institution Established: 1802

With the backdrop of a new administration and expanding nation, Jefferson needed a military establishment that he could trust, one where the officers espoused his political tenets and principles. The concept of a new national military academy became a reality as Jefferson and his fellow Democratic-Republicans sought to reform the US Army. On March 16, 1802, Jefferson signed a law entitled, "An Act fixing the Military peace Establishment of the United States."[14] Besides this aspect, the national government needed officers to lead the army that was serving on the new and expanding frontier in the West.

There were twenty-nine sections of the law, with the first twenty-six dealing with eliminating nearly a third of the officer corps, reorganizing regiments and branches of the army, and designating the Corps of Artillerists and the Corps of Engineers as separate entities. The final three sections of the law authorized the establishment of "a military academy" under the Corps of Engineers, which "shall be stationed at West Point in the state of New York." The law provided "that the principal engineer . . . shall have the superintendence of the said military academy, under the direction of the President of the United States," and that the secretary of war would "procure the necessary books, implements and apparatus for the use and benefit of said institution."[15]

Nestled among the Hudson Highlands and occupying the Revolutionary War garrison of West Point, the new academy was born. The school shared sacred ground and historic icons of the great American military victory twenty years earlier. Isolated on a tight turn on the Hudson River, the famous Plain was the stage for many future military, government, and business leaders to march, parade, and train in the art of warfare.

At first the United States Military Academy was a small, insignificant military school that struggled along for fifteen years underfunded, and undermanned. The school was nearly terminated due primarily to lack of congressional interest and oversight. Classes were small, some graduating only a dozen cadets as commissioned officers; in fact, in 1810 there were no graduates at all.[16]

The Academy Ascends

The academy survived the second war against Great Britain, the War of 1812, where many graduates performed well in leadership and engineering roles. In 1815 Congress finally provided sufficient funding for permanent granite barracks, called North and South, a mess hall, and a library-academy building. Enrollment increased as sons of America's elite and middle-class families began to take notice of the small school fifty miles north of New York City. The Corps of Cadets was still relatively small as the new buildings on the storied and historic Plain rose. More than two hundred future officers trained, drilled, and paraded in their dress gray uniforms and French "shako" hats.

After a major leadership failure by Capt. Alden Partridge, who argued and had open conflicts with members of the small teaching staff, a new superintendent, same as a commander, arrived. In July 1817 the academy's most influential person and greatest contributor assumed the superintendency: Capt. Sylvanus Thayer. (Thayer was a brevet, or honorary, major for his service during the War of 1812.) A graduate of the academy in 1808 (and Dartmouth College a year earlier), Thayer changed everything at the school that was now known as the US Military Academy. Prior to his arrival there was no standard curriculum, professional standards were lacking, and the instructors and the few professors were not the finest America had to offer. Cadets attended classes—some for less than a year—and upon successfully passing their graduation examinations were commissioned as officers into the US Army.[17]

Immediately Captain Thayer shook up the academy, and his spirit and influence remains today. During his tenure as superintendent, Sylvanus Thayer established a strong curriculum eventually based on engineering, an austere schedule, daily recitations of lessons, stern discipline, and complete conformity to the highest standards of conduct, honor, personal accountability, and professionalism in order to graduate and obtain a commission in the US Army. His success caused a rising trajectory for the school for the next hundred years. He established or furthered the Academic Board of professors and department heads, a Board of Visitors, and a cadre of outstanding officers, such as Capt. William Worth, who served as commandant of cadets for eight years under Thayer.[18] These officers helped Thayer establish the strong military and character skills and values officers needed in the new army.

Also, during the Thayer era some of the greats of American and military history attended the academy. Benjamin Bonneville, the great western explorer and cartographer, and George Washington Whistler (father of artist James Whistler) both graduated in 1819. Future Confederates Albert Sydney Johnston (class of 1826), Jefferson Davis, president of the Confederacy (class of 1828), Joseph E. Johnston (class of 1829), and future superintendent Robert E. Lee (also 1829) graduated during Thayer's tenure, as did future Union generals Robert Anderson, who commanded Fort Sumter (1825), cavalryman and frontier great P. St. George Cooke (1827), and Randolph B. Marcy (1832), an officer who led several explorations in the West.

Thayer resigned his superintendency in 1833 due to his frustration with President Andrew Jackson, who continually reversed Thayer's decisions regarding dismissing cadets and undermined discipline to protect the sons of friends and political patrons. To this day, no one person has had more influence and impact on the US Military Academy than Sylvanus Thayer during his record sixteen years as superintendent. Though not the founder, Thayer is properly known as the Father of the Academy.[19]

The great challenge that Thayer and other leaders faced was the admission process of the early years. A state, local, and civic or political leader would forward a name to the secretary of war who would select candidates for a nomination to the academy. Reporting to West Point in June each summer, candidates then had to pass an entrance examination. This was a very political process overwhelmed by patronage and favoritism. In 1843 Congress reformed the admission process by allocating members of Congress, senators, and representatives a nomination each. The reformed nomination process bypassed

Artist George Catlin was visiting his brother, a cadet at West Point, when he painted this scene in 1827. It is one of the earliest images to show the Superintendent's Quarters at West Point. Courtesy of the West Point Museum Collection.

US Military Academy in the 1820s; landscape by George Catlin. *Courtesy West Point Museum Collection, USMA.*

the secretary of war, who had no personal contact with these young men. The US president later had annual nominations to the academy. This did not perfect the system, but it greatly made the process more universal and less partisan.[20]

The first war that graduates served in was the War of 1812, but they were not in the higher ranks and positions. The conflict that truly established West Point as an institution that trained its men to lead armies at the highest levels was the War with Mexico in 1846. Numerous academy graduates served with distinction against Mexico. General-in-Chief of the US Army Winfield Scott said after conquering Mexico City, "I give it as my fixed opinion, that but for our graduated cadets, the war between the United States and Mexico might, and probably would have lasted some four or five years . . . whereas, in less than two campaigns, we conquered a great country and a peace without the loss of a single battle or skirmish."[21]

The swift victory in Mexico was truly an amazing achievement, with West Point–trained officers gaining the leadership and combat experience that would serve them later as field and army commanders during the Civil War. The young junior officers included Joseph Hooker (1837), George H. Thomas (1840), James Longstreet (1842), U. S. Grant (1843), and classmates George Pickett and George McClellan (1846).

The men from West Point also performed important civil works projects for the nation in harbor and river development, cartography, and surveys across the West for the transcontinental railroad. Graduates also served in the Indian Wars against the Fox, Comanches, Seminoles, and other tribes.

Of course, the greatest of all tests the academy graduates faced was the Civil War. In the days following the secession of several southern states leading up to the national crisis, some seventy-seven cadets refused to take an oath of allegiance to the United States in the spring of 1861. Eventually 304 graduates would serve under arms against the federal Union and US Constitution. During the Civil War and soon thereafter, Congress attempted on three occasions to cancel funding and abolish the academy, with some congressmen calling it a "den of traitors."[22] Tragically and ironically, the academy straddled both sides of the argument. West Point was damned for training many great Confederate officers and battle commanders, but then it also provided the successful Federal commanders who would bring victory for the Union.[23]

The post-war years saw a stagnation develop at West Point, with few innovations or new teaching methods. Also, the cadet culture of hazing increased to a level where bullies ruled the barracks and the night, lording over the weak and especially the newly appointed Black cadets. The sons and grandsons of generals such as Phil Sheridan, U. S. Grant, and Arthur MacArthur became special targets for hazing and abuse. Some of the officers and faculty disdained and tried to curb the practice of hazing; others saw it not only as a tradition and a rite of passage for all cadets but an essential tool of leadership and character development.

The professors and officers saw no reason to reform or change the school; after all, if the methods and atmosphere was good enough for the Civil War generation to defeat the Confederacy, then why change?

The same tactics were taught for decades based on Antoine Henri Jomini's treatises from the Napoleonic War. These lessons were the same ones that Grant, Sherman, and other Civil War leaders learned on the Plain forty years earlier. There were also few enhancements in infrastructure and major construction projects during the post-war years. The school was ruled by the

Academic Board of a half-dozen professors who had spent most of their careers teaching as opposed to serving in the army in the field. Thus, paternalism ruled above reform and innovation; the professors and tactical officers knew what was best for their young charges. The cadets had few freedoms and privileges, and considering their daily routine, they had little time to indulge in wanton behavior.[24] Like dictators over their departments, the professors ensured that any innovations or improvements the superintendents or the War Department offered were blocked. For the remainder of the nineteenth century the school was mired in the past and the glory of the national victory.[25]

• • •

Two events occurred in 1898 that had a profound connection to Douglas MacArthur personally and professionally. The first was the adoption of a logo and motto that MacArthur would treasure, serve, and personify his entire life. The second was the hazing and departure of a young cadet in the fall of 1898 whose demise two years later the family blamed on the brutal treatment he suffered at West Point. The latter event caused a public review of the academy's cadet life and a signaled a call to end hazing once and for all. MacArthur would dedicate his professional honor to discard this arcane and archaic practice, though he was unsuccessful in doing so.

As concerns the first event, the logo and motto: For nearly a hundred years, West Point had no standard emblem or insignia and no motto to encapsulate the meaning and purpose of the academy. In early 1898 the Academic Board was determined to design and codify a new image or symbol for the academy. On October 8 of that year, Secretary of War Russell A. Alger approved the heraldry recommendation presented by the Academic Board after a review. The new design incorporated the traditional helmet and sword of Pallas Athena along with the shield of the United States. An American eagle and a banner with the inscription DUTY HONOR COUNTRY and the founding date of the academy, MDCCCII (1802), completed the insignia. The correlation of the academy's new coat of arms the year before Douglas MacArthur's arrival there is an interesting prologue. Heralded as one of the greatest speeches in American history, General MacArthur's famous 1962 "Duty, Honor, Country" address is considered by many to be his masterpiece. Curious to the West Point and MacArthur story is the fact that many people mistakenly believe that the general originated these three words as a motto in 1962 during this address.²⁶

And now, to return to the hazing event: In 1898 nineteen-year-old Oscar L. Booz had informed his parents that summer training, "Beast Barracks," was truly bestial. Oscar's family related that "he expected to be hazed, but he did not want to be treated brutally." He called the upperclassman "brutes and bullies."²⁷ Cadet Booz was beaten badly in boxing matches and was knocked out with a severe blow to his solar plexus and had a concussion. The senior cadets forced him to consume a great amount of Tabasco sauce, causing his throat to become painful. He was verbally harassed—called a coward and other names. He was hounded for weeks even after summer camp. Booz finally resigned and returned home in the fall of 1898, seeking and receiving medical treatment. Booz could not work and could hardly talk and eat. He eventually developed tuberculosis in the throat. He died on December 4, 1900. His family alleged that hazing at West Point caused his death.²⁸

Oscar Booz's death caused public outrage, forcing the army to hold an inquiry and investigation that led to a congressional hearing in 1901. The fact that a young man died as a result of a tradition at West Point was appalling. Dozens of cadets testified before these hearings. One of them was Cadet Douglas MacArthur, who himself had been brutally hazed. It was this harsh and unrelenting world of strict and mindless discipline and autocratic rule that young nineteen-year-old Douglas MacArthur entered in June 1899.

CHAPTER 2

★ ★ ★ ★ ★

A MILITARY FAMILY

The greatest constitutional catastrophe in American history occurred in 1860 politically, and then militarily in April 1861 as the American Civil War erupted. The cause of the war was the forty-year debate over slavery: its future and expansion or containment, and then whether secession was constitutional or not. The crisis evolved into a regional problem, dividing the United States, north and south, based mainly on slave states versus free states. As fighting bloodied the land, more and more men flocked to the colors on both sides. One who wanted to serve was a sixteen-year-old boy hailing from Milwaukee, Wisconsin: Arthur MacArthur Jr.

The first MacArthur to have any association with the United States Military Academy was Arthur MacArthur Jr., father of Douglas. Arthur MacArthur senior, a federal circuit judge in Wisconsin, did not want his son to serve in the federal army, so he shipped young Arthur off to West Point for four years, where he hoped the boy could outlast the war. Arthur had already studied one year at a local military academy beginning in 1861 with the agreement that he would attend West Point if his father could secure him a nomination. No congressional appointments were available in the spring of 1862 from Wisconsin, so MacArthur Sr. took his son to Washington, DC, to present him before President Abraham Lincoln to seek a presidential appointment at the academy.[1]

Judge MacArthur first met Wisconsin senator James R. Doolittle, a friend, to arrange the meeting with the president. Previously, Judge MacArthur had written the president, "This is not a light or sudden impression with him," referring to Arthur Jr., "for he has been dwelling upon it or the Navy for the last two years, so that it has become the fixed bent of his inclinations."[2]

The MacArthurs met President Lincoln on June 3 in the White House and they soon learned that Lincoln had no nominations available for the current year. He did, however, offer an appointment for the class arriving in 1863. Young Arthur would not countenance such a delay. All he wanted to do was to join the army and fight. He received his wish.

Two months later, on August 4, 1862, Arthur MacArthur—who had just turned seventeen years in June—received a commission as a first lieutenant in the newly formed 24th Wisconsin Volunteer Infantry Regiment.[3]

• • •

"The MacArthurs are of Scottish decent," Douglas MacArthur wrote on the first page of his memoirs, *Reminiscences*. The elder Arthur was born in Scotland and arrived with his widowed mother in America at age ten in 1825. Settling in Massachusetts, young Arthur worked as a law clerk in Boston, became a lawyer, and was admitted to the bar in 1840 in his twenty-fifth year. The law became Arthur's weapon, and courtrooms were his battlefields.[4]

Gaining success and clients, Arthur Sr. opened his own law practice in Springfield, Massachusetts. The only military experience he had was with the Massachusetts militia for a year in the Western District as a captain serving as judge advocate (military lawyer).[5] In 1844 he married Aurelia Belcher, and the next year she bore Arthur MacArthur Jr., on June 2, 1845. Four years later the MacArthurs moved to Wisconsin, which had joined the Union only a year earlier, in 1848. Establishing his law practice in Milwaukee, Arthur soon gained prominent friends in the Democratic Party; he ran for lieutenant governor in 1855 and two years later was elected judge of the state's Second Circuit. Arthur MacArthur Sr. would be a judge the remainder of his life, ultimately being appointed by President U. S. Grant in 1870 to be an associate justice of the Supreme Court of the District of Columbia, from which he retired in 1887.[6]

Arthur Jr. began his military service in 1862 and retired after some forty-seven years in 1909 in the rank of lieutenant general.[7] The one major difference militarily between Douglas the son and his father Arthur was the US

Military Academy; the son was a member of the Long Gray Line and the father was not.

• • •

Arthur MacArthur's service during the Civil War was nothing short of brilliant, heroic, and sometimes even amazing and miraculous. He served in no less than seven major engagements with the 24th Wisconsin, from Perryville in October 1862 to his final fight at Franklin in November 1864, where he was severely wounded and so forced to end his front-line service for the remainder of the war. He rose from first lieutenant and eventually to lieutenant colonel in the volunteer service and received the honorary rank of brevet colonel in March 1865 for distinguished service. MacArthur was soon referred to as the "boy colonel."

He fought in many of the great engagements in the western area of operations, including Stones River in December 1862, Chattanooga in 1863, and the major battles during the Atlanta Campaign in the summer of 1864 at Resaca, Kennesaw Mountain, Jonesborough, and the siege and capture of Atlanta in early September. He served under some the Union's great commanders in the West, namely, Gordon Granger (West Point class of 1845), Phillip Sheridan (1854), George Thomas (1840), William T. Sherman (1840), and U. S. Grant (1843).[8] In the 24th Wisconsin there were few if any West Point graduates, which was true for most volunteer regiments, regardless of branch. Yet, academy graduates dominated the upper echelons of command on both sides of the conflict.

Arthur's first battle was at Perryville in October, followed by Stones River serving in Phil Sheridan's division in the Army of the Cumberland. After the Union defeat at Chickamauga in September 1863, the Confederate Army of Tennessee moved on to Chattanooga, Tennessee, and besieged the Union Army of the Cumberland. After the disaster at Chickamauga, President Lincoln selected General Grant to command all the federal armies west of the Appalachian Mountains. Grant realigned three separate field armies and shook up the command structure by relieving some and appointing other officers he knew and trusted. By the end of November, Grant was ready to break the Confederate siege and force his way out from Chattanooga.

The Confederates had some 48,000 men under the command of Gen. Braxton Bragg, West Point class of 1837, whereas Grant had assembled some 73,000 federal soldiers. The Confederates held the dominant terrain: Lookout Mountain to the west, Missionary Ridge to the east, and Tunnel Hill adjacent to Missionary Ridge. On November 23, two divisions under General Thomas attacked and took Orchard Knob.[9] Next a Union corps under Gen. Joseph Hooker, who had months earlier suffered a devastating defeat at Chancellorsville in Virginia, advanced up the steep slopes and rock cracks of Lookout Mountain. The rains days earlier had left a shrouded layer of clouds obscuring the rock ridge from the observers below. The fight for Lookout Mountain has since then been called, rightfully, the "Battle above the Clouds." Hooker and his forces took the mount as General Sherman, Grant's great friend, took the northern slopes of Missionary Ridge.

Grant planned to attack both Confederate flanks and then send a spoiling frontal attack in the center by Thomas's troops. Among the regiments ready to assault Missionary Ridge in the frontal attack was the 24th Wisconsin Infantry, with eighteen-year-old Lt. Arthur MacArthur serving as adjutant. In ranks some two miles long, the 24,000 men deployed in the low valley facing towering Missionary Ridge with its three lines of Confederate entrenchments as musket fire and artillery fire rained down on the attacking troops. What soon followed was one of the most interesting military feats in American history. Under the very eyes of Grant and other commanders observing from Orchard Knob on November 25, the attack, which was designed to merely capture the Confederate rifle pits at the base of Missionary Ridge, unfolded very differently than planned.[10]

As the federal forces attacked, the color bearer of the regiment fell; young MacArthur grasped the national colors and moved forward, and his commander and men followed. At one point he raised the battle ensign and called out, "On Wisconsin," which later became the official state motto and song. Up Missionary Ridge the 24th Wisconsin and other regiments trudged, while the Confederates watching and firing their weapons soon were overtaken by fear at the spectacle before them. Against great odds the Union regiments gained the crest of Missionary Ridge.[11]

Lieutenant MacArthur was not the only officer who led his men forward and up Missionary Ridge, but MacArthur was a target for the Confederates the moment he grasped the colors and waved them about. Up the steep ridge he scrambled with his Wisconsin men following him. At one point a canister round exploded only a few yards from him, throwing him to the ground. Shrapnel ripped through the flag, and the concussion blew his hat off. MacArthur received only a minor scratch.[12]

Arthur raised himself up and continued the charge up the ridge; the entire regiment followed. As the Union forces gained the top, many yelled out, "Chickamauga! Chickamauga," referring to the defeat that the Army of the Cumberland had experienced three months earlier. The regimental commander proudly recalled, "What flag was first, is perhaps not susceptible of demonstration.... I am satisfied that no standard crested the ridge sooner than that of the 24th Wisconsin." Routed, the Confederate army under General Bragg crumbled. Thousands surrendered, and many more fled.[13]

The men of the 24th Wisconsin were astounded by the assault up Missionary Ridge and especially by Lieutenant MacArthur's amazing feat that Wednesday. Capt. Edwin B. Parsons later declared, "Arthur was magnificent. He seems to be afraid of nothing. He'd fight a pack of tigers in a jungle. He has become the hero of the regiment."[14] Weeks later, Arthur was promoted to major, elected by the men of the regiment, skipping the rank of captain.[15]

Chattanooga and Missionary Ridge may have been the most heroic moments in Arthur MacArthur's life and career; however, his outstanding leadership was manifest throughout the Civil War and for decades afterward.

Grant's great victory at Chattanooga secured for him the promotion to lieutenant general and general-in-chief of the Union Army in March 1864. Leaving the western area of operations to General Sherman, Grant traveled east to assume command of all the Union forces. In the summer of 1864 Sherman commenced his campaign to capture Atlanta, one of the most important industrial and transportation cities in the South. Leading an army of some 70,000 veterans, Sherman fought several battles as he advanced into Georgia. Among his many units were MacArthur and the 24th Wisconsin Volunteers. During the engagement at Resaca on May 15, 1864, the regimental commander was wounded, and Major MacArthur assumed command of the regiment at age nineteen.[16] MacArthur was appointed lieutenant colonel of volunteers on June 4, which came with the authority and pay in-grade, though both were temporary and would end at the war's conclusion.[17]

At Kennesaw Mountain north of Atlanta, federal forces engaged the Confederates on June 27, 1864, where Lt. Col. Arthur MacArthur was wounded in the chest and right wrist. Rejoining the regiment, he soon resumed command through the capture of Atlanta. Serving under General Thomas's Army of the Cumberland, MacArthur marched north with his regiment to Franklin, south of Nashville, Tennessee. There on November 30, Confederate forces attacked but were repulsed and defeated. During the battle MacArthur again was in the thick of the fight. Charging forward mounted, Captain Parsons recorded, "I saw the Colonel sabering his way toward the leading Confederate flag. His horse was shot from under him, a bullet ripped open his right shoulder, but on foot he fought his way forward trying to bring down those Stars and Bars. A Confederate Major now had the flag and shot the Colonel through the breast. I thought he was done for but he staggered up and drove his sword through his adversary's body, but even as the Confederate fell he shot our Colonel down for good with a bullet through his knee."[18]

Franklin was MacArthur's last battle in the Civil War. His wounds were serious enough that he was sent home to Milwaukee to recover. He was able to rejoin the 24th Wisconsin Infantry for its mustering out in June 1865. He received honorary or brevet promotions to lieutenant colonel and colonel for distinguished service and gallantry in action; in addition, he served in both grades in the volunteers. After nearly three years he was a civilian again at age twenty.

• • •

Whether young Arthur MacArthur was imbued with the martial spirit or whether the profession of arms appealed to him, he soon sought a commission in the Regular Army rather than study and read for law, though he had passed the bar examination in Wisconsin. Gaining a commission for a non-academy graduate was not an easy process after the Civil War. In 1866 Congress established the army strength at 54,000 officers and men, based on twenty-two infantry regiments with a compliment of some twenty lieutenants each. By 1869 the army was reduced again, and many regiments were combined with others.[19] Through all this confusion, Arthur first received a commission as second lieutenant in the 17th Infantry in February 1866 and was promoted that July to captain. Captain MacArthur would serve mostly on the frontier as a captain for the next twenty-three years until he finally was promoted to major in 1889.[20]

During Mardi Gras in New Orleans, twenty-nine-year-old Arthur met Mary Pickney Hardy, a resident of Norfolk, Virginia. Seven years his junior, Mary was a daughter of the South whose entire family had been staunch Confederates during the war. One observer said that she was "a beautiful Southern lady." The captain and southern belle soon fell in love, and arrangements were made for a spring wedding at Riveredge, the family plantation on the Elizabeth River of Virginia. The wedding was hosted by Thomas Hardy, who accepted the "Yankee" captain as a son-in-law, but several of Mary's brothers refused to attend the ceremony. Known as "Pinky," Mary was Arthur's faithful partner for the next thirty-seven years.[21]

To this remarkable couple were born three boys. Arthur, the oldest, who became a naval officer, was born in 1876 at Mary's ancestral home of Riveredge in Norfolk. Malcolm was born in 1878 in Connecticut while the MacArthurs were on furlough and died in 1883 of measles at age five. Pinky became pregnant again in 1879 when the family was posted to Arkansas. She wanted to have the child born in her family's home, but the baby came early. On January 26, 1880, Douglas was born in family quarters of Arsenal Barracks, Little Rock, Arkansas.[22]

For the next two decades, Douglas and his family would live in a half-dozen different homes, including Fort Wingate in New Mexico Territory and other frontier forts such as Fort Seldon and then Fort Leavenworth. In Kansas Arthur attended the professional training school, after which he was posted to Washington, DC, where Captain MacArthur served in the War Department staff in the adjutant general's office. Douglas's pride in his father's service and his own experience growing up on the frontier was exaggerated in his personal memoirs, *Reminiscences*, published near the time of his death in 1964. He wrote, "I learned to ride and shoot even before I could read or write—indeed, almost before I could walk and talk."[23] This was a rather wild claim, but one can readily see the heart and soul of Douglas MacArthur. He was not only a soldier, a commander, sometimes a politico, and certainly a statesman; he was at heart a storyteller and a romantic cavalier.

One of his fondest stories from his youth was about the three-hundred-mile forced march from Fort Wingate in northwest New Mexico Territory to

The MacArthurs: front, Mary Pickney MacArthur with grandson Arthur on her lap, Gen. Arthur MacArthur Jr.; back row, Lt. Arthur MacArthur III, US Navy, his wife Mary Hendry MacArthur, and Douglas MacArthur, circa 1905. *Courtesy MacArthur Memorial.*

Fort Seldon on the Rio Grande near Las Cruces, New Mexico. He was a mere boy, only four years old in 1884, but the romance of infantry and cavalry marching during a time of fear as the Apache chief Geronimo was on one of his brutal campaigns against white settlers, across the Mexican border, captivated him.[24] There Arthur took command of the fort, having led his K Company, 13th US Infantry, to the small, desolate fort with his two sons and Pinky in tow.

In September 1886 Geronimo surrendered, and the crisis abated.

After two years at Fort Selden, Captain MacArthur and his family moved to Fort Leavenworth, Kansas, where Arthur joined the faculty of the US Army's Infantry and Cavalry School, which eventually became the Command and General Staff School. Arthur's service at Fort Selden brought forth a commendation from an inspector of the Department of the Missouri, Maj. George H. Burton, West Point class of 1865, who wrote, "Captain MacArthur impresses me as an officer of more than ordinary ability, and very zealous in the performance of duty. The company and post show evidence of intelligent, judicious, and masterly supervision."[25]

Pinky was happy to have her sons Arthur and Douglas improve their education at the better, formal schools at Leavenworth. Besides, the quality of life and the post quarters were much better than the New Mexico dirt-floored adobe cabin they had resided in. The great moment came for Captain MacArthur on July 21, 1889, seven days short of twenty-three years of Regular Army service, when his promotion to major occurred. The old promotion system based on seniority only, and not merit, finally yielded a vacancy for the forty-four-year-old.

The next year Major MacArthur received the Medal of Honor, officially awarded June 30, 1890, some twenty-seven years after his valorous actions at Missionary Ridge. If one reads the citation for Medal of Honor, it is easy to think that this action would never come close to resulting in the highest military decoration in the modern era: "First Lieutenant MacArthur, Jr., seized the colors of his regiment at a critical moment and planted them on the captured works on the crest of Missionary Ridge."[26]

The reason for the delay was a unique and somewhat embarrassing chapter in the Medal of Honor story. In the late 1880s the secretary of war instituted a policy that the aging Civil War heroes should be honored. With proper affidavits a soldier could submit an application for consideration for the Medal of Honor. The process was fraught with errors, and dozens of undeserving individuals self-applied and received the award. More than five hundred Union veterans and currently serving soldiers received the medal during this period. In 1897 a new secretary of war introduced a different standard whereby individuals could not nominate themselves. Veterans such as Arthur MacArthur rightfully deserved the recognition, but for some reason his commanders did not nominate him.[27]

Also in 1889, Arthur was assigned again to Washington in the War Department as an assistant adjutant general. It was during this time that Arthur III, age sixteen, determined to have a military career as his namesake. He applied for a nomination to West Point in 1892 but failed to obtain one. He then sought a nomination to the US Naval Academy in Annapolis, Maryland, from his father's home state of Wisconsin, the Oshkosh district, and succeeded. He would eventually graduate in 1896 and had a distinguished career of twenty-seven years in the US Navy.[28]

Douglas attended a public high school on Massachusetts Avenue and admitted later, "I was only an average student."[29] That all changed in September 1893 when Major MacArthur was transferred to Fort Sam Houston in San Antonio, Texas. Pinky enrolled thirteen-year-old Douglas in the West Texas Military Academy under the rector, Rev. Allen Burlesoa. Here Douglas excelled. Though receiving a classical education in Greek and Latin, he achieved outstanding grades, was quarterback on the football team, played baseball, and was top graduate in 1897. West Texas was a Christian military school located on Government Hill just north of the famous Alamo. Young Douglas achieved a grade score of 97.65 percent and received the graduating class gold medal for "the highest standing in scholarship and deportment."[30] Douglas said about his time in Texas, "My four years there were without doubt the happiest of my life.."

The year 1896 was a singular one for the MacArthur family. Major MacArthur was promoted to lieutenant colonel in May, the same rank he held in the volunteers some thirty years earlier. In June, Midshipman Arthur MacArthur III graduated from the US Naval Academy at age nineteen, and entered the navy. On August 26, 1896, Judge Arthur MacArthur Sr. died at age eighty-one in New Jersey.[31]

In 1897 Arthur MacArthur received orders for the Department of the Dakotas headquartered in St. Paul, Minnesota, but the family moved to the MacArthur ancestral home of Milwaukee.

• • •

In April 1898 the United States declared war on Spain. The reasons and causes of this conflict are complex and controversial, but simply put, the Cuban popular revolution against Spanish rule, and America's gambit for imperial expansion and the tragic explosion of the USS *Maine* in Havana harbor that February, caused a fervor with Americans stoked by the yellow press of the era. Known as the "Splendid Little War" of only ninety days, it was the basis for many other future American political and military events and conflicts. The war was also a major affair for the MacArthur family, where service in the Philippines for the next forty years would be a major place of duty for the MacArthurs and another second home for Douglas.

Though the major theater of operations was in Cuba and not the Philippines, it was the Pacific theater where Arthur served. Selected to command a brigade in the VIII Corps, Arthur MacArthur was promoted to brigadier general of volunteers on May 27, a temporary promotion for the duration of the war. Maj. Gen. Wesley Merritt, West Point class of 1860 and one of the boy wonders of the Civil War, commanded the expeditionary force against the Spanish Philippines. Some eleven thousand regulars and volunteers arrived in July and August 1898, and on August 13 Merritt launched an attack to capture the capital of Manila. Brig. Gen. Arthur MacArthur commanded a brigade of regulars during the attack, which basically was a staged battle negotiated between the Spanish commander and the Americans. Involved but not allied with the US forces were thousands of Filipino revolutionaries attempting to defeat Spanish rule and hoping that the Americans would help them toward independence.[32]

The peace was signed with Spain in December 1898 in Paris, France, ending the war. However, the Filipino nationalists were not involved in the negotiations for peace, and soon they revolted against American rule. In January 1899 Filipino insurrectionists attacked American soldiers, which initiated a three-year war that cost some four thousand American and sixteen thousand

Filipino lives. After nearly four years, the Filipino insurrectionists ceased fighting the Americans and peace was established. During the Philippine-American War, Arthur MacArthur, now a major general of volunteers, commanded the 2nd Division initially, and then became the department commander of Northern Luzon. In May 1900 he became the military governor of the Philippines.[33]

MacArthur commanded some seventy thousand American troops in the Philippines, where at times there were twenty-four thousand soldiers in the archipelago patrolling and fighting. The insurgent war was nasty and brutal. The major challenge that General MacArthur faced was the balance between fighting a vicious guerrilla war and trying to establish peace through pacification of the local populace. A slogan that emerged from this bitter war cleverly depicts the policy: "The schoolbook and the Krag." The schoolbook is obvious, but "the Krag" refers to the .30-caliber Krag-Jorgenson rifle, the standard infantry rifle used by American troops.

Another frustrating challenge that General MacArthur endured was the civilian commission headed by future president Howard W. Taft. The two men became bitter enemies over the politics and policies enacted by the commission and the realities of insurgent warfare.[34] The tragic relationship and bitter feud between MacArthur and Taft would cause more problems later in life. Arthur struggled to both win the war and establish a peace with the Filipinos, but he spent much of his time warring with Taft. Finally, on July 4, 1901, MacArthur left the Philippines to return home after three long years.[35] His son fifty years later also would have trouble with civilian oversight of the military.

When news of the war against Spain came to Douglas in Wisconsin, he wanted to skip his education and the admission process at the US Military Academy and enlist as a private in the war. Arthur told him, "My son there will be plenty of fighting in the coming years, and of a magnitude far beyond this. Prepare yourself."[36] Douglas MacArthur followed this council and did not enlist but began the admission process for an appointment to West Point.

• • •

In the summer of 1898 Douglas renewed the challenging struggle of obtaining admission to the academy. All his energy now focused on that pursuit.

"Always before me," he recorded in his memoirs, "was the goal of West Point, the greatest military academy in the world."[37] This year he began his nomination process for entrance in 1899, joining the class of 1903.

Previously, in 1896, the year before Douglas graduated from West Texas Military Academy, he sought an appointment for the class reporting in the summer of 1897 for West Point. That year, however, President Cleveland awarded his four appointments to other young men, passing over Douglas.

The next year, 1897, again he sought a presidential appointment, this time from President William McKinley, who took office that January. Again, the MacArthurs, father, mother, and young Douglas, orchestrated a full-court press with another line-up of prominent Americans. One of these was Senator Redfield Proctor of Vermont, who wrote, "All I can say is, that I know of no officer who better deserves the privilege of having his son educated at West Point than [Arthur] MacArthur."[38]

President McKinley rejected the nomination. Biographer Geoffrey Perrett explained that Douglas's failure to secure these nominations was for the good. "In the long term," Perrett wrote, "this rejection was probably the best thing that could have happened. At sixteen Douglas was too young to get the most out of West Point and not sufficiently well prepared academically."[39]

Now the only course of action available to the MacArthurs was a competitive nomination through Congress. In order to do this, Douglas had to establish residency in a congressional district that would support his nomination. Arthur's old home of Milwaukie was ideal because the congressman representing that district was a good friend of Judge MacArthur. Also, during the summer of 1897, Lieutenant Colonel MacArthur received orders to serve as adjutant general for the Department of Dakotas headquartered at St. Paul. The MacArthur family would move to Milwaukee so young Douglas could declare his residency in Wisconsin, take the competitive examinations, and secure a nomination.[40]

From his new home in Milwaukee Douglas sought a nomination to the academy from Wisconsin. The process was not complex, but it was challenging. Basically, each senator and representative had one nomination each year to West Point and the Naval Academy. The power to appoint a young man to one the federal academies was a great incentive for granting a great education to deserving young Americans. It also served as a means to reward favors to political friends or families who had means. Candidates and their families relied heavily on favorable assistance from powerful people, especially politicians.

In Milwaukee, Pinky and Douglas resided at the Plankinton House, arriving in October 1897. Lieutenant Colonel MacArthur traveled from St. Paul to visit his family as often as possible. Douglas after a few months became a resident of Wisconsin, a prerequisite for a congressional appointment. At this time the congressional district was that of US Representative Theobald Otjen. In Milwaukee the MacArthurs befriended a family that Gen. Arthur MacArthur knew as a boy, the Mitchells. US Senator John L. Mitchell had served in the 24th Wisconsin Infantry with Arthur during the Civil War. One year older than Douglas was William "Billy" Mitchell, one of the pioneers in American military aviation.[41] Billy Mitchell and Douglas were not close friends; in fact, they hardly knew each other, whereas their parents and grandparents were very close.[42]

In Milwaukee, Douglas went to work in 1898 to prepare for the rigid entrance examinations. He slaved away, hour after hour every day, studying, reading, practicing his lessons, taking preparatory tests, and doing all he could to prepare. His taskmaster was his mother, Pinky, his constant light and motivation. Near the end of his life, MacArthur recalled his feelings on the entrance test day in May 1898, "The night before the examination, for the first time in my life I could not sleep, and the next morning when I arrived at the city hall I felt nauseated."[43] Pinky sensed this and addressed this with her son. Douglas remembered, "But the cool words of my mother brought me around." He then rehearsed an amazing pep talk that perhaps became a foundational moment in his life, and his first major objective in life, to enter West Point. He recalled his mother's encouragement: "'Douglas,' she said, 'you'll win if you don't lose your nerve. You must believe in yourself, my son, or no one else will believe in you. Be confident, self-reliant, and even if you don't make it, you will know you have done your best. Now go to it.'"[44]

According to some individuals, Douglas MacArthur was one of the most vainglorious and arrogant people in history. This may be true in some instances, but as an eighteen-year-old seeking admission to West Point he was a mass of nervous anxiety. There were several times in his life where anxiety, self-doubt, and fear ruled him to a point where he even vomited. On June 7, 1898, the

Milwaukee Journal printed the test results. Douglas MacArthur scored sixteen points higher than the next applicant, with a total score of 93.3 percent.

Douglas was on his way to the US Military Academy—his dream fulfilled. Years later, Gen. Arthur MacArthur confided in his friend Gen. Peyton March, chief of staff of the army, that "He [MacArthur] told me that he started Douglas towards West Point the day he was born."[45]

CHAPTER 3

FACING THE BEAST

New Cadet MacArthur

The West Shore Railroad completed the tunnel under the Plain in 1882–83 that allowed more traffic, including future cadets, to reach West Point. In June 1899 a mother in her late forties and her nineteen-year-old son rode the rails along the scenic Hudson Valley on the West Shore line. They arrived at the station and then took a room at the West Point Hotel, built by Major Thayer in 1829. The woman, Mary "Pinky" MacArthur, would stay at the hotel for two years, through 1901, until her husband, Maj. Gen. Arthur MacArthur, returned from the Philippine wars. Douglas, the son, reported to summer training, notoriously known as "Beast Barracks," a few days later. For decades, Douglas MacArthur would be derided as a "mommy's boy" because his mother resided at the West Point Hotel at Trophy Point during his first years as a cadet. If this is true, then he was not alone, because Mrs. Ida Honoré Grant, wife of Brig. Gen. Frederick Dent Grant, also took a room at the hotel, because her son, U. S. Grant III, grandson of President Grant, was in Douglas's class of 1903.[1]

On Tuesday, June 13, all the new cadets—145 total—reported to the officers and upper-class cadets to begin the entrance process. This was the great day that Douglas MacArthur had been waiting for most of his young life.

However, the new world Douglas had envisioned was not what he faced. The severity and sometimes brutality of his first summer was a rite of passage for the new plebe class that continues today. The institution was going through a reformation, where the senior officer, the superintendent, clashed with the department heads and seasoned professors who often were much older than the commanding officer—later a colonel. The superintendent, Albert Mills, was only a first lieutenant when he arrived the year before. As Douglas MacArthur would experience in 1919 after returning from the Great War in Europe, Superintendent Mills faced the "old guard," the Academic Board, which one superintendent explained was like placing "one's head in the lion's mouth."[2] The school and garrison in the summer of 1899 was a small but formidable institution in tradition, reputation, and paternalism. We will now turn to a review of the academy at the turn of the century: its structure, faculty, curriculum, and atmosphere.

• • •

The 1899 *Annual Report of the Superintendent* outlined the academy's roster of seven professors (department heads), one associate professor, fifty-one commissioned officers who were staff and instructors, one master of the sword (Lt. Col. Herman Koehler), and one music teacher (also the commander of the West Point Band), for a total of sixty-two staff and faculty including the superintendent. On the first day of class, September 1, 1899, there were 325 cadets in the corps among the four classes.[3]

After a few months as superintendent, Albert Mills was promoted by the War Department to the rank of colonel—a temporary rank, whereas his permanent rank was captain. A year earlier Lieutenant Mills was severely wounded during the assault on San Juan Hill in Cuba during the Spanish-American War. A bullet struck him in one eye, leaving him with sight in only the other. Upon recovering, Mills was appointed superintendent, and he was nominated for the Medal of Honor for gallantry for his service in Cuba.[4]

Mills had graduated in 1879 from West Point, and some of the professors he oversaw as superintendent, including Peter Michie, Gustav Fiebeger, and Samuel Tillman, were teaching when he was a cadet twenty years earlier. Only forty-four years old, he was considered a young, inexperienced officer by the old guard professors. Mills made some drastic mistakes, such as ordering that

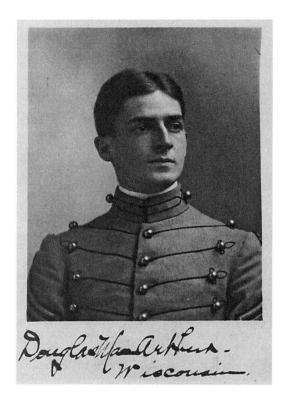

Cadet Douglas MacArthur.
Courtesy USMA Archives.

he have three votes on the Academic Board whereas all the other members held one vote.⁵

He also antagonized the professors with his quick and far-reaching decisions and the actions he made on his own. He was able to push through Congress a request for a large building appropriation for West Point that eventually totaled some $7.5 million in 1902 dollars. This measure resulted in a major building boom that changed the central area of the academy.⁶ The National Park Service historical sites survey of the academy in 1984 recorded, "The turn of the century was marked by the single greatest expansion and construction program ever undertaken at West Point."⁷

Just prior to MacArthur's arrival a new academic hall was completed in 1895. It replaced the previous academic building built in 1839 after the first academy hall had burned down in 1838. The first gymnasium was completed in 1893, along with the fencing academy that resembled a Norman castle with two towers and stood where the present-day Washington Hall is. Though small and primitive compared to a modern gymnasium, this facility allowed Douglas and other cadets to develop their physical prowess. The second official hospital was completed fifteen years earlier, in 1884, replacing the 1830 hospital built by Sylvanus Thayer.[8]

Cullum Hall, originally dedicated as Memorial Hall, was completed in 1898, the year before Douglas's arrival. An officer club was under construction during his cadet time and was completed the year he graduated. Most of the buildings, halls, and the Central Barracks had been around for decades. The school needed improvement with new conveniences and inventions of the modern world, such as electricity, gas lamps, and steam radiation. Indoor plumbing would come later.[9]

Even with these few new buildings and amenities the academy needed additional reform. Colonel Mills was one of the most reform-minded superintendents in West Point history. He challenged the paternalism and tradition of the institution, but he failed to break down the strict and austere authoritarian environment. Mills was a visionary who saw the need to expand the school physically and to increase the student-body "corps" to provide the US Army with quality officers for the growing imperial possessions gained through the Spanish-American War.[10] He deserves much credit for his significant achievements, though not one building was even commenced before he departed in 1906 after eight years as superintendent.

The other significant officer position during Cadet MacArthur's time was the commandant of cadets. The commandant was the head and chair of the Department of Tactics and responsible for military training and discipline. There were two commandants during MacArthur's time as a cadet, Otto L. Hein and Charles G. Treat, both graduates of West Point. The office and position of commandant dates to 1817 and was always the second most important leader and administrator at the academy. One of the previous commandants and longest serving was Capt. William Worth, for whom Fort Worth, Texas, is named. Though he was not a graduate himself, he served eight years as commandant under Sylvanus Thayer. The litany of historically significant former commandants is long, several of whom died in combat and three who served in the Confederacy during the Civil War.[11]

With power gained through their many years teaching at the school and membership on the Academic Board, the department heads were the next most significant and powerful individuals at West Point. For decades the board was the supreme governance body of the academy, second only to the Board of Visitors in creation. The professors were dedicated officers and were technically proficient in their academic fields, but many had outlived their military experience by being well into their forties and fifties, or older, as professors. Full of traditional decorum and academic knowledge, they had little to provide in training and the art of war. The tactical officers provided the training, leadership, and discipline the young cadets required for professional development. Yet, over the decades there was a growing disparity between the military instructors and training program, and the academic departments and classroom instruction. The tug-of-war between academics and the school of the soldier continues to this day. For the new cadets, classrooms, school texts, chalk boards, and rote memorization would come later—once they survived "Beast" and summer encampment.[12]

• • •

All new cadets faced the traditional ordeal of a couple weeks of "Beast Barracks," in which they suffered the harassment and ridicule of hazing and extreme workouts and training. Upon completion, they joined the rest of the corps in Summer Encampment with its training, parading, marching, company, and camp activities—which included social events with dances or "hops" and idling away the summer in their tents with boardwalk floors. The new cadets spent their entire summer in camp on the famous Plain of West Point.

For two weeks, beginning on June 12 and ending July 2, 1899, Douglas and the other plebes endured some eighteen days of training. The new cadets were subjected to "Beast" under the control and training of the first classmen, the lordly seniors, but were led directly by third classmen, only a year ahead. This was a rigorous training period learning the "School of the Soldier." There were also lectures on academic regulations, the "Blue Book" or the West Point Guide (the Bugle Notes of the day), and military protocol. What was called "preliminary training" was more attune to familiarization training, which involved the revolver and rifle marksmanship, and physical exercises. According to the *Annual Report of 1901*, "The new cadet drill instructors were especially selected members of the first class, acting under the immediate supervision of an assistant instructor of tactics."[13] Thus, the initial training during "Beast"

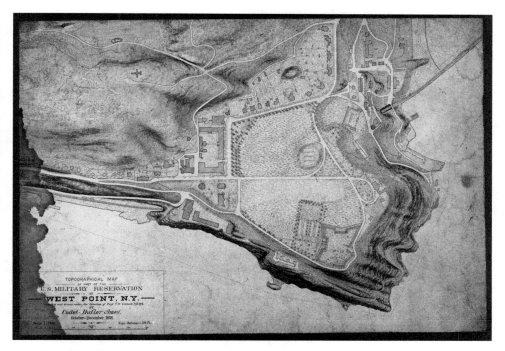

Map of West Point, 1891. *Courtesy USMA Archives.*

was by cadets but under officer control. The same was not true of Summer Encampment.

In early July, the new cadets began Summer Encampment, joining the other classes, except for the second classmen, who were away on their two-month furlough. Encamped in tents, they drilled, trained, and marched, along with some unscheduled time for playing cards, games of fun, recreational activities, and even dances with young ladies from all quarters of the region. There was also free time enough for young men to perform pranks and engage in sporting events. This relaxed time also allowed the upperclassmen, in this case the "Yearlings" or third classmen, the freedom to harass and haze the new cadets.[14] Over the decades, mischievous and mean-spirited upperclassmen had conceived some ingenious and often vicious methods of hazing other cadets.[15]

If a cadet was a son of politician or, better yet, a general officer, or was in some way noteworthy, the treatment was more intense and severe. Thus, the selection of Cadet Douglas MacArthur, son of a general officer and a war hero being a recipient of the Medal of Honor, was particularly inviting. "We always prepared a warm reception for the sons of well-known men," declared Robert E. Wood, class of 1900, a first classman the summer when Douglas arrived.[16] A year earlier, Cadet Philip H. Sheridan Jr., son of the famous Union Civil War cavalryman and general-in-chief until his death in 1888, entered the academy. Young Phil had to ride a broomstick around the area for hours mimicking "Sheridan's famous ride" during the Battle of Cedar Creek in 1864.[17]

Among the new cadets was George W. Cocheu from New York, one of some two hundred young men who took the entrance examinations at the academy. He recalled seeing "a tall, black-haired, erect boy of slightly over nineteen years of age." Forty years later, Cocheu said, "I can see him now, jauntily wearing a light-colored hat which in those days was called a 'fedora.' It was DOUGLAS MACARTHUR."[18] Cocheu would graduate and serve later with MacArthur.

Soon the senior cadets singled out MacArthur as a target for incredibly harsh and abusive treatment. Young Douglas stood nearly six feet tall and weighed 133 pounds in the summer of 1899. His unique character stood out and was recognized by others. "There was much speculation as to how Douglas MacArthur would act as a Plebe," wrote upperclassman Robert Wood. "He was without doubt, the handsomest cadet that ever came into the Academy, six-foot tall, and slender, with a fine body and flashing dark eyes."[19]

Historian and academy graduate Lance Betros wrote, "The first hazing . . . was, at best, a misguided effort to weed out cadets deemed unfit for the rigors of military life," but then later "hazing became more severe after the Civil War," where it became more common and increasingly brutal. Not only was this indignity and abuse practiced upon others, but it was tied to unauthorized barracks vigilante practices based on honor issues. Betros explained: "Both hazing and extralegal honor enforcement had the tacit support of many cadets, alumni, and even faculty, but they were blights on the institution and negative influences on cadet development."[20]

Some graduates and serving officers saw the importance of the cadets policing their own ranks, instilling discipline among the new plebe class, even if hazing was the manner and method. Col. Peter Smith Michie, a graduate of 1863 and long-serving professor of engineering, chemistry, and physics at the academy, told a congressional committee that as a cadet, "More often at that time it was for the purpose of having a little fun and bringing the new cadets to a realizing sense of their new position."[21] Perhaps the most damning support of hazing at West Point came from one of the great graduates of all times, John J. Pershing, class of 1886. Many of the men and officers who both endured and practiced this severe treatment at the turn of the century would later serve under Pershing in France during the Great War. Captain Pershing, who was a tactical officer at West Point before the Spanish-American War, declared, "I hope the day will never come when hazing is abolished."[22]

The third classmen soon began training and harassing the new cadets. At first, the tasks for Douglas MacArthur were simple, such as reciting pertinent information or explaining his father Arthur's career. He was ordered to lead a notional battalion through the tactics of battle. Then the exercises became more rigid and austere. During the summer training MacArthur was subjected to these forms of harassment several times. One day senior cadets ordered MacArthur to take a "sweat bath" where Douglas wore his full-dress uniform, and then donned his raincoat on a scorching summer day with all its humid and stifling heat.[23] The exercises, as they were called, that MacArthur and other cadets of his class endured were more intense and brutal than usual. One of these cadets was Ulysses S. Grant III, who underwent much of the same treatment.

These exercises were forms of athletic drills or calisthenics, some of which were from prescribed training routines. A spread eagle, or "eagling," required the subject to stand on his toes and then squat down with his arms extended and flapping like a bird, then rising. Another exercise was the "wooden willies" with a rifle. One had to raise the rifle to the firing position and then drop to the ready, repeating the exercise many times—perhaps more than a hundred.[24]

One evening in August, Douglas was forced to perform hundreds of repetitions of several exercises, especially some 250 "spread eagles." During this session he had to squat over a burning candle, lowering himself to the flame as he extended his arms, but not burning his trousers. After an hour of such abuse, he passed out. The upperclassmen dragged MacArthur to his tent, dropped him at the entrance, and fled. He was in so much pain that night that he groaned and cried out. Frederick Cunningham, Douglas's tentmate in the summer of 1899 and classmate, testified later before an inquiry, "Finally [he] asked me to throw a blanket under them [his legs] in order that the company officers could not hear his feet striking the floor." He also stuffed the corner of another blanket in his mouth to smother his cries. The next morning, MacArthur did not report the brutal treatment of the night before, but he fell out for the morning formation. The upperclassmen saw him and were either humbled or ashamed of their actions, or a combination of both. MacArthur earned their respect. For the remainder of the encampment, Douglas was left alone. "He gained the respect of all upperclassmen during summer camp that year," Cadet Wood recalled decades later. "I recall that all members of the class watched him for any sign of weakness, but he emerged from camp with flying colors. He showed himself a true soldier."[25]

These acts were not exactly torture, but they were abusive because they could have caused serious injury. Frederick Cunningham gave testimony of the severe hazing young Douglas endured. In late August, after two months at the academy, Cunningham resigned his appointment and departed. He wrote an unsigned letter to the *New York Sun*, a prominent New York City publication of the day, explaining the abuse that new cadets faced.[26] This letter, and the death of Oscar Booz the next year, prompted President William McKinley to order the investigation into the practice of hazing at West Point. Douglas MacArthur would be a reluctant witness at these military and congressional hearings.[27]

• • • *

The death of former cadet Oscar Booz in December 1900 created a public outrage especially in the press of the day. The accusations by the family, a local physician, and the family's minister caused Congress and the War Department officials to act. Fate's fortune dictated that Cadet Douglas MacArthur would be summoned to be a witness at the three hearings and inquiries held at West Point: two were Army, and the last was a congressional hearing.[28]

Superintendent Mills conducted an internal investigation held in mid-December 1900 shortly after Booz's death. The commandant, Lt. Col. Otto Hein, learned of Cadet MacArthur's ordeal during Summer Encampment and interviewed him during the academy investigation concerning hazing. MacArthur refused to provide any details or names of those who harassed him.[29] The code of silence was great among the Corps of Cadets—not informing on other cadets was an unwritten principle among these young men. But Mills and Hein were determined to clear West Point's good name.

On December 8, Mills wrote a report to the secretary of war outlining for the official record the results of the inquiry and the history of Cadet Booz's time at West Point. One point brought to light was that Booz was called "Bibles" by other cadets "and was made by them to suffer ridicule and persecution on account of his religious belief." During the hearings, the investigators often asked questions and probed the witnesses about religion as a cause for brutality toward Booz.[30]

The inquiry Colonel Mills conducted is best described as perfunctory, which did not thoroughly investigate the matter at hand. Mills did not have the means, time, or expertise to conduct a thorough investigation. He and his officers interviewed many cadets who were new cadets in 1898 (Booz's class) and who were upperclassmen who allegedly committed the hazing and abuse.[31]

Colonel Mills eventually denied any connection of Booz's death with the academy.[32] Later, in the *Annual Report of the Superintendent* completed for the year 1901, he provided a summary of how hazing had exacerbated in recent years: "In recent years, due in a measure to new conditions, it [hazing] had developed to an extent of severity never before attained, I believe, and in cases it was carried to extremes. All cadets have not been in sympathy with the practice, nor indulged in it, and but few in any class have carried it to a point of brutality."[33]

Unfortunately, as a review of his reports and his own witness statements reveals, Mills seemed more concerned with clearing the academy's name and reputation against the newspaper accounts and the Booz family's accusations. Of the allegations of cadets forcing Booz to drink inordinate amounts of Tabasco sauce, he declared, "I do not hesitate to assert that it is untrue." Mills regrettably looked upon both hazing and the hearings as a matter of honor and reputation. He did all he could to wage a campaign of damage control.[34] The academy's honor was more important to Mills than the safety and well-being of the cadets and finding the truth.

On December 11, Secretary of War Elihu Root, acting on orders from President Woodrow Wilson, directed that a court of inquiry conduct an internal investigation. The general-in-chief, Lt. Gen. Nelson A. Miles, appointed Maj. Gen. John R. Brooke, a forty-year veteran beginning with the Civil War, as chair. Soon a committee of military officers convened at Governor's Island in New York City to organize themselves and commence their work. General

Brooke was commander of the Department of the East at the time. He eventually convened the court at West Point and commenced interviewing witnesses. Cadet MacArthur was one of dozens of witnesses questioned.[35]

The military court of inquiry under General Brooke convened on December 28, at West Point. Along with MacArthur that day, two notable cadets and classmates were summoned to testify: Cadets Cocheu and Grant.[36]

At the time, Cadet Corporal MacArthur was academically first in his class and was a rising star in the corps. For him to face military officers, and then Congressmen, in a public hearing and answer questions concerning a traditional practice, as brutal at it could be at times, placed him in a difficult position. If Douglas accused serving cadets and described in detail what he endured, telling the truth, then he could be held in contempt among his fellow cadets and ostracized for doing that which was right and proper.[37]

However, some interesting evidence from the academy inquiry surfaced regarding the interviews undertaken by Lt. Col. Hein. On the morning of December 29, Hein appeared before General Brooke's military court of inquiry and testified that he had interviewed some cadets in the late summer of 1899 who had been hazed severely. Douglas and another cadet had been asked by Hein who had committed the hazing against them. Hein stated, "Mr. MacArthur had been subjected to brutal hazing. . . . These cases were investigated by the Superintendent and myself. The cadets were questioned . . . but from them no information could be elicited as to what hazing they had been subjected." During this session Hein explained the statistics concerning hazing at the academy: there were fifty-two cadets punished for hazing in 1897; in 1898 there were 129 reports of hazing, with twelve cadets punished and confined for thirty days.[38]

The same week that the army inquiry took place, the US House of Representatives decided to act due to the intense press coverage and literally dozens of newspaper articles condemning the academy and the army. A "select committee" was appointed with the commission "to investigate and report the alleged hazing and resulting death of Oscar Booz" and determine the truth "upon the subject of the practice of hazing." The committee was to investigate whether there had been criminal conduct by the cadets and whether negligence on the part of the officers of West Point was in fact true. The chairman was Republican Rep. Charles Dick of Ohio, a long-serving veteran of the Ohio militia and the new National Guard. He was also the chairman of the House Militia Committee, which sponsored some of the most significant legislation reforming the armed forces of the United States in the early twentieth century.[39] The main investigator was Democrat Edmund Driggs from Brooklyn, New York. Driggs was determined to find the truth regarding hazing at the academy and punish the guilty, especially those cadets involved in the death of Oscar Booz.[40] Being from New York, Driggs possibly saw the cruelty of hazing at West Point as an embarrassment to his home state. Also on the panel was Bertram T. Clayton, also a New Yorker, who was a graduate of the academy himself in the class of 1886 along with John J. Pershing.[41]

Of the three separate inquiries, the congressional hearing drew more national attention and had more authority to perform a thorough investigation. The select committee had subpoena authority to call witnesses and greater power to investigate not only the Booz case but also hazing as a practice at the academy. If some witnesses were obstinate, they could be found for "contempt of Congress" or perjury by misrepresenting the truth. These members of Congress were also responsible for the academy's budget and oversight of policies and regulations. The military court of inquiry, in contrast, did not have such authority.[42] Both panels called dozens of cadets to testify as witnesses. Many at the hearing, and especially the congressional committee members, knew who Cadet MacArthur was. At this time in January 1901, Douglas's father Arthur MacArthur was serving as military governor of the Philippines.[43]

Cadet MacArthur's testimony, in both the military court of inquiry held in December 1900 and the congressional hearings of January 1901, were recorded in an official government document. The select committee held hearings and sessions in Bristol, Pennsylvania, where the many witnesses—members of the Booz family and their associates—resided, on January 4, 1901. Next, the committee held sessions in Philadelphia on January 7 and 8. The committee then moved on to West Point, where hearings were in session January 14 through 19, 1901.[44]

Some practices of the entire hazing episode were revealed in this first military inquiry conducted by US Army officers. The questions of the inquiry addressed what the nature of the hazing was. Also, the investigating officers wanted to determine the cruelty and brutality that the cadets employed, and who the culprits were. The hearings were held to discover why cadets committed such brutal acts against their mates in the name of loyalty and discipline.

The battery of questions recorded in the 1901 *Special Congressional Report* was nearly as painful for MacArthur as the hazing itself had been. The committee members pummeled MacArthur with dozens of questions that he agonized over. One example: "Mr. MacArthur, we have received a great deal of evidence that you were severely hazed.... [Describe] the physical effect on you personally of the hazing at that time." Answering a question about how many eagling repetitions he had performed one night, he responded, "I should say, perhaps, 250 would be a good estimate."

A court member asked MacArthur, "Were you subjected to more hazing than any of the rest of your classmen?" His answer: "I think not; no sir." A strict review of the congressional hearings and the military court of inquiry reveals that no cadets in the years in question, 1898, 1899, and even 1900, endured the brutality and treatment that Douglas MacArthur experienced—except for Booz possibly. Many of the witnesses testified that MacArthur was the subject of several severe hazing sessions and other indignities.[45]

During the military court, General Brooke asked Douglas directly about his experience:

QUESTION:	"What were you required to do? Tell the court fully."
MACARTHUR:	"I was required, among other things, to make funny speeches, sir.... I was also required to stand in a constrained position and do what is known as exercising, to some extent."
QUESTION:	"What kind of exercising?"
MACARTHUR:	"What is known as 'eagling' and 'wooden willies,' sir."

MacArthur attempted to answer the questions as honestly as possible, but he was perhaps nervous and afraid of the outcome. Eventually, the questions turned to who hazed him and their names. He had been taught as a young boy to not turn on others, not to accuse or squeal about the misdeeds of others. Referring to his upbringing, MacArthur declared, "My father and mother had taught me those two immutable principles—never to lie, never to tattle." In his autobiographical memoirs, *Reminiscences,* published some sixty years later,

MacArthur recalled: "If the court insisted and ordered me to reveal the names, and I refused to obey the order, it would in all likelihood mean my dismissal and the end of all my hopes and dreams. It would be so easy and expedient to yield, to tell, and who would blame me?"[46]

According to his own account, "I knew then what to do. Come what may, I would be no tattletale." Before the battery of questions ended, Douglas became sick, as he had during his entrance examinations in Milwaukee more than two years earlier. Until his death in 1964, MacArthur maintained that he did not reveal the names of his tormentors. His many biographers stated that he only provided the names of those cadets who had already admitted their actions and were no longer in the corps.[47] However, this is not the case—it is not true. Cadet MacArthur did indeed provide the investigating panels with the names of those who harassed him. At first, he was coy, dismissive, and even artfully dodged their questions, but eventually, he had to face reality.

At one point he was asked whether he had fainted or not, whether he screamed out or not, and whether he sought medical attention. All these questions MacArthur denied or did his best to avoid or obfuscate.

Then the true test arose: Would Douglas name his abusers?

General Brooke asked directly, "Give their names."

MacArthur answered, "General, is it absolutely necessary that I give these names, sir? I don't see that they have any bearing upon the investigation, sir."

"This is not an ordinary examination, Mr. MacArthur. You are to reply to all questions as they are put to you!"

Douglas had no choice but to answer.

"Mr. Dockery, sir."[48]

This name had not been announced before: Cadet Albert B. Dockery from the state of Mississippi, who was still a member of the corps and in the class ahead of MacArthur.

General Brooke continued in his interrogation: "Who else?"

MacArthur responded, "That is all I can say to you, sir. There were other cadets, who have since left the corps."

Brooke bore down: "Who were they?"

Douglas relented, "Mr. [Walter O.] Boswell, Mr. [J.B.A.] Barry, and Mr. [James W.] Devall, sir."[49]

Of interest is the fact that three of the main abusers of Cadet Douglas MacArthur were Southern born: Barry was from Tennessee and Boswell was from Georgia. (The fourth named abuser, Devall, was from Louisiana.) Whether these cadets tormented MacArthur because he was a son of a Yankee war hero is not confirmed from the testimony or record.

MacArthur also provided the names of several cadets who had engaged in boxing contests that the cadets called "scrapping committees," where certain cadets targeted others for harassment, which, like hazing, became an arena for abuse. There was a scrapping during Douglas's plebe year where he served as second to Cadet Edward M. Zell, who was pummeled and beaten in the match. MacArthur named Zell and upperclassman James A. Shannon, both cadets at the time of the hearings. Zell later graduated with MacArthur in 1903. Both Shannon and Zell died later during active service. The boxing and scrapping exercises were held in discreet locations and at secret times to avoid the scrutiny of officers. One of the favorite haunts was the ruins of old Fort Putnam high on the hill above the main academy area. These cadets were acting as a second as in a duel, enforcing rules and gentlemanly expectations.[50]

During the congressional hearing, Representative Driggs took the opportunity to scold a cadet, making him the whipping boy for what he saw as a detestable practice at an institution that was intended to set a higher standard of fairness and decency. Cadet Albert Dockery took the stand and became the subject of some of the treatment he had heaped on others. His ordeal was not physical but verbal and public.

DRIGGS: "You are satisfied that you hazed Mr. MacArthur?"
DOCKERY: "Yes, sir."
DRIGGS: "You are also satisfied that he was sick after you got through hazing him?"
DOCKERY: "Yes, sir."
DRIGGS: "You heard that he had convulsions more or less?"
DOCKERY: "Yes, sir."
DRIGGS: "You didn't consider that at all cruel, did you?"
DOCKERY: "Well yes, sir."
DRIGGS: "Now, young man, for your own education, I want to tell you what I think it was; I think it was atrocious, base,

detestable, disgraceful, dishonorable, disreputable, heinous, ignominious, illfamed, odious, outrageous, scandalous, shameful, vile, violent, and wicked. That is all I have to say, Mr. Chairman."[51]

• • •

In the *Annual Report of the Superintendent of 1901*, Colonel Mills recorded the outcome regarding the accusation that hazing had caused the death of Oscar Booz: "The evidence adduced before the military court of inquiry and Congressional committee last winter showed that the allegations in the case which led to the inquiries were not true."[52]

Albert Mills wrote extensively about hazing and the investigations in his annual report, admitting that hazing was wrong, immoral, and abusive. He seemed unable to correct the situation and eradicate this unseemly practice, though he established some new measures in 1899, the year after Booz endured his hazing, and the same year as MacArthur's Beast Barracks and Summer Encampment. As commandant of cadets, Lieutenant Colonel Hein attempted to end hazing, scrapping, and extreme physical exercising of the new cadets. These measures were not effective; in fact, they caused a great unrest in the corps.[53]

Though the investigations and hearings were unsettling, the cadets maintained a form of power and unity in their ability to police their own ranks, employing hazing, boxing, and extreme exercises as tools. The officers of the academy, Congress, and the American public now wanted it otherwise. After the hearings, Congress passed a new law on March 1, 1901, giving the superintendent more power and authority to stop hazing. This act of Congress caused the modifications of academy and corps regulations in the Black (academy) and Blue (cadet) Books, respectively.[54]

A month later there was an incident in the cadet mess where a minor food-flinging contest caused a great deal of resentment among the corps, when a cadet was punished for not controlling this simple episode. On April 16, 1901, dozens of cadets marched to the superintendent's house west of the Plain and demanded mercy for the cadet. They cried out slogans and wild comments, and even dragged the Reveille Gun from Trophy Point, unlimbered it, and aimed it at the great house. No shot or shell was loaded, but a blast of powder was truly an act of defiance. Colonel Mills would not brook such disrespect, calling the incident a mutiny; he charged more than a dozen cadets with a major breach of discipline. With summary power by Congress, Mills did not convene a court martial but dispensed justice quickly. Five cadets were dismissed, and six others were suspended for a year. The idea of dozens of cadets taking matters into their own hands, showing such a deliberate act of open rebellion against authority, was seen by Colonel Mills and others as furtherance of cadet disobedience akin to hazing. The discipline of the corps was the main concern at stake.[55]

The Corps of Cadets was duly upset and tested the law and authority of the superintendent by seeking redress from Secretary of War Root with no success.[56]

Did hazing end at West Point?

No. But the most severe forms of the practice were less common.

As for MacArthur's opinion about these practices, he declared, "Hazing was practiced with a worthy goal, but with methods that were violent and uncontrolled."[57]

What is truly interesting about the Summer Encampment, Beast Barracks, and the hazing Cadet MacArthur endured is that no more than a hundred yards away from where he bivouacked, his mother, Mary "Pinky" Hardy MacArthur, lived in quiet rest and a level of luxury at West Point Hotel on Trophy Point. She was also residing there during the tribunals and hearings that took place during the winter of 1900–1901.

CHAPTER 4

THE CORPS

With Beast Barracks and Summer Encampment accomplished, the young cadets returned to their austere stone barracks, built some sixty years earlier. The second classmen returned from their summer furlough and joined the other three classes. Companies were formed with cadets from all four class years dispersed among the four companies of the cadet battalion. Cadet MacArthur was assigned to Company A with Capt. Edmund M. Blake, class of 1889, as tactical officer. Cadet Arthur Hyde was a first classman in the summer of 1899, serving as first sergeant over his company and its plebe squad. He recalled years later that summer cadre cadets were in a fuss over how to treat the new batch of cadets. Cadet Hyde also observed Douglas MacArthur among the many new plebes. "During camp I had had occasion to watch MacArthur's activities rather closely," he recalled forty years later, "and had been impressed with his attention to duty and his manifest determination to make good as a cadet." As a cadet lieutenant he planned to room with another cadet from his class, but he decided on a bold move. The new room assignments or "makes" occurred at the end of Summer Encampment. Cadet Hyde decided to offer his make to Douglas MacArthur, a plebe—an unusual move. "The invitation naturally came to him as a surprise, but in about a half hour he came to me to say he would accept."[1] Where did Douglas go during that half hour? He was off to the West Point Hotel and "asked for time to run over to the hotel to talk to his mother" about the invitation. He probably did not need to ask his mother, Mary "Pinky" Hardy MacArthur, for permission, but it was an unusual opportunity rooming with Hyde, a "firstie"; probably he was just confirming what he already knew was the right thing to do. A plebe rooming with an upperclassman had extra benefits; for example, firsties could keep their room light on an hour later, until eleven o'clock.[2] This was a huge advantage for MacArthur; more time he could study.

The two young men moved into the First Division stairwell of the Central Barracks on the third floor in the tower.[3] There were originally ten divisions in the old 1855 barracks with four rooms on each floor, going up to the fourth floor, a total of sixteen rooms per division, housing normally two cadets per room. The divisions were organized by squads within companies. The entrances were the division area's old barracks building, that eventually combined with additions in the 1880s and 1920s to make the Central Barracks the shape of a horseshoe or "U." The First Division, the most prestigious division, was where the senior cadets of the corps had roomed ever since 1851, when the barracks was completed. Cadet John J. Pershing, for example, lived there during his senior year in 1885–86 as First Captain over the Corps of Cadets. At that time all the entrance rooms into the barracks were numbered by a division number over the door. There were no hallways that connected the entire barracks or wing together. This building floor plan from the 1840s did not allow the cadets to rally or gather together indoors in large groups and have incidents or rumbles in the hallways. The First Division was the division of honor and a cause of jealousy among the corps.[4]

Hyde saw immediately the dedication and commitment Douglas showed. "My outstanding recollection of Doug in those days is of the earnestness of his purpose," Hyde wrote. "It was his ambition to be the number one man in his class, and in consequence his energy was directed to the attainment of that object."[5] MacArthur spent the entire plebe year with Hyde, and together they developed a warm and life-long friendship. Hyde commented years later, "Whatever Douglas MacArthur achieved in his military career, he has earned by those qualities which were so evident when he was a plebe." Other cadets realized that young Douglas was a standout even during his first year. Hyde continued that MacArthur had "a fine mind, marked ability, a determination to succeed, inexhaustible energy, the respect of his associates and an innate quality of leadership."[6]

Despite demonstrating outstanding traits and abilities, Cadet MacArthur was still a teenager with the foibles and foolishness of youth. Though MacArthur developed a great academic and service record as a cadet, he still broke rules, ignored regulations, dared to be outrageous at times, and even challenged the system on rare occasions. He was mischievous and adventurous, especially when away from the academy in New York City or on other trips. Fortune smiled on him never being caught during his misadventures.

Douglas often visited his mother "Pinky" during those first two years—if not every day, at least on Sunday afternoons. Rules and class privileges, accorded by rank and year, allowed certain opportunities. The underclassmen often risked the rules to have some fun and do daring exploits. On one occasion Douglas was visiting his mother at the West Point Hotel along with George Cocheu, his classmate and roommate during their yearling, or sophomore, year. The hotel was off-limits at times, so, Pinky often brought treats to the barracks area for Douglas and his friends, serving "fruit and other delicacies." On one Sunday afternoon the two were visiting Pinky and were eating on the back porch with some young ladies. Cocheu remembered that "a bellboy informed Mrs. MacArthur that the Superintendent was calling on her." This was Colonel Albert Mills. "All exits were closed and sealed for the winter," Cocheu remembered. "The only way out was through the cellar, so it was there that we ran, and we escaped, undetected, by crawling out through the coal chute."[7] This harrowing experience was just one of many that young Douglas had.

One of the most famous pranks in West Point history, and a fabulous legend among the Corps of Cadets even until today, involved MacArthur. His name is associated with this notorious cadet deed, though it is impossible to prove the connection. Historian D. Clayton James wrote: "For many years after his graduation he was credited with the best-known trick of that era at West Point—hoisting the reveille gun to the tower of one of the academic buildings."[8]

Sgt. Marty Maher, a physical fitness instructor who served at the academy for more than fifty years, wrote about the MacArthurs. He published a memoir entitled *Bringing up the Brass* and titled a chapter "Them MacArthurs." Maher wrote of the reveille gun incident, providing his opinion as to who accomplished this feat. It took "a detachment of men, working with block and tackles, most of a week to get the cannon down." The cadets emplaced the gun in one night, and Maher had his own opinion about who did it: "I don't know who did it, but I said then, and I still say, that Douglas MacArthur was the cadet with the most brains, the one who could have figured the thing out."[9]

Below the famous Plain of West Point there is a narrow trail that winds along the shore of the Hudson River. An ammunition and supply cart path during the Revolutionary War, in the nineteenth century it became known as "Flirtation Walk," where cadets strolled with female friends—and where many a proposal was made. Douglas narrated an interesting story from his autobiography, *Reminiscences*, sixty years later: "And that awful moment when a tactical officer caught me on Flirtation Walk publicly kissing a girl, and instead of reporting me for unbecoming conduct, just grinned and said, 'Congratulations, Mister MacArthur.'"[10]

Young and handsome MacArthur had several other adventures with those of the opposite sex during his cadet years. During his upperclassman years Douglas and some friends visited New York City. His classmates Charles Severson, who was his roommate at the time, and Emil "Dotty" Laurson "slipped away and swaggered into Rector's on Broadway, [and] shook hands with 'Diamond Jim Brady.'" James Brady was a wealthy gambling man and shady character in unsavory New York backstreets of questionable business dealings. Rector's was a famous and elite restaurant where Douglas called for "nine martinis." The astounded bartender asked, "Where are the other six?" Young Dotty Laurson, "striking a Napoleonic posture, bellowed out, pointing to the six waiting glasses, 'Their spirits are here.'" Douglas concluded his memory of the evening with, "And then we swanked out to a burlesque show. We loved it."[11] A burlesque show of that day was a very seedy affair.

An interesting romantic adventure occurred during Douglas's senior year in 1903. He had a blind date as an escort for a Miss Bess B. Follansbee, if that was her name after forty-two years. She narrated that in 1945 she had rummaged through a trunk and found a diary about her date with Douglas MacArthur decades earlier. By then General MacArthur was now famous and a household name to Americans.[12]

Arriving by train at the West Point train station, then by bus to the West Point Hotel, Bess soon met MacArthur, her escort for the evening. "We met the cadets outside and proceeded up the marble stairway" in Memorial Hall, later Cullum Hall. She recorded, "and then I saw the most beautiful ballroom," with a dance floor that "was smooth as glass and around the sides of the electric-lighted room were mahogany davenports trimmed with crimson velvet." She recalled "my first two [dances] were with Mr. MacArthur and I liked him." Then according to her dance card, she danced with a half-dozen other cadets.[13]

The next day Bess met Douglas at the West Point Hotel and was introduced to Mrs. MacArthur. Yet again, Douglas and other cadets had to scramble and hide when an officer visited the hotel. They hid in the basement, which Bess said "impressed me as very funny." Cadet MacArthur and his two fellow cadets returned from their temporary hideout, and Bess returned to New York City later that day with two cents remaining of her allowance.

Physical Fitness and Athletics

Anyone familiar with the legacy and contributions of Douglas MacArthur to the US Military Academy knows that athletics, sports, physical fitness, and military readiness were huge aspects of his own life and his professional attributes. He infused these skills and qualities in all his units he commanded and to soldiers who trained and served under him during his entire career. Cadet MacArthur, perhaps not the most capable, talented, and accomplished athlete, was nonetheless a letterman in baseball and served as a manager on the football team his senior year. He was diligent and gave his best, and most of all, over a fifty-year career serving his nation and army, he relished and was proud of his cadet years and the small part he played in West Point sports and athletics.

Cadets had to undergo physical fitness classes during their four years of study according to the academic curriculum. The plebes had to take fencing, gymnastics, wrestling, dancing, and boxing classes besides participating in company calisthenics, drill, and military exercises. These courses in athletics were administrated through the master of the sword, later the head of the Department of Physical Education. From the earliest days of West Point, the master of the sword and a small cadre of officers and instructors taught swordsmanship and other physical skills or exercises to the cadets. They participated voluntarily in other group sports that included baseball, soccer, lacrosse, football, tennis, golf, polo, and track. Some of these sports later became intercollegiate athletics programs.[14]

At West Point, sports and athletics as an academic or organized program began during the 1880s when Herman J. Koehler revolutionized physical training after he was hired in 1885 by superintendent Col. Wesley Merritt as a civilian instructor. Recommended for a commission in 1889, Koehler was the driving force behind the first gymnasium structure, the Gymnasium and Fencing Academy, completed in 1893. He also pushed for a larger and more modern gymnasium, which in 1910 came to pass, during the major campus building program by the architecture firm of Cram, Goodhue, and Ferguson. Koehler not only established and professionalized the athletics at the academy but, during World War I, was assigned by the War Department to travel extensively to all the recruit and mobilization depots to train cadre instructors in the proper skills and practices of unit physical training. Historians today view Herman Koehler as the father of physical education not only at West Point but for the entire US Army.[15] Koehler published manuals on physical training for the army that were used by hundreds of trainers at various depot training camps during the Great War.[16]

In 1901 Herman Koehler received a direct commission of first lieutenant during young MacArthur's cadetship. Koehler was still the Master of the Sword in 1919 when Brigadier General MacArthur returned as superintendent. Koehler served thirty-eight years at the military academy, retiring in 1923 as a lieutenant colonel and recipient of the Distinguished Service Medal.[17]

One of the staff members in 1899 was the legendary Marty Maher, who published a book about his fifty-five years at the academy. In 1955 a film based upon his life, *The Long Gray Line*, was released; its director was the renowned John Ford. In his book, Maher recalled Cadet MacArthur: "I still remember how Douglas MacArthur looked when I first laid eyes on him in 1899. He was a plebe in A Company then. Handsome as a prince he was—six feet tall . . . with dark hair and a ruddy, outdoors looks. You know he was a soldier even in his swimming trunks."[18]

Athletics was not part of the curriculum at the time, but it is when intercollegiate athletics was born. College competitive sports began in earnest after the Civil War and soon took hold between the two federal service academies. Many baseball enthusiasts believe that Abner Doubleday was the founder of the game, but the historical evidence does not support this myth. Regardless, Doubleday, an 1842 graduate of the academy, is forever linked to the game.[19]

College sports grew and matured in the later nineteenth century with baseball and football as the crowning contests.

Athletic competition boded well with the military culture of teamwork, discipline, and physical finesse. The very first Army/Navy football game was played in 1890—a Navy win. After the 1893 game, President Grover Cleveland ordered the match-up's termination due to a major ruckus by fans after the game. It was not until 1899, MacArthur's plebe year, that the rivalry was resumed after officials were convinced the fans would behave. On December 2, 1899, not only did Army defeat Navy, 17 to 5, at Franklin Field in Philadelphia, Pennsylvania, but the famous Army mule mascot was introduced. The mule, called "Big White," was ridden and walked about during the game, challenging Navy's goat mascot. Young Cadet MacArthur witnessed this most historic game and would all his life be a devoted fan to West Point sports.[20]

It was not until 1901 that the two military academics squared off in baseball, the more dominant American sport at the turn of the century. Douglas MacArthur played left field in this historic game played in Annapolis. Biographer William Manchester wrote of MacArthur, "All his life he would be fiercely proud of his varsity 'A.' Aged seventy, he wore it on his bathrobe the night before the Inchon landing."[21]

Young Douglas's great day of glory as an athlete came in spring of 1901, his third-class year. On Saturday, May 18, the Army baseball team faced the Navy team at Annapolis for the first time. The coach was Charles Irvine, a civilian under contract and a former professional baseball player.[22] The West Point officer charged with the baseball program was First Lt. Leon B. Kromer, an 1899 graduate, who retired in 1938 as a major general and chief of the Cavalry Branch.[23]

Left-fielder MacArthur was second in the batting order. The game commenced at precisely 2:30 p.m. As Douglas walked up for his first at-bats, Navy players and fans hooted at him, referring to his father, the general in the Philippines. "Every raincoat was swinging, every Navy voice joining the ribald ditty," MacArthur recalled:

> Are you the Governor General or a hobo?
> Who is the boss of this show?
> Is it you or Emilio Aguinaldo?[24]

West Point baseball team, 1901. Cadet MacArthur is seated at far right. *Courtesy MacArthur Memorial.*

MacArthur then grounded out to the Navy second baseman. The game was rather wild at times: two Army players were hit by pitched balls, including right-fielder Edward Zell, who was hit in the face and needed a substitute runner.[25] Navy scored a run in the third inning, but then the third hitter was Douglas, who walked to first with a base on balls, loading the bases for Army. He then advanced to second base with a fly-out to deep right field, and the lead runner scored. Then a wild throw from the right-fielder after the fly-out sailed over the catcher, allowing the runner ahead of MacArthur to score, while he bounded to third base. With MacArthur on third base, John Herr hit a clean single over the second baseman, driving MacArthur to home plate, scoring the third Army run of the inning.[26]

According to MacArthur, "I was no Ty Cobb, but in those days I could run." He admitted, but "the catcher threw wild, allowing me to go to third and I trotted home with what proved to be the winning run in a 4–3 contest."[27] Actually, Douglas's run gave Army a lead of 3 to 1 over Navy in the third inning.

The Army squad scored another run in the bottom of the sixth inning, making it 4 to 1. Then Navy scored two runs in the ninth but still lost the game to Army with a score of 4 to 3. For the day, MacArthur had no hits for three at-bats, one fly-out, one ground-out, and one base on balls. Douglas MacArthur did not score the winning run of the famous 1901 Army victory as he claimed; he scored the third of four runs total. One could accuse him of lying, or perhaps it was a failure of memory. For the season, MacArthur had thirty at-bats and eight hits, with a batting average of .266, near the bottom of the roster.[28]

Army vs. Navy Baseball Game, 1901

	1	2	3	4	5	6	7	8	9	R H E
Navy			1						2	3 11 3
Army			3			1			X	4 7 1

The next year, MacArthur played on the baseball team and earned his letter "A" in baseball. That fall of 1902, Douglas volunteered to serve as manager of the football team. At 135 pounds and lean, MacArthur would not have done well on the gridiron. It is interesting that this same year, his senior, he served both as cadet battalion First Captain, the senior ranking cadet in the Corps, and manager of the team. Both positions took a great deal of personal time. To serve as a lowly manager, responsible for cleaning soiled football jerseys, mending equipment, and watching the practices and games for endless hours in all weather conditions, was a major sacrifice of time, something unusual for a cadet who was excelling in all disciplines and the senior leader of his class and the Corps. MacArthur was a huge football enthusiast his entire life, especially with regard to Army football.[29]

Academics

One of the hallmarks of Cadet Douglas MacArthur's successes and achievement was academics. He did indeed graduate number one in the class of 1903, among ninety-three fellow cadets. One of the legends surrounding Douglas MacArthur's academic accomplishments has been noted by many peers, historians, and biographers. Arthur Hyde, MacArthur's first roommate, wrote forty years later, "In addition MacArthur enjoyed the distinction of having graduated with the highest scholastic record to be attained by any cadet in 25 years."[30] Biographer Arthur Herman wrote: "Some said it [MacArthur's record] was the most outstanding graduating record since Robert E. Lee's in the class of 1829. Most agreed it was the best in a quarter century."[31]

Rating Douglas MacArthur in comparison to other graduates of other eras is not reasonable, because curricula changed every dozen or so years, and grading and coursework evolved over time. There are also merits earned and demerits assigned, which on occasion meant the difference in graduating or not, dismissal or not, or being turned back for a year. Class standing was based on academic and performance grades and the merits/demerits earned or lost. The military courses and training drills were graded in the sense of earning merits or gaining demerits; they applied to mastery of a skill or subject, or shortcomings noted. The education and instruction of MacArthur's era was based on cadets learning or memorizing certain material and being prepared to discuss it, or recite in class session the next day.[32] Carrying his remarkable record from West Texas Military Academy, Douglas MacArthur was top of his plebe class of some 134 members. His performance was impressive:[33]

Subject	Class Standing
Mathematics	1
English	1
French	2
Drill Regulations	1
Conduct	2
Demerits ending May 31, 1900	11
Order of Merit	1

The classes were rated by the total number of merits or points that could have been earned each semester. For example, the highest rated discipline was math, with 400 points, whereas chemistry and other physical sciences such as mineralogy and physics rated only 225 merits. Humanities rated even less: English earned 50 points or merits, Spanish garnered 85, and French fetched 150 points. The system was used to determine academic weight and priority, which was also used to establish class ranking with this weighted scale. This system not only evaluated academic expertise but also judged character development and military leadership.³⁴

Classroom instruction at West Point during Douglas's time there was austere. Discipline was rigid and the learning climate was severe. Cadets recited their lessons, and there was very little interaction between students and instructors. In one exchange a cadet sought guidance and assistance, to which the instructor retorted, "I'm not here to answer questions, but to mark you."³⁵

Cadet MacArthur himself had some interesting academic adventures. Col. Gustav J. Fiebeger had been a chair of civil and military engineering since 1896, himself an 1879 graduate and engineer officer. One day in engineering class the cadets were studying Albert Einstein's Theory of Relativity. MacArthur narrated the episode:

> The text was complex and, being unable to comprehend it, I committed the pages to memory. When I was called upon to recite, I solemnly reeled off almost word for word what the book said. Our instructor, Colonel Fiebeger, looked at me quizzically and asked. "Do you understand this theory?" It was a bad moment for me, but I did not hesitate in replying, "No Sir." You could have hard a pin drop. I braced myself and waited. And then the slow words of the professor, "Neither do I, Mister MacArthur. Section dismissed." I still do not understand the theory.³⁶

This was probably a rare admission for such a senior professor and department head in a particular discipline.

Academically, MacArthur again led his class of 104 members his third classman (sophomore) year ending in 1901. Near the end of the spring term, MacArthur faced an academic dilemma. He had a mathematics class with the department head and professor, Lt. Col. Wright P. Edgerton, class of 1874, who had been appointed as professor in 1898. At that time if a cadet had reached a certain score or average at the end of the semester, the cadet was not required to take the final examination. Douglas learned, however, that he was scheduled to take the examination regardless of his class standing as number one in his entire class year in mathematics. Outraged and a bit arrogant, he marched to Colonel Edgerton's quarters and confronted him about the examination and his class record. The professor explained that class standing was only one requirement to be exempt from the final, but a cadet had to take the majority of the in-class quizzes. MacArthur protested, saying he was not aware of this second requirement. Because he had been sick that winter, he had missed some of the quizzes. Frustrated and angry, MacArthur declared to his superior that he would not be at the scheduled examination and stormed off to his barracks room. He swore to his roommate George W. Cocheu, "If my name is not off that list before 9:00 in the morning. I'll resign!" To MacArthur this was a matter of honor and not an academic problem.[37]

Ten minutes before the exam time the next morning, a messenger arrived with a note from Colonel Edgerton. Cadet MacArthur had been excused from the final. This incident, according to Cocheu, was a demonstration of personal honor "no matter how disagreeable." There were other tests and challenges of his life that confirmed that he was exceptional and that he had a mission to perform for the nation, the US Army, and his family's honor. This episode with the professor gave Douglas MacArthur the confidence that he could determine his future if he was resolute and hopefully also correct. As biographer D. Clayton James stated, "this incident" demonstrated Edgerton's forbearance "but also [was] the first known manifestation of MacArthur's acute sensitivity when his pride and honor seemed to be at stake."[38]

After two academic years MacArthur was at the top of his class. His third year, however, now called "Cow" by modern cadets, Douglas dropped to fourth in the class standing of ninety-seven members. The original group of 134 new cadets was decreasing every year. His class standing during the third year was thus:[39]

Subject	Class Standing
Natural and Experimental Philosophy	7
Chemistry, Physics, and Mineralogy	4
Drill Regulations	2
Drawing	24
Conduct	2
Demerits ending May 31, 1900	4
Order of Merit	4

The bright spot of this year's report card was his lower number of demerits, the best of all four years.

One of MacArthur's chief competitors in class standing was Ulysses S. Grant III, the grandson of the president and great victor of the Civil War. The two had much in common: they were both sons of senior ranking generals and heroes of the Civil War. They both excelled in academics and other duties at the academy. They both were destined for distinguished military careers and a great future of service. The crown jewel was scholarly standing at the end of each year and finally at graduation. Grant initially challenged MacArthur, but by their third year, Grant stood sixth in the class.

At West Point competition was a religion—honored, respected, exalted to a degree, and practiced with zeal. Arthur Hyde, Douglas's roommate his first year, recalled his dedication and his thirst for competition: "His time was devoted wholly to his academic and military duties."[40] Apparently young Douglas MacArthur arrived at West Point with the full intention and objective to graduate at the top of the class of 1903.[41]

Douglas MacArthur's final fourth-year class standing:[42]

Subject	Class Standing
Civil and Military Engineering	3
Law	1
History	1
Ordnance and Gunnery	1
Drill Regulations	4
Military Efficiency	1
Soldierly Deportment and Discipline	5
Practical Military Engineering	37
Conduct, First Class	10
Demerits ending May 31, 1903	27
Order of Merit	1

Cadet MacArthur achieved a sterling scholastic record of 98.1425 percent of maximum credits possible. His record was not at the top of all the cadets before and after him. In fact, in one register he was thirty-ninth overall from the classes of 1821 to 1949, out of some seventeen thousand cadets. Robert E. Lee was six places ahead of MacArthur. All in all, though, MacArthur excelled and accomplished much.[43]

Centennial: 1902

At the end of MacArthur's third year, in 1902, the United States Military Academy celebrated its centennial. The actual founding date of the academy was March 16, 1802, with an act of Congress creating the Academy at West Point. Academy officials elected to commemorate the great day in June during graduation week. The Centennial Commemoration was perhaps the greatest ceremonial and popular event in West Point's history to that date. One of the important players was the Association of Graduates, or AOG, founded in 1869 as a forum for class reunions and alumni social events. The academy made the centennial celebration a major national event, which attracted alumni, their families, dignitaries, and thousands of other people. Cadets at the time would especially cherish this magnificent week, including Cadet Douglas MacArthur.

The first day of the celebration, Monday, June 9, 1902, was Alumni Day. More than 350 graduates attended a luncheon at the new Memorial Hall along with their guests. During this event Cadet MacArthur served as a supervisor of cadets acting as escorts and guides for the older graduates and other visitors. Some of the alumni slept in the old Central Barracks, where Douglas had lived for three years.[44]

The next day, June 10, was Field Day, which included a baseball game between Yale College and West Point, wherein the Army team was trounced 15–4. This was the last year that MacArthur played on the baseball team. That evening was the "Graduation Hop," a dance in Memorial Hall, a major gala event. Secretary of War Elihu Root and Lt. Gen. Nelson A. Miles, the army general-in-chief, were the distinguished guests. Former superintendent and general-in-chief John Schofield attended as the president of the Association of Graduates. Both generals Schofield and Miles were Medal of Honor recipients, and several individuals in attendance would in the future be associated with the Medal of Honor.[45]

Centennial Day was June 11, Wednesday, one of the great days in West Point history. The grand event commenced with the arrival at 10:00 a.m. of President Theodore Roosevelt, at the train station at south dock. He was escorted up the steep hill to the Plain by a detachment of cavalry, interesting because "Colonel" Roosevelt led the 1st US Volunteer Cavalry "the Rough Riders" in Cuba during the Spanish-American War. Reaching the Plain, the president and his party stood on the review stand where Colonel Albert Mills, the superintendent, ordered the Corps of Cadets to "pass in review"—a pageant in itself. But first, President Roosevelt had a surprise. He called Cadet Calvin Titus forward "front and center." Without any warning, Cadet Titus stood before the entire Corps of Cadets. President Roosevelt descended the stand and presented the Medal of Honor to Cadet Titus, pinning it on the young man's uniform tunic as a short citation was read. Two years earlier Private Titus was a soldier serving during the Boxer Rebellion in China, and he was cited for his "gallantry at Peking, China, August 14, 1900, while a soldier with the Fourteenth United States Infantry."[46]

Roosevelt delivered a robust speech to the thousands of people gathered for the ceremony. He spoke of the importance of the military academy over the next hundred years, "This institution has completed its first hundred years of life. During that century no other educational institution in the land has contributed as many names as West Point has contributed to the honor roll of the nation's greatest citizens."[47] The ceremony included the unveiling of a Centennial Tablet by Roosevelt and the president of the Association of Graduates, General Schofield, class of 1853.

After the parade ended and as the cadets and others dispersed, MacArthur, two years ahead of Cadet Titus, approached him. Sizing up the young plebe, Cadet MacArthur exclaimed, "Mister, that's something," looking at the Medal of Honor pinned to Calvin Titus's uniform tunic.[48]

What is so interesting about this ending event of the academy's grand Centennial Day was the constellation of individuals associated with the Medal of Honor. Cadet Titus received the award from Theodore Roosevelt, who in 2001, some eighty years after his death, received the decoration for his actions on Kettle and San Juan Hills in 1898. The superintendent, Colonel Mills, himself received it a month later in 1902. In attendance were the aforementioned

Medal of Honor recipients John Schofield and Nelson Miles. Most fascinating was the comment that Cadet MacArthur made to Cadet Titus, as some forty years later Gen. Douglas MacArthur received the Medal of Honor for his "gallant leadership" during the Philippine campaign in 1942, as his father before him, Arthur MacArthur, received the award for his bravery in 1863 at Missionary Ridge. Arthur and Douglas MacArthur were the first father-and-son team to receive this, the highest award in military service. President Roosevelt's son Theodore Roosevelt Jr. received the medal for his valor in Normandy in 1944, the second father-and-son team. One morning on the Plain at West Point saw the amazingly unusual assortment of connections and individuals associated with the Medal of Honor.[49]

The formal centennial observances were over, but on June 12 the class of 1902 graduated and received its diplomas from President Roosevelt, who preferred being called Colonel Roosevelt. With the senior class graduated, the second classmen moved up, and the new First Captain of the entire Corps of Cadets was Douglas MacArthur.

Character and Leadership

One of the great missions of the US Military Academy is to develop leaders for the US Army. Leadership has been a key facet of the academy ever since Maj. Sylvanus Thayer established the fourth-class system where senior cadets lead and supervise the underclassmen. To really understand Douglas MacArthur's cadet service, his leadership qualities and achievements are key.

From his first day, when senior cadets saw Douglas MacArthur's manner and bearing, they realized his potential abilities. At the end of his plebe year, MacArthur was appointed "ranking corporal" for his yearling or third-class year. During his second-class year, MacArthur was appointed cadet first sergeant of A Company. The Corps of Cadets was small at this time; there were only some 450 cadets in four companies. The senior position commanding the entire corps was that of First Captain, above other cadet captains. The position was codified or more permanently established in 1872. Earlier in the academy's history cadets were in command positions, but they rotated among summer training and the academic terms. After 1872, several future army chiefs of staff served as First Captains: John J. Pershing, class of 1886; Charles P. Summerall, 1892; and Malin Craig, 1898. Pershing later served as the commander of the American Expeditionary Force during World War I.[50]

In later years, the position of First Captain would be an esteemed accomplishment, an incentive that propelled young Americans through their military or professional careers. During these years, serving as First Captain was strictly a military leadership opportunity and duty. There was regard and respect for those who served as the senior cadet, but the army and Corps of Cadets were so small that such positions were more routine than grandiose.[51]

The fact that the academy leadership selected Cadet MacArthur to serve as First Captain for 1902–03 was based on their opinion that MacArthur was the best candidate of the hundred remaining cadets of his class. The duties were challenging: he was responsible for the daily operation, discipline, and conduct of some 450 cadets. One of the most difficult leadership challenges is being over one's own peers. MacArthur and the young men were equals technically, though some had more years and time at the academy than others.

Early in Douglas's cadetship the officers and his peers recognized his great leadership ability. During his second year, as Cadet Corporal MacArthur drilled his squad. Capt. Edmund Blake was the tactical training officer of A Company, who observed, "There's the finest drill master I have ever seen." Captain Blake, an 1889 graduate and artillery officer, served in the Tactical Department during MacArthur's four years as a cadet.[52] The second school year ended in June 1901, but this year there was no "June Week," the normal graduation time, because the War Department had ordered that the class of 1901 graduate in February due to the ongoing insurrection and war in the Philippines. Since the time of the Civil War and even through World War II, wartime classes often graduated early before completing their full curriculum of four years. Later, in 1919, Superintendent MacArthur would face the terrible situation of the academy's near demise due to the early graduation of five classes in a year and a half.[53]

The leadership qualities of Douglas MacArthur were apparent to the upperclassmen early in his cadet years. Robert Wood, class of 1900, remembered MacArthur as a plebe: "We all recognized intuitively that MacArthur was born to be a real leader of men. With a magnificent brain and fine body

Class of 1903 visit to Gettysburg Battlefield, spring 1903; Cadet MacArthur in front row, far left, with stick in hands. *Courtesy MacArthur Memorial.*

and with all his sterling qualities of leadership, we felt he would rise to the top.... I knew him as a First Classman knows a Plebe, and I, too, felt sure he would make a great leader."[54]

In 1901 during his summer furlough Douglas visited his parents in Milwaukee for the first week of his sixty-day leave. Gen. Arthur MacArthur had returned from the Philippines in July and "Pinky" MacArthur left West Point, ending her two-year domicile at the West Point Hotel. It had been three years since the MacArthurs, including naval officer Lt. Arthur MacArthur, had been together as a family.[55]

Graduation day came finally on June 11, 1903. Cadet Douglas MacArthur was top in his class with a remarkable academic record. He and his fellow ninety-three graduates were bonded for life. To mention a couple of MacArthur's interesting classmates, Ulysses S. Grant III was sixth academically; fourth in class standing was Charles Telford, a Latter-day Saint from Utah who was involved with the minor protest in 1901, when several cadets fired the reveille cannon at Colonel Mills's quarters. He was punished by

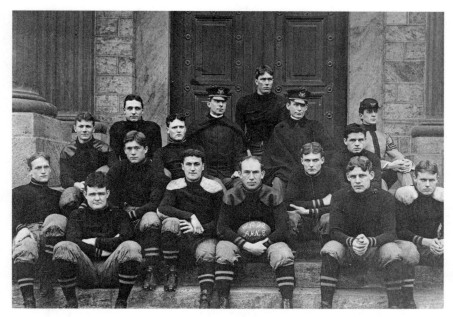

West Point football team, 1902; Cadet MacArthur upper right, in cadet uniform, served as team manager. *Courtesy MacArthur Memorial.*

Members of the class of 1903; Cadet MacArthur is second from right. *Courtesy MacArthur Memorial.*

being held back a year. Two classmates died in combat in the Great War in 1918, Emil Laurson and James Shannon. MacArthur's good friend Paul Bunker was in the army in the Philippines under MacArthur in the 1940s. Colonel Bunker surrendered to the Japanese on Corregidor only to die in a prisoner-of-war camp in Formosa in 1943. The first-ever American military flight fatality was Thomas Selfridge, who died in 1908 in an accident that also left aviation pioneer Orville Wright seriously injured. Lastly and tragically, fellow baseball teammate Edward Zell died by suicide in 1916 while serving on the Punitive Expedition against Mexican revolutionaries.[56]

Douglas MacArthur was commissioned and took the oath of office administered by Maj. Gen. Arthur MacArthur, his father. During the graduation ceremony, Secretary of War Root made these comments for the class of 1903: "Before you leave the Army, according to all precedents in our history, you will be engaged in another war. It is bound to come, and will come. Prepare your country for that war."[57] These words came true. Within a year of graduation Lieutenant MacArthur was in a firefight in the Philippines, killing several insurgent fighters. He would see action in Veracruz, Mexico, in 1914, fought in both world wars, and commanded all United Nations and US forces in Korea. Few American soldiers saw and experienced war as did Douglas MacArthur.

Leaving the academy must have been a difficult moment for Douglas MacArthur. Most graduates for more than two hundred years saw graduation day as one of the happiest days of their lives, which was probably true with MacArthur also. Yet, there was also a reverence and sorrow leaving because of his great admiration for the US Military Academy. His last roommate, George Cocheu, recalled Douglas's true sentiment: "He once told me that next to his family, he loved West Point."[58]

CHAPTER 5

★ ★ ★ ★ ★

CLASSMATES, CONNECTIONS, AND CAREERS

The class of 1903 departed the academy to their various postings to serve in the branches that the army had chosen for each new lieutenant. There were ten graduates including MacArthur who because of their class standing received commissions in the elite Corps of Engineers. Since the early days of West Point, the top branch of the army—and the most technical—was the Corps of Engineers. Previous high-standing graduates such as Joseph Totten, Sylvanus Thayer, George Washington Cullum, James B. MacPherson, and George McClellan became engineers, to name a few. Just a few years after their graduation in 1903 perhaps the greatest engineer in West Point history, George Washington Goethals, second in his class of 1880, would be appointed in 1907 by President Theodore Roosevelt to finish the Panama Canal.[1]

After graduation from the US Military Academy there was little opportunity for further military education. No basic course or formal school for new officers relative to their branch of service then existed, nor was there an established professional development plan—just service and on-the-job-training in one's assigned regiment and branch, fulfilling whatever the nation and the army needed. Rank and promotion were based primarily on seniority, though officer appraisals and ratings were becoming new tools for commanders to determine advancements, positions, and future assignments.

The assignments of MacArthur's class were typical. Most of the cadets were assigned to an infantry branch, thirty-six total; next among Douglas's classmates was the cavalry, some eighteen, half that of infantry. (The days of the mounted service were numbered by 1903.) Next came the thirteen who joined the Coast Artillery Corps. These branches were all combat arms though not called that at that time. Because of their branch assignments the odds were that these officers would cross paths many times in their careers.[2]

Second Lieutenant MacArthur and his classmates waited for their orders during their summer furloughs. What is interesting is that all the Corps of Engineers graduates, all ten including Douglas MacArthur, received orders to join the 3rd Engineer Battalion in the Philippines. The most academically successful cadets of the class were all ordered to the Philippines to serve in the same battalion, except Charles Telford, fifth in the class, who was commissioned cavalry. This was probably because he was a re-admit or turn-back from the class of 1902, not because of poor grades but for his involvement firing the reveille gun at Colonel Mills's quarters in 1901, an act of protest. All these very promising young officers would serve together for several years, including U.S. Grant III, as engineer officers in the Philippines and later in other units and places where their paths would cross again.[3]

Douglas departed for his well-deserved graduation furlough and traveled to San Francisco to visit with his father and mother. General MacArthur was then commanding general of the Department of the Pacific, headquartered at Fort Mason, a coast artillery post at the time on the north shore of San Francisco Bay overlooking the bay (which later would have a grand view of the Golden Gate Bridge). Coast artillery, as opposed to field artillery, was the up-and-coming, high-tech branch of the US Army. At West Point there was a Department of Ordnance where cadets received training on the huge siege and coastal guns that were arrayed near the shore of the Hudson River below Trophy Point. In 1899 the army installed four new 5-inch siege guns and two 7-inch howitzers with carriages and gun-mounts. Therefore, the graduates were familiar with the coast artillery branch as well as all the other branches of the service at the time.[4] Among Douglas's graduating class, several fellow lieutenants were assigned to the Coast Artillery Corps, such as Paul Bunker, who would be captured by the Japanese in the Philippines in 1942.

• • •

Douglas and his fellow new engineer lieutenants sailed for the Philippines aboard the USS *Sherman* and entered Manila Bay on October 28, 1903. They soon were assigned positions throughout the 3rd Engineer Battalion's companies, platoons, and detachments. Lieutenant MacArthur was assigned to the Department of the Visayas and reported to the department engineer, Capt. Thomas H. Jackson (class of 1899). There his duty was repairing a dock and a retaining wall at Camp Josman. He also served in other locations performing other duties. Just because MacArthur and others graduated from West Point, the nation's first engineering school, and conducted engineering projects while there, did not mean these new lieutenants were truly trained to be civil engineers and project managers. But as with any college education, one does not learn the profession and trade from schooling alone.[5]

It was an interesting time for service in the Philippines, with a bloody insurrection that had just officially ended the year before, a conflict that Douglas's own father had witnessed before becoming military governor. The American Philippine War was a brutal affair though it lasted only over three years, but the wounds especially among the local Filipino people took many years to heal. There was anxiety and bitterness from the war, in which four thousand Americans and tens of thousands of Filipinos died. After three years of vicious combat and guerrilla war, the people of the Philippines eventually realized they could not overcome the power and military might of the Americans. The Filipinos moved to reconciliation and pacification, and the Philippines became a prized American possession, regardless of the imperialism that the United States forced on the Filipinos.[6]

Young Douglas performed his duties as an engineer and soon learned to love the Philippines. He wrote, "The Philippines charmed me. The delightful hospitality . . . the amazingly attractive result of a mixture of Spanish culture and American industry." This may have been his opinion, a cheery outlook, but the truth was the jungles, hills, and remote areas of the islands were still dangerous places.[7]

Lt. Douglas MacArthur. *Courtesy MacArthur Memorial.*

Besides contracting malaria, MacArthur had his first deadly exchange, a firefight, that was his introduction to guerrilla warfare. While serving near Iliolo Harbor on Guimaris Island, MacArthur was in the jungle procuring pilings for a project. "The place was dangerous, being infested with brigands and guerillas," he wrote sixty years later. As he ventured along a jungle path with a veteran sergeant some distance behind, two armed banditos suddenly jumped him. A flash of gunfire like in the Old West erupted; whoever drew first is unknown, but Douglas wrote, "I was expert with a pistol. I dropped them both dead in their tracks, but not before one had blazed away at me with his antiquated rifle." The bullet ripped through the peak of his campaign hat. The sergeant rushed to the scene and saw the two dead desperados and looked "at my crownless hat still smoking from the blast." He walked up, saluted MacArthur, clicking his heels, and said, "in his Irish brogue, 'Begging thu Loo'tenant's paddon, but all the rest of Loo'tenant's life is pure velvut."[8] This story is very MacArthuresque and is included because his service and valor in combat is one of the most extraordinary in American history and a defining quality of his life.

After only a year MacArthur left the Philippines with several experiences, connections, and opportunities. The reason for his departure was his contracting malaria, for which he had been hospitalized. While convalescing, the young lieutenant met two Filipinos with whom he would later have close professional and personal relationships. Manuel L. Quezon and Sergio Osmeña were law students at the time, and both later served as presidents of the Philippines as a commonwealth of the United States before it gained independence. Of course, as an army engineer, MacArthur gained firsthand knowledge of the Philippines, the people, the culture, and especially the geography. He also experienced his first taste of combat. Though the small firefight was more a criminal incident, regardless, he coolly and deliberately took action and killed his two assailants.[9]

• • •

Returning to the United States, MacArthur reported to the Debris Commission in San Francisco and again resided with his parents. Maj. Gen. Arthur MacArthur was still commanding the Department of the Pacific. Promoted to first lieutenant in April 1905, Douglas worked for several different engineer officers, many of whom were graduates of West Point and who gave MacArthur excellent marks and appraisals for his services. In the next year, Lieutenant MacArthur had opportunities shared by few young officers. The War Department assigned him as aide to his father, who had been tasked to make a tour of Asia and the subcontinent of India and many nations and kingdoms on the Pacific Rim. He joined his parents in Yokohama, Japan, where the three MacArthurs departed on their Asian adventure on October 31, 1905. Their tour took them to several dozen countries, covering twenty thousand miles in less than a year. The purpose of the tour for Major General MacArthur was to study the military capabilities of Asia and advise the War Department on the people, politics, culture, national resources, and history of these nations and kingdoms.[10]

It was the greatest education a young career officer could obtain about the growing and modernizing nations in Asia, especially Japan, China, and India. The future march of history allowed Douglas MacArthur to understand the forces at work in the world he first saw at the turn of the century: nationalism, capitalism, communism, and the decline of imperialism. This was a mere year after the end of the Russo-Japanese War, which brought former medieval Japan onto the world stage as a modern power when it militarily defeated a European power: Czarist Russia.

Strategic thought in 1900 was based on military—more specifically, naval—power. Born at West Point in 1840, Adm. Alfred Thayer Mahan was one of the great military theorists of world power in the modern age. His father, Dennis Hart Mahan, taught military and civil engineering at the academy for more than forty years. Alfred Mahan was a graduate of the Naval Academy, second in his class of 1859. His 1890 publication *The Influence of Sea Power upon History 1660–1783* was the bible for global strategic thinking for the United States for decades. Mahan's masterpiece, along with the work of Emory Upton (class of May 1861), greatly influenced the US military establishment and led to numerous army reforms. Upton's *The Military Policy of the United States*, published posthumously, criticized US dependence on the militia and volunteers, and stressed the importance of a larger and better trained expandable federal army to serve the nation's needs in modern times. These works were crucial studies to the profession of arms at the turn of the century, becoming part of MacArthur's reading list. The global trek that the young lieutenant experienced in 1905–06 was a milestone in his life and learning.[11]

The first and last stops of the tour were in Japan, where Douglas saw firsthand the extreme loyalty and conviction of Japanese militarism. He recalled,

"I first encountered the boldness and courage of the Nipponese soldier," the very soldier he would engage in combat less than forty years in the future. "His almost fanatical belief and reverence for his Emperor impressed me indelibly."[12] It was this fanaticism that General MacArthur and the Allied forces fought and defeated in 1945. In fact, when MacArthur became military occupation governor in Japan, the nearly divine emperor was subservient to him.

He had visited Japan, Burma, French-Indo China, Singapore, Siam, Hong Kong, and India—and even crossed into modern-day Pakistan, going through the famous Khyber Pass.[13] MacArthur summarized this journey: "The experience was without doubt the most important factor of preparation in my entire life." In the course of all the meetings and engagements with the most powerful and the most desperately humble people, literally hundreds of places and thousands of people, MacArthur declared that "it was crystal clear to me that the future and, indeed, the very existence of America, were irrevocably entwined with Asia and its island outposts."[14] This was a course of education that West Point could not provide.

• • •

Douglas and his parents arrived in San Francisco in early August 1906 and recovered from their long, exhausting but amazing trip. Lieutenant MacArthur received an appointment to the Engineer School at Washington Barracks in Washington, DC. The army was trying to develop more professionally trained and educated officers, mostly based on the schools of Infantry and Cavalry Application at Fort Leavenworth. The Engineer School was similar, more of a trade school for skills and techniques than a strategy or leadership development course.[15]

MacArthur was a year ahead of his year group of West Point classmates and other officers, being appointed with more senior lieutenants. He joined a group of eleven other officers for the class of 1906–07. He may have been selected because of his standing and achievements at the academy. The commandant of the school was Maj. E. Eveleth Winslow, an 1889 academy graduate and career engineer. By the end of the course MacArthur had not done well. Unlike his time at West Point, he did not apply himself and dedicate his full energy to the school and training lessons. Part of the issue was his service as military aide to President Theodore Roosevelt. An occasional duty, "to assist at the White House functions this winter, such detail not to interfere with some regular work under the Department," it gave MacArthur the opportunity to meet many powerful and influential foreign leaders.[16]

Major Winslow wrote to the chief of the Corps of Engineers about MacArthur's performance, "I am sorry to have to report that during this time Lieutenant MacArthur seemed to take little interest in his course at the school and the character of the work done by him was generally not equal to that of most of the other student officers.... Indeed, throughout the time Lieutenant MacArthur was under my observation, he displayed, on the whole, but little professional zeal and his work was far inferior to that which his West Point record shows him to be capable of."[17]

What is most interesting about Major Winslow's appraisal is that he connected MacArthur's performance with his academic and military achievements at the Military Academy. Would he express this for a student officer who had attended Virginia Military Institute, or a direct commission officer who went to Harvard or Stanford University?

MacArthur and other West Point graduates who excelled were held to a higher standard, just as Douglas and other sons of generals were hazed more severely than the other cadets. Whether this is unfair or not, it was the situation that Douglas MacArthur had to face and overcome. His superiors, his peers, his soldiers, and the growing public expected more from him.

In August 1907 MacArthur was assigned to engineer district headquarters in Milwaukee, Wisconsin, where his father and mother lived. What appeared to be an important opportunity for him proved to be a near disaster for his career. Lt. Gen. Arthur MacArthur had been promoted to lieutenant general in September 1906, the highest rank of any officer in the army. However, President Roosevelt had not selected him to serve as army chief of staff due to the influence of Secretary of War William H. Taft, who had feuded with MacArthur years earlier in the Philippines. This, of course, was a discouraging situation, as the general was the most senior officer in the Regular Army, but he had no responsibility of command for the last two years until his retirement in 1909.[18]

Commencing his duties under Maj. William Judson, West Point class of 1888, Douglas once again slid into a slump that affected his career and reputation. He devoted much of his time to finishing the engineering courses that he did not complete at Washington Barracks. He also spent much time with his parents and soon neglected his duties, and Judson grew concerned. Later a major harbor project was underway at Manitowoc on Lake Michigan, some eighty miles north of Milwaukee. Douglas did almost anything he could to not serve and work in Manitowoc. Major Judson soon realized MacArthur's deficiencies and counseled him: "I spent many hours in conversation with Lieutenant MacArthur on engineering subjects. I gave him the best I had of knowledge in such matters, so far as I had to me and opportunity." MacArthur at one point requested more time away from his duties. Frustrated, Judson reported to his superiors that "Lieutenant MacArthur, while on duty under my immediate orders, did not conduct himself in a way to meet commendation, and that his duties were not performed in a satisfactory manner."[19]

Seeing the appraisal from Judson, dated July 18, 1908, MacArthur objected and wrote a rebuttal statement in August that Judson's "serious charge is not supported by specifications of any time. . . . I feel keenly the ineradicable statement blemish Major Judson has seen fit to place upon my military record . . . to deserve such drastic action." He sent it directly to the chief of the Corps of Engineers in Washington, ignoring his immediate chain of command, a very unprofessional action. For this he was also reprimanded.[20] Judson's report was part of MacArthur's official file, as was Major Winslow's Engineer School appraisal in Washington a year earlier. MacArthur did not address either of these episodes in his memoirs published the year he died, *Reminiscences*.[21]

In February 1908 Douglas had applied for a vacancy in a teaching position at West Point under his former professor Col. Gustav Fiebeger, who made the offer directly to Douglas. However, Col. Hugh Scott, class of 1876, the superintendent, denied the position to Lieutenant MacArthur because Fiebeger did not follow the proper process. Eventually, MacArthur received orders for duty at Fort Leavenworth in April 1908 to report to the 3rd Engineer Battalion, his former unit, that summer.[22] Just ten years later as superintendent MacArthur would have serious disagreements with Colonel Fiebeger on academy reforms.

Lt. Douglas MacArthur was spinning downward from the lofty heights he had attained at the academy at a young age. Even the US Military Academy would not accept him back. Fate smiled on him at Fort Leavenworth, though, as MacArthur took command of K Company of the 3rd Engineer

Battalion in the summer of 1908. He was finally with real soldiers again, and he thrived on the experience of conducting civil and combat engineering. During the next three years he turned his career around, advancing to captain in February 1911. Commanding soldiers, drilling, hiking twenty-five miles some days, building bridges, and teaching demolitions classes was exhilarating and profound. Commanding an engineer company of cheery but imperfect soldiers meant more to him than anything else: "I could not have been happier if they had made me a general."[23]

The leaders and officers at Fort Leavenworth were fair and demanding, which is exactly what Douglas MacArthur needed. He served under three officers, all graduates of the academy, whom he had earlier or later connections with. Col. Thomas H. Rees, an 1886 graduate and one of Gen. John Pershing's classmates, commanded the engineer battalion. Maj. Clement A. F. Flagler, of the class 1889, assumed command in September 1908, and he later commanded the 42nd "Rainbow" Division in France with MacArthur as a brigade commander. For a time, MacArthur served as battalion adjutant, the most important staff officer position in the army of the day. Finally, Lt. Col. Joseph E. Kuhn was commandant of the Mounted Service School at Fort Riley. He was top of his class of 1885 and was teaching military engineering at West Point when Douglas was a cadet.[24] MacArthur would teach engineering and a short course of a few weeks to the student soldiers in demolitions and field pioneering skills. He even wrote a draft field manual on field engineering and demolitions for the course. These connections with Douglas MacArthur and his army colleagues were based on a large part because of their West Point affiliation. In the spring of 1911 Captain MacArthur was appointed to the Board of Engineering and as head of the department of engineering at the Field Engineer School at Fort Leavenworth.[25]

Douglas had great personal and professional opportunities while at Fort Leavenworth, namely, to serve short terms of duty in San Antonio and in Panama. The American effort to complete the Panama Canal was proceeding under the leadership of Col. George Washington Goethals, class of 1880. MacArthur observed the progress of one of the greatest engineering feats in history. He met and observed Colonel Goethals, who during Douglas's cadet years was a major serving on staff at West Point as the engineering officer responsible for the physical facilities and infrastructure of the garrison.[26]

While in Panama he reunited with upperclassman Capt. Robert Wood, whom MacArthur praised: "I learned much of the complexities of large-scale supply from an old West Point friend of the class of 1900, Robert E. Wood, who later, as the head of Sears, Roebuck and Company, so revolutionized the system of retail sales."[27]

About the same time in the fall of 1912, his father, Arthur MacArthur, died. General MacArthur suffered a heart attack in front of his old warrior comrades at a reunion in Milwaukee for the 24th Wisconsin Volunteer Regiment of the Civil War. When Captain MacArthur learned of his father's passing, he recalled, "My whole world changed that night. Never have I been able to heal the wound in my heart."[28]

• • •

Fort Leavenworth had been a shot in the arm for Captain MacArthur and his slumping career, but in the fall of 1912 he transferred to Washington, DC, to serve on the engineering board, and then in April 1913 he was assigned to the War Department. He worked specifically for chief of staff Gen. Leonard Wood, a Harvard medical school graduate, army surgeon, Medal of Honor recipient (in 1886), and commander of the 1st US Volunteer Cavalry Regiment, the famous Rough Riders. Douglas was labeled as one of "Wood's Boys" by the opponents of the new staff system. MacArthur later recorded, "What attracted me most was working as Wood's assistant in his indefatigable crusade for military preparedness."[29]

In the spring of 1914, a difficult and complicated international crisis erupted in Veracruz, the main Mexican port city in the Gulf of Mexico. For several years Mexico had been ravaged by a revolution, and chaos reigned throughout the country. An incident occurred at Tampico with US Navy sailors on a routine supply and logistical task and overzealous Mexican harbor officers. The sailors reported the incident to their naval commander, who demanded that Mexican authorities apologize, which they did, but also required them to raise the US flag and fire a twenty-one-gun salute in homage—which the Mexican officials refused. Soon, this ridiculous circumstance became an international crisis.[30]

The Navy and State Departments recommended a full-scale invasion and capturing Veracruz, which President Woodrow Wilson approved in order to restore American honor. On April 22–23 more than eight hundred US sailors and marines attacked and took the custom house, the piers, and the other government and civic buildings in the harbor. Some 170 Mexicans were killed and 250 wounded: the Americans lost 19 dead and 72 wounded. The navy later awarded the Medal of Honor to fifty-five officers and enlisted men—a rather overzealous amount of valor for such a small campaign.[31]

Near the end of April, Brig. Gen. Frederick Funston arrived in Veracruz with a brigade of four thousand US Army soldiers, who established a perimeter defense and then improved the public works and facilities. The intensity of the situation did not dissipate even with a token eight thousand soldiers and marines at Veracruz. Into this volatile military and political melee came Capt. Douglas MacArthur. With the calamity in Mexico, General Wood tasked MacArthur to sail to Veracruz to ascertain what the needs were. The astonishing thing General Wood told MacArthur concerning the mission was that it was secret: no one, not even the local commander, General Funston, was to know of the purpose of the mission.[32]

Arriving on the battleship USS *Nebraska* on May 1, 1914, MacArthur soon learned that several locomotives were positioned south of Veracruz along a coastal railroad line near Alvarado, about 45 miles away. Confiding in Capt. Constant Cordier of the 4th Infantry Regiment, he outlined his scheme to make his way to Alvarado at night, evading Mexican soldiers and banditos. MacArthur wore his uniform, carried a Browning .45-caliber, semi-automatic pistol, and carried no money, gold, or valuables. He also persuaded three Mexican railroad men (an engineer and two firemen) to assist him for $150 in gold upon their return. He searched them to ensure they were not armed.[33]

On the night of May 6–7, MacArthur and the Mexican engineer departed and made their way south by handcar, crossing rivers by small boats, riding stolen ponies, swimming streams, and hiking when necessary. At Paso del Toro they reached the railroad line again and met the two Mexican firemen with a second handcar. Off they raced on the handcar, pumping the handles like a water pump. MacArthur recalled later, "We reached Alvarado shortly after one o'clock and there found five engines" or locomotives, two of which were not suitable, but "three were just what we needed—fine big road pullers in excellent condition except for a few minor parts which were missing."[34]

Capt. Douglas MacArthur in Mexico, 1914. *Courtesy MacArthur Memorial.*

The mission to find the equipment was successful and flawless, but the return was something totally different. At Salinas, about half the way back to Veracruz, five men—probably banditos—intercepted MacArthur and one of the Mexican railroad men, who both immediately fled. The brigands followed on foot, but only two were able to keep pace; therefore, MacArthur turned around and "I was obliged to fire upon them. Both went down." Douglas and his companion continued on foot until they reached the handcar and the other two men. Rushing along as the night wore on, "in a driving mist, we ran flush into about fifteen mounted men" and literally bumped into armed horsemen, where MacArthur was knocked down because of the crashing of men and horses. The banditos opened fire, and "three bullet holes [went] through my clothes, but escaped unscathed," he recalled. Blazing away at close quarters, one of MacArthur's men was wounded in the shoulder, but keeping his calm under fire, he shot and killed and the rest skedaddled.[35]

They reached Laguna by handcar when suddenly three caballeros charged up and "kept a running fight with the hand car. I did not return fire," he wrote. Finally, two of the riders fell away with their horses nearing exhaustion, but one bandito was "unusually well mounted, overhauled and passed the car." The desperado fired, forcing MacArthur to return fire. The rider and horse went down sprawling across the tracks. The captain and his amigos had to remove the dead rider and horse from the tracks. As daylight broke, they pushed their way to the American lines.[36]

After all this drama and danger, the American expedition stalled, and troops were retired from Mexico weeks later, so MacArthur's venture did not add to the outcome.

Several officers felt strongly that Captain MacArthur should be decorated for his gallantry and incredible reconnaissance in Veracruz. Captain Cordier recommended that MacArthur be awarded the Medal of Honor and wrote to General Wood about the mission, stating that if the navy could award some dozens of awards for gallantry, the army should do the same for MacArthur "for heroism displayed, for dangers braved, and for difficulties overcome." Which was all true.[37]

Now began a tangled web of correspondence, reports, and a formal board of review that ended in one of the most tragic and vindictive actions that Douglas MacArthur ever performed. General Wood approved the proposal for the award, and even General Funston wrote that "Captain MacArthur was acting in good faith, and any error of judgement he may have made in undertaking his hazardous expedition should not, in my opinion, cause him to lose the appropriate reward."[38]

Unfortunately, other officers did not feel the same. The new chief of staff, Maj. Gen. Hugh Scott, a former superintendent of the US Military Academy, convened a three-officer board to review the recommendation; chairing the panel was Col. Charles G. Treat, serving on the general staff at the time. Treat had been the commandant of cadets during MacArthur's last two years at West Point. Eventually the board unanimously voted to deny the proposal. Two of its members, including Treat, concluded that "the advisability of this enterprise having been undertaken without the knowledge of the commanding general on the ground" would, in the future, "encourage any other staff officer, under similar conditions, to ignore the local commander, possibly interfering with the latter's plans with reference to the enemy." Yet, the final decision lay with chief of staff Scott and the assistant chief, Maj. Gen. Tasker Bliss, class of 1875, who endorsed the board's finding.[39]

Upon learning of the results of the board and the chief's approval of the decision, MacArthur was incensed enough to write a scathing rebuttal on February 9, 1915, not only to the board but also to General Scott, berating the process for "rigid narrow-mindedness and lack of imagination."[40] He vehemently criticized the decision and in doing so demonstrated one of few times in his career, where he allowed emotion and anger to rule him. His reaction was disgraceful.

Captain MacArthur, then thirty-five years old and a dozen years out of West Point, was denied the Medal of Honor for perhaps the most daring and mostly solo act of bravery he would ever perform. His many awards and decorations of the future were in units, along with other soldiers and comrades, or while leading such units. This was the only time, on his own as an American soldier, that he executed an incredible mission, engaging more than a score of hostile gunmen and completing the task with total disregard of his own life and safety. Perhaps, because of his father performing his act of gallantry at age nineteen, a very young man, this circumstance weighed on him. Who knows in the course of a career as a soldier when one will ever be in a circumstance that requires or allows action of great valor at the risk of life?

As for a West Point connection to this story: the president of the review board, Colonel Treat, was the same officer serving as commandant of cadets who appointed Cadet MacArthur as First Captain in the summer of 1902 for his leadership and military excellence. Now thirteen years later, Treat rejected the recommendation of the Medal of Honor to that same individual. The benefit of doubt must be accorded to Colonel Treat's obligation of fairness and professionalism. In fact, two of three officers on the board were graduates of West Point. The connection is constant and persuasive.[41]

CHAPTER 6

FIGHTING IN FRANCE

Returning from Mexico in August 1914, Captain MacArthur assumed his duties on the general staff. About this same time war clouds erupted in Europe: The Great War had begun. In December 1915 MacArthur was promoted to major—a rarity to become a field-grade officer after only twelve years of commissioned service. Despite his fiery memorandum about the Medal of Honor, the senior leaders saw his ability and gave him duties of increasing responsibility and advanced him accordingly. Chief of staff Maj. General Hugh Scott wrote an appraisal: "Major MacArthur is a very well appearing, high-minded, conscientious and unusually efficient officer, well fitted for positions requiring diplomacy and high-grade intelligence."[1]

A new secretary of war assumed office in the spring of 1916, Newton Baker, one of the most effective and far-sighted secretaries in US Army history. Shortly after his arrival on June 30, 1916, Secretary Baker appointed Major MacArthur as the first-ever army public affairs officer in the newly established Bureau of Information.[2] MacArthur explained that he "became the liaison link with the newspaper men," and the press of the day. "I was expected to explain our national military policy to the country," and the major policy issue of the day was the National Defense Acts of 1903 and 1916, which helped establish the modern National Guard of the United States.[3]

By the time the 1916 National Defense Act was passed, the war in Europe was entering its third year of slaughter and desolation. Though isolationism was the official policy, President Wilson and Secretary Baker took steps to prepare for war. One of the great issues for the American people and Congress in early 1917 was the establishment of a draft, a peace-time conscription in preparation for war. The country had a draft during the Civil War. The war in Europe was dragging the United States slowly but surely into the maelstrom. In January 1917, Imperial Germany once again after two years allowed unrestricted submarine warfare against neutral ships trading with the Entente, or Allied powers. American ships, goods, and lives were now targets of a hostile policy and lay at the bottom of the sea. Major MacArthur joined a few others in pushing for the passage of the conscription act. A fellow officer remarked, "Make no mistake; it was the then Major Douglas MacArthur, Class of 1903, who sold the American people the Selective Service Act that was passed on May 18, 1917."[4]

Along with MacArthur was his fellow classmate Capt. Hugh Johnson, who worked closely on the legislation. Johnson was assigned to write the army's selective service implementation plan to manage the expansion of the army, which he did on five hand-written pages. Johnson was promoted to brigadier general and commanded an artillery brigade in the Great War. Later in his life Johnson became a journalist, a radio spokesman, and first director of the National Recovery Administration, a New Deal agency, in the Roosevelt administration.[5]

On April 6, 1917, President Wilson signed the declaration of war passed by Congress days earlier. America was at war against the Central powers, led by Germany. As millions of men entered the service, enlisting or by the draft, dozens of training depots and camps were established, along with new combat divisions consisting of two infantry brigades, and two regiments in each brigade, including an artillery brigade totaling some 27,000 men. These divisions were divided among the three main components: Regular Army, National Guard, and National Army (draftee). Major MacArthur and Captain Johnson were involved with the public information campaign during this process, which helped convince the governors and the adjutant generals of each state to support this war measure.[6]

The National Guard divisions had been previously organized by region, crossing state boundaries in some cases. The chief of the army's Militia Bureau was Brig. Gen. William A. Mann, class of 1875, and Major MacArthur struggled to find a resolution to one last organizational problem. Secretary Baker remarked, "I disclosed my puzzle to Major MacArthur, who was attached to my office at the time." MacArthur explained that the last organized National Guard division was the 41st of Oregon and Washington guardsmen. There were four regiments from four separate states that were not aligned with a division. MacArthur recorded his recollection that occurred in Secretary Baker's office: "I suggested that we take units from the different states so that a division would stretch over the country like a rainbow—from that time on it was known as the Rainbow Division."[7] The division would have regiments from Alabama, Ohio, Iowa, and New York, but eventually soldiers represented twenty-eight states, a true rainbow across the land. This was the 42nd "Rainbow" Division.[8]

Baker appointed MacArthur as chief of staff of the new division and promoted him to the rank of colonel by fiat. That evening Major MacArthur went to the Army and Navy Club in Washington for dinner. There he met Col. Briant H. Wells, class of 1894, and another colonel who was also a graduate of West Point. Both were serving on the general staff at this time. Learning of Douglas's promotion, the two took the eagle rank from their collars and pinned the new colonel, unofficially.[9]

The first commander of the 42nd Rainbow Division was sixty-three-year-old General Mann, who was later replaced in France by Maj. Gen. Charles Menoher, an 1886 classmate of General John J. Pershing, the commander of the American Expeditionary Force (AEF). Interestingly, despite a bitter feud later in their careers, it was MacArthur who first recommended to Secretary Baker that Pershing assume command of the AEF.[10]

Among the officers of the 42nd Division were several graduates who were friends, associates, or even classmates of MacArthur. Maj. Robert E. Wood, who was a first classman during Douglas's plebe year, had retired in 1915 but was recalled in 1917. Eventually, he rose to brigadier general and director of AEF transportation. Classmate Maj. Grayson Murphy served on the 42nd Division headquarters staff under MacArthur. Douglas had made rank quicker and attained greater responsibility than all his classmates and many other West Point officers who knew him as a cadet.[11]

• • •

Colonel MacArthur, the new and first chief of staff of the 42nd Division, labored greatly to organize a fighting unit consisting of four separate regiments from four states. The 165th Infantry, once the "Fighting 69th New York" of the famous Irish Brigade from the Civil War, along with the 166th of Ohio guardsmen, made up the 83rd Brigade. The other brigade, the 84th, commanded by Brig. Gen. Robert A. Brown, class of 1885, included the 167th Infantry from Alabama and the 168th of Iowa guardsmen. Douglas MacArthur would assume command of the 84th Brigade during the final campaigns of the war.[12]

The men and units were organized and trained at Camp Mills on Long Island, New York, in the late summer of 1917. These were chaotic weeks, but under Mann's leadership and MacArthur's energetic administration, the division was born. After several months of training, the division sailed for France in November. The 42nd was among the first four American divisions to reach France. But after it arrived, the AEF staff wanted to literally disembowel the Rainbow Division by transferring many of its experienced officers and thousands of the soldiers to the other three divisions in France to reach their full man-power level. The division would be designated as a "replacement division" and no longer would serve as a front-line combat division. By November 1917, the process of dismantling the division commenced. One of the first senior officers in the division to be transferred was Brig. Gen. Charles P. Summerall, commander of the 67th Artillery Brigade of three artillery regiments. An 1892 graduate of West Point who served as First Captain of his class, Summerall later was army chief of staff, whom MacArthur replaced in 1930. This was a severe blow to the division.[13]

Colonel MacArthur made visits to the AEF headquarters at Chaumont, France, arguing and clamoring with the staff for a reversal of this decision, insulting not a few staff officers in the process. Having connections in government at home, senior officers in the division and MacArthur also wrote letters to influential political friends, including letters to Secretary Baker. Not waiting for trans-Atlantic post to travel and knowing Pershing's chief of staff personally from their time in the Philippines, MacArthur made an unannounced call on Brig. Gen. James G. Harbord. He was able to convince Harbord, not a West Point graduate, and other key staff members to reverse their decision. MacArthur recalled later, "My action was probably not in strict accord with normal procedure and it created resentment against me among certain members of Pershing's staff." Yes, it certainly did, and it would haunt MacArthur later.[14]

On the AEF General Headquarters staff at Chaumont were several officers from the class of 1898, who soon created a "clique" because of their West Point association. They were labeled as the "Ninety-eighters" by other army officers, especially those on the front line. These officers were senior staff members who had great influence and often challenged the priorities and needs of the line units. There have always been clashes between staff and line officers in military affairs throughout history, but many of the officers at Chaumont raised their staff power to an art form. Among the "Ninety-eighters" were Fox Connor, the G3, who was responsible for operations and training, and Robert C. Davis, the adjutant general for personnel and administration, especially overseeing awards and decorations. Fox Connor would be a great mentor to future American military greats such as George Marshall, Dwight Eisenhower, and George Patton. This clique often challenged MacArthur on a personal basis.[15]

In February 1918, the 42nd Division entered the line in the Lunéville sector, becoming the first American division to experience combat. The chief of staff position of any major unit, especially an infantry division, is an incredibly demanding job with great responsibility as the principal staff officer under the commander. Ensuring the smooth and efficient management of the staff supporting an organization of 27,000 soldiers and all that goes with it is a fearful proposition.[16] The position entails many simultaneous processes and intense pressure. What the job does not specifically or traditionally involve was leading combat patrols, normally at night, between the battle lines. But that is exactly what Colonel MacArthur did.

Eventually, MacArthur participated in or led dozens of intelligence-gathering and reconnaissance patrols scouting the German lines, noting their machine gun and artillery positions, capturing enemy soldiers, and learning the immediate terrain of "No Man's Land." During these patrols, sometimes with French comrades, MacArthur was wounded twice by mustard gassing, for which in 1932 he received two Purple Heart awards—an award that he as army chief of staff helped establish through Congress.[17] (During the Great War, American soldiers wore Wound Chevrons on their right uniform sleeve.)

The 167th Infantry Regiment of Alabama National Guardsmen of MacArthur's 84th Infantry Brigade, 42nd Rainbow Division. From *Illustrated Review*, 4th Alabama Infantry, US Army, Montgomery, Alabama, 1917.

When MacArthur went on patrols in the battle area, he donned the most unorthodox combat uniform perhaps in the entire AEF. He rarely wore the standard M1917 steel helmet, instead, opting for a crushed service cap; he never carried the gas mask, even though he was gassed twice; he carried a riding crop and seldom his sidearm (a Browning .45-caliber pistol); he wore cavalry boots and wound a four-foot-long muffler his mother Pinky had knitted for him under his olive drab tunic. He also wore his West Point letterman's sweater with his "A" he earned in baseball nearly all the time during his service in the Great War.[18] This image he created may have been individualistic or intentional. MacArthur during his entire life was a showman and knew how to entertain. His actions were either a disdain for battlefield necessity, at least for himself, or a total disregard for his own life. His soldiers, however, loved his theatrics, calling him "The Dude" or "The Stick."[19] He ignored this attention and simply said one of his famous lines he often used, "It is the order you disobey that makes you famous."[20]

MacArthur's willingness to participate in these patrols drew criticism from others, then and even today. In a more direct commentary, biographer William Manchester wrote: "More and more he was delegating authority for operations, intelligence, and administration to majors and lieutenant colonels. There was a kind of madness in his method: he wanted the staff to be self-sufficient so that he would be free to cross no-land's-land with assault troops."[21] This, of course, is Manchester's opinion. The reality is that MacArthur gained a thorough knowledge of the battle area before operations and briefed the leaders accordingly.

A French commanding general objected to MacArthur's participation with night patrols, to which Douglas replied, "I cannot fight them if I cannot see them."[22] General Menoher, the division commander, praised MacArthur with these words: "Colonel MacArthur is one of the ablest officers in the United States Army and also one of the most popular."[23]

Colonel MacArthur and the 42nd Division endured several campaigns in the spring and summer of 1918, in what are commonly called the Ludendorff or spring offensives. With the collapse of the Russian empire in 1917, the Germans moved more than a million soldiers, thousands of artillery pieces, and mountains of equipment from the Eastern Front. The objective was to decisively defeat the Allies on the Western Front before the Americans could intervene effectively. When US forces arrived in France, the British and French leaders wanted the American "doughboys" to serve under their tactical command at no higher than regimental level. General Pershing was totally against this concept, called amalgamation, that would divide the American forces among the two major Allies and cause him to lose control of his soldiers. Yet, the British and French already had three years of combat experience in the trenches, and regardless of their poor fighting record, they had maintained the line of defense.[24]

In the spring of 1918 Pershing visited the 42nd Division and delivered instructions for the defense against the Germans. Turning to leave, Pershing said with a hoarse voice—"We old First Captains, Douglas, must never flinch." It was an interesting comment, referring to their similar status and experience as First Captains at West Point to drive home a leadership point.[25]

General Pershing made a surprise return visit to the Rainbow Division on June 21. After making an inspection of the soldiers and their work of loading thousands of tons of gear, tentage, caissons, and equipment, Pershing lashed out at MacArthur, "This division is a disgrace!" He continued, "The men are poorly disciplined and they are not well trained. The whole outfit is just about the worst I have seen."[26] Reeling, MacArthur was shocked at being reprimanded so severely by the army commander, a man whom weeks earlier confided in him their special relationship with the academy. Now Pershing turned malicious. "MacArthur," he raged, "I'm going to hold you personally responsible for getting discipline and order into this division.... I won't stand for this. It's a disgrace."[27]

Perhaps Pershing cornered MacArthur because he was on the scene and Menoher was not. Perhaps he personally expected more from MacArthur, as a former First Captain. Either way, upbraiding the nearest officer available was a clear indication of Pershing's abrasive leadership style.

Five days later a rather unpredicted action took place. On June 26, 1918, Pershing promoted Colonel MacArthur to brigadier general with a commission in the temporary national army. Brig. Gen. MacArthur was one of the youngest general officers in the American army. What is also interesting, during this same time, MacArthur's mother, Mary "Pinky," was waging her own campaign four thousand miles away. In faraway Washington, DC, Pinky wrote General Pershing a letter dated June 12, 1918, recommending, asking, even pleading Pershing to promote her son. "I am taking the liberty of writing you a little heart-to-heart letter," she began, explaining that Douglas "knows absolutely nothing whatsoever of this letter and its purport to you." She then asked Pershing to consider Douglas for one of the upcoming appointments for promotion. The first qualification she noted was her son's performance and sterling record at the US Military Academy. "You are familiar with Colonel MacArthur's record—that he stood first in his class upon graduation at West Point, and held this position in the class for four consecutive years at the Academy," she mistakenly claimed. In truth, during his second year Cadet MacArthur dropped to fourth in his class academically.[28]

Yet, Pinky was not finished; she continued to drive her point home, and she used an unsavory tactic to convince Pershing that Douglas deserved this promotion. She wrote of previous promotions in April 1918, where three junior officers in rank were promoted ahead of MacArthur, "including a classmate of

Brig. Gen. Douglas MacArthur in France, 1919. *Courtesy MacArthur Memorial.*

his (General Hugh S. Johnson)." She explained that "General Johnson is a fine, capable officer, but he graduated far below my son in the class of 1903 and is nearly a year younger in years."[29]

Pinky used the Military Academy as her main tool to prove to Pershing that her son was more deserving. The fact that class ranking is prominent among West Point graduates—even those who attended decades earlier—because of the small size of the Regular Army, an officer's performance at the academy was well known. Class standing should not be the determining factor of an officer's ability and future capability. But Mrs. MacArthur used a fact that was measurable and revered, but in so doing she placed her son above others by academic standing alone. The final ironic fact is, General Pershing did not receive or know about Pinky's pleading until sometime after he had promoted MacArthur.[30]

Just over a month later another circumstance with a fellow graduate would come to a head. Its resolution propelled Douglas MacArthur on a trajectory of great service in battle and resulted in a distinguished combat reputation. By late July 1918, General Menoher had become increasingly concerned about the commander of the 84th Brigade, Brig. Gen. Robert A. Brown, an experienced officer and former aide-de-camp to Gen. Arthur MacArthur in the Philippines. Brown was an 1885 graduate and a fine officer, but the stress of battle and command overcame him. In August he was relieved of command and returned to the United States. The newly minted Brigadier General MacArthur assumed command from an officer who was a close associate of his father's.[31]

• • •

By the summer of 1918, the war was not going well for the Germans, and their miscalculation about the United States was a strategic disaster. America's intervention turned the tide against the Central powers that led to eventual victory.[32] The failure of the Ludendorff offensives provided the switch or change of the initiative to the Allies. The Allied line held along the Marne River, especially the AEF supporting the French through a bloody June. On July 14, the anniversary of the French Revolution, Bastille Day, Ludendorff planned one final attempt to destroy the Allies, but the attack failed because the Allies had learned of it and unleased an artillery barrage, driving the Germans back on July 18. This is when the initiative of the Western Front changed hands.[33]

In September the AEF finally had its own sector of the Western Front, when the Supreme Allied War Council ordered Pershing to reduce the St. Mihiel salient. The Americans attacked on September 12 and in four days had pushed the Germans back even as they were withdrawing. That same day MacArthur was observing the battle from his headquarters when he had a historically serendipitous meeting with an American officer. Recalling the incident, MacArthur wrote about the tank support by an

American armor unit: "We followed a squadron of tanks, which soon bogged down in the heavy mud," but he soon met "an old friend who in another war over this same terrain was to gain world-wide fame, Major George Patton," in command of the tank unit. Watching the battle develop as artillery rounds burst near the two, Patton flinched as a shell landed even closer. MacArthur said to Patton, "Don't worry, major; you never hear the one that gets you."[34]

MacArthur was wrong in his declaration that he and Patton were old friends; they had never met before this, so they were not old friends and Patton was actually a temporary lieutenant colonel, not a major. Patton, of course, was a 1909 graduate of the academy who had an opposite academic record compared to Douglas. He was re-cycled his plebe year due to his failing grades in mathematics.

The success at St. Mihiel gave the Americans confidence and a false belief that the Germans were completely defeated. However, a month later the Americans would meet a determined German defense in the Meuse-Argonne.[35] Having commanded the 84th Brigade at St. Mihiel, MacArthur led his men into the Meuse River valley beginning on September 26, 1918.[36] On October 10 the Rainbow Division relieved the 1st Division, later the famous "Big Red One" of the Regular Army. The attack had not gone well for the Americans because, unlike St. Mihiel, the Germans made a determined defense forward of the famous Hindenburg Line. The Germans had three separate lines named after Wagnerian witches, the main line being the Kriemhilde Stellung. Along this line there were several commanding hills, the most significant and heavily defended being the Côte de Châtillon. As the 42nd Division advanced, the importance of this hill became clear. MacArthur himself described the tactical situation:

> This salient was dominated by the Côte de Châtillon stronghold which raked the Allied flank and thus stopped the advancing line of the American attack. Every effort to go forward had been stopped cold by this flanking fire. I carefully reconnoitered the desolate and forbidding terrain that confronted my brigade. There were rolling hills, heavily wooded valleys of death between the endless folds of ridges. I saw at once that the previous advance had failed because it had not been recognized that

the Côte de Châtillon was the keystone of the whole German position; that until it was captured we would be unable to advance.[37]

The division first approached the hill on October 11, and the next day MacArthur conducted his own reconnaissance, at which point he was wounded (for the second time) during a gas attack. He refused to be evacuated and endured the next few days of service while suffering from the effects of the gas with vomiting, no sleep, and great pain in his eyes, nose, and throat that caused coughing and wheezing.[38]

On the evening of October 13, General Charles Summerall, the commander of the newly established US V Corps, arrived at MacArthur's brigade headquarters. He was adamant in manner, wanting Côte de Châtillon to be captured the next day. A former First Captain like MacArthur, and a future army chief of staff, whom MacArthur would succeed, Summerall was an effective officer and leader. According to MacArthur, the general was "tired and worn, and I made him drink a cup of steaming black-coffee, strong enough to blister the throat. 'Give me Châtillon, MacArthur,' he suddenly said, his voice strained and harsh. 'Give me Châtillon, or a list of five thousand casualties.' His abruptness startled me. 'All right, General,' I assured him, 'we'll take it, or my name will head the list.'"[39]

The next day, October 14, the attack did not go well for the brigade. Some ground was gained, but Châtillon was not captured. That very night, General Summerall summarily relieved Brig. Gen. Michael J. Lenihan, commander of the 83rd Brigade. Lenihan, an 1887 West Point graduate, was replaced by Col. Henry Reilly, a friend of Douglas's at West Point in the class of 1904. Reilly had commanded the 42nd Division's artillery brigade previously. Now he was an infantry commander of several thousand infantrymen. After the war Henry Reilly would compile and write an outstanding history and account of the division during the war entitled *Americans All: The Rainbow at War*, published in 1936.[40]

Frustrated by the failure of the 84th Brigade and the overall tactical situation, MacArthur grew restless and rash. He devised a reckless plan to capture Côte de Châtillon—a night attack by a couple of battalions with bayonets fixed and no firing of their rifles. One of the battalions was from the 167th Infantry, guardsmen from Alabama. The commanding officer was hospitalized due to illness, and the regimental executive officer, Lt. Col. Walter E. Bare, a long-serving Alabama National Guard officer, was appalled at the order he received.[41] He narrated the situation later: "That night I received orders to take the Côte de Châtillon by night attack, using only bayonets, not a shot to be fired. I realized that it was impossible.... After explaining the impracticability of such an attack the order was rescinded. We were held up all day on October 15, 1918, by enemy machine gun and artillery fire."[42]

The attack was eventually cancelled by the division commander, General Menoher, who realized how foolish this dangerous gambit was.[43] When dawn arrived on October 15, the 84th Brigade renewed operations against the German position on the Kriemhilde Stellung. The major difference of this attack was the employment of tanks on the open valley floor to support the infantry attacks, which failed.[44]

The next day, October 16, was the day of days. MacArthur developed an operational plan for the final assault on the hill consisting of two battalions, one each from the Iowa 166th and Alabama 167th Infantry Regiments. These battalions were to assault simultaneously as a double envelopment or, as the Germans say, *Kesselschlact*. "The two battalions, like arms of a relentless pincer, closed in from both sides," MacArthur explained. "That is the way the Côte de Châtillon fell, and that is the way those gallant citizen-soldiers, so far from home, won the approach to final victory." Though MacArthur perhaps exaggerated, there is no doubt that this successful operation contributed to the defeat of Germany, as did the concurrent French and British campaigns.[45]

The official US Army records of the First Army for October 16, 1918, summary report read: "During the day our troops attacked along the entire front from Grandpré to Beaumont, Grandpre was taken, the Bois des Loges and the Côte de Châtillon were occupied.... G[eorge] C. Marshall, Colonel, General Staff, A. C, of S., G-3."[46]

The war lasted only four more weeks before Germany agreed to an armistice, to take effect on November 11, 1918. The last weeks of fighting were bloody, but the great German war machine collapsed militarily on all the fronts, causing the government politically and economically in the Fatherland to seek peace. The Allies sought to punish the Germans for starting the war, which was formalized in the Treaty of Versailles and was one of the leading causes for the Second World War and the rise of German fascism.[47]

As for Douglas MacArthur, the end of the war changed everything for him. He assumed command of the Rainbow Division for a few days, but then he was relieved by Maj. Gen. Clement A. F. Flagler, who earlier had served with MacArthur at Fort Leavenworth, where they made a professional bonding. The final chapter of MacArthur's service in the Great War has a very interesting twist of decisions, and connections with the US Military Academy that is the basis of MacArthur's personal and professional reputation.

General Menoher wrote a dispatch to his classmate John Pershing on November 6, regarding MacArthur's service and courage: "This record represents the unremitting endeavor of a very brilliant and gifted officer who has, after more than a year's full service in France without a day apart from his division or his command, and although twice wounded in action, filled each day with a loyal and intelligent application to duty such as is, among officers in the field and in actual contact with battle, without parallel in our army."[48]

With such accolades, Generals Summerall and Menoher also nominated MacArthur for the Medal of Honor. Menoher wrote a two-thousand-word letter of endorsement, dated October 30, 1918, and entitled, "Distinguished

Gen. John Pershing (USMA class of 1886), commander of the American Expeditionary Force, awarding the Distinguished Service medal to MacArthur in 1919. *Courtesy MacArthur Memorial.*

Services of Brigadier General MacArthur." This recommendation, supported later by General Flagler also, was denied by General Pershing. Biographer Arthur Herman unabashedly declared, "In the end, MacArthur did not receive it [the Medal of Honor]. It was Pershing, and Pershing alone, who finally blocked the award."[49] Menoher had also recommended that MacArthur be promoted to major general "for his field leadership, generalcy and determination during three days of constant combat (in front of the Côte de Châtillon) ... for his gallantry and determination in the field."[50] Amazingly, MacArthur nearly five decades later simply wrote, "I was also recommended for the Medal of Honor, but the Awards Board at Chaumont disapproved. It awarded me, however, a second Distinguished Service Cross, the citation more than satisfied my martial vanity."[51]

Unlike his arrogant and unjustified overaction against his first nomination for the Medal of Honor after the Veracruz expedition of 1914, MacArthur had obviously learned his lesson. He never again sought nor really cared about any awards and decorations that were presented to him, despite the rumors and opinions of others even to the present day.

General MacArthur walked off the battlefields in France with a second Distinguished Service medal, seven Citation Stars (later the Silver Star), two Wound Chevrons (later the Purple Heart), and a dozen or more foreign decorations including Frances's Légion d'Honneur (Legion of Honor) and the Croix de Guerre (Cross of War).[52] He emerged from the Great War as one of the most decorated soldiers in the American Expeditionary Force.

CHAPTER 7

★ ★ ★ ★ ★

CHAOS ON THE HUDSON

The challenges and situation that Douglas MacArthur inherited at the academy were tremendous. He eventually not only saved the school from its difficult circumstances but provided a powerful lesson of success against dire adversity. His accomplishments at West Point would propel him to greater renown while rescuing the US Military Academy that he adored from the ruin. During the space of eighteen months beginning in 1917, five classes graduated early due to emergency acts passed by Congress at the behest of the War Department. The expansion of the army from some 130,000 officers and enlisted men to more than four million by late 1918 greatly affected the academy. The US Army desperately needed officers, especially junior officers, to lead soldiers at the platoon and company levels in Europe. The War Department therefore pushed for the early graduations.[1]

Jacob Devers (class of 1909), who commanded the US Sixth Army Group in France during World War II, described the challenges MacArthur faced: "He inherited an old institution with a great heritage of success and tradition, but now reduced to a pitiable state as a result of the War Department."[2] The academy has been the army's main commissioning source for new lieutenants for a hundred years. Though some officers received direct commissions, the War Department and Congress had established a process for National Guard

Central Barracks at West Point, early 1900s. *Courtesy USMA Archives.*

and Reserve officers to gain commissions through the National Defense acts of 1908 and 1916. There was also a growing popular movement in the United States among upper-crust business and college students called the "Plattsburg Movement." Thousands of young men, mostly college students, gathered in upstate New York at their own expense to participate in voluntary military training. The army had sent a small cadre of trainers to assist and provide elementary training.[3]

When war commenced in Europe in August 1914, Col. Clarence P. Townsley, class of 1881, was superintendent, serving until June 1916. He was replaced by Col. John Biddle, also from the class of 1881. In May 1917, a month after the US declaration of war on Germany, Colonel Biddle was transferred to command a brigade of engineer regiments, and he eventually commanded all American troops based in Great Britain and Ireland.[4] On June 13, two weeks after Biddle was transferred to Europe, Col. Samuel Tillman returned to West Point to become the thirtieth superintendent. Tillman was sixty-nine years old, a member of the class of 1869, finishing third in his class of only thirty-nine graduates. He was a career engineer officer. In 1880 Tillman returned in a permanent faculty assignment at the academy, teaching mathematics and engineering. He soon became the head of the Department of Chemistry, Mineralogy and Geology, where he established a national reputation as a scientist and scholar, publishing many textbooks and papers. He retired in 1911 and was residing in Princeton, New Jersey, when the call to active service came.[5]

Before Tillman's arrival, the class of 1917 had already graduated 139 cadets on April 20, and then on August 30 the class of 1918 would graduate 151 young lieutenants destined to serve on the Western Front. These two classes are identified as the classes of April and August 1917. The War Department also asked Congress to reduce the curriculum from four years to three, then later to two years. These were War Emergency Acts, as they were called. Also, forty-two officers and other ranks were transferred from the Military Academy either overseas or to training camps. By the start of the school year in September 1917, there were three classes remaining, including the new plebe class that arrived in June. The first class of 1918 to graduate was on June 12, and later designated as 1918. A new plebe class arrived two days later. There were now three class groupings; two were technically yearlings or third classmen, and then the new cadets.[6]

The Upheaval

Adjutant Maj. William Ganoe narrated the shock that rattled West Point in October 1918 when a phone call came from the War Department. Ganoe heard a voice, "This is the Adjutant General, General Harris." Brig. Gen. Peter C. Harris, member of the class of 1881, told Ganoe alarming news. "You will graduate your two upper classes November first," Harris announced. Ganoe gasped, asking for clarification—then turned the phone over to Colonel Tillman. He pleaded, "Can't the order be held in abeyance or the date of graduation be postponed until I can discuss the eventualities with higher authorities?"[7]

The answer from General Harris, a man a dozen years younger than Tillman, was—no. "I'm sorry."

"Why, this means there will be no upper classmen in the Corps," Tillman protested, "We'll have only fourth classmen with a few months behind them." Harris apologized again. Tillman made his final plea: "I don't understand, why

Maj. William A. Ganoe, USMA class of 1907, academy chief of staff under MacArthur. *Courtesy USMA Archives.*

they are deliberately trying to destroy the Academy."⁸ Ganoe described in his book about MacArthur, in a chapter entitled "Crash," "Never in its precise production of officers through the previous hundred and sixteen years had the U.S. Military Academy been so battered and broken as in 1918."⁹

Harris then ended the call.

The extreme measure of graduating two classes early was a great sacrifice for the academy, but war always has sacrifices. Little did General Harris realize that in this same month of October 1918, his son, Capt. Charles Dashiell Harris, would be killed in France. Young Harris was only twenty-one years old when he died and was posthumously awarded the Distinguished Service Cross. Captain Harris was a product of the War Department's rush to commission officers into the war, graduating in August 1917 with 150 other classmates.¹⁰

Colonel Tillman referred to an issue caused by the war that was a huge problem for the academy's process and method of developing the leadership with the cadets. This was the system where senior cadets, the upperclassmen, had the task to train, mentor, and lead the younger cadets and develop them into experienced upperclassmen, who in turn did the same for the next generation of young men.

During his superintendency MacArthur also declared this same notion: "The prestige and influence of the upper classmen was impossible in a situation where there were no upper classmen. Cadet officers had never known the example of cadet officers before them."[11] The hundred-year method of more experienced upperclassmen leading the corps, which Major Sylvanus Thayer had instilled, was gone.[12] Ganoe declared, "The Corps had died November first 1918.... Not even a miracle could bring it back to life."[13]

That miracle would be Douglas MacArthur.

Colonel Tillman, Major Ganoe, and the other staff members did their best, but the demands of war caused another casualty, not in France but above the Hudson River. An American institution was deeply wounded, but not fatally. Tillman explained the significance of the year's challenges in the annual report of 1919, "at the end of the most unusual and eventful year in its history," which was probably true. He ended the report with this comment: "The system of instruction established through long experience was greatly dislocated by the war."[14] This statement was true and accurate, but Tillman's assessment was understated considering what really happened to the academy.

The bitterness portrayed by Tillman and Ganoe was real as more young lieutenants went off to war. In the year 1918, three classes graduated, one on June 12, then two more on November 1, as General Harris and Tillman discussed in their phone call. When the school year began on September 1, 1918, there were 940 cadets among the three remaining classes; the senior-most were technically the second classmen (juniors). After the November graduation of two classes, only the plebe class (429 cadets) was left—the most senior cadets at the academy despite arriving only five months earlier.[15] New cadets arrived in early November and were eventually graduated into two separate classes later. In sum, what remained were two groups of plebes (freshmen), who did not possess the experience, the training, and the leadership to act as upperclassmen over other cadets who would arrive in the future. Class integrity, structure, and cohesion were in shambles. The War Department policy had, according to historian Stephen Ambrose, "in effect...changed the

Academy from a military training university to a wartime military training camp for officers."[16] Maj. Gen. Sydney Berry, a superintendent in the 1970s and a 1948 graduate, understood the academy's desperate straits after the Great War: "World War I almost destroyed the Military Academy. Emphasis on quickly producing large numbers of officers for the War led to early graduations of five classes, disrupted the staff and faculty, and virtually turned West Point into simply another training camp for officers. The War ended with Fourth Classmen as the only members of the Corps of Cadets."[17]

Tillman throughout the Annual Report of 1919 referred to the challenges and confusion induced by the war, but he defended his decisions and minimized the actual situation. Others did not, such as professor of chemistry, mineralogy, and geology Col. Wirt Robinson, who addressed both the cadets' and instructors' anxiety: "The students are overtaxed and overloaded to the verge of breakdown, the instructors are exhausted and instruction deteriorates correspondingly.... Instructors, in particular, were subject to stress at West Point brought on by the war."[18]

After the graduation of all the upperclassmen in November 1918, it would take several years to restore the quality of leadership and expertise of the corps. Not only were the cadets graduated early without the benefit of the full educational program, but they were also segregated in unique categories as never before. These various classes wore different uniforms, not by choice but by events. When more than seven hundred new cadets reported at West Point in November 1918, there were not enough cadet gray uniforms and other articles, hats and caps, to issue to them. The only uniforms available at short notice were the standard-issue officer tunics, the M-1911 Campaign Hats and Sam Browne Belts.[19]

Within a month, the more junior class that had graduated on November 1 was recalled to West Point to undergo a special seven-month student officer training program. The 284 graduated officers begrudgingly returned to the academy and commenced the new, special officer course. These individuals would have technically two graduations, November 1918 and then June 11, 1919, when they completed their training course, receiving the designation of the class of 1919. They too wore the standard-issue uniform, as did the new plebes of November. To differentiate them as separate groups, officers from cadets, the new plebe class wore an orange stripe or band around the crown of their Campaign Hats. Soon the sobriquet of "Orioles," referring to the orange-breasted bird, would describe this class in academy lore. Thus, there were three different uniforms seen on campus the spring of 1919, defining three separate student groups.[20] Eventually, they all would be issued cadet uniforms.

Other factors accompanied the frustration and chaos of this time. The large class of new cadets of November 1918 wanted to serve in the war and expected a short training program and graduation in June 1919, after which they would be shipped off to France. Colonel Tillman explained: "These appointees were admitted without the usual mental tests and with the expectation and promise that they would be graduated the following June [1919 of this year]."[21] Because the war ended days after their admittance, the new plebe class was soon expected to meet all the standard requirements for entrance and graduation as other classes had done for decades. In March 1919, seventy-three cadets failed the entrance exams and were dismissed. But the major

Graduating Classes during World War I

Original Class	Admitted	Report Date	Class Designation	Graduates
1917[a]	186	June 1913	April 1917	139
1918[b]	210	June 1914	August 1917	151
1919	178	June 1915	June 1918	137
1920	319	June 1916	November 1918	227
N/A	350	June 1917	1919	284 graduated November 1918; returned as student-officers
N/A	424	June 1918	1920	271
N/A	425	Nov.–Dec. 1918	1921	17 (3-year course)
N/A	291	Nov.–Dec. 1918	1922	102 (4-year course)
N/A	30	June–July 1919	June 14, 1922	30 (3-year course)
1923	444	June–July 1919	1923	262 (4-year course)

Sources: Lance Betros, Carved from Granite, 119; Annual Report of the Superintendent, 1919, 3–4.
[a] In this class 24 cadets resigned due to the changes in curriculum.
[b] Some 85 cadets resigned from this class because of the curriculum; 73 additional cadets failed entrance examinations.

tragedy of this class was the mass resignation of eighty-five cadets in the summer of 1919 because they could not serve in the Great War. Also, their class would probably be required to attend three or more years of schooling at West Point. This was not what they bargained for, since they expected an "intensive course of eight months" and then to receive their commissions and enter the army.[22] Thus, more than a hundred new cadets left the "Oriole" class. Part of the confusion was the frustration of dozens of young men, who would not serve in combat against the enemies of their nation.[23]

The Aftermath

Once the Great War ended, the Military Academy had an entirely new challenge: future students, young men at this time, had many options for a college education, including great schools without the military obligation that the two federal service academies required. Competition for new cadets intensified when the war ended. The experience of so many cadets resigning in the past year, because of the termination of the hostilities and restoration of a four-year program, was a factor making the need to convince Americans to choose West Point. If the academy's curriculum, teaching methods, faculty expertise, and pedagogy were dated and inferior, then how could the academy attract the best candidates for future army officers? This was another factor Douglas MacArthur, or any other officer appointed as the new superintendent, had to face.[24] Did the faculty have the scholarly credentials of a modern American education system? Does being an effective army officer make one a proficient professor?

Col. Lucius Holt, the professor and head of the Department of English and History, was the only professor who held a PhD, and was a graduate of Yale, not West Point.

Leadership and Unity

"The Tactical Officer had been looked upon by the cadet as a sort of master ogre in a tower," recalled a staff officer who looked "to see whom he could devour." Over the decades tactical officers became far removed from the cadets, separating themselves from any meaningful contact with their wards. During

Thayer's day through the Civil War, unwed tactical officers resided in the cadet barracks. This gradually changed through the remainder of the nineteenth century. In fact, there was such a separation that when an officer observed a cadet making a mistake, committing an infraction, breaking a regulation, or not fulfilling a task, instead of making an immediate on-the-spot correction, the tactical officer (TAC) would go his desk and write out a "skin sheet" and forward it to the commandant for review. This was basically a written reprimand that turned into a formal charge sheet. The cadet would then receive the "skin sheet" through distribution with his penalty and punishment.[25] He had the right to an appeal known as "bellyaches," but this rarely happened. Thus, punishment hours or demerits were the outcome. There was little mentoring or counseling, scarce personal involvement, and a total lack of leadership. What character development was derived from this process? The cadets viewed the TACs as tyrants "who came to inspect and despoil."[26]

Lt. Col. Robert Danford concluded that something was amiss and later shared his concerns with General MacArthur. "Every morning I find on my desk a big pile of cadet explanations" for delinquencies and demerits. Danford reported that these "skin lists" were necessary in early times, but in recent times "it is utterly absurd." They were also typed by clerks or the officers, using more time and resources for such a derelict leadership process.[27]

Tradition and Opposition

West Point was in dire straits, which caused great concern on campus with the cadets, cadre, and staff, but also in the wider army and community, especially among the alumni. All colleges have loyal graduates, but the service academies' unique experience makes them different from most colleges. Because of intense military training, a grueling physical fitness program, and stringent discipline, the four years of training at West Point were unique compared to other American colleges. Their unique experience made the alumni especially loyal to West Point, and their memories were long.

Since 1869, West Point had been supported by an alumni organization, the Association of Graduates. Initially it was a society formed to host reunions and social gatherings so that old comrades could gather and celebrate their youth through parades, dinners, and graduation events during June Week.

The alumni were mostly concerned with maintaining West Point's reputation and status by safeguarding its history and legacy. "Tradition" was the watch word above all else.

The guardians of tradition and legacy distrusted unwanted change and reform, whether alumni or the professors of the Academy Board and cadre staff graduates. Many of the alumni were elderly, and they were almost universally unbending in their attempt to maintain West Point just as it was. A term arose in the last century that became part of the West Point lexicon: DOG, Disgruntled Old Graduate. Of course, not all West Point alumni were old, nor were they disgruntled. Yet, the term is appropriate for those alumni who were querulous and most vociferous in their criticisms of MacArthur's reforms.[28]

Even though the war disrupted the academy greatly, some aspects of the culture and tradition continued unabated. The cadets, though very junior and inexperienced, still attempted to enforce the integrity of the corps through hazing and ungoverned justice that they dealt upon their peers without law or rule, and administered at night, in darkness of the barrack rooms. Through decades of practice the cadets had established their own justice system; an as army lawyer explained, "Although the vigilante committees had no official recognition by the Academy, their existence was tolerated and its decisions unofficially sanctioned."[29]

Due to the graduation of the senior classes, the process of self-policing the Corps of Cadets was even more tenuous in the hands of new plebes with no or little experience. The chaos in the academy was also endemic to the corps itself, the reason why the school exists in the first place. The years ahead would severely test these young men and the institution itself. Earl "Red" Blaik, a cadet during these times, remembered, "For the cadets the winter and spring of 1918–1919 brought gloomy days mixed with hazing, a cadet suicide, personal grudge fights.... Certainly an air of melancholy prevailed."[30]

Academics

"At the beginning of the twentieth century," wrote historian Lance Betros, "the academic program at West Point looked much the same as it had for the previous eighty years."[31] As damning as this statement is, Betros was not alone

United States Military Academy poster by Frank Hazel, 1920s. Library of Congress.

in this assessment. Even before MacArthur arrived, criticism of the academy's educational manner and priorities were evident. The *New York Times* in 1919 questioned the graduates' ability to work effectively with the citizen-soldier of the Great War, saying, "During their four years' term the cadets see about as little of the world as the inmates of a convent." A proper education was not only scholarship in the classroom but also social contact and understanding and not "seclusion at the Military Academy."[32]

In 1920, after a visit the year before to the academy, Dr. Charles W. Eliot, emeritus president of Harvard University, criticized the school during a presentation he gave in Boston, noting "ill-prepared material [plebes]" and that "no school or college should have a completely prescribed curriculum" that offered little flexibility and innovation.[33] Eliot also denounced an obvious quality at West Point: "No school or college should have its teaching done almost exclusively by recent graduates of the same school."[34]

The issues that academic experts of the time observed concerning West Point dealt mainly with its exclusivity, paternalism, and rigid tradition of not keeping current with advances and innovations outside of the gray granite walls. What brought these defects to the forefront was the World War, which not only destroyed the class structure and morale of the Corps of Cadets but opened the question of the quality of the education that these sequestered officers received and whether it qualified them to lead a new, modern citizen-soldier into battle.

Besides the conflict and challenges due to the Great War, another enemy attacked Fortress West Point—an unseen foe that would have ghastly consequences for some 570 cadets and the hundreds of faculty members, staff, and their families residing at the post. In the fall of 1918 as the Great War was winding down, the Spanish flu arrived on campus. The resulting epidemic killed an estimated eighteen million people worldwide; some estimates place the total at fifty million. (The latter seems to be an outrageous figure.) At West Point there were two waves of the epidemic during the school year, first in October and then again in December, in which eventually every cadet, some 570, contracted the virus along with many staff and faculty falling ill also. Eventually, three cadets, one officer, and nine enlisted men died from the flu. Colonel Tillman outlined the affect the disease had on the academy by stating, "The total inadequacy of the Cadet Hospital was made evident again in the epidemic of influenza." This hospital had been constructed in 1884, and its modernization fell to Superintendent Douglas MacArthur.[35]

Historian Stephen Ambrose made an accurate commentary that "MacArthur's task was more difficult than Thayer's, for Thayer did not have to struggle against the tyranny of the past."[36]

CHAPTER 8

KING OF WEST POINT

Superintendent MacArthur

Returning to America, Gen. Douglas MacArthur would face a difficult and challenging assignment—one that he did not at first desire but that guaranteed his rank, which he highly desired to maintain. He moved quickly to evaluate and review West Point's current status, and then make significant, needed reforms and establish order. He soon instilled pride and confidence in the Corps of Cadets and the entire community. MacArthur addressed many problem areas and succeeded in reestablishing the four-year curriculum through Congress. He also developed the academy's first mission statement, and with the assistance of loyal subordinates, the commandant and adjutant (chief of staff), was able to challenge the control and power of the Academic Board, causing much friction. He nevertheless pushed reforms in academics, instructor teaching and advanced education, and military training away from the traditional Summer Encampment. He enhanced the academy's well-being and public image through visits from foreign dignitaries and heads of state, the US president, statesmen, and war heroes. By establishing an honor system in an attempt to end hazing and providing more privileges to cadets, he challenged the paternalism and tradition of a century. Athletic competition took precedence with corps sports, but his policy that every cadet must be enrolled in physical fitness activities was a major and lasting reform. MacArthur met the personal challenges in life of supporting an often onery elderly mother and courting a much sought-after lady of wealth and high society.

After every war in American history the military forces have been reduced in strength to a peacetime level. Sometimes the post-war manpower level was less than the antebellum strength. The US Army at the time of the armistice of November 1918 totaled more than four million soldiers; by July 1920, Congress had reduced it to 288,000 men.[1] With the reduction came the end of the temporary wartime commissions of the National Army. On June 30, officers in the Regular Army reverted to their permanent ranks. Both George Patton (class of 1909) and Dwight Eisenhower (1915) reverted from colonel to captain, their Regular Army rank. The next day both were promoted to major in the regulars.[2]

As the war ended, Brigadier General MacArthur also faced a reduction in rank, because his present temporary rank was authorized by legislation establishing the National Army. His rank was major in the Regular establishment before the war, and he could possibly revert to major when the turmoil and anxiety of the reductions ended. He was one of the youngest generals in the army and was regarded highly by all the soldiers and officers who knew him. What opportunities lay ahead once the famous 42nd Rainbow Division was inactivated?

MacArthur returned to the United States through New York City on April 25, 1919. Soon thereafter, summoned to the War Department in Washington, DC, he met with Gen. Peyton March, the army chief of staff. General March was an academy graduate of 1884, two years ahead of John Pershing—and, of course, they knew each other very well. Serving as the commander of the US First Army artillery, Major General March had been recalled stateside and on March 4, 1918, was appointed chief of staff.[3]

March told MacArthur that he was under consideration to be assigned superintendent of the US Military Academy. In his memoirs, MacArthur recalled March's comments as, "West Point is forty years behind the times. . . . Even the proud spirit of the Academy had flagged. In every way, West Point would be revitalized, the curriculum re-established."[4]

Initially, MacArthur was not pleased by the opportunity. He told March, "I am not an educator. I am a field soldier. Besides there are so many of my old professors there. I can't do it." To which March countered, "You can do it."[5]

General March was direct to his bewildered subordinate: "Douglas, things are in great confusion at West Point." He explained that he had spoken to Secretary of War Baker about the assignment and need: "Baker and I have talked this over and we want you to go up there and revitalize and revamp the Academy." Besides the fact that the school was in shambles, nearly ruined by the War Department and Congress graduating five classes early, March addressed another great concern, that West Point "has been too parochial in the past. I want to broaden it and graduate more cadets into the Army."[6]

This would be the greatest challenge Douglas would face during his superintendency, breathing fresh and revitalizing air into a weakened and run-down institution. Soon after his interview with General March, MacArthur wrote a letter to an officer of the 42nd Division about his new assignment. This letter, dated May 13, 1919, was reprinted in his *Reminiscences*, published in 1964 just before he died. The original letter is very different from the version in his book, which MacArthur sanitized. The former states, in part, "I was told to prepare myself to go to West Point as its Superintendent—so behold me in June ascending the throne as King of the Hudson." This is a rather interesting appellation he applied to himself, "King of the Hudson."[7] Wisely MacArthur accepted the assignment, because he could retain his rank: "I hold my rank and hope to continue to do so. Rumor has it that all the other general officers of the 42nd are to be demoted shortly."[8]

MacArthur's acceptance to serve as superintendent was initially based more on his career and his hope to maintain his rank of brigadier general than to be a reformer to restore the academy's curriculum and other necessary problems. However, he also understood the need to make reforms at West Point. In his first annual report to the War Department, MacArthur articulated his philosophy: "With the termination of the World's War the mission of West Point at once became the preparation of officer personnel for the next possible future war."[9]

The King of the Hudson Arrives

That first day General MacArthur walked to his office in the headquarters from his quarters, numbered Quarters 23 (now Quarters 100), he passed several buildings that had not existed when he was a cadet exactly twenty years earlier. Behind his house was a new gymnasium, completed in 1910 (now part of Arvin Cadet gymnasium). The first structure he walked by was North Barracks, also finished in 1910 (where MacArthur Barracks is today). Passing the barracks, on his right was the old Gymnasium and Fencing Academy, erected in 1893, which was a perfect model of a Norman castle of the eleventh century. He reached what is now Thayer Road and headed south, passing on his left a new academic building (Bartlett Hall), which was finished in 1913 and called East Academic Hall. What was missing was the 1836 Cadet Chapel that he knew as a cadet; it no longer stood there. Across the street was West Academic Hall (Pershing Barracks now), which he had attended for all his classes as a cadet. Approaching an intersection among the buildings, he could stop and look both left and right and see new granite edifices: to his right, two hundred yards away up on a hill was the new Cadet Chapel, and to his left stood the new indoor Riding Arena. Both were completed in 1910–11.[10]

MacArthur walked hundreds of times to his office past the six new major structures that were part of the major construction contract let in 1906 that changed the face of the US Military Academy. The architectural firm of Cram, Goodhue, and Ferguson was awarded a $7.5 million contract that commenced construction in 1909, including the new buildings located in the central area of old West Point on the historic plain. There were also other buildings and horse stables constructed at the cavalry field a mile south of main post. This contract also provided for several professor and officer quarters south and north of the central area.[11]

Passing the new academic building on the east, he arrived at the new headquarters building, completed in 1910.

• • •

Maj. William Ganoe was quite agitated as he paced the floor in the new headquarters building. The Great War was over, and he had not served in combat; in fact, he had not left West Point for that matter. Since 1916 he had served as the academy adjutant, one of six officers on the administrative staff. Though Ganoe missed the fighting war, it does not mean that the war did not affect him and the academy. West Point had faced its own battles, and after three years Major Ganoe was ready to move on. "My spirits were at a superlative low," he wrote. "Not only was the prospect black but the present was blue."[12]

Major Ganoe was blue because that morning, June 12, 1919, the new superintendent was due to arrive, a prospect he did not relish. The academy had gone through an upheaval during the previous two years after the United States declared war on Germany on April 6, 1917. Ganoe had experienced it all, assisting the elderly Samuel Tillman, appointed in June 1917 from retirement as the superintendent. Together they witnessed the decimation of the four-year academic program. Ganoe was loyal to Tillman, who was soon retiring again, this time with a promotion to brigadier general. "I was doing my best to help General Tillman move from the reservation into full retirement," Ganoe related.

What bothered Ganoe most was not that another officer was arriving as superintendent, but who that officer was. The name was known, and there were already comments by staff and faculty, such as "the appointment is fantastic. Looks like another effort to wreck the Academy." And then, "What possible qualifications can he have?" thinking of a non-scholar leading a college. "The Academic Board will make a monkey out of him."[13]

Major Ganoe knew the new superintendent; they had overlapped one year as cadets. He had not forgotten the striking and imposing cadet leader, the First Captain and top graduate of the class. Ganoe graduated well in the middle of his class, finishing 52nd of 111 classmates, rather unimpressive compared to the distinguished Douglas MacArthur. Now Brigadier General MacArthur, unlike Ganoe, had vast combat experience. Lady Luck and destiny had not smiled on Willian Ganoe, or so it seemed, whereas MacArthur was a hero and considered by many to be the greatest combat leader of the American effort. Regardless, Ganoe had fought his own battles, not in France but above the Hudson River; these battles were not bloody, but they were significant and critical.[14] The turmoil and confusion at West Point would only increase now with a new leader, Ganoe lamented: "Such was the state of affairs and feelings when it was announced that Brigadier General Douglas MacArthur was to be the new Superintendent."[15]

MacArthur reached the headquarters building and met Major Ganoe at the entrance. They entered through the main double doors and walked up the stone steps to the second floor, to the superintendent's office suite. MacArthur had never visited the administration and headquarters building before. He remarked to Ganoe, "Quite a castle. Slightly different from the little building with its church steeple of old." He referred to the former administrative building finished in 1870, which had been the headquarters when he was a cadet, and then demolished to make space for the present HQ. Eventually, Ganoe showed MacArthur the Academic Board Room just north of the superintendent's suite. Walking in, MacArthur said, "Privy Council," and then repeated again, "Privy Council."[16]

MacArthur was rather insightful here, because in this room he would face the distinguished department heads, some of whom had taught Cadet MacArthur. The idea of a privy council was perfectly appropriate regarding what he experienced during board meetings. MacArthur certainly saw the Nine Worthies of carved limestone above the fireplace in the Board Room. These figures, austere and warlike, looming overhead were themselves intimidating. Designed and sculpted by German-born American sculptor Lee Lawrie, they represented ancient and Medieval characters that looked over the shoulders of the board members, inspiring the warrior ethic.[17]

Adjacent to the Board Room was a spacious lounge, and beyond it, running east-west the entire length of the building, was the West Point Museum. The first military museum in America, founded in 1843, it displayed artifacts of bladed weapons, firearms, uniforms, and flags. With the Nine Worthies and museum weaponry in the headquarters, one could not deny the military themes of the academy.

"It seemed a day before quick steps clicked on the terra-cotta floor," Ganoe recalled, and "the General . . . swung into my office." Ganoe saluted, but MacArthur ignored it. They soon engaged in a conservation about their cadet days. "He wore no impressive uniform appropriate to the office of Superintendent," Ganoe observed, "although his clothing was neat and well pressed."[18]

Eventually, Major Ganoe asked General MacArthur if he would like to review the Corps of Cadets.

"For what purpose?" MacArthur asked.

"To greet and honor the new Superintendent," Ganoe replied.

MacArthur possibly thought about marching in parades when he was cadet. Then he said, "If memory serves me we didn't lack for ceremonies as cadets." MacArthur continued, "There was a constant excuse for turning out the Corps for a show."

MacArthur seemed to be quizzing himself. "What possible benefit can be found in an extra one for me? They'll see me soon and often enough. There are occasions when ceremonial is harassment, I saw too much overseas."[19]

And so the first decision General MacArthur made as superintendent was to cancel a parade of the Corps of Cadets in his honor that he found unnecessary and foolish. This was counter to the often-held view that MacArthur was vainglorious and arrogant; a haughty officer would have relished such a demonstration of pomp and ceremony.

Entering his spacious office with his swagger stick cradled in his arm, MacArthur surveyed his new command post. Ganoe narrated his boss's reaction: "His bright look was back as he stopped short and studied the large painted portraits of all the Superintendents since 1802, which formed a frieze under the high ceiling. It was an illustrious panel, including Lee, Beauregard, Schofield and Merritt. He stopped before each one as he examined the features . . . 'Quite a galaxy,' he said softly. . . . 'How will I ever have the face to perform the grave duties of Supe with these mighty dignitaries staring down at my every move, listening to my every word?'"[20]

Douglas MacArthur was absolutely correct in his assessment. How could he possibly rise to the level of these great officers, superintendents all, of the past? The names that William Ganoe mentioned are interesting, two Confederates and two Union officers, who fought on opposing sides. The superintendency of Pierre Gustave Toutant-Beauregard was the shortest tenure ever, only five days when the secretary of war relieved him on January 28, 1861. After Beauregard's home state of Louisiana's secession from the Union, fearing that he would take most of the Corps of Cadets south with him, he was dismissed. Douglas's father, Arthur MacArthur, served under John Schofield and Wesley Merritt, two great commanders revered at the time. Arthur was particularly close to General Wesley Merritt, who commanded the American forces that took the Philippines in 1898, where Arthur commanded a brigade under

Brig. Gen. Douglas MacArthur, thirty-first superintendent of the US Military Academy. *Courtesy MacArthur Memorial.*

Merritt. The position and office of superintendent had been held by a close-knit and select group of army officers. MacArthur was the thirty-first officer to serve as superintendent.[21]

The last and most important event that day dealt with Major Ganoe and his future service. Ganoe was not thrilled about serving under MacArthur—it was time to leave after nearly four years as instructor and adjutant at the academy. He wrote years later, "I was more than dismal over his [Tillman] going. Between sadness and fear, I was sure that serving anyone else was unthinkable.... Nothing could induce me to stay on. How absurd! He'd [meaning MacArthur] probably be glad to get rid of me."[22]

Ganoe had written his letter of resignation and had placed it on his superior's desk. Once in the large office, MacArthur saw the letter and asked, "Well, what's this?"

"Before I could answer, he shot out a question about the condition on the reservation. I answered," and an interrogation commenced. MacArthur pummeled Ganoe with many questions ranging from curriculum issues to the Cavalry Detachment to the observatory and even the Cadet Store. "The rapid-fire quiz kept on.... There was nothing of the severe or inquisitorial about his manner, no show of passion or hounding." After some time and many questions, Ganoe was baffled and finally said, "Sir, I don't know."[23]

MacArthur reached for the letter, "tore it into bits, threw them in the wastebasket and spoke with that low, compelling resonance, 'Chief, go back to your desk.'" In a few minutes MacArthur had confirmed Ganoe's knowledge of every facet of the academy and the military reservation, and how valuable he was to the new superintendent. He also promoted Ganoe from adjutant and created a new position in the academy's hierarchy: chief of staff. Maj. William Ganoe was the first USMA chief of staff and remained in position for the remainder of MacArthur's tenure, giving him seven years on staff at West Point.[24]

Among the Corps of Cadets MacArthur's arrival provided an interesting hint of change and reform. Cadet Earl "Red" Blaik, who graduated in 1922, was a plebe when the new superintendent took office. He later became the most successful football coach in West Point history and a life-long friend of MacArthur. "There was no ceremony, not even a review of the Corps," Blaik recalled of MacArthur's first days as superintendent. Not having to march in dress uniform on the plain was no minor occurrence.

Decades later, Blaik offered a sanguine account:

June 12, 1919 was a day of dramatic action on the Plain. Brigadier General Douglas MacArthur, age 39, took command of West Point. He replaced the retiring superintendent, Colonel Samuel Tillman, who had been a cadet during the Civil War. The oldest Supe had been relieved by one of the youngest.... We soon learned he was not one to soiree the Corps with unnecessary pomp and ceremony. Perhaps several days passed before the cadets saw this tall, striding officer of casual dignity on Diagonal Walk. But during those days West Point changed. The air was charged with renewed vitality. Days of frustration turned to days of purpose, and so it was to remain for the next three years.[25]

As superintendent, General MacArthur had the responsibility for all facets of the Military Academy and the West Point garrison. Governance was the first order of business.

Governance

The academy is and always has been a college, a liberal arts institution, and the first engineering school in the United States. Governance, the application of policies, and the assessment of practices and the enforcement of regulations and directives has always been essential. But, as historian Lance Betros wrote in his book *Carved from Granite: West Point since 1902*, "governance at West Point has never been simple or straightforward." Since the Academy is also a military school, governance is complex: "On the one hand, cadets live in an environment that steeps them in the traditional military virtues of loyalty, obedience and unity of purpose. On the other hand, they are encouraged to embrace the academic virtues of intellectual freedom, scholarly skepticism, and diversity of opinion."[26]

Governing the Military Academy was relatively simple when it began in the early 1800s. The first organized governance body was in 1817, when Major Sylvanus Thayer established the Academic Board. This board was initially very small, composed of only the superintendent, three or four department heads or professors, and the commandant of cadets. As time went on the board evolved into a unique entity, different from a normal army organization. Betros wrote, "For good or bad, the command arrangement defined by the Academic Board was unlike any other in the army. It was collegial, powerful, autonomous, and enduring."[27]

Though ad hoc committees and groups were appointed at times, it was the academic board that ruled the academy. It oversaw nearly every facet of the school: academics, curriculum, infrastructure, military training, uniforms, rations, and future projects. In comparison, the Board of Visitors, created in 1815 but not convened until 1817, consisted of outsiders—professors from other institutions, Congressmen, and distinguished experts appointed by the president of the United States that made recommendations and reviewed processes but had no control or authority.[28] The Academic Board in the early nineteenth century dealt mainly with academic and pedagogical issues, but as time passed its power grew, because its "influence over curricular matters soon spread to virtually every other area of governance at West Point."[29] This influence, according to Theodore Crackel, "continued to dominate governance until the end of the Second World War," whereas its "influence constituted a powerful counterweight to the prerogatives and initiatives of the superintendent." The board's "corporate nature . . . ensured that changes, particularly those relating to the curriculum, were incremental"—or glacial, in fact. Col. Samuel Tillman while a professor wrote, "The Board was the continuing, developing, and stabilizing factor of the Academy."[30] All decisions and prerogatives were important to the board, but the academics and engineering-based curriculum were especially sacred cows to the impervious knights of the Academic Board Room's rectangular table.[31]

The board's entrenched and stubborn adherence to tradition would be one of the greatest challenges that MacArthur faced during his superintendency, a bear staring down of a pack of wolves.

Leading the pack was Col. Gustav J. Fiebeger, who was absolutely determined to maintain the status quo antebellum, especially with engineering as the basis and foundation of the academic program. With the academy's curriculum decapitated from four years to less than two years of schooling within the wartime academic years, Fiebeger and his fellow board members were determined to regain some control over the academics of West Point.[32] Historian Clayton James wrote, "The consequence during the years 1919–1922 was a collision between an ambitious superintendent and a faculty . . . powerful and deeply entrenched."[33] MacArthur recognized the challenge he faced from the "Old Guard." He told Major Ganoe, "The professors are so secure, they

Academic Board Members 1919	
Civil and Military Engineering	Col. Gustav J. Fiebeger (USMA 1879)*
Modern Languages	Col. Cornelis D. Willcox (USMA 1885)
Chemistry, Mineralogy, and Geology	Col. Wirt Robinson (USMA 1887)*
Mathematics	Col. Charles P. Echols (USMA 1891)*
Military Hygiene	Col. Frederick P. Reynolds (U. Penn MD 1890)
Natural and Experimental Philosophy (Electricity, hydraulics, physics)	Col. Clifton C. Carter (USMA 1899)
Law	Col. George V. Strong (USMA 1904)
English and History	Col. Lucius H. Holt (PhD Yale 1905)
Drawing	Col. Roger G. Alexander (USMA 1907)
Ordnance and Gunnery	Capt. Charles Hines (USMA 1910)
Commandant of Cadets and Department of Tactics	Lt. Col. Robert M. Danford (USMA 1904)
Non-Academic Board Key Members	
Master of the Sword, Physical Training	Lt. Col. Herman Koehler

*Faculty during MacArthur's cadetship.

have become set and smug. They deliver the same schedule year after year with the blessed unction that they have reached the zenith in education.... But what have they added or improved since I was a cadet?"[34]

MacArthur was not underestimating the opposition he faced with the Old Guard. Ganoe, who again was a key witness of this episode, narrated and explained the wrestling match between the two rivals: "MacArthur went exploring the holy precincts of the pedagogical duchies"—the department halls, the sacred turf of the professors, where learning the processes and teaching techniques by instructors. "His visits became cheeky snooping ... unprovoked aggression" on the department domains. "What right had any Supe to question the true-and-tried practices of a century?" Ganoe reported the professors' attitudes that MacArthur "was an interloper and dictator. At best, he was dangerous to the very fundamentals of West Point."[35] These are rather heady observations by Ganoe, an accomplished literary figure who relished his prose and narrative ability. This sensational explanation is nevertheless accurate. The department heads were covetous of their fiefdoms.

The comments and quotes from William Ganoe's book *MacArthur: Close-up, Much Then and Some Now* (1962), offer a primary source for MacArthur's time as superintendent at the academy. Colonel Ganoe was later a remarkable writer and historian serving as such in Europe during World War II. He also wrote an outstanding history of the US Army, a revised edition of which was published in 1964, the year MacArthur died.[36] He declared in his preface to *MacArthur: Close-up*, "I took notes, memorized many of his words and started repeating his acts." One has to be suspect of a witness so long ago who based much of his story on his memory. Ganoe claimed that "many statements were so startling and original, they just naturally stuck."[37] Historian Roger H. Nye, later deputy head of the Department of History at West Point, wrote in his 1968 PhD dissertation about Ganoe's objectivity, "Ganoe's *MacArthur Close-Up* has become the leading interpretation of MacArthur's relationship with other Academy officials.... The meager official records tend neither to confirm or discount the validity of the pro-MacArthur bias of the Ganoe account."[38]

Fortunately for MacArthur's superintendency, Ganoe's manuscript was reviewed by retired Maj. Gen. Robert M. Danford, who was commandant under MacArthur, and who praised Ganoe's recounting.[39] Again, some critics will condemn Danford also because he too was a devoted friend and associate of Douglas MacArthur.

• • •

The first major challenge facing both Superintendent MacArthur and the Academic Board was securing a restoration of the four-year curriculum that had served the academy well for a century. When General March met with MacArthur in May, he directed Douglas to reinstate a three-year program when he assumed command. This he did in a recommendation on June 28, 1919, with Secretary of War Newton Baker's approval; it was implemented for the commencement of classes in September.[40]

This was the first step toward reestablishing stability and confidence for all involved. The restoration of the former four-year program would be a greater challenge, and MacArthur knew he could not do it by himself. This required a level of humility on his part. "Day and day, for long hours, I huddled with the Academic Board in formulating and applying their plans for revitalization."[41]

The board agreed with MacArthur that the four-year curriculum had to be reinstituted. "Through a long series of exhaustive discussions the Board endeavored to give proper weight to all phases of the life and activities at the Academy, and to evolve finally a logical coherent schedule." With much effort MacArthur and the board cajoled the support of Congressman John M. Morin of Pennsylvania, chair of the subcommittee for appropriations for both federal service academies. He was also president of the Board of Visitors for 1919, and in February 1920 Morin convened congressional committee meetings and hearings on the USMA's proposal.[42] MacArthur's skills serving as former chief of the War Department's Information Bureau was certainly helpful, as he recorded in the *Annual Report of the Superintendent*: "The Act making appropriations for the support of the Military Academy for the fiscal year ending June 30, 1921, contained the provision that 'The course of instruction at the United States Military Academy shall be four years.' Immediately after the presidential approval of this bill March 30, 1920, the Academic Board began its consideration of the nature and content of the four-year course."[43]

The reestablishment of the curriculum was one of the major victories that the Academic Board and MacArthur achieved together. The board supported the restoration of the four-year course of study because it was a step toward returning the academy to the antebellum foundation of proven success but, more so, out of tradition.[44]

There were other accomplishments also, especially in daily routine operations and education that these two major players of the academy achieved in unison. When it came to reforms, to radical changes versus proven ways or tradition, these two bulls locked horns. Not all the professors opposed MacArthur; a couple, not many, were reform-minded also. One was Col. Lucius Holt, the only PhD on the faculty, and one of the few faculty non–West Point graduates. On the subject of adding some courses apart from math, science, and engineering, as early as 1911 Holt wanted to introduce economics—and social and political science, especially psychology—into the curriculum. When MacArthur made this offer Holt enthusiastically aligned himself with the superintendent.[45]

Yet, there were times that the Academic Board Room turned into a war room. Tempers, egos, personalities, and military rank and position rose and faced off. Lt. Col. Robert M. Danford, a graduate of 1904, a year behind

Recommended curriculum 1920, adopted for the 1921 academic year.

THE FOUR YEAR COURSE OF INSTRUCTION

Time	1	2	3	4
8:00	MIL. ENGINEER-ING ½ A	PHILOSOPHY A / CHEMISTRY B	ENGLISH ½ B / HISTORY ½ B (Alternating)	MATHEMATICS A
	LAW ½ A		FRENCH ½ A	
			MATHEMATICS ½ A	
9:00				
9:15	MIL. ENGINEER-ING ½ B	Extension for Laboratory	Alternating	GYMNASIUM A (Exc. Sats.) MATHEMATICS B
	LAW ½ B			
10:00				
10:15		Ex. for Lb.	Alternating	GYMNASIUM B
10:30	MIL. ART AND HISTORY ½ A	PHILOSOPHY B / CHEMISTRY A	MATHEMATICS ½ B	LECTURES Saturdays only
11:00	RIDING ½ A+½ B Except Saturdays	Extension for Lab't'y	FRENCH ½ B	SURVEYING Last 38 days replacing English.
11:15	MIL. ART AND HISTORY ½ B		ENGLISH ½ A	FRENCH ½ A Alternating with ENGLISH ½ B
11:45			HISTORY ½ A	
12:00	PROFESSIONAL LECTURES Saturdays only			
12:15				DINNER
1:50	Alternating	Alternating	Alternating	DRAWING A
	ORD. & GUN. ½ A	SPANISH ½ A	HYGIENE ½ B	TACTICS B
	ECON. & GOVT. ½ A	RIDING B		Including PRACTICAL MIL. ENGINEERING. No study time available. Indoor periods 1 hr. each: 1:50-2:50. 2:50-3:50.
2:35				30 Periods begin Jan. 2.—Replacing riding.
2:50	ORD. & GUN. ½ B	SPANISH ½ B	HYGIENE B	FRENCH ½ B Alternating with ENGLISH ½ B
	ECON. & GOVT. ½ B			SURVEYING Last 38 days replacing English
3:50				

MacArthur, became commandant at MacArthur's request. Danford served as a member of the Academic Board and was a loyal supporter of the superintendent and his program and policies. Danford recalled a heated exchange during one of the board meetings: "One of the oldest members of the Board, always talkative and always critical, kept interrupting him [MacArthur] repeatedly at a Board meeting. The outbursts of dissension and arrogance bordered on the insubordinate. MacArthur took it patiently for as long as he could, then suddenly, he froze with indignation. 'Sit down, Sir,' commanded the Superintendent, 'I'm talking.'"[46]

The older board member was no doubt Colonel Fiebeger, head of the Department of Military and Civil Engineering, MacArthur's arch opponent on nearly every issue, every decision, and every recommendation of MacArthur's reforms.[47] Quietly and discreetly, Fiebeger referred to MacArthur as the "boy superintendent," and he used his power and influence in an effort to maintain the status quo of the academy and its traditions.[48]

MacArthur devised ways to win the joust with the Academic Board and at times was clever and cunning. For one such meeting, Capt. Louis Hibbs, MacArthur's aide-de-camp, asked the superintendent about an upcoming meeting, the agenda and time schedule, recommending a morning meeting. MacArthur responded firmly, "No! ... Call the meeting at 4:30 p.m. I want them to come here hungry—and I'll keep them here that way till I get what I want."[49] MacArthur could stiff-arm when he wanted.

Creating a Mission Statement

Organizations need a purpose, an objective to strive for and accomplish: in modern parlance, a mission statement. West Point as both a college and a military academy needed a direction, a purpose to follow. For decades the academy had survived without any type of official mission statement. Now in the twentieth century and having fought in a world war, the academy needed a mission statement, a standard to bring overall guidance moving forward. Such a statement would be a great first step in MacArthur's reform agenda.

MacArthur needed a guide, a path to follow in order to organize his efforts to pull West Point out of the morass it was in. For the first time ever, a superintendent devised and published a mission statement for the Military Academy. It was a year into his superintendency and ensconced in his first *Annual Report of the Superintendent* in 1920. Eventually, the academic board reviewed and approved the mission statement. The statement was published in italics with a short preamble MacArthur prepared:

> Estimating the situation as it exists today, the Academic Board approves the following statement of the function of this institution: *The function of the Military Academy is to live, in addition to that character-building for which it has long been famous, and in addition to the necessary military and physical training, such a combination of basic general and technical education as will provide an adequate foundation for a cadet's subsequent professional career.*[50]

In this annual report MacArthur laid out clearly, but not briefly, the state of affairs at the academy, his intent with reforms, and his overall objectives. "My assumption of the command of the United States Military Academy synchronized with the ending of an epoch in the life of this Institution." He cited the combat records of the graduates: "The excellence with which the Academy's mission has been carried out in the past has been testified on the battlefields of the world for a hundred years and more."[51]

The task ahead was daunting, but MacArthur saw early on a course to revitalize and reform West Point by building on the past values of the academy and molding it into a modern institution. He wrote in his first *Annual Report of 1920*: "In meeting this problem those who were charged with the solution undertook the task with a full realization of its seriousness. It was well understood that it was no light affair to attempt even in moderate degree to modify a status which had proved itself so splendidly for a century and more. It was understood that change under the guise of reconstruction was destructive unless clearly and beyond question it introduced something of added benefit."[52]

Reform was not for reform's sake; there had to be a purpose and a plan. The mission statement was a first step. One of MacArthur's objectives was to increase the size of the corps, having learned from the Great War that there was no guarantee of West Point's role in future and modern warfare. Along with an increase in cadets, a new modern Corps of Cadets would ensure that West Pointers would not only be a part of, but hopefully would lead, the new modern army. Following the peacetime reduction of the army, "The Military

Academy was left with the same authorized strength of 1,334 cadets that it had previously" before the war. MacArthur knew that West Point "cannot supply more than one-third of our officers even in times of peace." The Brigade of Midshipmen at the Naval Academy had an authorized strength of 3,136, more than twice that of West Point. He ended this point by declaring, "I regard a commensurate increase in the Corps of Cadets as the most necessary and constructive feature of a sound military policy that confronts the Nation today."[53] This was a battle that MacArthur lost in 1920 as superintendent; it was not until 1935 that Congress authorized 1,960 cadets in the corps, an increase of some 600 cadets.[54] Only during World War II did the Corps of Cadets equal the number of Naval Academy midshipmen.

The situation at West Point, especially with the chaos of reconstituting the Corps of Cadets and reestablishing the curriculum, meant that achieving some level of stability was the major issue for MacArthur and his team to address. Defining a mission and reforming governance were the main priorities, but there were other issues. The responsibilities that caused MacArthur and the staff added distress and were distractions, included hosting prominent visitors who, if handled properly, could be a great benefit to the academy.

Kings, Princes, and Protocol

West Point has always been a beloved American gem to visit, especially by foreign and national dignitaries, and so the end of the war brought a renewed flood of distinguished visitors to the academy. These visits have always caused a level of planning and coordination, and consumed resources, time, and dedicated effort.

Because of his youth, vigorous health, communication skills, and reputation as a combat leader and hero, Brig. Gen. Douglas MacArthur was the perfect ambassador to represent both the army and the academy to some of the most distinguished individuals of the time.

In October 1919 a call came to chief of staff Major Ganoe that within thirty minutes King Albert I of Belgium was landing by floatplane on the Hudson River at South Dock. The entire staff was in a state of hysteria as Ganoe informed MacArthur of the alarming news, to which Douglas replied, "the

King of the Belges? Well, well, we're getting up in the world." MacArthur watched idly by with a detached sense of humor as the chief frantically located a driver and military police escort, a boat, and a driver. Then MacArthur offered a recommendation: "This King of Belgium is, I hear, a mountain climber." Thus, Albert and his young son, Leopold, were escorted on a stroll among the Hudson highlands near the academy. The teen-aged Prince Leopold was delighted to walk along the trails around Fort Putnam, where the party had an amazing view of the Hudson below. As the royal party departed, King Albert presented MacArthur with an award, Order of the Crown, for his service in France during the war.[55]

Instead of the formulaic tour and parade, MacArthur required some creativity when showing West Point to guests and distinguished visitors. He wanted to adjust and cater tours for each visiting party and not always provide the standard exhibitions of the past.

A great example of this was when Edward, Prince of Wales and the future King Edward VIII of the United Kingdom, visited the academy in

The Prince of Wales (right), future king of Great Britain, and General MacArthur at West Point, 1919. *Courtesy MacArthur Memorial.*

1919. The prince was a young man at the time, twenty-five years old. This visit was scheduled, so MacArthur and his staff had some time to coordinate and plan. Ganoe recalled the superintendent instructing him, "This Prince, Chief, is a youngster at heart like any other lad." MacArthur continued, "The fact he was born to royalty can't change his natural boyish impulses and desires. He has the same longing for relaxation, freedom, and play.... He's not interested in buildings, grounds and ceremonies."[56]

MacArthur then hit on a novel approach for the Prince of Wales. He directed Ganoe to round up "four of your most engaging, personable cadets," all well-spoken. "I'm going to turn them loose at the proper time with the Prince" and let the young cadets enjoy a lively time with the young royal. He offered no restrictions, no guidance, other than complete freedom to ask anything and see anything.[57]

Ganoe's question was, "How, General, are you going to pry the Prince loose from his bodyguard?" MacArthur answered with a smile, "I'm not even going to try. It will just come to pass." Prince Edward arrived, and while he was in the mess hall, with all the commotion of hundreds of cadets, the four-cadet team whisked the prince away. For the next several hours they had a merry time marauding around post. The "five of them were giggling and bantering each other" when they returned. The "Prince thanked MacArthur with overflowing words and [a] broad smile."[58]

A special event occurred in 1919 that General MacArthur took pride in presiding over, though he had nothing to do with the concept or the process. The Republic of France wanted to express its gratitude to the American people at large and the armed forces, in particular, for America's support in the victory in Europe. The L'Ecole Polytechnique presented a replica of a monument that stood on its campus in France. The connection L'Ecole Polytechnique had with West Point was not new, as Captain Sylvanus Thayer had studied engineering and collected instruments and textbooks during his two years in Europe prior to his return as superintendent in 1817.[59] The gifted statue is impressive, depicting a French soldier of the Napoleonic era swinging a saber overhead while standing near a cannon with the French flag in hand. The statue was originally installed on the plain in front of the old Central Barracks where Eisenhower Barracks now stands. MacArthur's service in France made him the perfect ambassador for the monument's reception. For this special visit, MacArthur asked the commandant, Colonel Danford, to select four cadets fluent in French to act as escorts to the young French visitors to make them feel more welcome.[60]

Not only royalty visited the academy during MacArthur's tenure; the next best thing in America, the president of the United States, Warren G. Harding, came for a visit in September 1921. He arrived on the presidential yacht, USS *Mayflower*, commissioned in 1898 during the Spanish-American War, having sailed north on the Hudson River from New York City. A *New York Times* piece published the next day stated, "The President had never been to West Point. . . . The Mayflower arrived at West Point a few hours after authorities at the Military Academy received word of the President's impending visit." MacArthur and his staff hustled to prepare for the presidential visit, which included an escort of Black mounted soldiers of the Cavalry Detachment to escort the president to the parade field. Meeting the official party at South Dock were "Brigadier General Douglas MacArthur, Superintendent of the United States Military Academy and his mother." Then the Corps of Cadets of 1,400 in dress uniform passed in review: "With a click each battalion came to present arms, and the 'Star Spangled Banner' was played to the bare headed President." After the parade Harding changed into his golf outfit in the superintendent's quarters, and he then played a round on the golf course that existed at this time on the historic Plain.[61]

On December 10, 1921, Field Marshal Ferdinand Foch of France made an official visit to the academy during his tour of the United States and Canada. Foch was the chief of the Supreme Allied Council during the last year of the war after the American forces had intervened. It was under his stable leadership that the Allies coordinated their efforts to defeat Germany on the Western Front. MacArthur was a young but distinguished commander under Foch's lofty leadership, a field marshal of France. Now Brigadier General MacArthur hosted the famous victor of the war.[62]

Pomp and ceremony aside, though not perfect, the state of affairs at the academy were tenuous. A strong hand and team effort were necessary. MacArthur's desire to rescue and reform West Point was a major undertaking, and being still a young man, he had the energy and vision. MacArthur had a difficult road even with the few allies he had. The Old Guard resented much of his vision and his manner. Eventually, his leadership and brilliance in stating

Marshal Ferdinand Foch of France (left) visiting West Point, escorted by Superintendent MacArthur, in December 1921. *Courtesy MacArthur Memorial.*

and illustrating his position, and his patience, provided the opportunity to make major reforms at West Point. MacArthur knew the fertile ground was ripe for change and the conditions for reforms in cadet life, physical education, Summer Encampment, and realistic training was possible. Ahead lay the near impossible task to eliminate hazing among the cadets and establish a viable cadet-led honor system. Being a visionary, MacArthur developed his concept for West Point's future and a scheme to completely overhaul the academic areas with new halls, buildings, and public venues.

Life with Mother

The first personal order of business for the new superintendent was to see that his elderly and by then frail mother, Mary "Pinky" MacArthur, age sixty-seven, was properly housed in the academy's spacious Federal-style quarters. While Douglas was away at war in France she lived with the family of her son Commander Arthur MacArthur III of the US Navy, who was serving in the Atlantic on convoy duty. With Douglas's return she elected to reside with him at West Point since she knew the lay of the land very well, having lived at the West Point Hotel during Cadet MacArthur's first two years.

Now she resided in the largest and the most elegant quarters on West Point and one of the most historic homes in America. Built under the direct supervision of Sylvanus Thayer in 1820 for $6,500, its Federal-style architecture set it apart from the gray granite barracks and academic halls of Tudor or military gothic. The superintendent's quarters had experienced several renovations and expansions over time. The house was more than adequate for only two people, with two parlors, a music room, a kitchen, and an attached sunroom at the west end on the ground floor. The second floor was the living area with several bedrooms and bathrooms, even though indoor plumbing was not added until years later. This was a marvelous home for Pinky to live in and support her son. Because Douglas was a bachelor, his mother served as hostess for social and official functions.[63] MacArthur was not the first bachelor superintendent: Major Thayer holds that honor, and Col. George Washington Cullum, who served from 1864 to 1866, was an older bachelor. Thayer was also the youngest superintendent ever, at age thirty-two when he accepted the position, whereas Douglas was thirty-nine.[64]

Douglas would eat breakfast and read the newspapers at the house for most of the morning. His biographer William Manchester explained: "He worked in his mansion through most of the morning to give his staff a head start. Between 10:30 and 11:00 a.m. he came in and disposed of his mail in an hour. On his orders, envelopes were slit only half open, so he alone would read the contents; his answers were scrawled on the back of the envelopes, typed up and signed. From noon to 1:00 p.m. he kept his appointments. The next two hours were spent in the mansion with his mother. Meetings occupied him until 4:30 or 5:00 p.m.; then he watched the cadets at athletic practice, dined, and passed the evening in his study reading history, literature and military science."[65]

On one occasion MacArthur stopped a group of cadets on a leisurely Sunday afternoon. They were passing the superintendent's quarters when MacArthur engaged in an informal conversation. The cadets had just acquired a refreshing treat of ice cream due to the fact they now had some allowance money to spend. As they visited outside, from a second-floor window a strong female voice called out, "Douglas!" His mother cried out, "You must stop talking to those boys and let them go. Don't you see that their ice cream is beginning to melt?" Douglas replied, "I guess you'd better hurry along."[66]

Pinky lived with her son in the superintendent's quarters for most of MacArthur's tenure, until the forty-two-year-old bachelor married Louise Cromwell Brooks on Valentine's Day 1922. Once the newlyweds returned from their honeymoon Pinky MacArthur left West Point and Quarters 23 to the new family, Louise and her two children from a previous marriage. Pinky joined her other son, Arthur, and his family once again in Washington, DC.[67]

CHAPTER 9

★ ★ ★ ★ ★

REFORMING THE MONASTERY

Gen. Peyton March told Douglas MacArthur to "revitalize" the academy, meaning he was to improve, refine—or, more properly expressed, reform—West Point. Other than reforming the academy in a general way, what needed to be reformed? Besides the wreck of the corps by the Great War, there were a dozen reforms needed, from academics to military training, from ending hazing and breaking down paternalism to improving tactical officers' leadership and interaction with cadets, instilling the significance of physical fitness as a crucial component of readiness, and gaining a unity among the professors, tactical officers, and staff that would enhance teamwork and cooperation. MacArthur also had to provide a vision of the future for the academy with an expansive building program of academic halls, barracks, an armory, a hotel, and an athletic stadium abutting the river.

These were major reforms, and historian Lance Betros offered this commentary after providing a litany of MacArthur's contributions in only three years: "These heady accomplishments, any one of which would have stood out by itself, represented a body of reform unprecedented since Thayer."[1]

The best way to address General MacArthur's reforms at the academy is by a thematic approach. His overall influence, reforms, and leadership were so comprehensive, far-reaching, and lasting that a simple narrative may not tell the story properly and completely.

Storming the Wall of Paternalism: Creating the New Officer

The US Military Academy has been described as many things over time: a castle, a fortress, a citadel, a bastion, all military and defensive terms; but Douglas MacArthur used a religious metaphor. He referred to the academy as a monastery with its granite walls and confining paternalism. "They [the cadets] were cloistered almost to a monastic extent." Echoing this same theme, the *New York Times* asserted in May 1919, just before the new superintendent arrived: "We need less 'pipeclay' and less seclusion at the Military Academy—in one word, more democracy. During their four years' term the cadets see about as little of the world as the inmates of a convent. When they graduate they know little of human nature, and the only men they have handled are themselves."[2]

Having suffered through four years of rigid isolation as a cadet, MacArthur was determined to treat the current cadets as adults, provide them with some privileges and helping them gain maturation. The academy had ossified into a stern and harsh institution where cadets had little freedom, few choices, and only one sixty-day furlough after completing two long years within the walls of West Point. The new superintendent wanted to change the cadet world, so that "they no longer were to be walled up within the Academy limits, but were to be treated as responsible young men."[3]

Walls of granite were an outward symbol of the restrictions of paternalism so intrinsic to the US Military Academy by the early twentieth century. The professors and administrators looked upon the cadets as mere children requiring complete control and supervision. Lance Betros, himself a 1977 graduate, explained paternalism at the academy: "Academy officials modulated the cadets' living and working environment to nurture and mold the development of intellect, character, physical fitness, and professional skills. They believed they knew what was best for the young cadets; accordingly, they forced strict compliance with every detail and punished every violation."[4]

The monasterial life of the academy was not only obvious to General March and MacArthur, but a distinguished visitor observed this culture a decade later in 1931, which of course was after some of MacArthur's reforms had been reversed. Marshal Henri-Phillipe Pétain, the victor of Verdun in 1916, visited West Point with General John Pershing. Later Pétain made this observation, "I do not think that young men who are being prepared for the duties of an officer should be required to repeat the same gestures every day during four years." He said that this routine and culture was "so rigid that elasticity becomes impaired." The product that Pétain saw at West Point was "well-instructed and obedient subaltern and a first rate drill-instructor ... he has got to pass considerable time before he can break the rigid forms in which his nature has become crystalized and regain his mental vigor."[5]

Creating a new environment that would allow the cadets to have more freedom was, MacArthur believed, paramount to reforming the corps and creating a new army officer. He felt cadets should make choices over simple and ordinary aspects of life such as allowance money, free time on weekends, opportunities to leave the confines of West Point, and staying in "touch with life outside the walls of the institution." These were not a reform for reform's sake but rather the creation of a new model—the modern army officer.[6]

After serving in combat for more than a year, and seeing what war requires of leaders, MacArthur knew that West Point paternalism did not create an environment to develop the officer that modern war demanded. To improve the corps and prepare the cadets to be officers, a new type of officer had to be different from those of earlier generations, MacArthur had learned some serious lessons from his experience in World War I. The officer that West Point was producing, according to MacArthur, was not acceptable. "The problem which faced the authorities was, therefore, this: Have new conditions developed, have the lessons of the World War indicated that a changed type of officer was necessary in order to produce the maximum of efficiency in the handling of men at arms? West Point, existing solely as a source of supply and a feeder to the Army, if a new era faces the latter ... must of necessity train its personnel accordingly."[7]

The world was changing especially because of the war, and American citizen-soldiers would not suffer through the type of austere discipline that their fathers and grandfathers had experienced during the Civil War and afterward. In his memoirs MacArthur remembered his goal "to deliver a product trained with a view to teaching, leading, and inspiring the modern citizen in crises to become an effective officer or soldier."[8] He recognized that to be new officers in the new modern army with its growing technology and lethality on the battlefield, cadets needed more freedom of choice than allowed previously in their daily lives and routines.

MacArthur's observations are interesting relative to human nature and the cadets he oversaw. A question that came to his mind was, How can these young men develop into officers and, more importantly, into fearless, mature, and competent combat leaders? He saw the hypocrisy that the cadets faced: "At one end, we boast about a cadet's truth and honesty; and at the other, we don't trust him to go out the gates of this medieval keep." The standards of paternalism were not a distrust of the cadets but were in place to protect them, because it was assumed that they were not capable of navigating the perils beyond the safety of West Point's granite by themselves. "I have been unable to discover the need for this combination of a cloistered monastery and walled penitentiary," he said.[9] The images he painted are poignant enough.

In his 1920 *Annual Report of the Superintendent*, MacArthur explained the traits of the modern officer leading the citizen-soldiers, including "a new atmosphere of liberalization in doing away with provincialism, a substitution of subjective for objective discipline, [and] a progressive increase of cadet responsibility tending to develop initiative and force of character rather than automatic performance of stereotyped functions."[10] In his memoirs he continued this theme, copied from his first annual history as superintendent: "Conditions will require a modification in type of the officer, a type possessing all the cardinal military virtues as of yore, but possessing an intimate understanding of his fellows, a comprehensive grasp of world, and national affairs, and a liberalization of conception which amounts to a change in his psychology of command. This standard became the basis of the construction of the new West Point in the spirit of Old West Point."[11]

MacArthur attacked the provincialism that had stifled the academy since the Civil War. He knew cadets needed to gain the leadership and confidence to command soldiers, and he outlined his arguments thus: "It has been my policy to allow certain privileges to the upper-class cadets which would serve both as a relaxation from the rigid grind of study and training and as a means of keeping touch with the ways of ordinary life outside the walls of the institution.... Much of the criticism of narrowness and provincialism which has been directed at the Military Academy in the past has been due to the restricted range of interests possible for cadets during these four important formative years of their lives."[12]

Superintendent MacArthur began a program to liberalize conditions and allowed privileges to the upperclassmen that were small but necessary. "Improvisation will be the watchword," MacArthur declared as he began to make the changes during that first year. He did not do this alone. Lt. Col. Robert Danford, the commandant, agreed with and supported the superintendent's ideas. Danford recalled his relationship with his boss, referring to himself in the third person, "The Commandant worked closely and in the utmost harmony with the Superintendent." To liberalize the expectations, rules, and traditions in the cadet's world, MacArthur needed a commandant who understood and agreed with his reforms. "Almost every working day the two were closeted together in the inner office discussing matters" normally relative to the Corps of Cadets.[13]

Together they developed ideas about privileges for each of the classes, from plebes to first classmen. The first-class cadets were allowed a six-hour pass off West Point on weekends. Cadets could take horse rides during their passes and ride across the river using the ferry, thus having freedom to roam through the highlands on their own. The seniors created a social club called the First-Class Club that met in Church Hall (named after a professor) in the old Central Barracks for limited interaction with faculty and staff officers.[14] They were also allowed visits to officers' quarters for dinners and social events. The three upper classes were permitted to elect their class officers for the first time rather than the cadre officers appointing them. The corps was allowed to establish a cadet newspaper, *The Bray*, a play off the West Point mule mascot.[15]

MacArthur and Danford also revised the cadet regulations, the Blue Book. One day MacArthur charged Major Ganoe, "Chief, we're going to rewrite the Blue Book. We'll erase and insert to meet the times." Danford recalled, "We cut out about half the [Blue] Book, even to making some officers howl," meaning TACs and the DOGs, the disgruntled old graduates.[16]

One of the major privileges that MacArthur instituted was that all the cadets, plebes included, would receive an allowance of $5 monthly. He believed the cadets needed to learn how to manage not only time but money, to develop an ability to prioritize their efforts and make decisions on their own. His hope was that "they no longer were to be walled up within the Academy limits, but to be treated as responsible young men."[17]

The DOGs howled at the allowances and the time away from the walled safety of West Point, saying that these sterling young men possibly would be defiled by corruption in nearby New York City and the evil haunts there. "The most frenzied tirades arose over the unbelievable privileges extended," the alumni barked out ravenously. "They [the cadets] could rove all over the country and spend money like drunken sailors."[18] MacArthur had a different worldview because of what he had seen in the army: "In the Service we give the lowest private weekend passes to go wherever he likes and do whatever he likes, so long as his record is good." Can't cadets, future officers, be trustworthy with time off? "Throw as much responsibility on the cadet as he can carry," MacArthur taught, to "cause him to make independent decisions by developing his resourcefulness."[19]

As much as MacArthur championed reforms and especially a more liberal culture on campus, as a general officer and war hero, he sometimes remained aloof from the cadets. He attended sporting events and especially daily football practices, but he had little interaction with the cadets at times. As the future superintendent and chairman of the Joint Chiefs of Staff Maxwell D. Taylor recalled, the superintendent "never made an effort to impress his personality on the cadets . . . and only a few cadets were ever asked to his house." Taylor also recalled that cadets had few dealings with the charismatic superintendent. Earl "Red" Blaik, future head football coach and cadet under MacArthur, recalled MacArthur's lack of involvement with the Corps: "Neither I nor the vast majority of my class ever saw the general, except when he walking across the diagonal walk, apparently lost in thought, his nose in the air."[20]

Douglas MacArthur was the jailer that released the Corps of Cadets from the bondage of paternalism, bestowing privileges and responsibility on the young cadets, hoping to create a new type of officer that would lead the soldiers of the modern army.

Establishing Honor and Ending Hazing?

Perhaps the greatest football coach the US Military Academy ever had was Earl "Red" Blaik, a cadet during MacArthur's superintendency for one year who graduated in 1920. He offered his opinion about the challenges MacArthur faced as superintendent. "The most pressing problem for the new Supe was to ward off further War Department and congressional investigations into hazing," Blaik wrote in 1964 at the time of MacArthur's death. As a cadet he had an entirely different opinion of the circumstances in 1919, especially after a terrible event that had occurred earlier in the year. "The suicide of Cadet Stephen Bird," Blaik wrote, "had established the fact that harsh and even sadistic treatment was being condoned by upperclassmen in dealing with the Fourth Classmen."[21]

"Red" Blaik even forty years later was off course on this assessment. Hazing was a key issue that MacArthur tackled and eventually did more than any superintendent toward eradicating. Hazing was not the most pressing issue during MacArthur's term, but it was a major concern. The death of Stephen M. Bird on New Year's Day in 1919, six months before MacArthur's arrival, was an alarming event. It was one of the few suicides that the academy acknowledged in an era when such tragedies were not publicly expressed.[22]

MacArthur had a different idea of what was the greatest priority for reform. "The highest standards of honor were to be demanded as the only solid foundation for a military career," he declared. "In the final analysis of the West Point product, character is the most precious component." There is no doubt how Douglas MacArthur felt about honor as the life blood of an officer's worth and service. Whether always a perfect exemplar of what he preached, contemporaries and later historians have made their own observations. Regardless of his imperfections, MacArthur survived an ordeal that most Americans never imagined as a cadet. "I was hazed more brutally than some other members of my class," MacArthur recalled, "probably because my father held high rank. The animosity engendered in me against some of the hazers, who seemed to take delight in being cruel, can never be erased. It's a sad result for them and me."[23]

Hazing was defined by the US Military Academy Regulation of 1910 as "any unauthorized assumption of authority by one cadet over another cadet whereby the latter shall or may suffer or be exposed to suffer any cruelty, indignity, humiliation, hardship, or oppression, or the deprivation or abridgement of any right, privilege, or advantage to which he shall be legally entitled."[24] Nevertheless, it persisted as a practice that had existed for decades. In earlier years it was seen as a necessary tool for leadership and character development. Ending hazing was a difficult challenge. One could argue, though, that an honorable cadet would not haze other cadets in the brutal manner of the past.

Superintendent MacArthur knew that to end hazing and develop an effective honor system, the most important ingredient to the formula would be cadet involvement and acceptance. The corps was the key to the issue of honor, but without senior and experienced cadets the challenge was great. "The Military Academy had always depended on upperclassmen to carry in the Code and the traditions, and to instill these in the new cadets," declared Jacob Devers, class of 1909, who later commanded an army group of American and French forces in Europe. "There was no written code of procedure," Devers noted. "The morale of the student body, faculty, and staff was at a low ebb."[25]

MacArthur aspired to gain the support of the young men and invest them with ownership of the process with "group pride for the Honor of the Corps which is responsible for the maintenance of the high standards of individual conduct."[26] The way to gain support from the cadets began with the commandant; therefore, MacArthur turned to Danford, who recalled, "The matter of hazing was attacked" through meetings arranged by the commandant "for free discussion on the subject of leadership with the cadets." These group sessions were helpful, and "no effort was made to change the old customs of the Corps, but the Supe was determined that the Plebes would learn them in a decent, soldierly way, without arrogance or abuse."[27]

MacArthur and Danford worked closely together to eradicate hazing and develop a revolutionary plan to eliminate cadet-supported, unofficial, and unsupervised vigilante groups. After one such meeting with Danford, MacArthur gave this order: "Com, select a few cadets of the highest, all-around character, who are most respected and influential in the Corps. Let them be called an Honor Committee. Bring them here to my office where we can start things off."[28]

Thus commenced one of the great innovations that has set West Point apart from other colleges for more than a hundred years. As opposed to codes of honorable conduct handed down to students, as in other colleges, the system was conducted by the cadets themselves, with minimal officer supervision. The Honor Committee was officially established in the summer of 1922, just as General MacArthur was departing. An authority on academy history wrote, "West Point now had, for the first time an explicit honor code based upon reasoned consent." The committee's inaugural meeting was in the fall after MacArthur's superintendency. The concept, committee, policy, and mission were all envisioned and created by MacArthur and Danford. Interestingly, it would be another twenty-five years before the Honor Code was written down.[29]

When the senior class was assembled, MacArthur instructed them, probably seeing a sense of history on the occasion. "Gentlemen, you have before you the greatest challenge and responsibility I have ever known for men of your age." He counseled, "You can accomplish something neither the Commandant nor myself has the opportunity to do. You know from inside the Corps the possibilities and limitations of your sacred mission. Think over what I have said, talk among yourselves and keep the substance of this meeting confidential. Let us know your proposals at the next meeting."[30]

There was some resentment, as Blaik recorded: "Bitter feelings arose as the presentation of changes to the Class was vigorously resisted by the traditionists." Future superintendent and chairman of the Joint Chiefs of Staff, Maxwell D. Taylor, recalled that MacArthur's: "personal prestige carried the day and overcame the reluctance to cooperate on the part of those cadets who would resisted an intrusion of authority into the traditions of the Corps of Cadets of which they felt themselves the guardians."[31]

MacArthur took an enormous step in seeking cadet ownership of the honor system and establishing the Honor Committee, trusting cadets to conduct business in a mature and resolute way. MacArthur also had the comments and recommendations of the cadets recorded and published in a pamphlet, *Traditions and Customs of the Corps*, so all cadets could have a written standard to follow.[32]

Every Cadet an Athlete

What set apart Douglas MacArthur's attitude and approach to reforming the academy was based mainly on one major experience in his life: the Great War. His wartime experience was everything to him as an officer and leader. He spent a year in France fighting the Germans in several major campaigns and saw how leaders and soldiers failed because of poor physical fitness. Col. Samuel Tillman and most of the other members of the Academic Board had not served in this major conflict and had no clue what modern, total war required of men mentally and physically. MacArthur knew what a soldier experienced on the modern battlefield, and he also knew what standard and skills officers needed to produce effective combat leaders. Many qualities of combat are important, but physical endurance, fitness, and strength are essential to survive the awful toll of warfare. MacArthur shared his view of life through "the experiences of the World War that a course of training should be planned not only to fit future officers physically for the rigors" of combat. He stressed that mastering physical training as an officer was to "qualify them as physical directors and instructors for their future commands ... by which they can most speedily and efficiently bring their men to the necessary physical condition."[33]

A contemporary of MacArthur, Thom Yates, explained that the new superintendent was critical to the foundation of athletics at the academy and its reputation. Though overly praiseworthy, Yates wrote in 1942 while General MacArthur was commanding in the Southwest Pacific, "His love of sports, for their resultant physical and moral benefits, more than any other factor save of course his military genius, is why General MacArthur was given a scope of power and jurisdiction never before exercised by an American Army officer."[34] Yates's claim is probably true regarding MacArthur's involvement with sports: in his combat commands, at an academic institution, and then as president of the US Olympic Committee in 1928 as a serving army officer. Few officers have achieved these distinctions during their career.

While he was the head of an academic institution, MacArthur offered this judgment: "We seek the best in scholarship. ... We seek the best in physical training and stamina. I would even prefer the physical activities to the mental, all things being equal."[35] There was no doubt where MacArthur's priority was with physical training, though not all the superintendents had the same priority. Col. Clarence Townsley, superintendent from 1912 to 1916, pronounced that football was more injury prone than any other sport at the academy, with sixty-one injuries in 1912 alone.[36]

The great asset MacArthur had during his superintendency was the on-hand master of fitness, and training for the entire army: Lt. Col. Herman

Koehler. With hundreds of thousands of recruits reporting to dozens of training camps nationwide, the importance of physical fitness and readiness came to the fore. According to Marty Maher, the War Department took Koehler "out of West Point in 1918 and sent [him] to camps all around the country to show how physical training should be done."[37]

It was Koehler who made MacArthur's pursuit of universal athletics for all the cadets possible. According to Red Blaik, "MacArthur was fortunate in having for his Master of the Sword, as the Director of Physical Education at the Academy . . . Lieutenant Colonel Herman Koehler."[38] The goal was not to achieve expertise or mastery with intramurals, but for every cadet to improve his level of fitness. The saying or motto that arose, "Every Cadet an Athlete," is of unknown origin and authorship, though it was most likely MacArthur's inspiration.[39]

Athletics as a movement grew in America after the Civil War and colleges embraced this new form of education. Though still in its infancy, physical fitness as a discipline and necessary avocation for good health became extremely important to military training. The expansion and seriousness of athletics at West Point at the turn of the century evolved around what became known as "Corps Squad" sports, or competitive sports, meaning external contests against other college sports programs. At this time the Corps Squads were baseball, basketball, boxing, cross country, fencing, football, gymnastics, hockey, lacrosse, pistol, rifle, soccer, swimming, tennis, track, and wrestling, as opposed to club sports such as squash, skiing, handball, and water soccer (polo).[40]

Koehler during his career wrote a treatise in 1909, *The Theory and Practice of Athletics at the Military Academy*. Koehler's fitness program was based on a curriculum that included gymnastics, boxing, swimming, and fencing as required academic courses. The competitive Corps Squad sports were voluntary, and the superintendents prior to MacArthur allowed practice, but not at the expense of the daily schedule, with few exceptions to training or routine. Col. Albert Mills expressed that "members of athletic teams should give as much time to their studies and their military duties as other cadets."[41] Herman Koehler felt the same way, as one historian explained: "Koehler's main points—that competitive athletics were a complement to the overall physical program and that winning was not the principal goal—went unchallenged for many years."[42]

MacArthur envisioned athletics at two levels, apart from the standard physical education courses: first, there was competitive Corps Squad sports and, then the new program he introduced—intramural sports. Every cadet would participate in some type of athletic program, either intramural or squad teams. This was a revolutionary approach, as an observer noted: "MacArthur changed the whole face of physical training at the Point. . . . He established the most comprehensive and well-founded program of bodily development."[43]

Because this program was new and revolutionary it met severe opposition and resistance from the Old Guard professors, who swore that MacArthur was "going to turn the Academy into a school for games." One professor during an Academic Board meeting "had his teeth clenched and a jaw set ready to snarl back at the new Supe's contentions."[44]

The Corps of Cadets accepted the new program with little complaint because MacArthur tied sports and athletics to training and combat readiness. He also cleverly coined one of the most endearing statements, a pledge, that is now a verse, a catechism that every cadet since MacArthur's days as superintendent learns, memorizes, and lives:

Upon the fields of friendly strife
Are sown the seeds
That upon other fields, and on other days,
Will bear the fruits of victory

Some twenty years later while living in the Philippines, Field Marshal MacArthur received an inquiry whether he authored this stanza and had it engraved in stone over the main entrance to the gymnasium. He replied: "I completely reorganized the athletic system and placed it on the broad and comprehensive basis which has been followed in that institution ever since. I, myself, composed the couplet which marks the entrance to the gymnasium."[45]

Blaik explained what MacArthur's intentions were: "While MacArthur was determined every cadet should be athletic as a requisite to becoming a well-rounded officer, his interest in sports was keenest at the varsity level." No truer statement could be made about MacArthur's love for competitive sports. MacArthur stated in the *Annual Report of 1922*, his last as superintendent: "The importance of intercollegiate athletics, has, however, not been overlooked." He wrote, "Nothing more than competitive athletics brings out the qualities of leadership, quickness of decision, promptness of action, mental and muscular coordination, aggressiveness, and courage.... The value of the intercollegiate contests is two-fold: first, in stimulating and vitalizing corps morale; and second, in establishing interesting contacts with other institutions of the same collegiate grade as West Point."[46]

William Ganoe narrated an instance where MacArthur manipulated the eye test results for candidate athletes on the Corps Squad so they would be admitted to West Point.[47] He was unabashed in his support of intercollegiate teams. "I will be bold and frank in seeking candidates with athletic reputation and background," he said, adding, "We have nothing to hide" regarding recruiting the best athletes possible.[48]

The intramural program, called Company Sports today, was a singular innovation that improved the health and athletic quality of the young men. The program has endured for a hundred years with modern-day practices, leagues, playoffs, trophies, team shirts, and jerseys where the cadets proudly display, for example, F-4, or F company, 4th Regiment, the "Frogs" insignias. No other college at the time in America had a student body participate in such a disciplined and organized program. Today, nearly a thousand cadets—men and women—compete in corps (squad) sports in the National Collegiate Athletic Association; the remainder of the corps are involved in either club teams of company sports.

MacArthur's great love of and regard for competition during his tenure failed in the most important outward symbol of athletics possible at West Point. The Army football team lost all three years to the Naval Academy team. In fact, Army did not score a point against Navy in all three games, though the team had defeated Navy in the years before and after MacArthur's time.

Academics and Professors

Of all the reforms that MacArthur envisioned and instilled, perhaps the most difficult and entrenched were those academics guarded by tradition and by the professors of the Academic Board and worshipped by the Old Guard. Upon his arrival, MacArthur was the "Boy Superintendent" and seen as an upstart.[49] Department heads opposed many things about MacArthur, but one of the most resented was his unannounced visits to the classrooms and the department domains. "MacArthur would suddenly appear in a classroom, take a seat in the rear, and start making notes," then he would meet with the instructor and "offer suggestions on ways to improve his teaching methods." This of course was a clear violation of protocol in the view of the faculty, where "his presence and counsel were obviously abhorred by some teachers."[50] Historian Theodore Crackel further explained MacArthur's interference: "He quizzed professors concerning the courses taught by other departments, inspected their instructors in the classroom, and commandeered their officers for non-academic purposes."[51]

With these comments, one would wonder what possible authority would a commanding officer have over his command? Professor Holt of the English Department and a few others welcomed the superintendent's reforms and had relished the opportunity for years to improve academics.[52] Others, however, viewed their classrooms as fiefdoms and greatly resented MacArthur's intrusions.

Many of the alumni soon learned of MacArthur's unorthodox methods, especially when articles appeared in the *Army and Navy Journal* condemning his interference. "They resented his efforts at reform—both on the academic side and in the area of cadet life," wrote one commentator.[53] How absurd it seems today that professors and department heads would be so militant and proud of their smaller domains that are part of the greater monastery, to the detriment of progress and education. These department spaces were still public space, and the superintendent was the steward.

MacArthur sought to drag West Point into modern society through sports and academics by introducing outside influences and initiatives to the static world of West Point. He took several other measures to accomplish this; one was having other academicians in prominent universities review the academy's new curriculum. The superintendent welcomed suggestions and criticisms by outside authorities, such as emeritus Harvard University president Dr. Charles Eliot, as mentioned earlier.[54]

One major field that General MacArthur pushed in academics was the priority of the social sciences and technology. Professor Holt offered new courses in economics and government, which MacArthur supported.[55] MacArthur himself saw the importance of aviation in the Great War and intro-

Col. Gustav Fiebeger, class of 1876, professor of civil and military engineering and MacArthur's chief opponent regarding reforms at the academy. *Courtesy USMA Archives.*

duced a new course on aerodynamics. In his class of 1903 was Thomas Selfridge, the very first military aviation fatality, who died in 1908 in a flying accident at Fort Myer with Orville Wright. For years some faculty members pushed to introduce aviation courses at the academy. With the new head of the Department of Natural and Experimental Philosophy, in 1917, Col. Clifton C. Carter (class of 1899), the time was ripe for another attempt. Since electricity, hydraulics, and physics were the standard curriculum, MacArthur approved the proposal by Colonel Carter to establish a course with eighteen lessons on aerodynamics, which was taught for the first time from April 15 to June 4, 1921.[56]

One of the most visionary and revolutionary reforms Douglas MacArthur made was having academy professors and instructors spend time at other colleges and universities to observe and gain knowledge of new techniques and innovations beyond the paternalistic confines of West Point. The new policy required that department heads make a month-long visit to another institution of higher learning.[57] In addition, newly assigned "instructors should spend the first year of their West Point detail at civilian colleges and universities in order to specialize in the particular study in which they were going to instruct."[58]

During the academy's hundred years no official had ever established such a radical measure. The mere idea that Military Academy faculty needed assistance in refining their scholarship at other colleges was a difficult measure to swallow. One professor complained, "A whole month.... How would the department get along while he was gone?"[59] This was a perfect example of the resistance that any reforming superintendent would have faced, whether it was Douglas MacArthur or another officer. Whether the human emotions of pride or arrogance controlled the professors and MacArthur is certainly possible, with MacArthur's supposed interference and the professors' stubbornness.

The new superintendent enacted another action that was progressive for West Point and well-meaning. He wrote a very thorough report after his first year that outlined the curriculum, programs, and overall status in academics, physical education, and future reforms needed. This was an amazing critique for its time, recorded in *The Annual Report of the Superintendent* of 1920. He forwarded this document to ninety-two distinguished educators in the United States, whereby most of them approved MacArthur's proposals. Major Ganoe was part of this effort, and his commentary was: "I know of no one who would and could have bearded the lions [professors] in the way without any other weapons than his moral courage and mental acumen. Not once did he shrink or take a step backward.... He got his curriculum, but not the hearts of the Old Guard."[60]

Ganoe's appraisal is seconded by an instructor who saw firsthand the reforms that MacArthur made. Future combat commander Jacob Devers relished the idea of academy professors visiting other colleges: "When the new orders had been carried out, and the fresh breezes had carried off some of the old, stagnant air, the individuals involved in the changes began to see the wisdom and validity of the demands of the young Superintendent."[61]

Most of the reforms MacArthur imposed remained in force after his departure, but a few were reversed. In fact, other superintendents following MacArthur's innovations later introduced some important measures such as gaining accreditation and joining the National Collegiate Athletic Association.

Training the Corps for Modern War

Being that the academy was a military school and beyond the sphere of all other colleges in America, except the U.S. Naval Academy, military training was paramount to the mission and development of future army officers. Combat arms training with weapons and current tactics of the time had been the foundation of the school of the soldier for more than a hundred years, often expressed in drills, parades, and reviews on the historic Plain. Training through the period of World War I still resembled exercises from the Civil War, where formations were trained with precision and flare, not tactical expertise. MacArthur recognized this immediately: "We are training these cadets for the past, not the future.... How long are we going on preparing for the War of 1812?"[62] The wars of the late nineteenth century were less conventional in nature and included guerrilla and insurgent actions against the Indian tribes and in the Philippines. "For someone just returning from war," such as Brigadier General MacArthur, "watching the summer encampment of 1919 must have been disorienting" if not totally preposterous.[63] In a somewhat humorous manner, MacArthur also questioned, "Of what possible benefit is Cadet Summer Camp?"[64] To a combat veteran like MacArthur, training on the Plain "was a ludicrous caricature of life in the field."[65] Eventually, there were several components to MacArthur's reformation of military training, which improved qualities among the officers as well as for the cadets themselves. Another reform was cadet training with realistic and modern methods away from the parade ground. MacArthur declared that "with the termination of the World War the mission of West Point at once became the preparation of officer personnel for the next future war."[66]

The relationship between the tactical officers (TACs) and the cadets was unacceptable. Besides being an "ogre in a tower, peering," Ganoe commented, "to see whom he could devour," the tactical officer was "harder to approach than the manager of a chain store."[67] The method of dispensing justice with "skin sheets" of demerits and cadet responses, or "bellyaches," caused MacArthur to take a drastic measure according to the traditionalists. The commandant, Danford, recommended that the young TACs establish an orderly room in the barracks and interact with the cadets in person, to serve and

Cadet summer training. *Courtesy USMA Archives.*

mentor them properly. When MacArthur heard this proposal, as Danford recalled, his reply was "Do it!" Both MacArthur and Danford saw the relationship of TAC and cadet as a company commander to his soldiers, "thus teaching cadets an important duty in handling the American soldier."[68]

Following this action MacArthur made one of the boldest reforms in West Point history. He determined to have officers, not upperclassmen, train the new cadets during Beast Barracks. No doubt influenced by his own experience as a cadet and the abuse he survived, MacArthur instituted this change in the summer of 1920. Coupled with this move he also established a new training program for the most senior class at Camp Dix in New Jersey. These were radical changes that he ordered Danford to carry out.

Summer Encampment had been more than training, drilling, and parading on the Plain; it was a festival, and a major social event of the year for the entire West Point community. Most evenings there were dances, or hops, illuminations, fireworks, and many social activities that the cadets, faculty, families, and especially young ladies, all enjoyed. "Summer [Encampment] was the social season at West Point," remarked Theodore Crackel, "and climaxed at the end of the encampment with a grand ball."[69]

It was almost sacrilege to terminate Summer Encampment as it was. MacArthur announced it at an Academy Board meeting that "dropped like a bomb" with a silence that soon changed as "the DOGs bayed to high heaven and snarled." Over the course of time every stratagem was used to convince MacArthur, the "high-handed autocrat," that he had "taken it upon himself single-handed to uproot tradition after tradition." The professors and alumni invoked the glories of the past. Summer training on the Plain "was good enough for the Lees, Grants and Pershings, but it's not good enough for MacArthur."[70]

Whether tradition or reform ruled the day for summer training, the impact was significant. Perhaps the true test should come from the cadets themselves. In *The Howitzer* class album for 1922, the cadets included a several-pages overview of their training during their cadet years. This class saw many unsettling changes during its time at West Point: "Although at times things did not seem as bright and as easy as we have been accustomed to have them and, especially so to those who had seen old Summer Camp at the Point, still that is what we were sent to Dix for—to see a little of that which we have to meet with in the service.... And above all, perhaps, stands the fact that the future officers got to see the viewpoint of the enlisted man, to see his side of the army game."[71]

An interesting aspect of the major change of training sites was MacArthur's declaration that the Academic Board had no say in the decision. Instead, the "only ones who are officially responsible for the cadet's military training are the Commandant and myself." He boldly stated that "no system of logic perceived any rightful part the Board can have in this move."[72]

MacArthur and Danford were the military commanders responsible for the cadets' training. MacArthur as superintendent was responsible for the entire academy and all its affairs, as commander and senior officer in charge. No matter the howling and criticism, only one officer has final authority. As for military matters and training, a recent combat veteran and commander of large units in the late war would best know what officers require in training and discipline.

A Vision of the Future

Douglas MacArthur's far-ranging reforms affected every facet of the academy, causing great concern for some, but overall these changes were as necessary as they were significant. Yet, MacArthur saw and wanted more. He laid out a plan, a vision during his three-year tenure he had for the future that few superintendents perceived before or since. In his *Annual Report of the Superintendent 1921*, MacArthur elaborated his concept for a completely new campus above the flow of the Hudson River. He laid out a scheme that was enthralling, expansive, brilliant, expensive, and ambitious. It was all-encompassing across all the domains: new granite barracks, a quadrangle of a new mess hall, a cadet store and a drawing academy, a new addition to the gymnasium, a huge new cadet armory, an ordnance laboratory and machine shop, officer apartments, and lastly the crowning achievement, a new athletic stadium.[73] This entire scheme MacArthur estimated at $6 million for the coming year's appropriations. He also envisioned as a separate project a new hotel to replace the aging West Point Hotel at Trophy Point and another Memorial Hall similar to the 1900 structure now called Cullum Hall.[74]

The grandiose stadium would be constructed at water level at Gees Point along the old ammunition path, now Flirtation Walk. Conceived mostly for football games, perhaps also soccer and lacrosse, this stadium would seat thousands of fans and architecturally would resemble Soldiers Stadium in Chicago. The vision included the docking of passenger ships and ferries disgorging hundreds of football fans to watch the games.

This incredible plan of an entirely new academy campus did not come to pass. Though never approved, MacArthur's ambitious plan opened the door for many construction projects just a few years after his departure, which included the first phase of the Cadet Mess Hall, 1925–29, and the Thayer Hotel, completed in 1926. The football field, Michie Stadium, was completed in 1924—not where MacArthur wanted it, but above the central area of campus west of Lusk Reservoir. MacArthur did in fact oversee the new hospital that was constructed in 1921–23.[75]

Before Christmas 1921, MacArthur received word that he was being transferred to duty in the Philippines and would depart after the June 1922 academy graduation. At age forty-two, General MacArthur, one of the most eligible of American bachelors, met Louise Cromwell Brooks, who was a friend and confidante of General of the Armies John J. Pershing. She served as a hostess in Washington, DC, on occasion for the bachelor army chief of staff. She had other suitors besides Pershing himself, including his handsome young aide, Col. John G. Quekemeyer, known as both "Quek" and "Harry." Graduating from the academy in 1906, Quekemeyer served as Pershing's aide-de-camp in France and was wounded in the Meuse-Argonne campaign. Louise seemed to have an attraction or appetite for West Point men. She flirted with Pershing, a man thirty years older, and had a romantic fling with Quekemeyer, but she eventually married another West Pointer: Douglas MacArthur.[76] The wedding took place in Florida on Valentine's Day 1922 in a chapel decked with flags from West Point and the colors carried by the 42nd Rainbow Division. How proper it was for the superintendent to have academy symbols witness such a unique and solemn occasion was interesting.[77]

The final commentary of General MacArthur's tenure as superintendent is a tragedy. Two cadets, James L. Baum of the class of 1922 and Denis B. Totten of 1923, died within two months of each other, both from self-inflicted gunshot wounds. Whatever reason or cause for these two young people to take their own lives is unknown.[78]

Reforms and Reversals

Col. Roger Nye, a professor at the academy, more than forty years later claimed, "By the summer of 1921, MacArthur had so completely drained the faculty and alumni of good will that he could no longer innovate and was instead waging a defense of all that he changed."[79] This may seem like a severe commentary, but much of it is in fact true. MacArthur's reforms were alarming to many. Besides breaking down paternalism and allowing the cadets more freedom, leisure time, and time away from the school, his termination of the festive Summer Encampment drew great criticism. MacArthur's moving the advanced military training to larger military installations in New Jersey annoyed many cadets, faculty, and even families of the West Point community. Historian Theodore Crackel explained: "This abrupt uprooting of the encampment—and with it the summer social season—engendered such resentment among the Academy's officers and their wives, and among the old graduates, that the traditional policy was reinstated by the War Department in 1922, even before MacArthur had left for the Philippines."[80]

Besides the older professors and others who heaped criticism upon MacArthur, even younger officers found reasons to disapproval of the sweeping reforms. Capt. Omar Bradley, an artillery instructor, lamented the end of Summer Encampment but also considered the campaign against hazing misguided—that cadet discipline was handled best as in the past, among the shadows of the barracks. Bradley had been a cadet a decade after MacArthur and so did not witness the cruel treatment that Douglas and his generation of cadets endured. Bradley also denounced the favoritism that the superintendent showed for athletes, especially one Walter E. French, a standout player on the football team whom MacArthur subtlety directed would not fail a course at the academy.[81] French left West Point a few months after MacArthur departed in 1922 and did not graduate.

The new superintendent, Brig. Gen. Fred Sladen, class of 1890, thirteen years older than MacArthur, lost no time in reestablishing Summer Encampment in the summer of 1922, though abbreviated. Sladen recorded in the *Annual Report of the Superintendent* for 1923, "In accordance with decision of the War Department, the cadet summer camp was established in the Fort Clinton area of this Post in the latter part of June 1922." Sladen recorded what his main reason was for the reversal: "The return to the traditional practice of establishing a summer camp at West Point proved an unqualified success."[82] He then devoted several pages justifying his decision and actions. He ended his narrative saying, "In brief, the experience of the summer has proved conclusively that the practice, prevailing for more than a century before 1920, of maintaining a summer camp at West Point for military instruction was based upon sound principles."[83] His main point here was, briefly, if the summer training was good enough for cadets of the past one hundred years, it was good enough for the current cadets. Tradition ruled in Sladen's mind. Naturally, many members of the academy community were happy because pleasure and tradition were more important than effective and realistic combat training.

For MacArthur summer training was for one purpose: to prepare young officers for combat. Social enjoyment and tradition were not important to him. He had an experience that few of the faculty and staff had had, seeing soldiers die because officers and leaders were weak or made mistakes. The fact that older graduates, faculty, and family members were upset about MacArthur's reforms proved that these changes were either drastic or correct.

Sladen also reversed other less significant reforms MacArthur made, such as senior cadets carrying cash and the weekend six-hour passes. Even so, MacArthur had accomplished his mission: "The new West Point [rose] in the spirit of the Old West Point." A historian summarized the long-term ramifications of these reforms: "In the big scheme of things, however, these reversals and modifications did little to slow the process of reform that MacArthur had set in motion."[84]

Much has been made of MacArthur's departure after only three years as superintendent. Pershing had notified MacArthur of his pending duty in the Philippines. Even Pershing had concern with MacArthur's radical reforms and his overall performance.[85]

MacArthur's mission as directed by Gen. Peyton March was to reform West Point, which he did. His task was not to gain acceptance or appease the old graduates and Academic Board. His decisions and policies were not meant to alienate any group or bring ruin to the institution, but to reform the school and drag West Point into the twentieth century. Those who were delighted at his departure and sought the return to the status quo obviously did not have the responsibility or the vision that MacArthur had. Few of his detractors had served in the Great War and understood and experienced modern warfare. Two of his most ardent critics were his replacement, Fred Sladen, and the serving chief of staff, General of the Armies John Pershing.

Was MacArthur's removal Pershing's doing? This is an interesting question to explore. There was no standard tour at the time; superintendents came and went, often after a year or two. Pershing assumed duties as chief of staff in July 1921 and determined by November to replace MacArthur, after only two years and five months as superintendent. The purported reason was that MacArthur was on the list of general officers for an overseas tour. His duty in the Philippines was based on a newly created office with little authority and only five hundred men to command the Military District of Manila. Some historians, and admirers of MacArthur, argue that Pershing was jealous of Louise Brook's romance with MacArthur. This is hardly the case, because the orders came in November and she and Douglas had only met that month at a football game. Pershing's decision may have stemmed from an incident that fall when MacArthur appeared before a congressional committee but failed to make an office call on Pershing at the War Department, though he tried. Pershing chastised MacArthur for violating army protocol, and MacArthur apologized in writing. But that was not good enough for the temperamental chief of staff, whose enormous ego took the minor slight as a personal attack. What is really interesting is that Pershing's censure came the same day that he issued the order for MacArthur's transfer. Months later Pershing wrote an evaluation where he stated that MacArthur was "a very able young officer with a fine record of courage," but he also "has an exalted opinion of himself."[86] This line also defines Pershing himself.

Pershing was troubled by MacArthur's amazing success and the regard that many officers, soldiers, and politicians held for him. There is little doubt Pershing wanted him gone. Historian Arthur Herman recorded, "To what personal bitterness over Louise may have influenced" Pershing's regard toward MacArthur in his triangular romance "is, of course, impossible to determine." MacArthur's reforms took a new life later, as historian Stephen Ambrose stated: "Slowly his innovations would be restored, his ideas accepted. If Sylvanus Thayer dominated West Point in the nineteenth century, Douglas MacArthur dominated it in the twentieth. The chief difference was that Thayer had sixteen years in which to impose his personality and ideas, while MacArthur had but three."[87]

An interesting feature is MacArthur's own assessment of his service of three years as superintendent and his legacy. "My work of reconstruction is almost done," he admitted to Louise before their marriage. "I have made West Point almost human and in so doing I have turned the enormous resentments that greeted [me] at the end of the war into words of sympathy and praise." He ended by saying, "Long after I am dead and moldering the Corps will call me the Father of West Point."[88] This has not come to pass, of course; Sylvanus Thayer remains the true Father of West Point. But MacArthur was accurate in writing as he departed for the Philippines in September 1922, "On the ashes of Old West Point I have built a New West Point—strong, virile, and enduring."[89]

Douglas MacArthur's tenure as superintendent was the apogee of his relationship with the US Military Academy. After 1922 for the remainder of his life MacArthur continued his relationship with, love for, and contributions to the academy, but this was much less than during his time at West Point. For the next forty years almost to the day, his influence was by association with other members of the Long Gray Line, using the values and principles he both learned as a cadet and endorsed as the superintendent. His greatest service was mentoring other graduates and his interaction through correspondence, public events, and being a model of "Duty, Honor, Country."

CHAPTER 10

★ ★ ★ ★ ★

MENTORING THE LONG GRAY LINE IN PEACE

"In was early in October 1922 when the transport *Thomas* docked at Pier Five in Manila," MacArthur wrote in his *Reminiscences* forty years later, "and once again the massive bluff of Bataan, the lean gray grimness of Corregidor were there before my eyes in their unchanging cocoon of tropical heat."[1]

The theme of returning to the Philippines would be one of the great motivations of MacArthur's life and career as a US soldier. Seeing the prominent and memorable Bataan and Corregidor as he did in 1922 would not be the last time he had this experience. In 1928 and again in 1935 and 1937, he would return to the Philippines for military assignments. In 1942 during World War II and the Japanese onslaught, MacArthur would leave Corregidor and the Philippines under orders from the president of the United States, Franklin D. Roosevelt. Once in Australia General MacArthur made the historical promise, "I shall return." On October 20, 1944, he and a large American force did return and liberate the Philippines from a brutal occupation by Imperial Japan. MacArthur's service and time in Philippines is one of the most enduring qualities of his life.

MacArthur's arrival was almost nineteen years to the day from when he first touched the shores of Manila Bay as a second lieutenant recently graduated from the academy. Like West Point, the Philippine archipelago of hundreds of islands was another home. Returning as a brigadier general, he was now the commander of the Manila District.

One of the main experiences that MacArthur had during this two-year tour was an assignment to put his engineering and West Point education in topography to work. He had orders to conduct a thorough and detailed survey of Bataan Peninsula, an area he had visited before. Serendipitously he now became personally knowledgeable with terrain he and the forces under his command would defend against the Japanese in 1942. When the order came to the staff, one officer was shocked, declaring, "Why that's a job for a younger engineer officer and not a brigadier general!" Maj. George Cocheu, no less than MacArthur's roommate his Yearling or second year at West Point, declared this. When Cocheu asked what MacArthur would do, he replied, "Obey it, of course. It's an order."[2] MacArthur was not happy about his assignment, but for a year he performed the task, recalling, "I covered every foot of the rugged terrain, over its trails, up and down its steep mountainous slops, and through its bamboo thickets."[3]

It is interesting that Major Cocheu, a close friend and erstwhile roommate of Douglas, was now a subordinate and a member of MacArthur's staff. In the course of twenty years since their graduation MacArthur had advanced rapidly, held positions of great responsibility, commanded troops in combat—even a brigade of some twelve thousand soldiers—and received a dozen decorations for bravery. Not that Cocheu was a lesser man, but his fortune and destiny were completely different. He did not serve in combat during the First World War. He received no high decorations and held no important posts, but rather standard positions of lesser responsibility. Yet, during their tour together in the Philippines, they remained close friends. Only a former fellow cadet could advise and counsel his commander and classmate as did George Cocheu. Another close West Point friend who served on MacArthur's staff was Maj. Robert C. Richardson, who graduated in 1904. He and Douglas spent three years together at the academy and knew each other well. Richardson served as the G-1 over personnel and administration and had served on the faculty twice at West Point, and then he was commandant the Corps of Cadets from 1929 to 1933. In World War II he commanded a corps and later was commander of the US Army Forces in the Central Pacific Area under Adm.

Chester Nimitz. Richardson was another academy alumnus who was a peer but now subordinate to Douglas. The bonds of the academy were stronger than position or rank.[4]

The Philippine Department commander was Maj. Gen. George Read, an 1883 academy graduate and MacArthur's former commander at Fort Leavenworth. The project of mapping Bataan was related to the recent treaties signed in Washington and potential war plans dealing with Japan especially, known as Plan Orange, the color for Japan. There were two paths that Douglas followed: his association with academy graduates and his profession. These were his paths for all his life.[5]

He also renewed his acquaintances with two Filipinos he had met as a young lieutenant, and who would have significant roles to play in his career and the war effort later. As a senior military commander, he developed stronger relationships with Manuel L. Quezon and Sergio Osmeña, key players in politics for decades, both of whom would serve as president of the Philippines.[6]

The year 1923 was a difficult one for the MacArthur family even in distant Philippines. Mary "Pinky" MacArthur became gravely ill, so Louise, Douglas, and Louise's two children (from her first marriage) made a quick trip home to America. Yet, even in her later sixties, Pinky recovered and the MacArthurs returned to the islands. Louise's dissatisfaction with the Philippines and the marriage grew and intensified.[7]

In December 1923 Douglas MacArthur received a personal body-blow. His older brother, Capt. Arthur MacArthur III, died of appendicitis while stationed in Washington, DC. At age forty-seven years, Captain MacArthur, a recipient of the Navy Cross during World War I, had served a quarter-century in the navy and was destined to future greatness.[8]

That September MacArthur assumed command of the Philippine Division with three regiments—two Filipino, and the 31st US Infantry Regiment of mostly Americans. MacArthur had been a brigadier general for six years and was hopeful for promotion to major general. His mother Pinky was even more desirous; she wrote General Pershing another "mother for son" letter. Pershing did not reciprocate with a nomination for MacArthur's promotion.[9]

Pershing was the most famous and respected American soldier since U.S. Grant, and with the solo rank of General of the Armies, he was alone at the top in rank and power, a consummate officer, dedicated, proficient, and an effective leader. The trick of fate was that in September 1923 Pershing turned age sixty-four, then mandatory retirement age. Soon after Gen. Frank Hine's assumption as army chief of staff, Douglas MacArthur was selected for promotion to major general, the youngest in the army.[10]

Just a week after Pershing's retirement in the fall of 1924, MacArthur was nominated for promotion; his second star was pinned on his uniform on January 17, 1925, ten days short of his forty-fifth birthday. Soon thereafter, Douglas, Louise, and the children left the Philippines for a brief new assignment in Atlanta, Georgia.[11]

• • •

The War Department assigned MacArthur to be commander of the IV Corps Area in Atlanta, Georgia. He had not lived in the South since his high school days in San Antonio, Texas. Louise MacArthur did not care for the Philippines and wanted to return to her high-society life in the United States. She was trying to convince Douglas to leave the army and establish a career in the private sector. Louise and the children joined him in Atlanta, but not for long, as the marriage was unraveling.

While at this post, MacArthur received a request from the US Military Academy to verify his wounding on October 12, 1918, during the Great War. The superintendent who replaced Fred Sladen and his staff were compiling service records of graduates of their awards and decorations, which included the wound chevrons Douglas was awarded for the two gassings in France. The request came through the adjutant general's office in Washington in July 1925 and asked for documentation. Why would West Point want these documents? The academy had always maintained records and documents of its graduates' service and other matters. MacArthur's service and especially his valor during the war must have been very important to the school. Few colleges in America were concerned with such details of military service.[12]

A few weeks later Douglas was reassigned to the III Corps Area Command in Baltimore, Maryland, where Louise had grown up and where her family lived. The MacArthurs moved into Rainbow Hill, owned by Edward T. Stotesbury, Louise's stepfather, a wealthy investment banker who was worth more than a hundred million dollars.[13] At Rainbow Hill the marriage deteriorated further because Louise was back at home in her life of wealth and privilege. MacArthur was an adoring stepfather to her two children and seemed to fit in well with her family, but Louise was in her element of high society, where MacArthur felt awkward and estranged. One advantage of living in Baltimore was that Pinky MacArthur was residing in nearby Washington, DC. Douglas's duties in Baltimore were not overwhelming but soon he faced a very difficult trial—literally.[14]

In the fall of 1925 MacArthur was summoned to a duty that he later declared "one of the most distasteful orders I ever received." This duty was to serve on the panel of the famous Billy Mitchell court martial. Many today believe that William C. Mitchell was the father of the modern US Air Force, but in 1925 he faced judgment for disobeying orders. The Milwaukee MacArthurs, especially Judge Arthur MacArthur, knew the Mitchells very well and were friends through a couple of generations. John Mitchell, father of Billy, served with Lieutenant Arthur MacArthur in the 24th Wisconsin Volunteer Infantry Regiment during the Civil War. Though Douglas and Billy were only a year apart in age, they had not known each other well in their youth because the MacArthurs were serving on the frontier during Douglas's adolescent years.[15]

Billy Mitchell was a pioneer in army aviation, a highly decorated hero from the war, and as a brigadier general was a senior commander of the Army Air Service in France. In the 1920s Mitchell was a key player in aviation tactics and the development of airpower. He was convinced that aircraft as a weapon and strategic force would determine the outcome of future wars. He met great resistance from senior army leaders entrenched in ground fighting, but Mitchell was determined and was successful in several bombing tests. Arrogant and condescending in his manner, he became obsessed with his objective and said so publicly. His superiors ordered him to cease his public statements, which he did not.[16]

In the spring of 1925 while serving at Fort Sam Houston, Mitchell made several damning statements to the press about the failures of leadership of both the army and the navy regarding pilot safety, funding, inadequate training, and unsafe equipment. Mitchell charged that the military leaders through "incompetency, criminal negligence and almost treasonable administration of the National Defense by the War and Navy Departments" caused several fatal accidents.[17] Harsh words from a determined man.

The trial convened in Washington, DC, in the fall of 1925 with a West Point alumni line-up on the court. President of the board was Maj. Gen. Robert Lee Howze, a Medal of Honor recipient and graduate of 1888.[18] Of the ten serving panel members, seven were graduates of West Point—all older than MacArthur. According to historian Arthur Herman, Mitchell hated "the West Point clique" because even after the war, the top strata of the army was dominated by academy graduates as was his court-martial panel.[19]

Mitchell was found guilty by a two-thirds majority. There was some evidence that MacArthur voted to acquit, which is addressed in many history books and MacArthur biographies. Fiorella LaGuardia claimed that slips of paper found in the jury room trash had a no vote in MacArthur's handwriting.[20] MacArthur claimed, "I did what I could in his behalf and I helped save him from dismissal." But MacArthur condemned Mitchell's manner in his defiance: "That he was wrong in the violence of his language is self-evident; that he was right in his thesis is equally true and incontrovertible." The great lesson for MacArthur from the Mitchell trial was his absolute belief that "it is part of my military philosophy that a senior officer should not be silenced for being at variance with his superiors in rank and with accepted doctrine."[21]

Louise MacArthur attended the trial to support her husband but also because it was a media circus of the day, which she enjoyed immensely. By this time Louise and Douglas had grown apart in most ways. The two most important women in Douglas's life finally fell into a serious division during his tour at Baltimore. Louise later in life had plenty to say about both Douglas and his mother, stating that the marriage was doomed due to "an interfering mother-in-law." Louise eventually moved to New York City while Douglas remained at her family residence near Baltimore, a strange situation to say the least. The marriage would never recover. Pinky was still residing with her son Arthur's widow, Mary McCalla MacArthur, in Washington, DC, during this time.[22]

• • •

Gen. Douglas MacArthur had an experience during his career that no other army officer had—a rather unique opportunity. And the reason that the opportunity came his way was his great support of athletics as superintendent of the US Military Academy. In September 1927, while MacArthur still was commanding III Corps in Baltimore, the president of the American Olympic

Committee died. The upcoming Olympic Games for 1928 in Amsterdam, Netherlands, were less than a year away. MacArthur knew that his leadership in the significance of sports at the academy prepared him for such a role. "The emergency was acute due to the imminence of the games," he wrote in his memoirs forty year later, adding: "I had never lost my keen interest in sports, and attention had been attracted by the intramural system of athletic training which had been installed at West Point during my tour as superintendent. The system had been largely adopted by the leading colleges of the country, and throughout the garrisons and the camps of the Army."[23]

Corroborating this fact was biographer William Manchester, who wrote, "The other [Olympic Committee] members, knowing of the General's strong support of athletics at West Point, offered him the position."[24] The October 1927 issue of *The Olympic* heralded and praised MacArthur's appointment as president of the American Olympic team "for his known efficient and business-like organizing ability. . . . No better choice could have been made by the American Olympic Committee for its president."[25]

Fortunately, army "chief of staff, General Charles P. Summerall, agreed to place me on detached service," MacArthur elaborated. Why? Summerall knew that MacArthur was the perfect candidate and would be a great public motivation for the US Army, and it was a great morale boost for him personally.[26]

For the next year Douglas MacArthur was technically still III Corps commander, but in reality, his entire life centered around preparing the US Olympic team for Amsterdam. In this he had his hands full with the many issues, personalities, and international politics ahead. He led a team of 280 athletes—236 men and 44 women—in 96 events scattered among 15 separate sports. This was a colossal challenge for MacArthur, not being a professional or experienced athletic manager at the international level, regardless of his love for collegiate sports. The complexity of working with so-called amateur athletes had its problems. Among the team members were five graduates of West Point: Sloan Doak, class of 1907, and Harry D. Chamberlain, 1910, in riding; and Peter C. Hains, 1924, Aubrey S. Newman, 1925, and Richard Mayo 1926, in the modern pentathlon. Hains and Newman had been cadets during MacArthur's superintendency.[27]

Commencing with the opening ceremony on July 28, 1928, through August 12, the US team garnered twenty-two gold medals, more than twice the number of any other nation. The same was true with the eighteen silver medals and sixteen bronze medals won by the team—for a total of fifty-six medals—which made the US team first among nations in the total medal count. The American team nearly doubled the number of medals won by second-place Germany's thirty-one medals. One of the great American athletes was Johnny Weissmuller, who later played Tarzan in a dozen Hollywood films and won two gold medals for swimming on the 1928 team.[28]

The 1928 Olympic Games were a tremendous achievement for the team and the United States. General MacArthur received great accolades for his efforts and leadership. Returning on the ship USS *Roosevelt* in September, he received a letter from General Summerall, chief of staff, congratulating him on his great success with the Olympics: "I can best voice what is universally recognized that you alone are responsible" for the amazing performance, "infusing the spirit and resolution and will to win." Summerall ended by stating, "You have not only maintained the reputation that Americans do not quit, but that Americans know how to win."[29]

MacArthur, now back in the United States, faced two major life changing events: orders for Manila, where he would serve as commander of the Military Department of the Philippines, a relished dream of his; and Louise's desire to divorce him. Just six months after MacArthur departed for the Philippines, Louise Brooks MacArthur traveled to Reno, Nevada, and obtained a divorce from her husband of eight years. As for MacArthur, in his book *Reminiscences* he simply declared, "In February 1922 I entered into matrimony, but it was not successful, and ended in divorce years later for mutual incompatibility."[30]

• • •

"I found Manila as bright and lively as ever," MacArthur recorded in his memoirs upon his third tour of duty in the Philippines. Being a single man at the age forty-eight, he had personal lifestyle adjustments. He recorded, "I lived in a spacious set of quarters with my inspector general, Colonel Charles H. Patterson, a West Point classmate," with two junior officers, who "formed a gay and lively group, and were a source of constant pleasure to me."[31]

It seems strange that the department commander of the entire Philippine archipelago would room with other officers, young lieutenants and a classmate who was two grades subordinate to him. Patterson was a Coast Artillery officer detailed to the Inspector General's Department, who was responsible for investigating infractions of regulations and official policies, to report abuse and incidents of negligence by the leaders and soldiers, and then to report to the commander such violations. One would think there was an issue with military protocol and fraternization of a commander living with a subordinate, but possibly the classmate connection assuaged all this for Douglas.

During his nearly two years in the Philippines, MacArthur's main purpose and work was preparing its defenses while caring for the soldiers in the American protectorate. The obvious threat to the Philippines in the late 1920s was Japan, with its growing thirst for economic independence and its aggressive policy to dominate vulnerable nations that had resources necessary to Japan's imperial objectives. The United States became Japan's main source for oil and other raw resources during the 1920s.[32]

MacArthur as department commander was saddled with Plan Orange, the theoretical war plan focused on Japan, and what both army and navy warplanners estimated or anticipated as a Japanese threat against American interests in the Pacific, especially the Philippines. MacArthur had dealt with Plan Orange earlier when he was serving as Manila District commander between 1922–25, when he surveyed much of Bataan on foot. He now had direct responsibility for the operational execution of the plan. Basically, if Japan attacked the Philippines, then the plan called for the navy to withdraw to Hawaii or to the West Coast of the United States, but the army forces were to defend the Philippines at all costs while waiting for reinforcements.[33]

MacArthur considered the plan "rotten" according to the commander of the Philippine Division, Maj. Gen. Johnson Hagood. MacArthur proposed that the only way to provide adequate defense of the islands was by recruiting and training a large force, a hundred thousand native Filipinos. MacArthur and Hagood were more than just serving together in the Philippines; their West Point connection allied them. Hagood was an 1896 graduate, an artilleryman who had returned to the academy as an instructor in 1901, halfway through MacArthur's cadetship, and they knew each other. Like so many academy graduates and classmates, MacArthur's meteoric rise and rank did not seem to challenge his friendship and comradery with fellow West Pointers.[34]

During his short tour as department commander MacArthur did his best with the available resources. He recorded the full situation he faced: "With the possibility that the Philippines could easily be caught in the middle of a struggle [war] for power, we trained and maneuvered such forces as we had. They were, however, pitifully inadequate, and Washington apparently had no clear-cut idea with reference to Philippine defense."[35]

MacArthur understood but would not concede the notion that US authorities would sacrifice the Philippines to gain time. According to William Manchester, "MacArthur never accepted the implied sacrifice, and from 1928 onward the chief obstacle to Japanese conquest of the Philippines was his implacable will."[36]

This all changed in late 1930 when MacArthur became army chief of staff.

• • •

On August 5, 1930, while still in Manila, MacArthur received this radiogram: "President has just announced your detail as Chief of Staff to succeed General [Charles] Summerall." This news may not have startled him, but he had some doubts, at least according to his 1964 book. "I did not want to return to Washington, even though it meant four stars of a general. . . . I wished from the bottom of my heart to stay with the troops in a field command."[37] His selection as chief of staff, the only officer with the rank of general in the entire army at the time, took a curious route to that August day.

Just a few days earlier, MacArthur had been notified that he was selected to command the Army Corps of Engineers as chief of engineers. The message came through the adjutant general of the Department of the Philippines, Col. Edward Aloysius Brown from Massachusetts, who graduated with MacArthur in 1903. Unlike Douglas at the head of the class, Brown finished second from the bottom of ninety-three. Initially a Coast Artillery officer, in 1918 Brown transferred to the Adjutant General Corps and served in it for the remainder of his career, until he retired for disability in 1934. Brown was one of several classmates or West Point friends serving under MacArthur in the Philippines.[38]

MacArthur did not want to return to the US Army Corps of Engineers, even though it was his commissioning branch, saying he was "very proud to have been in the Engineer Corps, but having cast my lot with line." Colonel Brown with his years of service in the War Department in personnel recommended strongly to Douglas to accept the position. In the aftermath of the

Cadets in a civil engineering class. *Courtesy USMA Archives.*

1927 great flood in the Mississippi Valley, and the subsequent Flood Control Act, the task of improving American dams and levees was critical. MacArthur knew that if he accepted the chief of engineer position, he would never be considered for army chief of staff.[39]

Eventually, MacArthur decided to reject the offer, not wanting to return to the Corps of Engineers. He forwarded his response to General Summerall, saying that the chief of engineers position called for "outstanding engineering ability." He explained he did not have the experience and credentials to gain the "confidence of the engineering profession at large." He later recorded "that Eddie Brown was disgusted. He said Washington would never forgive me, that I had dug my own professional grave." His old classmate was absolutely correct in his assessment for any other officer in the US Army, but MacArthur's luck and his gut feeling were different: "It was a wise decision I took, both for me and ... for the government." Just two weeks later, MacArthur received the request to serve as chief of staff. He commented in his memoirs, "Eddie Brown was wrong, too, about Washington."[40]

The behind-the-scenes and back-room game that transpires for such important political or governmental positions is both interesting and complex. General Summerall determined around the end of July 1930 that MacArthur was the best choice, due to his date of rank, relatively young age compared to other major generals, and the fact he had strong political connections and knew Washington inside moves—and because he was a war hero. Summerall then convinced Secretary of War Patrick Hurley, who was relatively new in the position, that MacArthur was the best choice.[41]

Hurley and others convinced President Herbert Hoover that MacArthur was the right man. But there were enemies and detractors in the administration who passionately voiced strong opposition to MacArthur. The most important of these was none other than retired General of the Armies John J. Pershing. The strife between these two men, though mostly from Pershing, once against raised its ugly head. Though fellow graduates and First Captains of the Corps of Cadets, Pershing opposed the appointment. Regardless of Pershing's unofficial influence, President Hoover said about his decision to appoint Douglas MacArthur, "I therefore searched the Army for younger blood, and I finally determined upon General Douglas MacArthur. His brilliant abilities and his sterling character need no exposition from me."[42] Eventually, even Pershing relented, stating lamely, "Well, Mr. President, he is one of my boys. I have nothing more to say."[43]

Douglas MacArthur became the thirteenth army chief of staff on November 21, 1930.[44]

CHAPTER 11

CHIEF OF STAFF

Saving the Army

One of the great challenges the United States faced in the 1930s was the Great Depression, which began with the stock market crash in 1929, a year before MacArthur returned stateside. The slow slide into the abyss of bank failures, loss of life savings, and record unemployment ravaged the nation. Millions were without means amid growing despair, causing huge problems socially, economically, and politically. A major political issue was an expanding antiwar movement and spread of pacifism due to the awful slaughter of the Great War. The new machines of war among the industrialized nations had caused so much death and destruction, and the accompanying trauma seized so many people and nations with horror and hatred of war.[1]

General MacArthur walked into a toxic office environment regardless of the fact that it was the highest position in the US Army. Gen. Charles Summerall and his leadership style created an atmosphere that according to historian Geoffrey Perrett "had never gone beyond the unreconstructed leadership style learned at West Point in his youth, which consisted of a bullying manner.... Summerall drove men, rather than lead them."[2] For Douglas MacArthur his first days as chief of staff involved two major tasks: first, to ensure that his mother "Pinky" had an easy move into Quarters One at Fort

Myer, the abode for the army chief of staff; second, to establish a personal staff that mirrored his personality and leadership style.

After a half-dozen years living with her son's widow and family in Washington, DC, Pinky moved into the second of two of the most historic homes owned by the US Army, the superintendent quarters at West Point and Quarters One.[3] Douglas's first official act as chief of staff was a task of a dutiful son; he arranged to have a sun porch added to the second floor of the house and the installation of an elevator "for the convenience of his aging mother." Pinky at age seventy-eight required some amenities.[4]

His second immediate issue was creating his own staff of officers and a few civilians that he either trusted or respected, though he was willing also to include new faces. It has been a practice since "time immemorial" whereby senior people use staff members they already know, who follow them from post to post. This was not always true with MacArthur. Coming from the Philippines he had to create his "general's household," which he soon called "my gang." US Military Academy graduates such as MacArthur had strong associations, friendships, and comradery, especially among those of the same class or class groupings. There is no real evidence in the historical record that MacArthur used West Point as a litmus test, a prerequisite for selection on his staff, or that he favored graduates over other officers. Mentoring junior officers and leaders is a major responsibility in the profession of arms, and MacArthur was one of the most distinguished mentors in American history.

Maj. Dwight David "Ike" Eisenhower, class of 1915, arrived at the War Department in November 1929, just after the October stock market crash. His position was executive assistant to Maj. Gen. George Van Horn Moseley, the principal military advisor to the assistant secretary of war, Frederick Payne. By 1931 Ike was supporting these two officials and MacArthur; he recalled, "My office was next to his [MacArthur's;] only a slatted door separated us." When Eisenhower was needed, MacArthur "called me to his office by raising his voice."[5] It was not until 1933 that Eisenhower became MacArthur's executive secretary.

• • •

MacArthur's greatest achievement as chief of staff occurred during the first year of President Franklin Roosevelt's administration, in 1933, though his entire tenure as army chief of staff was plagued with serious challenges and problems. Much of it was caused by the Great Depression and its spiraling descent into bitter misery and misfortune. He faced many attempts by two administrations to castrate the army, either reductions in funding and manpower or terminating research projects, modernization, and new technological advances. When forced to decide between funding for manpower or new technological innovations, MacArthur always fought to save soldiers over new tactical developments such as armored forces and aviation. In 1931, in order to appease the budget vultures, MacArthur begrudgingly ended the development of a provisional tank corps at Fort Meade under the American pioneer of armored warfare, Maj. Adna R. Chaffee Jr., who had been a plebe attending the academy with Cadet MacArthur, graduating in 1906.[6]

Later that year MacArthur faced even a more serious challenge, when Hoover's cabinet and Congress wanted to reduce the officer corps in the regular army from twelve thousand to ten thousand to save $24 million in manpower costs. He argued in a written statement, "Trained officers constitute the most vitally essential element in modern war, and the only one that under no circumstances can be improvised or extemporized."[7] Taking care of soldiers and mentoring officers meant a great deal to MacArthur. He was always discovering ways to improve morale and to inspire and develop character and teamwork. During his first two years as chief of staff, he instituted and conceived several ideas based on historical precedence that would inspire and reward soldiers.

MacArthur in 1931 devised the idea for a new military award for meritorious service and for wounds in combat. He and the staff members of the Quartermaster General Office settled on a design incorporating the purple ribbon and heart used on Gen. George Washington's Badge of Military Merit, presented near West Point at the New Windsor Cantonment in 1782. "Douglas MacArthur, the prime mover behind the revival of the Purple Heart, was twice wounded by gas while fighting in France," wrote historian Fred Borch. However, MacArthur was against the so named Purple Heart as a posthumous award; he declared it was not "to commemorate the dead, but to animate and inspire the living." The chief of staff pushed the concept through the War Department channels, and on the bicentennial of George Washington's birth on February 22, 1932, hundreds of veterans gathered in New

Windsor to receive their decoration in person; thousands more medals were mailed to other recipients. The Purple Heart replaced the "wound chevrons" worn on the uniform sleeve to recognize those wounded in action during World War I. Beginning in 1942 the Purple Heart was presented to any American servicemember who was wounded or killed in action, and no longer for meritorious service.[8] "No action taken by me while I was chief of staff," MacArthur wrote, "gave me greater satisfaction than re-establishing the Order of the Purple Heart. It had not been in use for a century and a quarter."[9]

If one decoration was not enough for General MacArthur, he devised another, the Silver Star Medal, also approved in 1932. In earlier conflicts a small 3/18-inch "citation star" was attached to the campaign ribbons. This was an award for gallantry in action. MacArthur recommended to Secretary of War Patrick Hurley to establish the Silver Star to replace the citation star. On July 19, 1932, just ten days before the Bonus March problem—discussed next—the war secretary formally approved the Silver Star "for gallantry in action . . . which citation does not warrant the award of a Medal of Honor or the Distinguished Service Cross."[10]

• • •

In 1932 General MacArthur faced one of the most difficult experiences of his life and career, this one concerning a popular movement among a deprived group of American veterans whom he swore were pawns or surrogates of Communist agitators. "The most poignant episode during my role as Chief of Staff was the so-called Bonus March," MacArthur recalled.[11] In fact, the Bonus March incident of 1932 is perhaps the only event most people knowledgeable in American history cite in regard to MacArthur's five years as chief of staff. The Bonus March is engraved into American historical memory as an overt use of government force against an innocent, peaceful popular movement. Though basically true overall, there is much more to the story, and victims were also the instigators, as in most civil unrest incidents. Biographer Geoffrey Perrett summarized that "nothing in MacArthur's long military career was as controversial as his action in routing the Bonus Army and driving it out of Washington in July 1932."[12] Arthur Herman wrote, "The image of MacArthur as would-be dictator and trampler of the poor and unemployed took root and spread."[13]

Army Chief of Staff MacArthur during the Bonus March incident in 1932. *Courtesy MacArthur Memorial.*

Regardless of all the above, this episode is also a West Point story, through and through. MacArthur and dozens of academy graduates took part, including Majors Eisenhower and George S. Patton; the actual commander of the troops, Brig. Gen. Perry Miles, class of 1891; and the superintendent of the Washington police force, Pelham D. Glassford, class of 1904, who knew MacArthur personally as a cadet. Douglas's classmate U.S. Grant III, a lieutenant colonel, as an army officer was an official in the District of Columbia government.[14]

In 1924 Congress had passed a law for a "bonus" that would be paid in 1945 that was roughly a few hundred dollars up to a $1,000 for each veteran, based on overseas service and time in uniform. These veterans did not want to wait until 1945; they needed and wanted the cash—now.[15] Thousands of people, veterans and family members, descended on Washington, DC, where city officials—especially police superintendent Glassford, from his personal account—provided food, blankets, and fuel, ignoring the veterans' illegal squatting in several condemned government buildings downtown. Even MacArthur and the army issued some goods "to provide further shelter." MacArthur wrote, "I issued tents and camp equipment to be set up on Anacostia Flats. I also ordered out a number of rolling kitchens to relieve any acute suffering." Congress complained, and Secretary of War Hurley reversed MacArthur's action. Also, in June MacArthur met with Walter W. Waters, the Bonus Marchers' unofficial leader, a veteran from Oregon, who agreed that the veterans would leave if the protests turned violent.[16]

By July MacArthur and many of his staff were convinced that this was a Communist movement more than innocent veterans clamoring for compensation. There were Communist radicals involved trying to insight a larger social agenda, but they were a small minority. After nearly two months of deadlock and rising tension, the House of Representatives passed a resolution to pay the veterans, but the Senate rejected the measure. The Bonus people were deeply disappointed, but no violence and unrest occurred. In fact, many began to leave Washington and return home. Railroad companies provided cheap fares for the marchers, and Congress provided funding to aid in their return.[17]

Still, thousands of protestors remained, and government officials became more anxious about their presence. On July 16, Congress adjourned, making the hope of congressional action impossible. By the end of July, the Hoover administration had enough and pushed to remove the protesters from squatting in abandoned government buildings that were due for demolition. Serving as director of public buildings and public parks in the district, overseen by the US Army, was a classmate of MacArthur, none other than U.S. Grant III. Lieutenant Colonel Grant forwarded a directive that the Bonus Marchers had to depart the parks and other government grounds under Grant's control.[18]

On July 28 the district commissioners ordered Police Superintendent Glassford to clear the buildings known as Camp Glassford on Pennsylvania Avenue. One of the commissioners that issued this order was Herbert B. Crosby, whom Glassford reported to, a graduate of the academy in 1893 and a retired major general. Police arrived at the site, and eventually violence broke out; Glassford himself was injured by a brick to the head. About midday the situation escalated and two protestors were shot by police officers—both died from their wounds. Regardless of the many stories of exaggerated injuries and deaths, these were the only direct loss of life in the entire affair.[19]

An order issued at 2:55p.m. from Secretary Hurley to General MacArthur directed:

> The President has just now informed me that the civil government of the District of Columbia has reported to him that it is unable to maintain law and order in the District. You will have United States troops proceed immediately to the scene of disorder. Cooperate fully with the District of Columbia police force which is now in charge. Surround the affected area and clear it without delay. Turn over all prisoners to the civil authorities. In your orders insist that any women and children who may be in the affected area be accorded every consideration and kindness. Use all humanity consistent with the due execution of this order.[20]

Always a man of action, MacArthur moved quickly and issued orders to General Miles, commanding the 16th Infantry Brigade at Fort Myer. The fact that General MacArthur attended the removal of the marchers in person has caused great fervor for decades. Even Major Eisenhower, his military secretary, entered the fray: "I told him that the matter could easily become a riot" and that it was "highly inappropriate for the Chief of Staff of the Army to be involved in anything like a local or street corner embroilment." In a more vulgar version Eisenhower declared, "I told that dumb son-of-a-bitch not to go down there." He recorded, "I told him it was no place for the chief of Staff."[21] MacArthur said to several officers on the scene, especially General Miles, that he would "take the rap if there should be any unfavorable or critical repercussions."[22] Was his presence on the scene necessary to fulfill this? No. But MacArthur was a man of action and would never shirk from his duty as he saw it.

By 4:30 p.m. mounted troops commenced their sweep of Pennsylvania Avenue, with Major Patton serving as second in command, sabers drawn. Five

Renault tanks and the infantry with fixed bayonets moved through the area, pushing all people before them. On hand were thousands of citizens, onlookers, like spectators at a sporting event.[23]

President Hoover from the beginning, as did most everyone, wanted no violent solution to the ordeal. Orders were sent to MacArthur and the commanders to not cross the Anacostia Bridge, but they were confusing or not delivered, or possibly MacArthur ignored them.[24] As evening came, Hoover ordered that the army troops not cross the drawbridge until all the women and children had evacuated the large camp. It was well after dark when the soldiers crossed the Anacostia River, as most of the people had departed. The troops used tear gas at the large camp, which ignited some tents and debris, causing the burning of the camps. MacArthur claimed, "The rioters set fire to their own camp," which is not at all likely, as he could not possibly know. Regardless, MacArthur on his own authority sent his men across the bridge to clear the large refugee camp.[25]

By 11 p.m. the camp was clear; the Bonus Marchers had either fled or were forced out of the city. Then MacArthur and Secretary Hurley conducted a press interview at the White House. The *Washington Daily News* reported the next day, "What a pitiful spectacle.... The mightiest government in the world chasing unarmed men, women, and children with Army tanks. If the Army must be called out to make war on unarmed citizens, this is no longer America."[26] Eisenhower recorded in his journal two weeks later, "A lot of furor has been stirred up by the incident but mostly to make political capital."[27]

The next day Hoover severely criticized MacArthur and Hurley in the White House. The president knew in this election year he could never recover from the political disaster of the Bonus Marchers. MacArthur even offered to resign his commission and office, but Hoover declined this and defended MacArthur's actions publicly.[28]

MacArthur recorded in his official report two weeks later, "This mission was substantially accomplished and with no loss of life or serious casualty, after the arrival of the troops, among either the civilian or military elements involved."[29] Even the Communist agitator John Pace echoed this fact: "General MacArthur put down a Moscow-directed revolution without bloodshed, and that is why the Communists hate him even today."[30]

The American Communists were not the only ones who were angry and threatened by Douglas MacArthur. The very next day, after hearing about the expulsion of the Bonus Marchers, Democratic presidential candidate Franklin D. Roosevelt took a phone call from fiery and capricious Sen. Huey Long from Louisiana. After the call, Roosevelt remarked to his aides, "We have to remember all the time that he's really one of the two most dangerous men in the country." An aide asked for clarification, to which FDR announced, "The first is Douglas MacArthur."[31] Because of the Bonus March, many key political figures turned to Roosevelt during the election of 1932—and he crushed Hoover handily.

It was a distasteful event, but one must admit compared to other civil riots or disturbances in American history, especially with the January 6, 2021, attack at the national Capitol in mind, the manner in which the army handled this event was deliberate and well executed with minimal injuries. The fallout from the Bonus March created another major problem for Douglas MacArthur, personally and professionally. That very summer of 1932, the newspapers and journalists turned on MacArthur, and Hoover, like sharks. The most vicious and critical accounts came from Drew Pearson, a notorious Washington insider and muckraker, who wrote that the army's involvement was "unwarranted, unnecessary, arbitrary, harsh, and brutal." He characterized MacArthur as "dictatorial, insubordinate, disloyal, mutinous, and disrespectful of his superiors in the War Department."[32] After months of relentless attacks, MacArthur struck back—not by words in public print but in legal language. He sued Pearson and his associates for libel in court for $1.7 million, an enormous sum at that time—any time, for that matter.[33] Soon Pearson and his publisher were on the ropes, and they searched for a way to escape the growing legal actions that MacArthur had marshaled. The answer came when they discovered an insidious scandal that could ruin MacArthur's career forever. Pearson learned that the army chief of staff had a girlfriend, a young, beautiful woman from the Philippines whom he had maintained secretly in a Washington apartment for three years, until the romance waned. All this came to a head in the summer of 1934.

Prior to MacArthur's departure from the Philippines in 1930, he met Isabel Rosario Cooper, an enchanting young actress with the stage name "Dimples," who had starred in several films in the Philippines and had been a dancer in nightclubs in China. The much older MacArthur, by then divorced, became very attracted to Isabel, whose father was American and mother Filipino. He arranged for passage to the United States on the SS *President Filmore* from Manila to New York City, where he met her on December 9, 1930. The passenger manifest recorded her age as twenty-one years old.[34]

MacArthur soon housed her in a plush apartment in Washington and discouraged her from wandering out or shopping. Perhaps his major concern was his mother learning of this affair with a young woman nearly thirty years his junior.[35] The romance soured, and Isabel left for California to act in American films. About this same time Drew Pearson discovered MacArthur's great secret and was prepared to use it against him. Eventually, MacArthur paid Isabel $15,000 to buy her silence and took possession of his love letters and other mementos. Then off to California she went for fame and fun. Tragically, in 1960 she took her own life by overdosing on drugs.[36]

The story should have ended there, but some historians and MacArthur detractors have fed the flames to make the story more than it is, to destroy MacArthur's reputation historically. They accuse him of keeping an underaged minor, a girl of sixteen when they met and when she came to America. It is hard to determine, but their claims are groundless. The most knowledgeable authority on Isabel was the late Carol Morris Petillo, who was also an expert on Philippine-American history. She had interviewed the Cooper family and found other evidence of Isabel's age and history. Petillo recorded in a note regarding Isabel's family that "considering her fame in Manila, however, it is likely she was at least a few years older [than age sixteen, and birth year of 1914] and may later have moved her birth date forward for professional purposes."[37] She was at least eighteen when she met MacArthur, but more likely twenty-one years old in 1930.[38]

Why is all this important? Why does anyone care whether an older man had a romantic fling with a younger adult woman? Adm. William Leahy, no real friend of Douglas MacArthur, learned of the affair and MacArthur's lawsuit. He disagreed with MacArthur's ending the libel suit, saying, "He was a bachelor at the time," and added, "All he [MacArthur] had to do was say 'so what?'"[39]

• • •

One of the great opportunities that came to MacArthur in 1933 was to return to West Point and speak at the graduation ceremony on June 13, 1933. To deliver the commencement address at the academy was no light thing. Typical speakers were presidents, secretaries of war, and occasionally congressmen or the army chief of staff. The graduation was exactly thirty years and two days from when Cadet MacArthur received his diploma as top of his class of 1903. Since graduation, fourteen of his classmates had died:

		Age			Class Ranking
Ferdinand Williams	1 June 1906	25	Accidental gunshot, pistol range		10th
Thomas E. Selfridge	17 Sept. 1908	26	First military aviation fatality		30th
Reynolds J. Powers	12 Feb. 1912	32	Service, Philippines		39th
Edward M. Zell	12 March 1916	25	Suicide, Mexican Punitive Exp.		57th
Clifton M. Butler	28 Jan. 1917	36	Service, Mexican Punitive Exp.		73rd
Scott Baker	2 June 1917	35	Service, San Francisco		12th
Emil Laurson	13 Aug. 1918	38	AEF France		19th
James A. Shannon	8 Oct. 1918	39	KIA, AEF France*		36th
Truman W. Carrithers	17 Oct. 1918	36	Service, Washington, DC		66th
Walter V. Gallagher	21 Oct. 1918	38	AEF France		61st
Carl Boyd	12 Feb. 1919	40	Service, France		60th
Samuel M. Parker	15 Feb. 1928	48	As a businessman		40th
Quinn Gray	22 Oct. 1929	51	In California		38th
George R. Guild	5 Aug. 1931	50	In Buffalo, New York		89th

*Posthumously awarded the Distinguished Service Cross.

MacArthur's class of ninety-three graduates had lost fourteen members of the Long Gray Line in thirty years. Tragically, Edward Zell on the baseball team with Douglas took his own life while on border duty just days after the raid at Columbus, New Mexico, led by Pancho Villa, the Mexican revolutionary leader. Doubly tragic was the fact that Zell had married Priscilla Williams, the sister of Ferdinand Williams, who was a classmate and who himself had died ten years earlier, the first of the class to pass on.[40] Also noteworthy was the death of First Lt. Thomas Selfridge while flying a Wright Flyer with aviation pioneer Orville Wright at Fort Myer, Virginia. Orville was seriously injured but Selfridge died.[41]

Now General MacArthur stood on the base of Battle Monument on the famous plain of West Point addressing the 346 cadets. Along with him was Secretary of War George H. Dern, former governor of Utah, and Maj. Gen. William D. Connor, superintendent, who was six years older and an academy graduate of 1897. Connor had a distinguished career and had been considered for army chief of staff when MacArthur was appointed. He served as commandant of the Army War College before he was appointed thirty-sixth superintendent in 1932 and retired in 1938.[42]

Before a crowd of some five thousand people—cadets, parents, friends, staff, and faculty—MacArthur based his remarks on the current crises of the economic depression and rise of militarism threatening peace. He said: "Pacific habits do not insure peace nor immunity from national insult or aggression. Any nation that would keep its self-respect must keep alive its martial ardor and be prepared to defend itself. . . . As the necessity of National Defense is sacrificed in the name of economy, the United States presents a tempting spectacle."[43]

He carried on the theme of a "spectacle" not so much as a notable or unusual concept but more as transitory moment, a curiosity, or a dramatic eye-catching quality. Noting the movement of some nations toward aggression, he spoke of others trying "an alignment" that "may lead to another World War, and that war would find a score of nations ready for the sack of America." Not spouting national sentiment as a basis, MacArthur clearly wanted to defend the United States as the chief priority, that the military was "solely for the preservation of peace." He condemned defense cuts and economic measures that threatened the overall defense budget and were "substituted for petty provincial politics."[44]

MacArthur then turned to the main audience before him, the 346 graduating cadets and 1,200 other underclassmen, with the solemn statement: "Today you bring to the army its annual increment of youth, vigor and fortitude, the things that make West Point the soul of the Army."[45] Ever a student of history, MacArthur gave a cautionary comment: "A good soldier, whether he leads a platoon or an army is expected to look backward as well as forward, but he must think only forward. The next war will be won in the future, not in the past."[46]

Moving forward was MacArthur's exhortation to the class of 1933 and all the other cadets listening. He may have perceived as many others that day, that it was likely that the four classes assembled on the West Point plain would see vicious combat in the future. Many would give their lives in these conflicts. He blessed them in his way, "Good luck, my dear young comrades-in-arms: happy landings and God be with you."[47]

Among the cadets of the class of 1933 were several who would make a name in army and military history. Graduating 231st in the class was Harold K. Johnson, who survived the Bataan Death March in 1942 and three years in Japanese POW camps. Johnson commanded a cavalry battalion in Korea, receiving the Distinguished Service Cross and Bronze Star, then rose to be army chief of staff in 1964, retiring four years later. Ranked 176th in the class was William O. Darby, one of the pioneering officers and first commanders of the Army Rangers in World War II. He led Ranger battalions in North Africa, Sicily, and Italy, received two Distinguished Service Crosses for bravery, and was killed by enemy artillery two days before German forces surrendered in Italy on May 2, 1945. At the time he was colonel and serving as assistant commanding general of the 10th Mountain Division at the Po River. Darby was promoted to brigadier general posthumously; the present-day Camp Darby of Ranger School is named in his honor.[48]

MacArthur's return to West Point was a great day for him, as he cherished his time among the gray granite buildings and cadets clad in gray. His professional relationships with the staff and faculty had remained important to him. Gen. Jacob Devers capitalized on this very thought of MacArthur's great regard for the professional and personal relationships he had with academy officials. "The influence of any person at any institution is," wrote Devers in 1964, after MacArthur's death, "of necessity, effected through his relationships with those others who are concerned with any phase of the life of the institution."[49]

MacArthur took this principle to heart especially with the permanent staff. In the spring of 1934, Capt. Philip Egner, the bandmaster at West Point, had reached the mandatory retirement age of sixty-four. As busy as MacArthur was as chief of staff, he took the time to congratulate and thank Captain Egner for his twenty-five years leading the band and serving as Teacher of Music. The

US Military Academy does not have a music department, but starting with fifers and drummers during the American Revolution, music has always been part of the West Point experience. What became the West Point (USMA) Band was established in 1817 and has been part of the pomp and ceremony since, especially performing at concerts and parades. MacArthur wrote to Egner, "I could not allow you to pass to the retired list without expressing the grateful appreciation of the War Department, as well as my own, of the faithful and efficient service you rendered the Government as Teacher of Music at the United States Military Academy . . . as Teacher of Music and as Leader of the Band endeared you to the cadets and won the commendation of your superiors."[50]

MacArthur continued in his great regard and interest in the academy, especially as chief of staff, by which he had great control over many aspects of the army. He requested Capt. Garrison Davidson, class of 1927, to come to Washington to talk about football. Davidson became head football coach in 1933 after MacArthur's graduation visit. MacArthur requested reports on the team, statistics, and updates from Coach Davidson. MacArthur in return offered to assign officers with playing or coaching experience to the coaching staff at West Point. Davidson declared later that his coaches were "professional army officers first and amateur coaches second." Twenty years later, "Gar" Davidson served as one of the reforming superintendents.[51]

• • •

After Roosevelt won the election of 1932, during the transition period, his counselors and advisors basically demanded that the new commander-in-chief summarily remove MacArthur as army chief of staff. MacArthur had completed his first full term, so theoretically he could be replaced, though the president can make changes at any time. Secretary of Interior Harold Ickes had a visceral hatred of MacArthur, saying he was "the type of man who thinks that when he gets to heaven, God will step down from the great white throne and bow to him into His vacated seat."[52]

Roosevelt's political agenda and New Deal programs included the Civilian Conservation Corps (CCC), a plan to have hundreds of thousands of people work on federal conservation projects and receive government pay in the process. The law passed in Congress on March 21, 1933, the administration's first major legislative victory. Roosevelt wanted the CCC operational by July 1, which required coordination among the Departments of Labor, Agriculture, Interior, and War, and many other agencies. The army was assigned to establish dozens of camps and provide two-week induction or training courses for some 250,000 volunteers. MacArthur was at first against the president's program, believing that it provided no professional value for the officers and soldiers tasked in the program, and insisted that there would be no military training conducted.[53]

It did not take long for MacArthur to realize that this was a major government program, and it actually had some advantages for the army. He stressed the fact that people, especially the officer corps, were the foundation of any military force.[54] As with most adventures and projects, MacArthur moved with speed and determination, tasking his staff to establish the camps, deploy the cadre, allocate the equipment and transportation necessary, and appoint the best officers to command and direct the training. Some 200 railroad trains and 3,600 army trucks were employed to support the project. Many of the trainees were veterans of World War I and Bonus Marchers, a rather dubious connection.[55]

Praise for the program came from Major Eisenhower, who realized the army's benefit in supporting the CCC training: "We will lose no officers or men (at least this time) and this concession was won because of the great numbers we are using on the Civilian Conservation Corps work and of Gen. MacArthur's skill and determination."[56] Over the months the two men developed a friendship and were at times very open to each other. MacArthur wrote, "In my own case, whatever differences arose between us, it never sullied in slightest degree the warmth of my personal friendship for him."[57]

In 1934 there was forecast a reduction of some $80 million for defense, which MacArthur fought and lobbied Congress against. Finally, he made a direct appeal to Roosevelt. MacArthur recorded an exchange with the president wherein "I felt it my duty to take up the cudgels. The country's safety was at stake, and I said so bluntly."[58]

In the verbal joust with Roosevelt, MacArthur remembered, "The President turned the full vials of his sarcasm upon me. He was a scorcher when aroused. The tension began to boil." An argument ensued, with nerves, voices, and intensity increasing. What occurred next was one of the most fascinating and perhaps foolish comments Douglas MacArthur made in his life, to none other than the president of the United States: "I spoke recklessly and said something to the general effect that when we lost the next war, and an American boy, lying in the mud with an enemy bayonet through his belly and an enemy foot on his dying throat, spat out his last curse, I wanted the name not to be MacArthur, but Roosevelt."[59]

General MacArthur (left), Secretary of War George H. Dern of Utah, and, seated in the automobile, President Franklin D. Roosevelt. *Courtesy MacArthur Memorial.*

Whether there was a pause not, as MacArthur narrated, "The President grew livid. 'You must not talk that way to the President!' he roared." Douglas knew he was wrong and admitted it, and even offered his resignation. Then amazingly Roosevelt relented, "Don't be foolish, Douglas," and said it was possible to work on a compromise budget. As they departed, Secretary Dern said to MacArthur, "You've saved the Army." Reaching the steps outside the White House, MacArthur experienced, for the third and last time in his life, a paralyzing nausea that began to creep over him, causing him to vomit on the steps of the president's residence.[60]

To everyone's surprise, Roosevelt announced in a press conference on December 12 that Douglas MacArthur would continue as chief of staff for another year to complete a few important projects.[61] Roosevelt expressed his reason: "I am doing this in order to obtain the benefit of General MacArthur's experience in handling the War Department legislation in the coming [congressional] session."[62]

• • •

Being a student of history and tradition, MacArthur recognized the importance that West Point played in the development of the professionalism of the officer corps. "It is not too much to say," he wrote, "that the reputation of the American officer corps for probity, integrity, and a high sense of honor and duty is traceable in large part to General [Sylvanus] Thayer's influence." Of course, he meant Thayer's success in developing officers at West Point and its profound legacy for more than a hundred years.[63]

In 1935 MacArthur convinced Congress to expand the Corps of Cadets from 1,374, about the level when he was superintendent, to 1,960 cadets. He had hoped to double the size of the corps, but that attempt failed. Yet, this increase was significant to him and the army, as he declared in the *Annual Report of the War Department* that graduates of the US Military Academy "have been imbued with the conceptions of duty, integrity, and patriotism which constitute the very basis of West Point training and which these graduates have in turn transplanted into the Army." Continuing, he said, "in a very real sense that institution has thus become the heritage, not merely of those who happen to be its graduates, but of every officer in the service."[64] This quality of the founding of the academy did not escape him. In this legislation he also requested that every graduate dating back to 1802 receive a bachelor's degree that would be recognized by other academic institutions and the new wave of accreditation that was growing.⁶⁵

MacArthur as army chief of staff helped provide funding for many other features at West Point, the new barracks completed in 1936, now called Scott Barracks, and a combination barracks and reception hall, now Grant Hall; additions to the 1910 gymnasium and the superintendent's house, known now as Quarters 100; and a line of officer family quarters running north toward the cemetery.⁶⁶

One of the most obvious and dramatic features MacArthur first proposed and then saw to fruition was a majestic mural in Washington Hall, the cadet mess. The sheer scale of the work is overpowering: 70 feet long by 35 feet high, covering 2,250 square feet. "General Douglas MacArthur more than any other person made possible the actual execution of the West Point Mural," wrote Thomas Lofton Johnson. In 1935, during MacArthur's final year as chief,

Mural in West Point's cadet mess, Washington Hall, dedicated in 1936. *Author's collection.*

funded by a grant from the Federal Art Project, a subcomponent of the Works Projects Administration (WPA), the contract provided $30 weekly for the artist and $20 for an assistant. The artist, "T L" Johnson, was selected by a panel that included the superintendent, Maj. Gen. William Connor, the Academic Board, and Juliana Force of the Whitney Museum of American Art in New York. As a basis for the mural, Johnson referred to Sir Edward Creasy's 1851 book *The Fifteen Decisive Battles of the World: from Marathon to Waterloo*, which was very European-centric. Johnson added two additional battles, Gettysburg in 1863 and the Marne of 1914.[67]

After a year of research and planning, Johnson learned that Congress did not resubscribe this specific project. With no money, and trying several other options, Johnson obtained an office call in Washington, DC, with General MacArthur. After hearing the situation, MacArthur remarked, "West Point must have that Mural," and then transferred $1,800 from the Army Athletic Association to the WPA account. The Army Athletic Association usually supported army athletes who participated in international sporting events such as the Olympics. With these funds, Johnson finished the mural, and it was dedicated in June 1936 during graduation week by none other than General of the Armies John J. Pershing, MacArthur's vacillating, mercurial mentor, and former antagonist.[68]

Summarizing MacArthur's love and commitment to the academy, historian D. Clayton James wrote, "During the years 1930–35 . . . in the office of chief of staff [was] a general who was one of the most enthusiastic supporters the United States Military Academy ever had."[69]

CHAPTER 12

★ ★ ★ ★ ★

THE FIELD MARSHAL PREPARES FOR WAR

Assignment to the Philippines in 1935 after his tenure as chief of staff was Douglas MacArthur's fourth posting to the islands. This voyage across the Pacific was one of the most important passages in his life, personally and symbolically. While on the ship bound for Manila, he met Jean Faircloth, a petite woman of thirty-five years, from Murfreesboro, Tennessee. Soon Jean would become the most important person in his life. Accompanying Douglas on the long voyage was Pinky MacArthur, his eighty-three-year-old mother, then failing in health.

MacArthur's official title was military advisor to the Commonwealth Government of the Philippines. In 1934 Congress passed the Tydings-McDuffie Act, which created the Philippines Commonwealth with a constitution approved by popular vote. The 1934 act allowed the Philippines nearly autonomous power and promised complete political independence from the United States in 1946. MacArthur's position had been recommended by President-elect Manuel L. Quezon but channeled through the War Department and approved by President Roosevelt. MacArthur's role would be separate from the US Army's Philippine Department commander's position that he had held from 1928 to 1930, but MacArthur would have authority to advise the department. The new commonwealth government held a ceremonial inauguration on November 15, 1935, which MacArthur attended.[1]

Three weeks after the MacArthurs arrived, on December 3, Mary "Pinky" MacArthur died in the Manila Hotel.[2]

Douglas recorded in his memoirs a simple declaration: "Our devoted comradeship of so many years came to an end.... I later brought her remains home to Virginia, where she rests beside my father in the soil of Arlington." It was actually two years later, in 1937, that he accompanied her remains back to America. As clinical as the above description implied, Douglas was shattered at the passing of his mother. "Mother's death has been a tremendous blow to me," he wrote a friend. "My loss has partially stunned me and I find myself groping desperately but futilely.... For the first time in my life, I need all the help I can get."[3] This was not the Douglas MacArthur who charged up Côte de Chatillon in France or fought off banditos in Mexico and in the Philippines. Eventually, Jean Faircloth would fill the void that overwhelmed him in the Philippines.

MacArthur's role was not a direct command responsibility; he was to lead a US military mission, an advisory group. Though not a completely independent nation, the Philippines was treated as such. Thus, MacArthur was advisor to a semi-foreign government appointed by its president. The military mission was to prepare the defense posture of the Philippines. Secretary of War Dern explained that the Philippine mission was to "aid without assumption of additional authority, an attitude that would faithfully conform to our disinterested attempt to contribute toward the development of the Philippine Islands of a status of complete independence." This military mission came with a price tag, of course; Congress allocated defense appropriations, which before World War II were a constant matter of debate and political arm-wrestling.[4]

One reason MacArthur was selected as military advisor was his reputation and personal prestige as former chief of staff; he was also selected for his experience and abilities. Even if he had no or little official authority, army officers and Filipinos listened to him—at first. MacArthur's drive and motivation were based on the fact that "he was devoted to the Philippines and the Filipinos."[5] He had lived and served six years in the Philippines, and his father had been governor-general and part of the initial American invasion force in

1898. As advisor he could plan, advise, and consult the commonwealth government to improve the Philippine national defense forces. This was a hybrid situation where MacArthur and many of his military personal staff, such as Ike Eisenhower, were active officers but serving or supporting the commonwealth—a true military mission.

Besides his salary as an US Army major general, some $8,000 per annum, he received from the commonwealth some $18,000 annually in compensation and $15,000 more for expenses. This was quite a sum for that era.[6] MacArthur had agreed to a six-year term, and a contract was drafted that involved a performance bonus at the end of this term, based on the percentage of overall defense appropriation for the Philippine Commonwealth from Congress through 1941. Secretary Dern had approved the contract, and Roosevelt was aware of it. The payments were made much later in 1941. Part of the negotiation with MacArthur was that President Quezon agreed to a promotion and rank in the new Filipino army: Field Marshal Douglas MacArthur. The new exalted grade was MacArthur's idea. After having served as a four-star general, and then reverting to major general, MacArthur probably saw this as a logical step for one who had held the most senior rank and position in the US Army and was now in a separate commonwealth army.[7]

The field marshal was no longer a common soldier or an ordinary American citizen for that matter. Though he worked nearly every day and attended to his duties unless he was ill, MacArthur seldom worked a full day either in his office or at his penthouse. For relaxation he read from his more than eight thousand volumes of history and literature and took long walks.[8] At the Manila penthouse he often wore his beloved West Point robe with the letterman "A" on it. Over the years he had to replace these robes, which were issued to the new cadets.[9] As he had worn his letterman's sweater under his tunic on the Western Front, he wore his academy robe at home.

• • •

Several officers accompanied MacArthur to the Philippines, voluntarily, but risking their own careers, because MacArthur's stock was waning and not gaining. For most officers who served under MacArthur, loyalty was the greatest magnet. The best example of this was Major Eisenhower, who followed him from Washington and who was joined by Maj. James B. Ord, a great friend

MacArthur and Lt. Col. Dwight Eisenhower (right), MacArthur's chief of staff, in the Philippines as military advisors. *Courtesy MacArthur Memorial.*

and fellow classmate of the USMA class of 1915. Like Eisenhower, Jimmy Ord was a brilliant staff officer. MacArthur had met Ord in France in 1931 while on a visit as chief of staff. Ord was fluent in Spanish and was known for "his quickness of mind and ability as a staff officer." Ike and Ord were friends to begin with, but their Philippine service under MacArthur galvanized them into a formidable team of efficient staff officers. Ike as chief of staff and Ord as assistant chief served well and diligently, though their positions had no opportunities for commanding troops—the apogee of leadership. MacArthur recognized this dynamic team and treasured his great luck to have them. James Ord's connection to West Point began generations earlier with his grandfather, Maj. Gen. Edward O. C. Ord, class of 1839, and a corps commander under Gen. U. S. Grant at Vicksburg. Fort Ord in California was named after him. James Ord's cousin James G. Ord was a member of the class of 1909 with George Patton and retired as a major general in 1946 after thirty-seven years of service.[10]

MacArthur and his team had a huge task to establish a Filipino defense force and prepare it for modern warfare, while safeguarding an archipelago of thousands of islands with hundreds of passages by sea and with diverse landscapes of jungles, wide plains, and mountainous terrain, all engulfed in a tropical climate. Many officers and experts for years decried the mammoth challenge to defend the Philippines. The small force of some twenty thousand US Army regular troops stationed there was the nucleus for defense, but it did not answer to MacArthur as advisor. The famous Philippine Scouts of native Filipinos commanded by American officers was the foundation that MacArthur built upon.[11]

MacArthur had dealt with the defense of the Philippines for decades, ever since his first tour in 1903 and War Plan Orange, which he still opposed. He knew that only through congressional funding and War Department priority would the proper defense of the Philippines come to pass. He also knew that manpower was not a problem, because the Filipinos wanted independence and their service as soldiers would help secure that desire. For more than a decade, the perceived threat to the Philippines and Far East Asia had been Japan. Marshaling sufficient soldiers was not the great challenge, but training, equipping, and maintaining a modern force of at least 100,000 men and all its support components was daunting. He commenced building an army through recruitment and education, to include one of MacArthur's great legacies: the Philippine Military Academy.

The rich heritage and connection of the Philippines and the US Military Academy was thirty years old by 1936 when MacArthur with President Quezon's knowledge and approval moved forward on the creation of the Philippines' own national military academy. "The Academy, to be built along the lines of West Point," wrote Filipino historian Jose G. Syjuco, "was a major proposal of General Douglas MacArthur."[12] Since 1815 West Point had admitted foreign candidates to the Corps of Cadets, and since the annexation of the Philippines as a US protectorate in 1898 there had been young Filipino cadets at the academy. In 1908 Congress passed legislation with directives allowing the admission of Filipinos to the academy. The first such was Vicente Lim, who arrived in the summer of 1910 and graduated in 1914. He was later killed by the Japanese in 1944. Following Lim, more than a dozen Filipinos attended and graduated through 1936. Several of these Filipinos were cadets during MacArthur's superintendency, including Pastor Martelino, who graduated in 1920, class standing 66 of 271 fellow classmates. After he had served in both the United States and the Philippines armies in many positions, Colonel Martelino was selected by President Quezon and General MacArthur to be the first superintendent of the new academy.[13]

President Quezon signed Act No. 1, dated January 11, 1936, the first National Defense Act, which included in Article 5, sections 30 and 31, the authorization of the academy: "There shall be established a military training school to be named the Philippine Military Academy, for the training of selected candidates for permanent commission in the Regular Force. The student body in the Military Academy shall be known as the Cadet Corps of the Army of the Philippines."[14]

The Tydings-McDuffie Act authorized not only a superintendent and commandant of cadets but also the dean of professors of the Corps of Cadets, a position that West Point would not have until 1945. The academy was established in the city of Baguio in central Luzon. The legislation limited the Corps of Cadets to 350, even allowing for foreign cadets to apply. The most important quality was that the Philippine Military Academy was to mirror the US Military Academy as MacArthur laid it out. The first graduating class was in 1940 with seventy-nine newly commissioned officers.[15]

The academy ceased to exist after the Japanese occupation in 1942 but was reestablished in 1946. Tragically, Colonel Martelino was captured by the Japanese in December 1944 and tortured for weeks for refusing to support the Japanese Imperial forces against the Americans. He was executed on January 7, 1945, only three days before MacArthur's forces landed on Luzon. His name appears on a bronze plaque at West Point attached to MacArthur Barracks that honors graduates, American and Filipino, who lost their lives fighting the Japanese in the Philippines during World War II.[16]

Once he was established in the Philippines, Major Eisenhower was promoted to lieutenant colonel on July 1, 1936, serving a chief of staff of the military advisory office to the Philippine Commonwealth. James Ord, assistant chief of staff, was promoted to lieutenant colonel on the same day. Another promotion occurred a few weeks later, which caused Eisenhower great indignation against his chief. Douglas MacArthur was officially commissioned a field marshal in the Philippine army on August 24, 1936, an honor that no other American ever held. This official promotion was a major disappointment for Eisenhower, who had counseled MacArthur not to accept. He endeavored "to persuade MacArthur to refuse the title since it was pompous and rather ridiculous to be the field marshal of a virtually nonexisting army."[17]

Over time Eisenhower became more and more disgruntled with his position and with MacArthur. In September 1936 MacArthur and Eisenhower had an episode that involved West Point itself. Maj. Gen. William Connor, then the academy's superintendent, requested through MacArthur that Eisenhower serve as commandant of cadets. MacArthur replied to Connor that Eisenhower was needed in the Philippines because his "duties [were] of the gravest importance. He could not adequately be replaced."[18] MacArthur did not inform Eisenhower of this request, and when Ike learned of the general's interference, he was furious. Eisenhower himself apparently had no desire to serve as commandant of cadets, saying, "I wanted no part of that. . . . The Commandant was merely [the chief trainer and disciplinarian of the Corps] and I had no ambition to get into that kind of business," despite MacArthur's meddling.[19]

Eisenhower's frustration deepened, and he grew restless, wanting to leave the Philippines and MacArthur. He complained of MacArthur, "He gets frantic in the face of difficulty, even if the difficulty is only an imaginary one and displays an exaggeration of glee when he believes things are shaping up to glorify his name, or increase his income." The interesting point about income is rather hypocritical of Ike because the main reason he remained in the Philippines was the extra income he received as an advisor—$980 monthly, but far less than MacArthur's monthly rate of $3,000.[20]

• • •

It was time to take Pinky MacArthur home to the United States and bury her next to Gen. Arthur MacArthur in Arlington, Virginia. President Quezon was making a trip to the United States to conduct business for the commonwealth, seeking audiences with President Roosevelt and members of Congress. Field Marshal MacArthur would accompany him, along with Capt. Bonner

Fellers, a November 1918 academy graduate who was the liaison between Quezon's office and MacArthur. Fellers would serve during the last half of World War II with MacArthur in the Pacific campaigns.[21] They departed by ship on January 25, the day before MacArthur's fifty-seventh birthday.

One of the benefits of this trip to the states was MacArthur's renewed association with Jean Faircloth. They were married on April 30, 1937, by a deputy municipal clerk in New York City. It was a simple affair, and he wore a civilian suit. After their wedding breakfast at the Hotel Astor, Douglas MacArthur drove his bride "home"—to West Point.[22]

Of all the possible locations and sites to take his new wife to visit, especially when in New York City, MacArthur chose his spiritual home: the US Military Academy. Jean recalled in an oral history interview years later: "We went to West Point. . . . We drove up there and the interesting thing, I've always thought was—that when we went through that gate, they came to attention even though the General was in civilian clothes."[23]

She recounted visiting the grounds and the famous plain, but "there wasn't a cadet . . . to be seen." Jean reported that no one engaged or talked to them at all, not even the superintendent, Maj. Gen. William D. Connor, who was aware of their visit.[24] It was obvious that Douglas was so proud of both his new bride and his spiritual home that he wanted to share them both on that special day. He made no record of the visit.

Jean Faircloth MacArthur was an amazing woman, not only because she married, loved, and tolerated such a dynamic and controversial man. She became the rock of his personal life, counselor, and cheerleader when he needed such. Douglas wrote of Jean and the marriage: "It was perhaps the smartest thing I have ever done. She had been my constant friend, sweetheart, and devoted support ever since."[25]

In the spring of 1937 Douglas and Jean returned to the Philippines, in a continuation of what would be a pivotal year for MacArthur. At this same time official correspondence arrived from the War Department announcing that Major General MacArthur would be reassigned to a stateside position, probably as an area corps commander again. This was a difficult dilemma for MacArthur. His mission to create a Philippine defense force remained before him. To MacArthur it was like Arthur his father, a task handed down from father to son. His options were two: return to the United States, or retire. On

December 31, 1937, Douglas MacArthur retired from the US Army after thirty-four and a half years of active service. He received a letter of gratitude from President Roosevelt:

Dear Douglas:

With great reluctance and deep regret I have approved your application for retirement effective December 31. Personally, as well as officially, I want to thank you for your outstanding services to your country. Your record in war and in peace is a brilliant chapter in American history.[26]

The new year of 1938 rolled in, and developing a professional military force in the Philippines continued. Then a shock came the end of January when Jimmy Ord died in an aircraft accident while flying to visit the Philippine Military Academy at Baguio. The aircraft's single-engine failed, and it crashed. Eisenhower was devastated, "I lost my right hand," he wrote in his journal. "He was my partner on a tough job, who furnished most of the inspiration needed to keep me plugging away. With him gone much of the zest has departed form a job that we always tackled as a team, never as two individuals."[27]

Such are friends and comrades in arms, and such are West Point classmates.

Later that year Eisenhower visited the United States due to medical issues with Mamie, his wife. There he lobbied for more funding and material from the War Department; he also fished about for his next assignment because it was time for Ike to return to the real army. Before his visit to America that summer, Eisenhower recommended a replacement for Jimmy Ord as assistant chief of staff: Maj. Richard K. Sutherland, a graduate of Yale who gained a commission in the Regular Army when America entered the war in 1917. He and Eisenhower had served together in the War Department when Sutherland was in the G-3 division in war plans and operations, and they became great friends. Little did Ike know in 1938 what role Sutherland would have in events in the year to come.[28]

Upon his return to the Philippines, Ike shared with his boss the latest news about the West Point football team and upcoming season. MacArthur had remained fanatic about Army team sports: listening to games on the radio when he could, writing to fellow graduates about the latest sports gossip, and advising coaches on teams and players. The coach for the 1938 season was newly hired William H. Wood, who replaced future superintendent Capt. Garrison Davidson, class of 1927, whose team had lost to Navy in 1936, 7 to 0, the year before. Overall, "Gar" Davison was a successful football coach while serving as an army officer.[29]

Wood had been a cadet for one year during MacArthur's superintendency. An All-American fullback who graduated in 1925 from the academy, Coach Wood had a successful record his first year, with eight wins and two losses. The supreme game of the football season was against the US Naval Academy's team, played on November 26, 1938, in Philadelphia—which ended in an Army victory, 14 to 7.[30] MacArthur encouraged Wood that after "an almost lifetime experience with West Point football has given me a perspective that along certain lines of general principle might be of some assistance." Coach Wood routinely corresponded with MacArthur during his three years as head coach.[31]

During the 1939 season MacArthur provided advice to the coach that sounded more like a tactical battle plan than a sporting event: "Too often both Notre Dame and the Navy have gone on the field against West Point knowing precisely where our attack would fall and being drilled to the last degree of minutia in defending therefrom."[32]

Wood's tenure was short because the 1939 and 1940 seasons were losing records, especially against Navy, the supreme game of the year. In fact, to West Point fans, then and now, a successful season is measured by the Army-Navy game alone.

Commenting on MacArthur's great love of the academy's sports and his life-time loyalty, D. Clayton James observed: "MacArthur's detailed messages of advice to West Point football coaches would continue regularly through the war years ahead, regardless of whether the general was in a bomb-racked tunnel on Corregidor or a mosquito-infested jungle hut in New Guinea."[33]

Replacing Wood in 1941 was Coach Earl "Red" Blaik, a cadet during MacArthur's superintendency, who was hired by superintendent Brig. Gen. Robert Eichelberger. Perhaps Eichelberger's greatest accomplishment during his short fourteen-month tenure was to select West Point's most winning coach ever. Eichelberger, a graduate of 1909, would later command a corps and then the Eighth Army under MacArthur in the Pacific war.[34]

• • •

The specter of war was obvious by 1939 following Germany's aggression against Poland in September and Japan's continuing brutal campaign in China. The threat to the Philippines and other American possessions in the Pacific was Japan, which made preparing for war somewhat easier. The planning and preparations that MacArthur's advisory group and the military department staff followed were focused solely on Japan's growing aggression. President Quezon discussed and schemed with his close advisors to negotiate an alliance with Japan through a neutrality pact that would hopefully safeguard the Philippines from invasion and conquest. Quezon and MacArthur disagreed on this course, which caused a serious division as time went on.[35]

MacArthur was absolutely convinced that Quezon was wrong, and that the Philippines was defensible: "The responsibility, however, for the defense of the Philippines, so long as it remains an integral part of the United States is federal and devolves upon the American Government."[36] It was a difficult situation for both men, who both loved the Philippines but approached the defense issues differently: one as a politician and the other as a soldier.

Eisenhower became tangled in an attempt by some influential Filipino politicians to have MacArthur either recalled or his position as military advisor terminated. According to Ike's life-long friend and ally, Capt. Lucius Clay, a graduate of the accelerated three-year class of June 1918, "When MacArthur found out about it"—that is, the politicians approaching Eisenhower—"from that moment he had no use for Eisenhower." Although Eisenhower had refused to support the attempt at removing MacArthur, the relationship was doomed between the two men. Clay claimed that the new assistant chief of staff, Major Sutherland, "deliberately tried to convince MacArthur that Eisenhower was trying to knife him in the back."[37] Clay would later attain full general rank, four stars, and serve as military governor of occupied Germany, where he orchestrated the Berlin Airlift of 1947–48.

Whether Sutherland poisoned MacArthur against Ike or it was a natural flow of events, the comradeship was then beyond redemption. Eisenhower received orders in May 1939 to report to Fort Lewis, Washington, in early 1940. Sutherland was the new chief by the end of 1938, and Eisenhower became operations officer, Ord's former position, though he was senior to Sutherland. Eisenhower raged with anger and pain in his journal: "After 8 years of working for him, writing every word he publishes, keeping his secrets, preventing him from making too much of an ass of himself, trying to advance his interests while keeping myself in the background, he suddenly turns on me."[38]

In September 1939, two important events occurred that would affect Eisenhower's life and career for the next six years. In Europe, World War II commenced with Adolf Hitler's aggression to fulfill his Nazi strategic dream of *Lebensraum* by invading and annexing western Poland. Eventually, Eisenhower would lead the Allied effort in western Europe to crush Hitler's Third Reich. More immediately, Gen. George Marshall was sworn in as army chief of staff, and Ike would become his great protégé. Eisenhower, Marshall, and MacArthur make an interesting American triumvirate of generals and commanders: MacArthur in the Pacific commanding the major land force theater, Eisenhower leading the colossal Allied forces in Africa and Europe, and Marshall supervising and supporting both. MacArthur was Marshall's peer in age and commissioned service, whereas Eisenhower's professional relationship with the new chief was so much better and smoother than his experience with MacArthur overall. Much has been written about the MacArthur–Eisenhower years: the great early successes, then the greater rupture and differences. John S. D. Eisenhower, son of Ike, West Point graduate of 1944, and historian, addressed his father's caustic, petty statements, and accounts found in his later writings about MacArthur in this way: "Ike was articulate, especially with the written word ... [but] I do not believe that everything he said in these pages represents his lifetime views of Douglas MacArthur."[39]

As for MacArthur, he wrote in Eisenhower's departing efficiency report: "Superior.... In time of war this officer should be promoted to general rank immediately."[40] He also wrote a personal note to Eisenhower: "I cannot tell you how deeply I regret your leaving. Your distinguished service has been characterized at all times by superior professional ability, unswerving loyalty and unselfish devotion to duty."[41] As much as MacArthur seemed gracious at

Eisenhower's departure, both men knew there had been a rift. Eisenhower's last words were: "I got out clean—and that's that."[42]

• • •

What became known later as the "Bataan Gang" began to form in 1939. It would become famous during World War II, composed of a half-dozen select officers who would serve MacArthur for the duration of the war. In his memoirs MacArthur never criticized or denigrated his staff and fellow officers, even when some richly deserved it. Before the Japanese invasion in 1941, his primary and personal staff that would serve with him throughout the war materialized. He described them in this way: "My staff was unsurpassed in excellence, and comprised such outstanding figures as Sutherland, chief of staff; Marshall in Supply [G-4]; Casey of the Engineers; Willoughby in Intelligence [G-2]; Aiken in Communications; Marquat in Artillery. No commander was ever better served."[43]

Of interest is the fact that only one officer of the original Philippine advisory staff was a graduate of West Point. Hugh Casey, called "Pat," was in the accelerated class of June 1918. The list above did not reflect all the staff officers in the Bataan Gang or in MacArthur's later, larger wartime staff.[44] Most of these officers were not graduates of West Point, but they were effective, hard-working, diligent, and sometimes judgmental and aloof, especially to outsiders who were not in the Philippines. The gang was obsessive in one area: they were totally loyal to the boss and would become a kingly court more than a staff for most of the war. Lt. Col. Richard Marshall, who graduated from the Virginia Military Institute in 1915, proved to be an exceptional staff officer as assistant chief of staff. MacArthur greatly admired his service, saying, "As a personality, Marshall was less aggressive, less dominant than Sutherland," using compromise and persuasion as his tools rather "than the brusque" manner of his chief.[45]

• • •

The war in Europe intensified when Germany invaded Denmark and Norway in the spring of 1940, followed by the low countries and France. Great Britain's expeditionary force had entered the fight and along with the French army was smashed by the German Wehrmacht's ground and air forces. The press the year before called the amazing and quick defeat of Poland "Blitzkrieg," or lighting war. The Great War had endured over more than four years of stalemate with millions of casualties on the Western Front. In 1940 Germany crushed both the British and French armies in six weeks. World War II was underway in earnest.

On the far side of the world, Field Marshal MacArthur was deeply concerned about events in Europe, but he was even more concerned by Japan's growing belligerence and aggression in China. Preparing the Philippine defenses for war was one major responsibility; the other was adhering to the War Department's war plans. This was War Plan Orange #5, or WPO-5, a new version of the previous plan. After the German victories in Europe in 1940, American war planners, both army and navy, initiated Rainbow 5. Basically, the plan theorized that American strategy in Europe was to support Britain and France and was offensive in nature, whereas the Pacific war was defensive. Of course, this plan infuriated MacArthur, whether Pacific-centric or not; he often decried the United States priority and emphasis on Europe. He was a devoted disciple of Asia and the Far East and had been since his 1904 tour with his father. Now, being responsible for the defense of the Philippines, he was perhaps overtly anxious for his stewardship.[46]

In the fall of 1940 MacArthur realized that his efforts to convince the War Department in Washington of the situation in the Philippines were not enough to allow preparations for an adequate defense. Though at times he spouted overly confident slogans and statements to the press, he also realized the truth. He was concerned the United States was providing more military aid to Great Britain and other Allies, rather than to the Philippines. He wrote a reporter, "The history of failure in war can almost be summed up in two words: Too Late." An example of what MacArthur experienced was supply of antiaircraft guns that were critical, receiving only four from a request for sixteen.[47]

The path to war increased in 1941 as events accelerated in Europe and the Far East. General Marshall as chief of staff considered recalling MacArthur to active duty.[48] Marshall advised President Roosevelt of the need to have the most experienced officer lead a new military command, the US Army Forces in the Far East. Marshall lamented the strategic situation in the far Pacific. "Both the Secretary and I are much concerned about the situation in the Far

Before the war, Gen. Jonathan Wainwright, left, wearing the campaign hat, and MacArthur, observing prewar maneuvers in October 1941. *Courtesy MacArthur Memorial.*

East," Marshall wrote to MacArthur on June 20, 1941, ironically the day before Nazi Germany invaded the Soviet Union. Marshall continued, "During one of our discussions about three months ago it was decided that your outstanding qualifications and vast experience in the Philippines makes you the logical selection for the Army commander in the Far East."[49]

On July 24 Japan sent occupation troops into French Indochina, controlled by the Vichy government in France, by then a puppet state of Nazi

Germany. This move for Japan was to secure much-needed oil, rubber, and other raw materials for its economy and growing war industry. Reacting quickly to Japan's aggression, President Roosevelt enacted trade restrictions and embargos on oil and raw material against Japan. These American actions were the final reasons and most significant events that drove Japan to war.[50]

In July 1941 MacArthur's beloved army reached out to him. On July 26, Field Marshal MacArthur was reinstated to active duty in the rank of major general, US Army, and the next day he was promoted to lieutenant general and assumed command of a new area command in the Far East. A message from Marshall read: "Effective this date there is hereby constituted a command designated as the United States Army Forces in the Far East. This command will include the Philippine Department, forces of the Commonwealth of the Philippines."[51]

MacArthur, the newly minted lieutenant general—a rank he never held before—could not rest on his laurels. He and his Bataan Gang had great tasks ahead of them not only militarily but also politically and diplomatically, because of the wavering Filipino leadership.[52]

MacArthur detested War Plan Orange and how it was merely a holding action mainly on the Bataan Peninsula to secure Manila Bay until reinforcements would arrive. MacArthur had fought against the plan and convinced the War Department to allow his army to make an active defense of all the islands of the entire archipelago, especially the beaches of Luzon at Lingayen Gulf. MacArthur, Marshall, and the War Department wrestled with this proposal all summer after MacArthur's recall and assumption of command. MacArthur's suggested changes to Plan Orange were approved that October, and the official notification was hand carried to Manila.[53]

By December 1941 MacArthur's command, though growing and recruiting more young Filipino men, was not very impressive. He commanded some 102,000 troops, most of whom were Filipinos in the new Philippine army. The foundation was 17,000 Americans of the Regular Army and 5,500 in the Philippine Scouts, which were part of the US Army. Stationed in the Philippines was the 4th US Marine Regiment, which was understrength by some 800 Marines. These were the units of the Far East Command in late 1941.[54] The Asiatic Fleet under Adm. Thomas C. Hart did not answer to MacArthur.

The Far East Air Forces on the day of the Japanese attack consisted of 35 new B-17 heavy bombers, some 40 older medium bombers, 175 fighter and pursuit aircraft, and 60 utility and support airframes, for a total of nearly 300 aircraft.[55]

The anxiety and fear of attack gripped many in the defense establishments, in the United States—especially Hawaii, then a territory—and for MacArthur himself in the Philippines. With the warnings from the War Department, MacArthur made a bold and personal decision that was against his nature regarding his alma mater. The annual Army-Navy football game, the greatest game of the year, was scheduled for what was a Sunday in the Philippines, November 21, 1941, to be played in Philadelphia. Going against his supreme love of academy sports, especially his devotion to football, he canceled the local radio broadcast and gatherings at the post and bases under his control. This was a dire decision for MacArthur, foretelling his belief that times were dangerous. Navy won the contest, 14 to 6, with the Navy goat parading about in victory.[56]

The Japanese strike at Pearl Harbor on December 7, 1941, was one of the most significant events in American and world history. At the exact time, but a day later because of the international date line, December 8, Japanese air forces attacked the Philippines. These two raids were part of several major separate operations and invasions by Japanese Imperial naval and army forces throughout the Pacific rim. By December 10, Japanese troops had struck Hong Kong, the Dutch East Indies, Malaya, and the Philippines. These attacks were enormous and complicated logistical operations involving hundreds of ships, thousands of aircraft, and hundreds of thousands of troops.[57]

In Manila, according to MacArthur, "Every disposition had been made, every man, gun, and plane was on the alert."[58]

CHAPTER 13

★ ★ ★ ★ ★

MORE WAR AND VICTORY

In 1904 the Russo-Japanese War commenced hostilities when the Japanese Imperial Navy attacked the Russian fleet at Port Arthur in Manchuria, three hours prior to Japanese officials delivering a declaration of war. The same situation occurred on December 7, 1941, against the United States. The declaration was to be delivered by the Japanese ambassadors by 1 p.m. Washington, DC, time, which was 8 a.m. in Hawaii, and 3 p.m. December 8 in the Philippines. The chronology of this day has become a major issue for historians of the two major American commands that the Japanese attacked that day. In fact, historian John Costello in his book *The Pacific War* devoted an entire chapter to the timelines of Hawaii, Washington, Tokyo, and Manila, play-by-play like for a football game. One can find any evidence one wants in the events of that day. The most repeated and supposedly egregious development in the Philippines that day was how most of MacArthur's bombers and three-fourths of the fighter aircraft were destroyed (seventeen B-17s were far away at Mindanao). The entire story is complicated and remains controversial.[1] Therefore, for this telling the story is short and summarized.

Gen. Douglas MacArthur was the senior officer and commander of all army personnel and units in the Philippines and was responsible for everything related to them. Subordinate commanders share the senior officer's responsibility to a degree to execute his orders and directives as given. Warnings and messages began about possible attack at 3:40 a.m. on December 8, when MacArthur received a call from Brig. Gen. Leonard Gerow, chief of war plans in the War Department. For the next ten hours, through early afternoon, chaos, miscommunication, personalities, and unrealistic expectations ruled among MacArthur, Sutherland, his air chief Maj. Gen. Lewis Brereton, and other staff members. Sutherland, then a brigadier general, as gatekeeper to MacArthur's time and presence, prevented direct and immediate communications; and then Brereton later blamed everyone but himself.[2] The recipe for this failure had plenty of cooks and enablers. The American bombers and most of the fighters did in fact launch by midmorning to conduct local coastal reconnaissance, hoping to engage enemy forces detected by radar. Brereton demanded an air strike against Japanese airfields in Formosa (Taiwan) in a desperate counterstrike. The problem was not just to attack bases on Formosa of the Japanese 5th Air Group, but also how to deal with Imperial Naval squadrons of the 11th Air Fleet that were carrier based. The Japanese attack occurred at midday after the B-17s and fighters had landed and were refueling at Clark and other airfields when they were destroyed.

There is no doubt that Sutherland was obstructive, protective, and difficult as chief of staff. Brereton was erratic and overanxious, making a half-dozen calls and a couple of visits to Sutherland and MacArthur that morning and wanting to launch his entire air fleet to attack Japanese airfields on Formosa. MacArthur's shortcomings, besides leadership failures, include his recollection and narration of the events that day decades later. He claimed not receiving certain messages even though official records prove some of these calls and messages reached him or his office. Sutherland's role as chief of staff was to minimize disruption, oversee and allocate functions, and at times be an usher to the boss—in peacetime. That morning, however, Sutherland acted more the prison warden, denying and challenging essential coordination and decisions. He saw MacArthur as a king and himself as chief courtier.[3]

Brereton was new to the command, not accustomed to MacArthur and Sutherland. Also, he was at a party, drinking until just an hour prior to the first warnings arrived. This was unacceptable and irresponsible, especially when over the past two weeks there was little doubt that Japan would soon strike.[4]

As much as some have criticized or defended certain players, Brereton's pleas to launch his aircraft to attack Formosa is interesting, because the Japanese bombers were grounded that morning due to fog. So how could American pilots find and bomb the airfields at Formosa with the fog covering the target area? MacArthur did authorize a wise move in midmorning to send a reconnaissance mission to Formosa to ascertain and photograph the latest targets and objectives before committing the entire air fleet into an unknown combat situation.[5] The best employment of these limited aviation assets that day were combat patrols and reconnaissance missions to safeguard air and ground forces. Why deploy and attack the enemy hundreds of miles away when there were so many unknowns on this first day of the war?

Another obvious factor that many have missed is that MacArthur had only thirty-five new B-17 bombers, consisting of four squadrons, and only a hundred fighters of various types and operational status. This was hardly a sufficient force to defend the Philippines. Even if none of the American airplanes were destroyed, the vast armada that the Japanese employed would have destroyed and neutralized MacArthur's air fleet eventually before reinforcements could come from Hawaii or Australia. These bombers were the first of several scheduled deliveries of aircraft to the Philippines. As mentioned, half the bombers had been deployed to airfields on the large island of Mindanao. MacArthur had ordered Brereton to ferry the remaining B-17s away from Luzon, but he failed to do this, and MacArthur failed to follow up or insist on this directive. This is indicative of the entire unraveling of leadership and command responsibility that day.[6]

In his memoirs MacArthur outlined the lack of sufficient aircraft, logistical support, and training, and the obsolete airframes available. This is all true, but he also took full responsibility for the disaster that occurred. He even defended Brereton: "A number of statements have been made criticizing General Brereton, the implication being that through neglect or faulty judgment he failed to take proper security measures, resulting in the destruction of part of his air force on the ground.... Such statements do an injustice to this officer."[7]

Yet, when MacArthur learned of the destruction of aircraft at Clark Field and Brereton's failure to deploy to Mindanao as ordered, he berated him on the phone, a rare moment for MacArthur. Another factor besides poor leadership and communications was fate and luck that governed affairs that day against the Far East Command.⁸ This simple narration may not answer all the questions and issues of this fiasco on the first day of the war in the Philippines and MacArthur's command.

• • •

A few minor Japanese landings began in isolated areas on December 10, 1941, before the major landing two weeks later at Lingayen Gulf on Luzon. Also, on that day, December 10, the first West Point graduate was killed in action after the official declaration of war. Captain Colin P. Kelly Jr., class of 1937, was the pilot of a lone B-17 bomber that bombed several Japanese warships but was shot down in the process. MacArthur later awarded Captain Kelly with both the Distinguished Service Cross and the Distinguished Flying Cross posthumously. A month later, another academy graduate, Lt. Alexander "Sandy" Nininger Jr., class of 1941, was killed on January 12, 1942, fighting on Bataan. He was the first American to be awarded the Medal of Honor in the war, though others later received the medal for bravery at Pearl Harbor and other actions.⁹

Beginning on December 22, Japanese soldiers from two divisions of the Fourteenth Army landed at Lingayen Gulf, and then advanced south across the central plains of Luzon. The commander, Lt. Gen. Masaharu Homma, a determined and experienced officer, led the first wave of some 43,000 men, who met and then overcame American resistance near Lingayen.¹⁰ Perhaps the greatest error and poor decision that General MacArthur made during the entire war occurred in the opening stages of the Japanese campaign to capture the Philippines.¹¹ MacArthur's concept to defend the entire island of Luzon at the beaches was a fatal mistake. He also relocated a horde of provisions, supplies, ammunition, and material forward to support several Philippine divisions consisting of mostly Filipino soldiers. The Japanese stormed ashore with tanks, vast resources, and complete air superiority, and with combat veterans throughout. Within days the situation was dire for the US Army Forces Far East (USAFFE). Having insufficient armored forces, no heavy artillery up front, and no airpower overhead, MacArthur made a critical decision, a reversal, on December 24. He had no choice but to withdraw his forces from the central plains to the Bataan Peninsula and then combine these units with more southern forces also enroute to Bataan. Thus, the mistake was rectified with the American/Filipino forces withdrawing successfully to Bataan during a two-week maneuver. As regrettable as was MacArthur's decision to defend the beaches, the greatest failure was the appalling loss of hundreds of thousands of tons of abandoned logistical resources. The situation was plagued by unforeseen changes that caused quick decisions that exacerbated the logistics problem on Bataan caused mainly due to the lack of and poor planning of vehicles and transportation. MacArthur was soon feeding not only 40,000 defenders as the original plan proposed, but now 40,000 more from the Lingayen beaches, including additionally 26,000 displaced civilians to support.[12]

Christmas week MacArthur made two major decisions that reflected the desperate state of affairs in the Philippines. Wisely, he declared Manila an open city on December 25 to save this majestic and historic city from the ravages of war. On Christmas Eve MacArthur and his staff began preparations to relocate the headquarters to Corregidor and, more specifically, inside Malinta Tunnel, an underground defensive structure. Constructed in 1940–41, the main tunnel was 1,400 feet long and 30 feet wide with 25 laterals, each some 400 feet long.[13]

MacArthur reorganized the ground forces that were converging on Bataan by the first week of January 1942. He established two main commands, I and II Corps, under Maj. Gen. Jonathan "Skinny" Wainwright and Brig. Gen. George Parker, respectively.[14] Well-designed defensive positions were manned, but they were without air support, adequate ammunition, supplies, and with only a few tanks on hand. By the end of 1941 Adm. Thomas Hart had removed almost all his naval forces from the Philippines, and Brereton had finally redeployed his remaining aircraft to other airfields farther away from Japanese attacks. Wishful thinking would not defeat the Japanese. The only hope that MacArthur, his 80,000 men, and the Philippines had was reinforcements that were on the way according to Plan Orange.

• • •

After the December 1941 attacks on US and Allied territories in the Pacific, the entire Allied effort reeled, losing ships, fortress cities, and armies to the Japanese in the first months of 1942. The US Navy had received a near-mortal blow at Pearl Harbor and would take time to recover. Some attempts were made to reinforce the surviving Pacific forces by assembling a mighty armed effort in Australia, which then also was under threat by the Japanese. The strategic situation forced the Allies to make a decision: Japan or Germany? Which had priority, the Pacific or Europe? President Roosevelt and Prime Minister Winston Churchill of Great Britain met in Washington and determined that Nazi Germany was the supreme enemy, inaugurating the "Germany First" strategic doctrine. On December 23, 1941, the same time MacArthur was deciding to withdraw to Bataan, the warlords of the two great Allies met and decided that "our view remains that Germany is still the prime enemy and her defeat is the key to victory.... The collapse of Italy and the defeat of Japan must follow."[15] The Pacific theater would go on the defensive, biding time for men and resources. MacArthur challenged and berated the "Germany First" strategic doctrine at the time and for the remainder of his life.[16] Yet, the Allies directed that the remaining Pacific outposts should fight and defend themselves with any means available.

The overall question was, could the Allies, or more specifically, the United States, reinforce the Philippines? Marshall related to MacArthur on December 27, "The president again personally directed the navy to make every effort to support you. You can rest assured [the] War Department will do all in its power in the Far East to completely dominate that region."[17] Roosevelt declared on December 29: "I give to the people of the Philippine Islands my solemn pledge that their freedom will be redeemed and their independence established and protected.... The United States Navy is following an intensive and well planned campaign against the Japanese forces which will result in positive assistance to the defense of the Philippines."[18]

Newly minted Brig. Gen. Dwight Eisenhower in the War Department stated on January 22, 1942, "We've got to go to Europe and fight, and we've got to quit wasting resources all over the world—and still worse—wasting time." This policy meant the War Plans Division now under Eisenhower recommended a limited effort to relieve the Philippines, and possibly did his best, knowing this effort was nearly impossible.[19] The many messages and updates from the division were vague and not forthright. After the war a reporter asked MacArthur if he believed the promises from Washington. His response: "By God, I did believe it.... I see now I may have deluded myself."[20]

• • •

On Corregidor MacArthur, his immediate staff, and hundreds of other American and Filipino service members, men and women, worked and quartered in Malinta Tunnel. The MacArthurs initially slept in a house on Topside near the old barracks and golf course, but soon moved to a smaller bungalow on Bottomside near the tunnel entrance due to air raids and bombardments. Soon a ballad or ditty set to "The Battle Hymn of the Republic" circulated among the soldiers on Bataan. It gave General MacArthur a new sobriquet that he would never escape.

DUGOUT DOUG

Dugout Doug MacArthur lies shaking on the Rock
Safe from all the bombers and from the sudden shock
Dugout Doug is eating of the best food on Bataan
    And his troops go starving on.
    (Chorus)
    Dugout Doug, come out from hiding
    Dugout Doug, come out from hiding
    Send to Franklin the glad tidings
    That his troops go starving on!

Of course, this ditty was not at all accurate, fair, or true, but soldiers in the midst of miserable combat were very creative and facile about the truth. There are numerous accounts of MacArthur leaving the tunnel during Japanese air raids to observe and encourage the anti-aircraft gunners.

On December 29, the Japanese unleashed an intensive bombardment on Corregidor where one observer recorded, "He stayed through the bombing, 'protected' only by a thick hedge around the yard. Once a direct hit went through the house, landing in his bedroom and shattering the whole building." Another officer remembered, the bombings "didn't faze him at all."[21] After another attack President Quezon criticized MacArthur for risking his life, to which he replied, "The Japanese haven't yet made the bomb with my name on it."[22] In a more serious vein, MacArthur recorded, "In war, to be effective it must take the form of a fraternity of danger welded between a commander and his troops by the common denominator of sharing the risk of sudden death."[23] MacArthur made only one visit to Bataan in January 1942 to observe and provide guidance. By then the major combat forces were defending the peninsula adequately. The Japanese under General Homma had been stopped, but soon reinforcements and more combat power would prove decisive against the stubborn American defense. In contrast, Allied strongholds and entire nations and colonies had already fallen to the Japanese. British possessions such as Hong Kong, Burma, Singapore, and the Dutch East Indies comprising also western New Guinea were all overrun by the end of February. But the Philippines held out and soon became a rallying cry for the Allies against Japanese aggression.[24] Defeat and surrender were inevitable without reinforcements and support.

In late February 1942, General Marshall recommended that MacArthur escape to Australia to command the forces assembling there. He refused. For a couple of weeks, the drama played out, and finally, President Roosevelt ordered MacArthur to leave.[25] MacArthur had no choice. "For three weeks I postponed my leaving until Marshall responded with the information that the situation in Australia called for my early arrival."[26] MacArthur would not escape by submarine but by PT Boat, Torpedo Patrol, a small craft made of plywood with no armor for protection, but which was fast and maneuverable. Eventually the Bataan Gang of Sutherland, Marshall, Huff, Hughes, and Willoughby and others, totaling eighteen people excluding the MacArthurs, departed on March 11, 1942. That evening they boarded four rather motley PT boats commanded by Lt. John Bulkeley, US Navy, who would receive the Medal of Honor for overall actions in the Philippines.

As MacArthur prepared to board PT-41, his thoughts turned to General Wainwright and their days at West Point together. In his memoirs he recorded, "He had been a Plebe at West Point when I was a first classman and later became First Captain of the Class of 1906." He told Wainwright earlier, "Jim, hold on till I come back for you." Regrettably he knew time had run out for them; it was "too late for the battling men in the foxholes of Bataan."[27]

On March 12, 1942, the day after MacArthur's departure, Col. Paul Bunker, MacArthur's classmate and subordinate, recorded that "General [George F.] Moore called a conference of regimental commanders at 11:00 and told us that MacArthur left last night for Australia, with most of his staff" and his family. Always loyal to his friend, Bunker declared, "Now to convince our men that he had not deserted. . . . It would be bad for our men's morale if they put the wrong interpretation on his leaving."[28] As the months passed in the Philippines and the Japanese gained the upper hand, Bunker never lost faith in friend Douglas. "If anyone can help us it is MacArthur. He is our only chance."[29]

Paul Bunker became a prisoner when General Wainwright surrendered Corregidor on May 5, 1942. He lowered the flag flying over Corregidor and tore a section away and burned the rest. During his captivity Bunker hid and preserved the part of the flag that he had sewn into his uniform. He gave part of it to a fellow officer before his death by starvation on March 16, 1943, the anniversary date of West Point's founding in 1802. He received the Distinguished Service Medal in 1944 posthumously, and his remains were interred in West Point Cemetery in 1948.[30]

The tragic reality of the American surrender of first Bataan, and then Corregidor, was the aftermath. The ignominious death march of Bataan survivors, where thousands died or were executed by the Japanese, remains a memorial of cruelty even today.[31] The final capitulation of General Wainwright's entire Philippines command at Corregidor occurred on May 9, 1942, and was a great blow to the United States and the Filipino people. To Douglas MacArthur, who was safe in Australia, leaving his soldiers in the midst of a battle galled him deeply, beyond understanding. What was equally worse was the surrender, an event that haunted him for years: "The bitter memories and heartaches will never leave me."[32]

• • •

When MacArthur arrived in Australia three things awaited him: a hearty welcome as a hero from the Australian people and its leaders; no real armed force as promised; and the Medal of Honor. The most extraordinary moment in MacArthur's arrival was a promise he made as he declared, "The President of the United States ordered me to break through the Japanese lines and proceed from Corregidor to Australia. . . . I came through and I shall return."[33]

In Canberra, the Australian capital, a special dinner was hosted by Prime Minister John Curtin at the Government House to honor MacArthur. During the event the American ambassador to Australia, Nelson T. Johnson, announced that President Roosevelt had awarded the Medal of Honor to Gen. Douglas MacArthur.[34] At age sixty-two he received the highest decoration that the United States can bestow on a soldier. It was the same that his father Arthur received in 1890 for his actions as an eighteen-year-old lieutenant in 1863. This was the third time he had been recommended for the medal: first in 1914 for gallantry during the American intervention at Vera Cruz; and then in 1918 during World War I, but downgraded by General Pershing.

The story of how Douglas MacArthur received this decoration is long and complicated and has been reviewed by scholars and others. There is no denying the fact that the reason that he received the award was not based on his personal courage "above and beyond the call of duty" but, as his citation reads, because he "displayed conspicuous leadership in preparing the Philippine Islands to resist conquest." The impetus behind the awarding was General Marshall, army chief of staff, "to offset any propaganda by the enemy directed against [MacArthur's] leaving his command and proceeding to Australia."[35]

The theme of the Medal of Honor and academy graduates continued with General Jonathan Wainwright. In June 1942 General Marshall had also nominated Wainwright for the decoration for his valiant leadership in Bataan and Corregidor. Succinctly, Marshall had already written a citation and forwarded it to MacArthur for his endorsement. MacArthur refused to do so based on the fact that Wainwright had already been awarded the Distinguished Service Cross.[36]

There is no doubt that this action was hypocritical for MacArthur, and this was another low point in his life and career. Later, in 1945 after Wainwright's release from a prisoner of war camp, Marshall again resurrected this action, and this time MacArthur offered no resistance.[37] MacArthur and Wainwright were two of nine academy graduates who received the Medal of Honor during World War II.

As noted, the second thing that awaited MacArthur in Australia was a barely existent army. American forces, mostly army, were no more than 25,000 men and 250 aircraft. The majority of these were logistical and quartermaster soldiers, many engineers, and air ground crews. There were parts of two divisions, the 32nd and 41st, both National Guard infantry divisions totaling 16,900 men, with more enroute to Australia. These were untrained and poorly equipped units with officers and leaders from their home states, many of whom would not remain in command. The US Army Air Forces were not much better off because the aircraft were older models and needed repairs or were newer but dismantled, yet to be assembled.[38] Eventually, Maj. Gen. George Kenney assumed command of the air forces under MacArthur. The two leaders would work admirably together.

The last consideration was how popular MacArthur had become—an instant hero. Upon his arrival in Australia, he was engulfed by throngs of people. The same was true at home as his name and service gripped Americans. His popularity was tied to his academy connections. His former roommate Rev. Arthur Hyde in April 1942 wrote from New York City: "I had a letter from West Point a couple of months ago saying the Academy is being inundated with inquiries about you in your cadet days, and asking me as your first room mate for any recollections of incidents, serious or humorous, that I might be able to furnish."[39] Former roommate Col. George Cocheu wrote him on May 7, 1942, from the War Department in Washington, "In the past few months, I have been literally besieged by writers of all kinds regarding information on you."[40]

Another connection to West Point materialized in three separate nations to honor General MacArthur. On June 13, 1942, the United States Congress, the Parliament of Australia, and the Philippine government in exile proclaimed MacArthur Day, celebrating forty-three years to the day that young Douglas MacArthur took the oath as a cadet on the plain at West Point in 1899. There were parades, fireworks, and festivities, especially in New York City and Milwaukee. The joint resolution in Congress was sponsored by Wisconsin senator Robert M. LaFollete Jr., connecting with MacArthur's ancestral home.[41]

MacArthur took a moment to further his connection and admiration with West Point. He remembered the great service and sacrifice that fellow graduates had devoted who served in the Philippines under his command. He wrote a simple message to Maj. Gen. Francis B. Wilby, the superintendent for most of the war period. Wilby had graduated with the class of 1905, so he and MacArthur knew each other as cadets. In a message dated May 30, 1942, from Australia, MacArthur expressed his gratitude for the members of the Long Gray Line who served in the Philippines. He wrote: "My grateful thanks to you all. The graduates of West Point who served under me in the Philippine campaign were worthy of its heroic past. The United States Military Academy always presses towards the front when danger threatens."[42]

An honor came to Douglas MacArthur through George Cocheu in the fall of 1943. Cocheu wrote, "As you perhaps know the people of Knoxville [Tennessee] on the 15th [October] presented to the University of Tennessee a replica of the bust of you already at the Military Academy." He explained that Brig. Gen. Bonner Fellers, class of 1916, had orchestrated the gift and that Cocheu represented MacArthur. "Taking a leaf out of your speech at our 30th reunion at West Point," Cocheu explained, "the War Department has decided that I am too old to be of any further use." Cocheu soon retired at age sixty-five, being two years older than Douglas.[43]

• • •

The war and relieving the Philippines were foremost on MacArthur's mind. The promise he made using the first person "I shall return," though ridiculed then and now, was his personal pledge, a matter of honor. Liberating the Philippines became an obsession with him. MacArthur's anger about the fall of the Philippines never left him. A year later he recalled his pain to Gen. Bonner Fellers: "I could have held Bataan if I had not been so completely deserted.... I am sick at heart at the mistakes and lost opportunities that are so prevalent."[44] This attitude both haunted and inspired him. He was determined on two main points: maintain some type of command and control in the Pacific, and keep his promise to liberate the Philippines. During these dark days in Australia as his army in the Philippines slid toward eventual defeat and surrender, he turned back to former and pleasant memories. In a letter to classmate George Cocheu, he reminisced about their academy days, "In these days of stress my thoughts turn back more and more often to the boys I grew up with and so dearly loved."[45]

On March 30, 1942, Marshal and Adm. Ernest King, the newly appointed chief of naval operations, after major disagreements and the age-old interservice rivalry, divided the Pacific and organized it into operational areas. This command structure was more than an American issue; the organization also involved the United Kingdom, Australia, New Zealand, and what remained of the Dutch armed forces. Adm. Chester Nimitz, commanding the Pacific Fleet from Hawaii, would be commander-in-chief of the Pacific Ocean Areas (POA), basically the entire Pacific Ocean and its dozens of island chains and thousands of lesser isles. MacArthur would command the Southwest Pacific Area

(SWPA), which included major areas of seas along with the huge land masses of Australia, New Guinea, all of the Dutch East Indies, Malaysia, and—lastly—the Philippines archipelago.[46]

These were joint commands not only of land, sea, and air forces but also Allied or coalition forces. MacArthur received great support from Australian Prime Minister Curtin, who knew full-well that MacArthur and the Americans were the saviors of his continent nation. "Without any inhibitions of any kind, I make it quite clear that Australia looks to America, free of any pangs as to our traditional links or kinship with the United Kingdom." This statement was both bold and true, and Australians under MacArthur's command would be the first Allied troops to stop the Japanese onslaught.[47] Technically and fundamentally, he was right, but the dynamics of vast ocean areas and huge land masses that required both major land and naval forces determined the arrangement. But MacArthur had another idea. "I decided to abandon the plan completely, to move the thousand miles forward into eastern Papua, and stop the Japanese on the rough mountains of the Owen Stanley Range of New Guinea—to make the fight for Australia beyond its own borders."[48]

• • •

The first year of the Allied effort in the Southwest Pacific Area would have achieved little without the Australians. It was months before the full complement of the 32nd and 41st Infantry Divisions reached Australia and were combat ready. MacArthur's air units took months to arrive, organize, and then conduct operations. The US Navy stopped a Japanese carrier force at Coral Sea in May, whose intent was to capture Port Moresby in southern New Guinea. Later the great and decisive battle of Midway in June turned the tide, at least in the naval war.[49]

In the meantime, only small and partially equipped Australian militia battalions were in New Guinea when eighteen thousand Japanese landed in July 1942 on the north coast at Gona. The Japanese objective was Port Moresby on the southern coast, which was across the steep and forbidding Owen Stanley Range rising to twelve thousand feet above the tropical jungles. The only way south over these knife-edge peaks was the Kokoda trail, whose summit was at eight thousand feet. More a foot path than a road, the Kokoda was a narrow, winding track that could not support vehicles. Over the next few months, the

Australians defended Port Moresby and then drove the Japanese back through the hellish jungles and across the high ridges. Australians fought malaria and dysentery as well as the Japanese, losing hundreds of men. Allied airpower and surface forces were also able to defend Milne Bay at the far eastern tip of New Guinea. These two ports, Milne Bay and Port Moresby, were crucial to both sides, but the Australians with some American assistance defeated the Japanese attacks.[50]

Serving under MacArthur was Gen. Sir Thomas Blamey, a hardened and crusty Aussie who was Allied ground commander, and another Australian, Vice Adm. Herbert Leary, who commanded the Allied naval forces. These were token positions as far as MacArthur was concerned because he would not allow any American forces to serve under Blamey's control, nor did he have any foreign officers serve on his primary and direct staff.[51] The Bataan Gang was in charge.

One of MacArthur's greatest battles was not against the Japanese but with the US Navy. He went through several naval component commanders until he finally gained the services of Adm. Thomas C. Kinkaid, who commanded the Seventh Fleet. Kinkaid, an experienced officer and 1908 graduate of the Naval Academy, worked very well with MacArthur from November 1943 on. Then there was Adm. Daniel Barbey, the amphibious assault commander, a 1912 Naval Academy graduate, who along with Kinkaid served admirably with MacArthur for the remainder of the war. Gen. George Kenney soon took command of the US Fifth Air Force and became one of MacArthur's most trusted commanders and friends.[52]

MacArthur's first major offensive was to capture two Japanese strongholds on the north coast of New Guinea: Gona and Buna. He faced considerable problems, one of which was leadership. The commander of the 32nd Infantry Division was Maj. Gen. Edwin Forest Harding, a 1909 graduate of West Point with George S. Patton. Harding was not aggressive enough for MacArthur, who tried to motivate Harding on several occasions; it soon became apparent that Harding was not up to the task. In early November 1942 MacArthur relocated his headquarters to Port Moresby to command more effectively. He now demanded more progress and turned to his senior commander for results.[53]

One of the most important subordinates who served under MacArthur in the Pacific war arrived in the theater of operations in late September. Maj. Gen. Robert L. Eichelberger was soon promoted to lieutenant general solely on MacArthur's recommendation. General Eichelberger served under MacArthur the remainder of the war. It is a rare situation where a former superintendent of the US Military Academy served under another former superintendent in combat. Their relationship at first was amicable and professional, but over the next several years Eichelberger came to detest MacArthur, though the latter promoted Eichelberger, awarded him, and made him commander of a field army.[54]

Eichelberger graduated from the academy in 1909 with some of the great combat commanders of World War II, such as Patton, Jacob L. Devers, and William H. Simpson. As a young officer he became a temporary lieutenant colonel during World War I and served in the Siberia expedition fighting the Bolshevik insurgents, for which he was awarded the Distinguished Service Cross for gallantry.[55] Eichelberger's superintendency was not long, being appointed in November 1940 along with his second star. His short time at West Point was unremarkable except for one major accomplishment that would involve MacArthur for decades to come. He hired Earl H. "Red" Blaik, who had been a cadet during MacArthur's superintendency, as football coach. Blaik, who eventually became the most successful football coach in West Point history, and MacArthur would soon commence a wartime correspondence trading game highlights, football gossip, and game films. After the attack on Pearl Harbor, Eichelberger demanded to be transferred to a combat command, leaving the academy after only fifteen months.[56]

The war years were beneficial to the US Military Academy in many ways. Some of the best and brightest young men clamored to serve and fight, and West Point (along with the Naval Academy) was the best way to obtain a commission and the leadership traits for combat. In early 1942 President Roosevelt, Congress, and the War Department did "not like to have West Point become subject to the criticism of being a place of refuge, where boys can go for four years and not be shot at." Later that year Roosevelt authorized the curriculum to change from four years to three years to provide more officers for the war effort. Similar to as in the Great War but not as drastic, two classes graduated early in 1943, the January and June classes.[57]

Undoubtedly, the athletic program at West Point benefited from the war, during which some of the great athletes and teams of all time played. The football squad under Blaik ranked number one in the nation in 1944 (through 1947 as well); Army defeated Navy in 1944 with the assistance of two of the greatest players in college history: Felix "Doc" Blanchard and Glenn Davis, who were consecutive Heisman Trophy winners. These two legends were running backs, "Mr. Inside and Mr. Outside." Doc Blanchard was Mr. Inside, graduating in 1945; Glenn Davis, Mr. Outside, graduated in 1946, coinciding with the years they each received the Heisman Trophy.[58]

On January 1, 1945, in a lengthy letter to MacArthur, Red Blaik, now a colonel in the organized reserves, wrote about the "Game of the Century." The Army and Navy teams were ranked nationally #1 and #2 respectively. They faced off on December 2, 1944, just as American troops under MacArthur were fighting on Leyte and others were preparing for the invasion of Luzon in the Philippines. The Army team defeated the Navy squad 23–7 in Baltimore. Blaik wrote, "Your congratulatory cable to the West Point team sent the spirit of the Corps of Cadets to an all time high." Obviously, the great fan of Army football had lost no time to express his regards to the coach in New York. Blaik, the proud and sometimes smug coach, wrote, "After the [19]42 Navy game I recall having written you that our squad lacked the will to win and that it was reflected by a spirit of lassitude in the Corps. The Corps this year was belligerent, and it went out to beat the Navy." The corps, of course, was more than just the football team; it was the entire student body. Blaik added that he would send the general the Notre Dame and Navy game films to watch.[59] Blaik and MacArthur would remain pen-pals for decades.

• • •

General Eichelberger soon saw that General Harding's leadership of the 32nd Infantry Division was appalling; he faced the personal dilemma of dismissing his subordinate, a tough situation for any commander, especially a friend and classmate.[60] The Australians took Gona in early December 1942, and American troops under Eichelberger captured Buna on January 2, 1943. General Harding was not the only casualty of MacArthur's first victory; more than two thousand Americans were killed and wounded. This was probably MacArthur's deadliest campaign per capita of troops employed.[61] The battle

Observing the casualties of war, the part of his profession MacArthur detested. *Courtesy MacArthur Memorial.*

for Buna inspired MacArthur to skip strongly held enemy positions and leapfrog or skip past them to less defended locations and thus isolate these hard-targets.

After the costly victories at Gona and Buna, MacArthur focused more attention on Rabaul, the major Japanese base on the far eastern tip of the island of New Britain. Through 1943 MacArthur's main objectives and battlegrounds were in the eastern half of New Guinea, still controlled by the enemy, and several larger islands such as New Britain and the Admiralty Islands. Rabaul, the key Japanese hub, was a base for hundreds of aircraft, nearly 77,000 army soldiers, and 21,000 naval personnel and dozens of ships that came and went.[62] Initially the Allied effort was directed at attacking and capturing Rabaul, but then the strategy shifted with Operation Cartwheel: the Allied objective became to isolate the Japanese forces there as on other islands, and then liberate all of New Guinea.[63]

Beginning in June 1943 MacArthur's campaign in New Guinea advanced across two thousand miles in eight months from Lae and the Huon Gulf westward. To conduct Cartwheel and keep it a purely American effort, MacArthur created the Sixth US Army under Lt. Gen. Walter Krueger. A year younger than MacArthur, Krueger had enlisted in 1898 during the Spanish-American War and gained a direct commission in 1901, two years ahead of MacArthur. Although not having combat service, Kreuger was one of the most respected officers in the army. MacArthur devised the "Alamo Force," which was basically the Sixth Army under Kreuger as the principal fighting unit.[64] The Alamo Force avoided strong enemy positions and bases at Wewak and Hansa Bay by leap-frogging hundreds of miles to assault Hollandia. This was a brilliant operational move. Overall, Cartwheel netted Japanese losses of some 2,900 aircraft, fifty warships, and some 100,000 men.[65] Major operations continued in New Guinea through the summer of 1944 with landings at Aitape and Hollandia on April 22, and Wakde Island on May 18; the US Navy's Third Fleet took the remaining islands in the Solomons, including Bougainville.[66]

Now came the great strategic decision that MacArthur had waited for: to return to the Philippines. In July 1944 President Roosevelt called for a conference in Pearl Harbor to outline the final approach and invasion of mainland Japan. Admirals Nimitz and William D. Leahy attended with FDR as well as MacArthur, where they discussed the strategic options to defeat Japan. The first option was the central approach across the ocean to Formosa (Taiwan) that the navy planners and especially Adm. Ernest King, chief of naval operations, adamantly recommended. MacArthur argued that his option was to

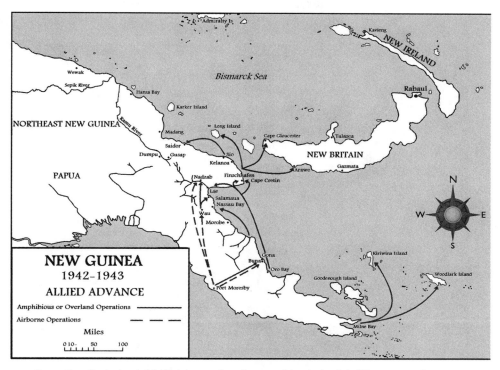

Operation Cartwheel, 1943-44, was the climax to MacArthur's brilliant campaign to isolate Rabaul. MacArthur's forces of the Southwest Pacific Area advanced along the northern coast of New Guinea. *Map created by Hyrum H. Fleek.*

ignore Formosa and liberate the Philippines. He pointed out that some 300,000 Japanese and hundreds of aircraft were based there and would threaten American lines of communications and supply. Nimitz and others were moved by MacArthur's manner and points, but Roosevelt had briefings in Washington from the Joint Chiefs of Staff, who favored the central advance. MacArthur in a last-ditch attempt asked for a few minutes with FDR in private. He declared to his old boss that King's plan involving Formosa was both foolish and strategically unsound and reminded Roosevelt that it was an election year. Besides, he added, "the nation will never forgive you if you approve this plan which leaves 17 million," people subject to Japanese brutality. "It would ruin you." This was a bold move by MacArthur, but Roosevelt took the bait.[67] MacArthur's recollection was much simpler and modest about the

In July 1944 at Pearl Harbor, President Franklin Roosevelt (far right) and Adm. Chester Nimitz (center) watch as MacArthur briefs them on his plan to invade the Philippines rather than the navy plan to bypass them for Formosa (Taiwan). MacArthur's option was accepted, which led to the invasion of Leyte Island in October 1944. *Courtesy MacArthur Memorial.*

conference decision: "Admiral Leahy seemed to support what I said, and the President accepted my recommendations and approved the Philippine plan."[68]

• • •

By September 1944, the Joint Chiefs had approved the invasion of the Philippines at Leyte for October 20. When the great day came, MacArthur would go ashore with the troops, as he did at Los Negros in February 1944 and during several other landings. The famous photographic image of Douglas MacArthur wading ashore from a landing craft at Leyte is now iconic. He strode up Red Beach at 2:30 p.m., met some soldiers and liberated Filipinos, and said, "I have returned." He then made his way with his staff following behind to a command post of the 24th Infantry Division and there met Maj. Gen. Frederick A. Irving. There was small arms fire nearby as General Irving gave MacArthur a tactical

As in World War I, MacArthur often visited the front while it was still under enemy fire. Meeting soldiers in Los Negros in 1944. *Courtesy MacArthur Memorial.*

battle update: the division had fifteen men killed in action and thirty wounded by that time. Irving's men had advanced about three hundred yards from the beach. They were now facing concrete gun emplacements and deadly machine guns. After a short time, MacArthur and his party retired to the beach.[69]

Fred Irving just two years earlier was the commandant of cadets at West Point under Superintendent Eichelberger. Irving had led the 24th Infantry Division in the battle at Hollandia earlier in April, and he now served under

MacArthur and staff come ashore at Leyte hours after the initial landings on October 20, 1944. *Courtesy MacArthur Memorial.*

Eichelberger's newly formed Eighth Army that would assume control of the Leyte operation in December 1944. Seven years later, in 1951, General Irving would become academy superintendent and deal with a major cheating scandal centered on Blaik's football team. Thus, there were two former, and one future, superintendents in the invasion of Leyte.[70]

MacArthur, back at the beach during a gentle rain, took a radio microphone and made history again. He announced to the world that his promise had been fulfilled. "People of the Philippines: I have returned. By the grace of Almighty God, our forces stand again on Philippine soil." He then referred to President Sergio Osmena at his side, the new president of the Commonwealth of the Philippines. And then he made a battle cry: "Rally to me. Let the indomitable spirit of Bataan and Corregidor lead on. . . . Rise and strike. Strike at every favorable opportunity. For your homes and hearths, strike! For future generations of your sons and daughters, strike! In the name of your sacred dead, strike! Let no heart be faint. Let every arm be steeled. The guidance of Divine God points the way. Follow in His name to the Holy Grail of righteous victory."[71]

Some eight thousand miles away in Washington, DC, and three months later, former roommate George Cocheu, wrote, "You gave your word that you would return to the Philippines. There was only one answer—you would."[72] Three days after MacArthur's rally call, one of the greatest sea battles in history occurred, if not the largest. From October 23 to 25, some 180,000 seamen on 285 warships and hundreds of aircraft were engaged in a battle that raged day and night and spelled the effective end of the Japanese Imperial Navy's offensive might.[73]

As the campaign on Leyte continued, MacArthur received word that he had been promoted by an act of Congress to the new rank of General of the Army with five stars. His date of rank was December 18, 1944, two days behind George Marshall, and days ahead of Eisenhower and of Henry "Hap" Arnold of the US Army Air Forces.[74] Eventually, five officers in the US Army would wear the rank; all but one, Marshall, were West Point graduates.

Next came Luzon.

The American troops landed at Lingayen Bay on January 9, 1945, with other landings south near Manila Bay and at other locations. The Japanese had some 260,000 troops on Luzon alone. They were poorly supplied, with little armor and artillery, and virtually no air force. Even so, Allied progress seemed to bog down, and MacArthur constantly pressured General Krueger to increase the speed of the advance. Krueger was a cautious man, but eventually he organized a "flying column" led by Brig. Gen. William Chase's cavalry brigade of the 1st Cavalry Division to hasten to Manila and take the city. An armored spearhead reached Manila on February 3, and MacArthur planned to have a victory celebration for the next day. However, the Japanese defenders had another idea. Their resistance in the city provided stubborn and deadly. Manila was the only urban combat for the American forces in the Pacific. It would take a month to defeat the Japanese defenders, which reduced Manila to rubble by the end of February 1945. A perilous combined airborne and amphibious operation on Corregidor began on February 16 and within days secured the former American bastion.[75] The fighting on Luzon would continue until Japan ceased fighting in August.

MacArthur experienced the waste and brutality of war in a personal way that most soldiers did not see. As American forces fought street by street through Manila, he was there with the troops. "I was anxious to rescue as much

American airborne troops land on Noemfoor Island, a small spit of land near New Guinea. On July 2, 1944, members of the 503rd Parachute Infantry Regiment were dropped from 400 feet above ground level, causing more injuries than their actual battle wounds. *Courtesy MacArthur Memorial.*

as I could of my home atop the Manila Hotel, [and so I] accompanied a leading patrol of the division," he recalled. Enemy fire from the hotel pinned the patrol down, then "suddenly, the penthouse blazed into flame." A Japanese colonel detonated an explosive charge, killing himself and destroying the penthouse. "I watched, with indescribable feelings, the destruction of my fine military library, my souvenirs, my personal belongings of a lifetime." This moment was truly devastating.[76]

• • •

MacArthur was planning and preparing for the largest amphibious assault in history, the invasion of Japan called Operation Downfall, when Brig. Gen. Thomas Farrell arrived from the United States with a sensitive and top secret briefing for MacArthur. Farrell, who taught at West Point in the mid-1920s,

Mrs. Jean Faircloth MacArthur, Douglas's second wife, and the general, during the war. Note the B-17 Flying Fortress bomber nose-art, "Bataan."
Courtesy MacArthur Memorial.

informed MacArthur in nontechnical terms about the atomic bombs and their ability to destroy a city, vast military resources, and perhaps killing tens of thousands of people.[77]

Estimates are not exact, but some 135,000 Japanese died from the two atomic bombs that destroyed Hiroshima and Nagasaki.[78] In bombings with conventional ordnance by hundreds of B-29 bombers, nearly 100,000 Japanese died in firebomb attacks weeks earlier in March 1945. As for MacArthur, the new devastating weapons were abhorrent and probably immoral. He felt that the atomic bombs "were completely unnecessary from a military point of view."[79] But this is not true. Nearly all military leaders at the time and most historians since have held that the Japanese would have never surrendered short of an all-out invasion, where hundreds of thousands of their Allies would have been killed, and perhaps millions of Japanese, before government leaders would sue for peace.[80] As the newly appointed Supreme Commander Allied Powers (SCAP) in the Pacific as of August 15, MacArthur would preside over the surrender of Japan and the end of World War II.[81]

CHAPTER 14

★ ★ ★ ★ ★

AMERICAN SHOGUN

"Of all the amazing deeds of bravery of the war," proclaimed British Prime Minister Winston Churchill, "I regard MacArthur's personal landing at Atsugi [airport] as the greatest of the lot." Hyperbole or not, Churchill was an outstanding commentator on such deeds. Even though advanced parties of American engineers and signalmen had arrived at Atsugi on August 27, followed by elements of the 11th Airborne Division flown in the next two days, there was no complete assurance as to how the thousands of armed Japanese soldiers would act on August 30, when General MacArthur's unarmed party landed at 2 p.m. Atsugi airfield had been a base for kamikaze pilot indoctrination and training; there were still thousands of Japanese soldiers on hand. Hundreds of armed soldiers lined the road that MacArthur's convoy passed by, and as the procession approached, they turned their backs on the vehicles, a sign of Japanese respect and obeisance. The possibility of a sniper or an errant soldier who could have killed the general was real. It was indeed a brave act.[1]

MacArthur outlined some critical aspects regarding the pivotal month of August 1945 for the Japanese people, their armed forces, and the role of the emperor in the surrender. The two atomic bombs that were detonated above Hiroshima and Nagasaki on August 6 and 9 were critical to the surrender process, convincing the Japanese government, especially the emperor, that resistance was hopeless and to seek peace. The Allies were adamant that Japan

MacArthur arriving at Atsugi airfield in Japan on August 30, 1945. Unarmed and without a proper escort, the general's party was met by hundreds of armed Japanese soldiers. British Prime Minister Winston Churchill proclaimed this as an act of courage during the war. *Courtesy MacArthur Memorial.*

surrender unconditionally, restating so at the Potsdam Conference held in Germany in late July.

By mid-August, the Soviets had finally declared war on Japan and began marching troops into Manchuria, and the government in Tokyo had accepted the Potsdam demand of unconditional surrender and even endured an armed military coup by fanatics who tried to stop a public radio announcement of surrender by Emperor Hirohito to the Japanese people scheduled for August 14.²

For MacArthur, the welcome news of the surrender was a great and joyful moment, despite all the time, effort, and planning for the great invasion. The US Army was marshaling hundreds of thousands of troops, hundreds of ships, thousands of aircraft and landing craft, and mountains of supplies that were suddenly rendered moot. MacArthur's way of war was over, and he knew it.³

• • •

MacArthur now stood on Japanese soil for the first time since 1905, when he was a first lieutenant serving under his father, Gen. Arthur MacArthur, while they were making their famous Asia tour. MacArthur was well-acquainted with Asia and had visited many of the lands in question. He was probably better informed on the history and culture of Pacific rim peoples than most American officers. However, he could not speak Japanese, he never lived there, and he had limited association with Japanese people and culture. He was influenced by Abraham Lincoln, one of his heroes, who believed that the governing and occupation of a former enemy should be magnanimous and not brutal. This principle would guide him for more than for five years as military governor and supreme commander in Japan.

Next came the great show and the ceremonial termination of the war. MacArthur ordered that no Allied commander could accept surrender of Japanese troops in local or isolated areas. He wanted to have the supreme Japanese authorities representing Emperor Hirohito surrender all their forces at one place and one time. President Harry Truman appointed MacArthur as presiding authority for this colossal and historic event. Nazi Germany had ended with several surrender negotiations by separate German commanders with local American, British, and Soviet elements: General Eisenhower accepted the surrender of the German armed forces (Wehrmacht) from Col. Gen. Alfred Jodl in a college building in Reims, France, then serving as Ike's headquarters. It was a low-key affair, and the documents agreed upon were whisked away to Berlin to be further notarized by Adm. Karl Donitz, Adolf Hitler's successor of the Third Reich. There were also surrenders in Berlin, Italy, and northern Germany.⁴

In preparing for the ceremony, MacArthur said, "I had received no instructions as to what to say or what to do."[5] As the occupation and surrender process continued, the Allies learned of the status, numbers, and locations of their POWs. MacArthur ordered Gen. Jonathan Wainwright and British Gen. Arthur E. Percival, recently released from camps in Manchuria, flown to Tokyo. In the New Grand Hotel lobby MacArthur later recorded, "I was just sitting down to dinner when my aide brought me the word that they had arrived. I rose and started for the lobby, but before I could reach it, the door swung open and there was Wainwright. . . . I took him in my arms, but when he tried to talk his voice wouldn't come." After a moment Wainwright expressed his shame about surrendering at Corregidor, which MacArthur dismissed. Wainwright asked about serving on active duty once again and commanding an army corps, to which MacArthur replied, "Why Jim, your old corps is yours when you want it."[6] It was a poignant moment. Two old soldiers embraced as comrades; they were only three years apart in age and graduation from the academy, both were First Captains of their classes, and both were recipients of the Medal of Honor for the same service—gallant leadership.

The idea of conducting the ceremony on American property in the form of the USS *Missouri*, a new and powerful battleship, was the perfect platform. The ceremony itself was rather simple, not a courtly affair. The major Allies sent their representatives, admirals, generals, and even a Canadian colonel. Representing the United States was Fleet Adm. Chester Nimitz, while MacArthur was Supreme Commander, Allied Powers. Thus, the end of the great ocean battlefield and theater of war fought across the vast Pacific was conducted by an army officer.

In Tokyo Bay were hundreds of warships, mostly American, demonstrating the might and power of the conquering Allies. The Japanese delegation, civil and military, came aboard, subdued and respectful. Assembled in every nook and corner of the gray painted superstructure were hundreds of sailors in their white jumpers, common seamen witnessing the historic event. On the deck were scores of officers, mostly US Navy, but dozens from American, British, Australian, and other nations standing in their pressed khaki and crushed service caps. At exactly 0900 hours Douglas MacArthur strode like a colossus across the teak deck to the microphone and commenced the proceedings with his opening remarks: "We are gathered here, representatives of the major warring powers," he read—from a prepared speech, which was unusual for him because he usually memorized his remarks—"to conclude a solemn agreement whereby peace may be restored." The pages rattled in his hands as he spoke in an atypical monotone. He then directed the senior Japanese official, Mamoru Shigemitsu, to come forward. The elderly statesman wobbled up due to his wooden prosthetic leg and signed the instruments of surrender—two of them—exact copies.[7]

Then MacArthur approached the table with six separate signing fountain pens. He signed his name, "Douglas" with one pen, then "Mac" with a second, and then "Arthur" with the third. There were two copies to sign, thus six pens. After signing with the first pen, he called for General Wainwright and gave it to him. The second went to British General Percival. Another went to the National Archives in Washington. Two pens were forwarded to the US Naval Academy and his beloved West Point. The last pen was for Jean MacArthur. MacArthur recognized the significance that both academies played in producing officers, especially the senior commanders, who led the major commands that won the war. Admiral Nimitz, representing the United States, had graduated in 1905 from Annapolis. The US Military Academy pen resides today in the West Point Museum.[8]

He then ended the ceremony by saying, "Let us pray that peace be now restored to the world, and that god will preserve it always. These proceedings are closed."[9]

Today at the US Military Academy in the courtyard of Taylor Hall, the headquarters building, are two bronze plaques commemorating the surrender. One is attached to the wall and bears a summary of the 1945 ceremony, with the list of signatories by names and nations including General of the Army Douglas MacArthur, Supreme Commander, Allied Powers, at the top. Below on the slate stones is a circular plaque representing the location on the deck of the USS *Missouri* where the table stood. These two plaques are replicas of the originals, which are mounted on that historic battleship, now a floating museum to the war in Pearl Harbor. The West Point replicas were installed in 1947.

• • •

If there is one major accomplishment that excels far and above any other contribution that Douglas MacArthur made in life, it would be his tenure as

The end of World War II occurred on the deck of the USS *Missouri* in Tokyo Bay on September 2, 1945, presided over by the commander of the Allied powers, Gen. Douglas MacArthur. Two bronze plaques at West Point memorialize the surrender. *Courtesy MacArthur Memorial.*

military governor of occupied Japan. Few soldiers and commanders in American history had the opportunity to reform an entire country on every level—government, economy, society, law, civil rights—and even write a constitution. Historian Arthur Herman wrote, "Above all . . . [was] his role after Japan's surrender in World War Two, when he used a combination of firmness and diplomatic skill to bring modern democracy and the traditions of an open society to that defeated country."[10] D. Clayton James, MacArthur's most thorough biographer, wrote about MacArthur's own opinion about his service and success in Japan, "There had been many indications in the general's remarks as he grew older that he remembered as his finest hours these spent helping a new Japan."[11]

For more than five years Douglas MacArthur basically single-handedly ruled Japan. As reforms and new institutions rose, the Japanese assumed more authority, freedom, and autonomy—but his presence and influence were still there. The peace and security of the land came first, which meant deploying Allied occupation troops, who were mostly American. At the same time, there was the demobilization of the Japanese Imperial forces and the repatriation of prisoners of war, Allied and Japanese. Then there was the absolute necessity of providing food, shelter, medical care, law and order, and good government for the defeated Japanese. One of the paramount and immediate tasks was to round up, investigate, indict, and try the senior Japanese officials accused of war crimes in military tribunals. This included the most delicate and politically significant early decision MacArthur ever faced: should Emperor Hirohito be indicted and stand trial?

The issue of the emperor's role in initiating hostilities in China in the 1930s, then the attacks against Allied nations in 1941, remains to this day. His part in ending the war is another point for review. Douglas MacArthur as a young lieutenant visited Emperor Taishō's court, the father of Hirohito, in 1905 during Gen. Arthur MacArthur's tour of Asia. Now forty years later MacArthur had the authority to determine if the emperor, who was worshiped as divine by many Japanese, should stand in a tribunal's docket to be judged by the governments he warred upon. MacArthur had to balance the demands of justice, truth, and the attitudes of the Japanese people as he considered Hirohito's fate against the base passion of revenge as a motive of the Allies. He finally came to the proper conclusion: that to sway the prideful and traditional Japanese subjects to accept the new order, to move toward democracy willingly, the emperor should not hang. He saw the reality of the situation even before the surrender. "I have no desire whatever to debase him [Hirohito] in the eyes of his own people, as through him it will be possible to maintain a completely orderly government."[12]

Regardless of MacArthur's humane claim, many in the American government felt otherwise. In September 1945 Congress passed a joint resolution "declaring that it is the policy of the United States that Emperor Hirohito of Japan be tried as a war criminal." Even Eisenhower concurred with this sentiment in November as the new army chief of staff and directed MacArthur to gather evidence enough to sustain an indictment.[13] If no one else in the United States government saw this proposal as a terrible mistake, MacArthur did. Replying to his new superior, army chief of staff Eisenhower, his erstwhile

MacArthur welcoming the defeated Emperor Hirohito in his office at Dai Ichi, in Tokyo, circa 1945. *Courtesy MacArthur Memorial.*

secretary and former chief of staff, MacArthur wrote in January 1946, "No specific and tangible evidence has been uncovered with regard to his [Hirohito] exact activities which might connect him in varying degree with the political decisions of the Japanese Empire during the last decade." MacArthur explained some other points and added his opinion how charging Hirohito would be a political and cultural disaster. "His indictment will unquestionably cause a tremendous convulsion among the Japanese people, the repercussions of which cannot be overestimated. He is a symbol which unites all Japanese. Destroy him and the nation will disintegrate."[14]

Emperor Hirohito was spared. Others were not.

Two senior military officers, generals Tomoyuki Yamashita and Masaharu Homma, were both tried in Manila, not in Tokyo. As supreme commander of the Far East MacArthur was convening authority and would make the final determination. Homma was the commander of the Japanese invasion and occupation forces in the Philippines in 1942. He was charged with war crimes against civilians and prisoners, and especially at the surrender of Corregidor, where many Americans and Filipinos were murdered. But the great atrocity laid at Homma's feet was the Bataan Death March and the murder of an estimated eight thousand prisoners, and the abuse and death of thousands more because of lack of food and medical care. The Bataan Death March was a terrible symbol for Americans and Filipinos. Debate has raged over whether MacArthur and the Allies should have charged Homma at all. He was nevertheless found guilty, but his conviction was appealed to the US Supreme Court, which confirmed the conviction with two dissenting justices. Homma was executed by a firing squad on April 3, 1946.[15]

Yamashita was a different case; he was not charged with ordering war crimes or atrocities, but for not controlling his soldiers who committed such. It was a new and novel accusation: that a commander failed to supervise or control his soldiers to conduct themselves according to the laws of warfare. In fact, the Japanese had never ratified their acceptance of the Geneva Convention and presumably cared little about the laws of land warfare. Yamashita was held responsible for the violations of the laws of war by his men whom he failed to control. He was convicted and hanged on February 23, 1946, in Los Baños in the Philippines.[16] In an interesting twist between General Yamashita and the US Military Academy, General MacArthur ordered that Yamashita's sword "be forwarded to the US Military Academy as able memento of the service rendered by its sons in the vital struggle which proved so decisive in the war with Japan."[17]

In Tokyo the tribunals commenced in early 1946 under MacArthur's authority and were designated as the International Military Tribunal for the Far East. The trials were not conducted well and dragged on for two and a half years. Finally, in November 1948, sentences were handed down for twenty-eight high-ranking Japanese officials, including former prime minister Gen. Hideki Tojo, the mastermind and agent provocateur of Japanese aggression. Eventually, all the defendants were found guilty; some, such as Tojo, were executed while others received prison terms.[18] MacArthur's role in the tribunal was minor once the governing charter was established; he was to approve the verdicts and then carry out the sentences. He wrote in his memoirs that "the principle of holding criminally responsible the political leaders of the vanquished in war was repugnant to me."[19] He saw indicting civilian leaders as a form of revenge by the victors, whereas military leaders were more likely to commit battlefield atrocities. Yet, his opinion here ignored the landmark Nuremberg Tribunal for the German leaders: civil and military. This set a new standard for the crime of "waging aggressive war" of which Japan was definitely guilty.

The final judicial process ended three years after the surrender and consumed much labor and took great patience, but the business of saving Japan from its history continued. The immediate threat MacArthur and Japan faced was the encroachment of the Soviet Union and its aggressive desire to gobble up as much of Asia as possible. Good government along with military might and policy would secure Japan from conquest.

• • •

The "Gaijin Shogun," warrior overlord of all Japan, aka General MacArthur, may not have had a gated palace as Emperor Hirohito had, but a space of dignity, a symbol of power and command, was in order. Such was the case with Dai Ichi, or Number 1, in Tokyo. Built just before the war as an insurance building with splendid offices and air conditioning, it was one of the most magnificent buildings to survive the war. The Supreme Commander Allied Powers (SCAP) headquarters moved into Dai Ichi with MacArthur's offices on the top, sixth floor, with a commanding view. The MacArthurs—the general, Jean, and their son Arthur IV, resided in the American embassy five minutes away by automobile from Dai Ichi. MacArthur worked at least part of every day, and soon developed a routine. Like a king coming to court in a large black Cadillac, what became a procession attracted hundreds of people daily.[20]

MacArthur's staff had evolved since the end of the war. The most obvious change: Lt. Gen. Richard Sutherland was gone, no longer chief of staff. Soon after the surrender, Sutherland retired and returned to the United States. Though an effective and proficient officer, Sutherland quarreled with nearly all the senior officers, and his toxic leadership created a terrible atmosphere among the staff. MacArthur was not totally blind to this, but Sutherland had been effective and loyal for several hard years. Gen. Richard Marshall assumed the position for less than a year. In 1949 Lt. Gen. Edward "Ned" Almond took over.[21] Both were graduates of the Virginia Military Institute.

MacArthur's many great tasks included demobilizing millions of Japanese military personnel, and gathering and disposing of thousands of tanks, artillery pieces, and the remaining enemy naval vessels and aircraft. He also oversaw the repatriation of hundreds of thousands of prisoners of war and displaced persons from all over Asia. A bitter but welcome duty was to liberate and care for thousands of American and Allied soldiers and civilians held throughout the Japanese domain. As mentioned, MacArthur administered and presided over the war crimes tribunals of senior-ranking Japanese officials, both military and civilian. He also supervised the writing of the Japanese Constitution, an amazing achievement for anyone, usually done by statesmen, lawyers, or government professionals, but rarely a soldier. The Japanese Constitution is a remarkable story and perhaps his crowning achievement as military governor of Japan—an American shogun.[22]

The constitution had a double birth, one cobbled together and impoverished, that would not have endured the test of time. The second birth had MacArthur's direct hand in it. As soon as the Occupation commenced, committees and officials assembled Japanese and American military and civil affairs officers. They basically revised and updated the former governing instrument, the Meiji Constitution, and presented it to SCAP for approval in January 1946.[23]

MacArthur successfully blocked the US State Department from hijacking the process, arguing that his staff and others on-site were better suited to perform the task. Whether right in this or not, history has confirmed his success. MacArthur rejected the first draft, and then took a more active role. Several of his staff members, namely generals Courtney Whitney and Bonner Fellers, two of his trusted advisors, helped him. Eventually, MacArthur with their assistance developed an outline that gave women voting rights, established the common rights of collective bargaining or unions, and guaranteed freedom of the press, religion, and many other articles from the US Constitution. He then called for a general election on April 10, 1946. The constitution also validated the role of the Emperor to "act in all important matters only on the advice of the Cabinet," which truly meant Hirohito was powerless without a proper government.[24] In a type of preamble, similar to the US Constitution, the Japanese version read, "The Emperor shall be the symbol of the State and of the unity of the people, deriving his position from the will of the people with whom resides sovereign power."[25]

As the election day approached, MacArthur publicly declared in early March 1946, "It is with a sense of deep satisfaction that I am today able to announce a decision of the Emperor and the government of Japan to submit to the Japanese people a new and enlightened constitution which has my full approval."[26] Seventy percent of the eligible citizens, men and women, cast their vote, and thirty-eight women were elected to the House of Representatives.[27] MacArthur knew the significance of the accomplishment: "It is the single most important accomplishment of the occupation, for it brought to the Japanese people freedoms and privileges which they had never known."[28]

Another major objective that MacArthur espoused was to keep the Soviet Union out of Japan. He would not allow Japan to become like post-war Germany, divided into two nations, one democratic and the other a Communist satellite. MacArthur, supported by President Truman and his administration, indeed blocked the Soviets from annexing any part of Japan. MacArthur later recalled, "I would not allow the Russians any part in the control of Japan."[29]

One of the great lessons the Allies learned from the occupation of Germany after World War I was not to punish the defeated foe. Rather than exact severe penalties and burdensome reparations from the defeated people and their war-weary economy, the post-war doctrine was to rebuild and reform. The great and famous Marshall Plan, known formally as the European Recovery Program of 1947, provided $13 billion to war-torn Europe with food, and economic programs, to rebuild and to introduce democratic government to the former Axis nations. The plan also provided money and material to Allied and formerly occupied nations such as Denmark, Norway, and France, which were devastated by the war. It was a huge success.[30]

Japan did not benefit from the Marshall Plan or any major reconstruction program or funding like it from Congress. MacArthur did not have the same amount of support, bureaucracy, and funding that Europe received. For the first two years his Far East Command budget supported minimal reconstruction, until 1948 when Congress provided $530 million through a program entitled the Economic Rehabilitation of Occupied Areas, meaning Japan, the Philippines, and other lands. Regardless, MacArthur here again, without similar assistance as in Europe, created a reborn Japan that emerged with a vast new infrastructure and modern facilities.[31]

By the time of the outbreak of war in Korea in June 1950, MacArthur's staff and key component commanders of the Far East commands had greatly changed. Gone were most of the Bataan Gang except for Sydney Huff, Charles A. Willoughby, and William F. Marquat, none of whom were academy graduates. The main West Point officers were Far East Air Forces commander George Stratemeyer of the class of 1915, with Eisenhower and Bradley; and Walton Walker, class of 1912, who assumed command of the Eighth Army when Robert Eichelberger retired in 1947. MacArthur's key advisor was Gen. Ned Almond, who became the chief of staff of the Far East Command in 1949.[32]

• • •

MacArthur and his family thrived in Japan, where they lived well in the American embassy. Arthur IV was a boy of seven when he arrived in Japan and soon acquired an interest in music rather than the activities his father preferred. Jean and the general watched films most evenings, the latest from Hollywood. Douglas enjoyed reading and tolerated formal dinners for visiting dignitaries.

True to his nature, MacArthur also had time for West Point. He was thrilled to learn the latest news and developments at his spiritual home, especially sports. His correspondence with Coach Blaik continued after the war. The 1945 season was a highlight for the general, where the Black Knights on the Hudson defeated Navy 32–13 on December 1, securing the national championship. The very next day MacArthur sent Blaik a radio message praising the victory with great hyperbole, "The streets of Tokyo have rung as never before with cheers for the magnificent success of your champion of teams." Unless the streets were filled with American soldiers, it is a wild stretch to think that multitudes of Japanese citizens knew anything about American football and that Navy was playing Army. He continued, "A great tradition still continues to grow. My affection to you all, MacArthur."[33]

In the spring of 1948 MacArthur continued his obsession with West Point sports, primarily football. He wrote Blaik that following the games and providing game plays and pointers was important to him and was "one of the few bright moments of relaxation that fall to my lot." He was such a fan of the academy that Jean MacArthur would order a new academy robe every few years when his old one wore out. She recalled she ordered the robes "all these years from the Cadet Store at the Academy, even during the war years. His 'A' was always put on at the Academy (this . . . he won in baseball as a cadet)."[34]

MacArthur again portrayed his supreme loyalty to the football squad after the 1949 Army-Navy game played on November 26. The Army team won 38 to 0 and was ranked fourth in the nation. He sent Blaik a message the next day, full of exuberance: "Every Army pulse is stirred; every Army heart is thrilled; every Army hope is gratified. Signed MacArthur." Indeed, MacArthur was proposing that every soldier in the US Army cared whether a college team won a football game.[35]

Beyond sports and outlandish messages to coaches, MacArthur had other connections with the academy during the occupation of Japan. Ret. Col. Chauncey L. Fenton, a graduate of 1904, wrote MacArthur in May 1947 about a proposal he had concerning the academy. Fenton had retired in 1944 after forty years of service, with his last assignment being professor of chemistry since 1928 at the academy. Serving as president of the West Point Alumni Foundation and the Association of Graduates, Fenton asked MacArthur for his assistance on behalf of West Point. The letter is genuine evidence of MacArthur's strong ties to the academy and how others saw that same connection. Quoting a portion of Fenton's appeal: "Following the war there have been the customary attacks upon our national institutions, including the Military Academy. Those who regard West Point as one of the buttresses of American liberty, justice and democracy are often reminded of the need to resist the forces which would tear down West Point and the ideals for which it stands. . . . Statements emanating from nationally respected leaders as to what West Point contributed to the winning of World War II, will always have a great effect in allaying unjustified criticism."[36]

Fenton had known Douglas since their cadet days, graduating one year later, and they had remained friends. Looking to the future, Fenton saw the significance of the sesquicentennial approaching in 1952. MacArthur's reputation in 1947 was unassailable, having played a major role in defeating Japan. Fenton connected the two points, as he had written asking MacArthur for a statement or article to support the academy's preparation for the anniversary a few years off. Fenton requested:

> Furthermore, in 1952 the Military Academy will celebrate its Sesqui-Centennial Anniversary. At that time it is proposed to publish a Golden Book memorializing the Military Academy and the work of its graduates, Statements such as I have in mind would comprise a significant part of such a volume.
>
> I am writing you as one of the distinguished graduates of West Point who by your high position was able to observe the work of thousands of graduates at all echelons of command. Your own cadet life has served as a base of departure for an outstanding military career. I consider that it would be a real service to West Point if you would provide us with a statement of what West Point had meant to you and to the nation in providing the leadership which made possible the victory in World War II.[37]

MacArthur replied a week later, stating that he would support the request, and saying, "The carping insinuations of criticism in the aftermath of the war will amount to little in the years to come when passions have somewhat cooled." He declared that the academy's "accomplished fact of victory, to which West Point leadership and tradition contributed so overwhelmingly, will be the criterion which will serve to reaffirm the complete trust and confidence with which the United States regards the Military Academy." He then forwarded the remarks he had given earlier, on Founders Day on March 16, 1947. The annual celebration is when graduates gather to honor the founding of the academy in 1802. MacArthur wrote to Fenton, "It has no literary value and makes no effort at delimiting and analyzing West Point's greatness."[38] During the long course of the US. Military Academy's existence there have been several attempts to either minimize its service or to outright end it. In 1947, though not stated directly by Chauncey Fenton, there were many factors affecting the academy's well-being, especially in recruiting new candidates after the demobilization of World War II and defense spending cuts. Probably at no other time in its history did West Point not reach its authorized strengths in recruiting, which occurred due to the rise of ROTC and the post-war GI Bill; both offered an attractive way for veterans and college-aged men to attend school. Not directly stated in this correspondence, the possibility of the post-war issues may have caused Congress and other entities to question the academy's viability or challenged its funding and any type of increase or new infrastructure.[39]

In reply to a letter dated July 30, 1947, from Coach Blaik, MacArthur addressed the most recent attack on West Point. "I have noted your concern about the future of the Academy," he wrote. "Many attacks, basic as well as superficial, have been made upon it in the past but all have failed." As perhaps the greatest supporter of the academy during its long history, Douglas MacArthur declared, "The record of West Point is so invincibly successful that the American people will not permit what would amount to its practical destruction.... You may rest assured that I would throw the fullest weight of any influence I possess to prevent it [termination]."[40] In another letter to Blaik in 1950, MacArthur declared his loyalty to West Point: "As time goes on, I find my own faith in and devotion to the Academy, and what it stands for, only deepening and becoming more confirmed."[41]

Such unhappy news from Chauncey Fenton and "Red" Blaik gave way two weeks later when MacArthur received another letter from a classmate and great friend, George Cocheu. Therein, Cocheu reported cheerfully that he had attended the graduation on the Plain of the class of 1947. This class was the last of the World War II classes that did not complete the traditional four-year program. The year before, in 1946, with the war over, more than six hundred cadets were divided into two classes, 1947 and 1948. The first would finish the three-year wartime curriculum, and the other would stay another year and be the first post-war class to return to the four-year course of study.[42]

Cocheu narrated, "I have just returned from a most delightful 'June Week' at West Point," which was June 3, as he continued, "You may be interested to know that [Maj. Gen.] Max[well] Taylor, the 'Supe', read your inspiring message sent on the occasion of the 145th anniversary of the Academy. The effect was profound. There is a movement on foot to have this message read each year as a part of the ceremony of swearing in the new cadets."[43]

Cocheu then urged MacArthur—the most famous academy graduate living at this time—to return to the United States the next year, in 1948, for the class of 1903's forty-fifth anniversary and reunion. MacArthur did not attend June Week in 1948; he had been away from America for ten years at that point.

The idea of using MacArthur's speech from the 1947 Founders' Day celebration in Japan for future swearing in ceremonies was an amazing offer for General Taylor to make. Yet, it never materialized into a standard tradition at the academy.

CHAPTER 15

THE FALL

If Douglas MacArthur had retired from active service the day after the Japanese surrendered in September 1945, he would have changed history: American, military, and his own. The sting of Korea and the confrontation with President Harry Truman would not have happened as it did. Many today, mostly Americans, are very critical of MacArthur mainly because of his public criticism of the policies in the Korean War that led to his falling out with Truman. But then Japan would not have had the amazing transition and accomplishments he initiated, oversaw, and conducted. Even into his late sixties, MacArthur made an enormous impact in post-war Japan and the Far East. To this day the Japanese, Filipinos, and Australians sing his praise. Had he resigned and gone home to the United States after achieving so much in Japan, again, he would have been celebrated for the remainder of his life. MacArthur quite possibly could have been elected president of the United States. But he did not. How long he intended to stay in active service is unknown; he probably had not thought it through. He was seventy years old when his last grand military adventure occurred in June 1950.

• • •

The Korean War has often been called the "Forgotten War," which is probably true. Some, even MacArthur, referred to it later as a "police action," a term not used by any official during the conflict though the press did. Others call it a stalemate and limited war. In historical parlance the Latin expression *status quo antebellum* is a term used to describe conditions after a war or conflict that really did not change anything except those who died and the damaged wrought—the same or very similar conditions that existed before the fighting more or less remained after the peace. Another interpretation of Korea is more to do with historian neglect, and it being overshadowed more than being forgotten. The vast and overwhelming Second World War before, and the longer, bloodier, and more controversial Vietnam War a decade later, eclipsed the Korean conflict and cast it into historical limbo. Korea was a new type of war that ushered in a military era of limited objectives and power instead of employing all available means against one's enemy. Some soldiers were not ready for this significant change in strategy and policy.

As for General MacArthur, the war was his downfall, which was not so ignominious at first. Over time, the weight of his actions and decisions have become a shadow obscuring his reputation and service of more than fifty years. His magnificent, storied, and often controversial career climaxed with his refusal to live the basic tenet of soldiering: obeying the orders of those above him.

"It was early morning Sunday, June 25, 1950, when the telephone rang in my bedroom at the American Embassy in Tokyo," MacArthur recalled. Like the Philippines nearly a decade earlier, the call to war came, literally. Learning the details, MacArthur pondered the significance. "How, I asked myself, could the United States have allowed such a deplorable situation to develop?"[1] Was he thinking militarily, politically, or diplomatically—perhaps all three? There is no doubt, as commander of the Far East Command, which encompassed the Korean Peninsula, it was as much his failure as that of any other policy maker, government official, or diplomat—even the president of the United States. It was a collective failure in the face of a pure case of ruthless Communist aggression.[2]

Korea is largely consigned to a major geographical feature, a peninsula that darts southward like "a dagger pointed at the heart of Japan." In 1910 Japan annexed Korea, which has experienced many invaders and occupiers over centuries, including Chinese, Mongolians, and then the Japanese through the end of World War II. The Japanese occupation was severe and brutal, especially once war had come.[3] After World War II there was a tug-of-war between Soviet and Communist Chinese intentions and those of the Western powers' strategy of halting communism, the age of "containment." After the Japanese occupation troops departed, American forces entered and established a short-lived military government in Korea, which was replaced by the Korea Military Advisory Group (KMAG), led by Brig. Gen. William L. Roberts, a 1913 academy graduate.[4] The 38th parallel became the demarcation between a northern occupation zone dominated by Korean Communists with Chinese combat experience and Russian equipment and support. The south was led by Syngman Rhee, whose regime proved to be unprincipled and immoral at times but was propped up by American support. The hope of both north and south was for a united Korea under their faction, but by 1950 Korea was hopelessly divided. The Communist north under Kim Il-Sung sought and gained support from the reluctant Chinese premier, Mao Zedong, and the Soviet Union's Joseph Stalin for an attack on South Korea. In January 1950, Secretary of State Dean Acheson made a pronouncement in a public venue outlining the United States's strategic interests in Asia, but in doing so Acheson omitted Korea. The Communist chiefs saw this as a statement that America would not intervene militarily if South Korea were invaded, which further convinced them to strike.[5]

Communist North Korea was well prepared for offensive operations, with 150 Soviet T-34 medium tanks and some 100,000 combat troops, some of whom were combat veterans against the Japanese. The north's Korean People's Army (KPA) also had an air force of 180 aircraft, of which 120 were fighters and medium bombers. Organized, trained, and disciplined, the KPA was deployed for the attack. Across the border, the South Korean, or Republic of Korea (ROK), forces were not prepared for intensive combat operations, having only 65,000 combat soldiers, no aircraft, few armored vehicles to speak of, and limited artillery.[6] Neither side had a navy. The American occupation forces under MacArthur in Japan consisted of four understrength divisions that had served so long in a constabulary role that they were not trained and fully equipped for combat operations. The only advantage that the Far East Command had was its 1,100 combat aircraft and a score of capital warships.[7]

Thus, on June 25, 1950, before daylight, the KPA crossed the 38th parallel dividing the two zones and hostile action commenced that would continue for the next three years. Within days the ROK divisions on the border were overwhelmed by tanks and artillery supporting massed infantry moving south like a snowplow. American advisors reported the disaster in the making. There was an obvious intelligence failure, and American reaction took a few days as President Truman, the Joint Chiefs of Staff (JCS), and MacArthur groped through the problems and options. Eventually, on June 27 air and naval assets went into action while the United Nations passed a resolution bringing international condemnation against the North Koreans for the attack. The UN also formed defensive measures for South Korea. Fortunately for the American-led international effort, the Soviet representative had boycotted the Security Council meetings over the admission of Communist China and could not block the resolution—a mistake the Russians would never repeat.[8]

The next day Seoul, the capital of the south, fell to the Communist invaders. MacArthur boarded his Lockheed C-121 aircraft, *Bataan*, on June 29 and flew without escort fighters to Suwon airfield south of Seoul to make a personal reconnaissance of the battle area. "I commandeered a jeep and headed north toward the Han River," and for several hours he saw the action across the Han River, recalling, "The South Korean forces were in complete and disorganized flight." His report to the president and the JCS that he wrote on the flight back to Japan was a bold statement of the rout of the ROK army and the necessity for the "introduction of United States ground combat forces into the Korean battle area." On June 30 Truman ordered ground forces to the Korean Peninsula.[9]

The UN designated a new command structure on July 7, the United Nations Command (UNC), and authorized President Truman to appoint a commander. The next day the JCS recommended the appointment of MacArthur as the first UN commander-in-chief in history.[10] The North Koreans continued the advance, but their momentum slowed as a perimeter formed around the key port city of Pusan and stopped the onslaught. The combined use of airpower and escalating numbers of combat troops in the "Pusan Perimeter" helped bolster the defense. The ground commander was Lt. Gen. Walton Harris Walker, class of 1912, a feisty infantryman turned tank commander in World War II. He commanded a corps under General George Patton in Europe and later served in Japan commanding the Eighth Army.[11]

General MacArthur meeting UN troops in 1950. The officer talking to MacArthur is US Marine Col. Lewis "Chesty" Puller, commanding the 1st Marine Regiment at Inchon and Chosin Reservoir. *Courtesy MacArthur Memorial.*

By early July MacArthur realized that the only way to save South Korea was to go on the offensive. He formulated a plan to strike the North Koreans by an amphibious landing, his specialty during World War II. Besides landing at Inchon by the X Corps, MacArthur briefed the JCS that the concept included the Eighth Army under Walker, which would attack from Pusan Perimeter, and eventually the two forces would join at Inchon and along the 38th parallel; this was the best option.[12] The plan, designated Operation Chromite, faced staggering odds, mainly with the tides that rose some twenty feet daily, leaving mud flats surrounding Wolmi-do Island, one of the first objectives. MacArthur conferred several times with the JCS and naval officers, all of whom had major reservations. "My plan was opposed by powerful military influences in Washington," he wrote later.[13] He boldly defied the naysayers in Washington when he asked for more reinforcements: "I will, on the rising tide of the fifteenth of September, land at Inchon and between the hammer of this landing and the anvil of Eighth Army, I will crush and destroy the army of North Korea."[14] MacArthur did exactly what he promised by the end of October 1950.

• • •

Biographer Geoffrey Perret wrote about the significance of MacArthur's success at Inchon, "There is one day in MacArthur's life when he was a military genius: September 15, 1950."[15] Historian Stanley Weintraub, no fan of MacArthur, declared, "More glorious for MacArthur than Côte-de-Châtillon in 1918 or Leyte in 1944 was Inchon."[16] Inchon was an amazing victory; combined with Walker's Eighth Army near-simultaneous breakout from the Pusan Perimeter, the North Koreans in days were reeling and routed. Yet, the day before the invasion, aboard the USS *Mount McKinley*, as he had been at earlier climatic moments of his life, MacArthur was ill. Wrapped in his West Point robe with the large "A" for warmth and perhaps psychological comfort, the great warrior was probably seasick because the invading fleet entered a tremendous storm, a typhoon that blasted through.[17] Despite the tides, the enemy, and the risk, the element of surprise and superior leadership brought an unprecedented victory.

The 5th US Marine Regiment went ashore at Wolmi-do Island at 0530 on September 15, which caused the fall of the north's KPA. In less than two weeks Seoul was recaptured as the KPA fled north to escape being crushed between Walker's advancing horde and General Almond's X Corps' swift attack east across the peninsula. The tide of war shifted so quickly that political leaders on both sides struggled to envision the near future. With this incredible strategic opportunity before them, the United Nations, encouraged by Truman and his cabinet, approved a resolution on October 7 to allow MacArthur's UNC to invade the north with these words, "The general posture of the United Nations forces should be one of liberation rather than retaliation."[18] Sensing victory, the JCS had already forwarded orders to MacArthur on September 27 concerning his next mission: "Your military objective is the destruction of the North Korean Armed Forces. In attaining this objective you are authorized to conduct military 'operations,' including amphibious and airborne landings or ground operations north of the 38th Parallel in Korea."[19]

The American-led UNC marched north across the 38th parallel after the defeated Communist North Koreans. But this was not the end of the story.

MacArthur observed the challenging and extremely risking landing at Inchon of September 15, 1950, aboard the USS *Mount McKinley*. Maj. Gen. Edward Almond, a Virginia Military Institute graduate of 1915, looks through binoculars at the landing. Almond was both MacArthur's chief of staff and commander of X Corps, the main amphibious force. *Courtesy MacArthur Memorial.*

The Communist Chinese under Mao Zedong would not allow North Korea to fall or be annexed into a capitalist democratic state uniting all of Korea. Plans and threats were underway. Soviet advisors and more aircraft augmented the gathering and growing Chinese Volunteer People's Army (CVPA), a new name for the Chinese forces in Manchuria, numbering well over 200,000 men. These soldiers the Chinese government claimed were volunteers organized to stop the American "imperialistic" intentions and aggression in North Korea. Mounting evidence gained by American intelligence agencies that the Chinese would possibly intervene became more obvious.[20]

In early October, with many political, diplomatic, and military developments escalating, President Truman decided to have a conference with his military leaders. General MacArthur received a message with only a few days' notice to travel to Wake Island for a meeting on October 15, with no explanation of its purpose.[21]

There already was some tension and stress between MacArthur and the Truman administration. After the North Korean invasion, the differences deepened. Chief among them occurred at the end of July, when MacArthur visited Gen. Chiang Kai-shek and his Chinese Nationalist forces on Formosa (Taiwan) after having been defeated by the Communists and fleeing from the mainland. His staff also inspected the Nationalist forces to determine their state of readiness. This became a great political and diplomatic issue, a drama of misunderstandings that crippled MacArthur's reputation with the Truman administration, especially the State Department.[22]

Another problem occurred with Truman and his advisors over a letter MacArthur sent to the annual meeting of the Veterans of Foreign Wars in August 1950, before the invasion of Inchon. Truman complained, "The whole tenor of the message was critical of the very policy which he had so recently told [Averell] Harriman he would support." Days later Truman himself ordered MacArthur to withdraw the letter.[23] The drama continued at the conference on Wake Island when the two leaders, political and military, gathered.

• • •

Truman and MacArthur had never met, but their relationship was already strained by the missteps MacArthur had made and by Truman's advisor Gen. Omar Bradley, chairman of the JCS, who had a visceral hatred of the general and his politics.[24]

At the airfield on Wake Island, MacArthur and Truman met and had a warm greeting. During their time together MacArthur apologized to Truman for the misunderstanding about the letter to the Veterans of Foreign Wars. When MacArthur saw that Secretary of State Dean Acheson and Secretary of Defense George Marshall were not present, he realized the true nature of the meeting—politics. Truman was slumping in the polls as his approval ratings declined in a congressional election year. MacArthur's popularity after Inchon was tangible, and the president, a consummate politician, tried to take advantage of the moment.[25]

The discussion turned to whether Communist China would intervene now that UN forces had crossed the 38th parallel and were advancing toward the Yalu River and Manchuria. The latest intelligence estimates were reviewed, and MacArthur replied that the Chinese had some 300,000 troops in

Manchuria but that only about 60,000 had crossed the Yalu into Korea. There was no evidence of major logistical support, nor indications of trucks or convoys. Armored columns and heavy artillery were not observed. MacArthur also made the grandiose statement that would haunt him later: "The formal resistance will end throughout North and South Korea by Thanksgiving.... It is my hope to be able to withdraw the Eighth Army to Japan by Christmas."[26]

Nothing was really solved at the Wake Island conference, which lasted only a few hours and required a great deal of traveling. Biographer D. Clayton James concluded, "In the long run, the Wake meeting contributed more to alienating Truman and MacArthur than to improving their relationship."[27] In the months and years to come these two Americans would become bitter enemies.[28]

• • •

Flushed with victory at Inchon and Pusan, the UNC forces moved northward along two major avenues of advance. By October 25 Walker's army had captured Pyongyang, the North Korean capital, and the X Corps commenced its advance north supporting Walker's flank.[29] The clash finally materialized in late October, when ROKA units encountered strong and substantial Chinese troops and captured several who were obviously not North Koreans in language, uniforms, and ethnicity. "The most disquieting feature of the situation," MacArthur recalled, "was the indication that an estimated three fresh divisions, apparently consisting of Red Chinese troops, had joined the battle."[30]

By November 1950 there was now no doubt that the Chinese Communists had intervened strongly, with perhaps hundreds of thousands of light infantry. On November 24, the day after the Thanksgiving holiday, MacArthur flew to see Walker at his headquarters at Chongchon River to observe conditions and receive reports.[31] He returned to Japan, and soon after that the UNC major offensive "died suddenly on the night of November 25, when strong Chinese forces unleashed a surprise assault against Walker's right flank."[32] Now known as the Second Chinese Offensive, the attack was massive. The forward South Korean units were decimated, though they fought bravely.

As November ended with UNC forces fleeing south, Truman and his administration were extremely vexed by the news in Korea. There was great concern about South Korea and the possible threat against the new Japanese democracy. This shift soon manifested itself in directives from the JCS, if not the president himself, that laid serious military restrictions on MacArthur's forces.[33] An example was the restriction that was issued concerning the bombing of bridges. MacArthur and his staff knew that major supply and logistical support was coming from Manchuria to sustain the North Koreans. Soon a battle of wills and minds occurred between MacArthur and the Pentagon. "The only way to stop this reinforcement of the enemy is the destruction of the bridges by air attack," MacArthur demanded. But the answer came back that his pilots could only bomb the "Korean end of the Yalu bridges."[34] The Far East Air Force was not allowed to make air strikes against Chinese depots across the Yalu. Also, American fighter aircraft were not allowed to make "hot pursuit" of Soviet MIGs once they crossed into Manchurian "sanctuaries."[35]

Disgusted, MacArthur asked to be relieved of his command. This request was ignored by the JCS, so MacArthur remained. He wrote with intoning eloquence seething with rhetorical disgust, "For the first time in military history, a commander has been denied the use of his military power to safeguard the lives of his soldiers and the safety of his army." His chief of staff convinced him to not send the dispatch.[36]

The ground war suffered through the bitter Korean winter as the Eighth Army and X Corps retreated south. Fortunately, some 105,000 American and ROK troops had been evacuated from Hungnan on the east coast by December 24, along with 350,000 tons of supplies—an American version of Dunkirk.[37] An earlier glimmer of hope was the extraction of the 1st Marine Division and regiments of the Army's 7th Infantry Division, which fought their way south from Chosin (Changjin) Reservoir during a three-week frozen ordeal.[38] These two stories were the only uplifting news in the hard fight, however dwarfed by the disaster.

The frustration MacArthur felt at the overall strategic change, and the inability to defeat the enemy with the combat power and means available, caused him to make several missteps in November and December. During press interviews, he voiced his confidence that the drive to the Yalu was proper, that Chinese intervention was a violation of international law, and that the JCS restrictions impeded his command and its ability to succeed on the battlefield. Some of the main media sources were *U.S. News and World Report* and the United Press, which released reports December 2–8. In one such report,

MacArthur stated to an editor that "results [were] largely from the acceptance of military odds without precedent in history—the odds of permitting offensive action without defensive retaliation."[39]

Truman was furious, charging that MacArthur was "shooting off his mouth." In his memoirs, he wrote, "I should have relieved him then and there. The reason I did not was that I did not wish to have it appear as if he were relieved because the offensive failed."[40] Truman and the JCS soon issued directives, on December 29, that all public and press statements be cleared through proper authorities and "to exercise extreme caution" for all government matters military, diplomatic, and civil to follow.[41] To MacArthur "this message seemed to indicate a loss of the 'will to win' in Korea. He felt that President Truman's resolute determination to free and unite that threatened land had now deteriorated into defeatism."[42] The Communist Chinese intervention into Korea seemed to take the wind out of Truman's sails, and for that matter, those of his administration and the United Nations' effort. The fear of escalation with the USSR and Europe's vulnerability overwhelmed the thinking.

The next piece of bad news came just before Christmas, when word arrived that Lieutenant General Walker had died, killed in an accident when his jeep collided with a truck. Walker was making a visit to award his son the Silver Star Medal when the accident occurred. Capt. Sam Sims Walker, an academy graduate of the class of 1946, who would later rise to full general during his distinguished career, received the word that his father and commander had been killed. Congress promoted the older Walker to the rank of general posthumously.[43]

The new commander of the Eighth Army, the main force of the UNC, was Lt. Gen. Matthew Ridgway, who graduated in the accelerated class of April 1917, just as the United States entered World War I. Ridgway as a young captain served under MacArthur as an assistant professor of Spanish in the Department of Modern Languages and had the additional duty of athletic director.[44] Ridgway had a meteoric career through World War II, starting at the rank of lieutenant colonel in 1941 and rising to lieutenant general and command of the 82nd Airborne Division and then the XVIII Airborne Corps by the end of the war. When word reached the Pentagon that Walker had died, Ridgway was a major general and army deputy chief of staff for administration under Gen. J. Lawton Collins, the army chief of staff. He was whisked away to Korea, promoted to lieutenant general again, and assumed command of the Eighth Army engaged in vicious combat. It was actually MacArthur who made the decision to have Ridgway assume command by calling General Collins and requesting him by name. MacArthur also called Ridgway and told him, "I look forward with keenest anticipation to your joining this command. Your welcome by all ranks will be the heartiest."[45]

The military situation was dire through the winter, especially when Seoul again fell to the Communists in early January 1951. General Ridgway was able to turn the tide by late January, launching major counterattacks. Seoul was liberated by UN forces on March 15 as the Chinese momentum slowed, though they tried other major offensives later through the spring of 1951. Through all the misery of retreat and the resurgence, MacArthur was very hands-off with Ridgway. He told Ridgway upon his arrival in Japan, "the Eighth Army is yours, Matt. Do what you think best."[46] Even the leaders in Washington seemed to bypass MacArthur as the theater commander and instead communicated more often directly with Ridgway.[47]

• • •

The Eighth Army and other UN forces under Ridgway advanced north once again. On February 15, MacArthur asked the JCS for permission to bomb the city and transportation depot of Rashin, near the Soviet border. His request was denied. He asked for approval to engage other targets through the end of February, thinking that with the recent success of Ridgway's counterattacks, the administration would drop the limitations on his command. MacArthur was wrong. Even the prospect of crossing the 38th parallel again caused division between MacArthur and Washington, where the latter "saw no profit in unnecessarily calling the attention of the United Nations to the 38th Parallel."[48]

In mid-March Truman was determined to reach out to the Chinese and seek some type of negotiation process to end hostilities. A draft statement was prepared by March 19 and was circulated among the various levels of government. On March 24, American officials learned that days earlier MacArthur had issued "a routine communique" from Japan, intended for the Chinese, that announced his own peace offer to the Chinese.[49]

The backlash was immediate and overwhelming from foreign governments and resulted in absolute rage in Washington. Truman had come to the end of his patience with MacArthur. "It was open defiance of my orders as President and Commander in Chief," Truman lamented later in a letter to an associate. "By this act MacArthur left me no choice—I could no longer tolerate his insubordination," Truman declared, which "was not just a public disagreement over policy, but deliberate, premeditated sabotage on US and UN policy."[50] Truman was completely right and justified in this regard. MacArthur had crossed the line. The president is commander in chief according to the Constitution, not a field commander. Yet, Truman waited and took no action for several days other than consulting with his advisors, who discussed the issue back and forth in a fit of indecision. They knew that MacArthur was a hero to most Americans and an icon to the conservatives and Republicans. MacArthur's defiance, intended or not, became a rallying cry for the administration's enemies.[51]

The final straw came two weeks later. The general had replied to a request of Republican House leader Joseph Martin of Massachusetts to comment on a speech Martin had given recently. MacArthur wrote confirming Martin's points, ending with this summation on war and his opinion of the current conflict. "If we lose this war to Communism in Asia the fall of Europe is inevitable," MacArthur wrote. "Win it and Europe most probably would avoid war and yet preserve freedom. As you pointed out, we must win. There is no substitute for victory."[52]

Representative Martin entered the House chamber and read MacArthur's letter on April 5, quoting the critical comments in the letter the general had for the administration and the conduct of the war. Truman was incensed and raged on his own warpath. "Rank insubordination. . . . The time had come to draw the line." Truman recorded in his memoirs, "MacArthur's letter to Congressman Martin showed that the general was not only in disagreement with the policy of the government but was challenging this policy in open insubordination to his Commander in Chief."[53] There was nothing in the letter that was new or unknown by the administration, but the fact that MacArthur's criticisms were now public was the final blow.[54]

For three more days Truman wandered through a political maze of indecision, frustration, and anger, discussing with his advisors, military, and policy wonks. Finally, on April 10 Truman determined he had to act regardless of the political and public fallout. Now the question was, how? The manner of notification was the next dilemma the president faced. Truman held a news conference at 1:00 a.m. on April 11, Washington, DC, time (Japan was thirteen hours ahead of Washington). The White House staff provided copies of the statement, which read:

> I deeply regret that it becomes my duty as President and Commander in Chief of the United States military forces to replace you as Supreme Commander, Allied Powers; Commander in Chief, United Nations Command; Commander in Chief, Far East; and Commanding General, U.S. Army, Far East.
>
> You will turn over your commands, effective at once, to Lt. Gen. Matthew B. Ridgway.... My reasons for your replacement will be made public concurrently with the delivery to you of the foregoing order and are contained in the next following message, HARRY S. TRUMAN[55]

Regardless of Truman's intentions, the plan went awry. Secretary of the Army Frank Pace was in Korea to visit the troops and would then fly to Japan to deliver the message in person to MacArthur, but Pace did not receive the message in time. The press and reporters broadcast the news on commercial radio, more speculation than facts, about MacArthur's relief. On Wednesday, April 11, in Japan Col. Sydney Huff, the general's personal aide, heard the news on the radio. The MacArthurs were hosting a senator at a luncheon at the embassy when Huff passed the word to Jean MacArthur by telephone. She then whispered the news to MacArthur as the guests looked on. He remarked to her, "Jeanie, we're going home at last."[56]

One can only imagine the pain and shame that a man of Douglas MacArthur's stature and renown suffered from such an undignified manner of his dismissal. "No office boy, no charwoman, no servant of any sort would have been dismissed with such callous disregard for the ordinary decencies," MacArthur lamented in his memoirs years later.[57]

Arriving in the United States on April 17, MacArthur's reception and regard by the American public was the same as in Japan—overwhelming. He was the hero returning from the wars of freedom and liberation. The Republicans had invited him to speak before a joint session of Congress on April 19, the anniversary of the battles of Lexington and Concord.[58]

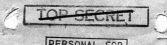

PERSONAL FOR

11 April 1951

FLASH

PERSONAL FROM: JOINT CHIEFS OF STAFF (PERSONAL FROM GENERAL BRADLEY)

PERSONAL FOR : GENERAL MACARTHUR

NUMBER : JCS 88180, 11 April 1951

I have been directed to relay the following message to you from President Truman:

"I deeply regret that it becomes my duty as President and Commander-in-Chief of the United States Military Forces to replace you as Supreme Commander, Allied Powers; Commander-in-Chief, United Nations Command; Commander-in-Chief, Far East; and Commanding General, U. S. Army, Far East.

You will turn over your commands, effective at once, to Lieutenant General Matthew B. Ridgway. You are authorized to have issued such orders as are necessary to complete desired travel to such place as you select.

My reasons for your replacement, will be made public concurrently with the delivery to you of the foregoing order, and are contained in the next following message. Signed Harry S. Truman."

MCN: 85871

TOO: 110510Z (111410I)

TOR: 110542Z (111442I)

DECLASSIFIED BY:
JCS-CCS DECLASSIFICATION
WORKING GROUP
DATE 6-Jun-71

"PARAPHRASE NOT REQUIRED.
CONSULT CRYPTOCENTER BEFORE DECLASSIFYING."

INDEXED BY MacARTHUR ARCHIVES

The official order of April 1951 relieving MacArthur of the UN command and all his positions in the US armed forces, signed by President Harry S. Truman. *Courtesy MacArthur Memorial.*

Wherever MacArthur visited he was mobbed by tens and even hundreds of thousands of citizens. The outrage against Truman was palpable and ubiquitous. The president's approval rating, already in the shadows, darkened even more. The White House was flooded with more than eighty thousand letters from citizens, most of them in support of MacArthur and damning Truman.[59] The news coverage of the day and political outrage increased until such time that MacArthur entered the Capitol. The popular interest was amazing considering that few households had television sets in 1951. There were an estimated twenty million viewers—and many times that number tuned in by radio. Just after high noon, General MacArthur was introduced to the two assembled houses of Congress, who rose in a tumultuous roar—friend and political foe alike.

With only two days' notification that he would address the Congress, MacArthur managed to write one of the greatest speeches in American history. There are phrases and passages he had already used in many cables, messages, and press releases over years, but it was a masterful document with the substance focused on limited war in modern times, indecision, appeasement, and the folly of allowing the Communists advantages when democracy and liberty were at stake. MacArthur declared,

> Efforts have been made to distort my position. It has been said in effect that I was a warmonger. Nothing could be further from the truth. I know war as few other men now living know it, and nothing to me is more revolting. I have long advocated its complete abolition, as its very destructiveness on both friend and foe has rendered it useless as a means of settling international disputes.... But once war is forced upon us, there is no other alternative than to apply every available means to bring it to a swift end. War's very object is victory, not prolonged indecision. In war there can be no substitute for victory.... There are some who for varying reasons would appease Red China. They are blind to history's clear lesson. For history teaches with unmistakable emphasis that appeasement but begets new and bloodier war."[60]

He then likened aggression by one nation and appeasement by the other as blackmail, where there are "successively greater demands, until, as in blackmail, violence becomes the only other alternative." This was the political level of war, but then he moved to soldiering. He recalled instances in the field and on the front line when he met the fighting men, for whom the obvious circumstance of limited war was hard to understand. He remarked, "Why, my soldiers asked of me, surrender military advantages to an enemy in the field? I could not answer." MacArthur then moved toward a conclusion addressing those people who had suffered: "Of the nations of the world, Korea alone, up to now, is the sole one which has risked its all against communism. The magnificence of the courage and fortitude of the Korean people defies description." There was a huge burst of applause in the chamber. He continued, "Their last words to me were, 'Don't scuttle the Pacific.'"[61] His faith and view was that Asia was equal to or more important strategically than Europe.

General MacArthur finished his last formal and official public address as a soldier before Congress with an allusion to his youth, where his incredible career all began, at West Point—his spiritual roots and foundation for all of his life:

> I am closing my fifty-two years of military service. When I joined the army, even before the turn of the century, it was the fulfillment of all my boyish hopes and dreams.
>
> The world has turned over many times since I took the oath on the plain at West Point, and the hopes and dreams have long since vanished, but I still remember the refrain of one of the most popular barracks ballads of that day which proclaimed most proudly that old soldiers never die; they just fade away.
>
> And like the old soldier of that ballad, I now close my military career and just fade away, an old soldier who tried to do his duty as God gave him the light to see that duty. Good-bye.[62]

The general left the rostrum amid a tumultuous and thunderous roar from Congress, as loud as the guns on the Western Front. MacArthur was right about one point; he did eventually fade away.

• • •

The Korean War continued for two more years after MacArthur's departure. He was followed by three other West Point graduates who commanded the UNC forces. Ridgway was the most successful, as both a commander and as a subordinate to national policy from Washington. These commanders too had to shoulder the burden of stalemate, indecision, growing battle losses, and the political realities of limited war that eventually cost some thirty-seven thousand American lives and hundreds of thousands of Korean lives, both north and south, besides the Chinese and other engaged nations. One of Korea's legacies is that the same type of limited war policy overshadowed the war in Vietnam—at least the American effort. This means General MacArthur was correct in his assessment and decisions. Despite his frustration that led to his dismissal, MacArthur admitted later during a congressional hearing that civil authority was supreme and any other position "of this Government is a treasonable concept in my mind." Therefore, Truman was justified in relieving his obstinate and insubordinate field commander. But the real question is, what led MacArthur to the point to question and challenge authority?[63]

The answer may lie with his loyalty and the oath sworn as a cadet on the Plain at West Point in 1903. MacArthur's opinion, interpretation, and regard for the motto Duty, Honor, Country perhaps holds the mystery at the center of his soul. There is an interesting passage in D. Clayton James's first biographical volume, *The Years of MacArthur: 1880 to 1941*. He laid out how critical character development and leadership were to MacArthur's faith in the principles of his Duty to his Country and the Honor he saw as central to the academy's mission: "The common thread running through his forty-two years of military service [through 1941] and the most predictable trait of his future was his unashamed, wholehearted dedication to duty, honor and country.... His fervent adherence to them was paramount in every significant decision and action of his career. In this sense, he was a veritable incarnation of the spirit of West Point.... Supremely dedicated to duty, honor, and country, [he] would not hesitate to sacrifice his career for those principles."[64]

Few commentaries describe MacArthur's faithfulness to the values learned in his youth at the US Military Academy. Admittedly, this chapter does not relate as much tangible evidence about the MacArthur and West Point connection as do other chapters. The Korean conflict was his downfall, causing his relief by the commander in chief during an armed conflict, a disgraceful consequence for a soldier. But as James stated, MacArthur felt so strongly that he was willing to jeopardize his status and reputation to prove that national policy and combat operations in Korea were wrongheaded—even immoral. And he did so.

Chapter 16

★ ★ ★ ★ ★

HOME AT LAST

One would think that General of the Army Douglas MacArthur at age seventy-one, after fifty-two years of service in uniform and not having been home to the United States for the previous fourteen years, would welcome the rest and relaxation of retirement. This was not the case. MacArthur immediately launched a crusade. His mission was to inform the citizens of America of the dangers of limited war: of appeasement to communism, of the reckless and irresponsible politicians in power, and the need to defend American values, rights, and freedoms and, by proxy, its allies. His primary objective was Harry S. Truman, president of the United States, to demonstrate how foolish, irresponsible, and perhaps even how wicked and immoral Truman's policies and intent were.[1]

In this vast effort he was aided by an unplanned development: his enormous popularity among many Americans and politicians countrywide. The day after his speech before Congress, April 20, 1951, he and Jean traveled to New York City, where they paraded along the long, canyon-like avenues, drawing a crowd estimated at more than seven million people—more than those who cheered Charles Lindbergh in 1927.[2] This was just the beginning of a national tour in which he was invited to scores of cities to speak. MacArthur was greeted by masses of people in a dozen states from Texas to Wisconsin to Washington State. He spoke in football stadiums, auditoriums, and theaters, in state legislatures, and on streets. MacArthur was like a rock star of the future, only a few years before Elvis Presley and other rock-n-roll bands canvased the nation. In the midst of this grand tour and personal crusade he was summoned to Washington, DC, to appear before a Senate hearing.[3]

The hearings convened on May 3 in the Senate Office Building, where MacArthur testified for three days. The Republican political enemies of Truman hoped this hearing would damage the president beyond repair. Truman's appeal and popularity were in the ditch anyway. The general answered dozens of questions and gave evidence making strong points about the true nature of war, the policy with China, and the conduct of the war in Korea. He denounced the administration as having no viable policy regarding the Korean conflict or the greater Pacific theater to deal with Communist aggression and stressed that military commanders required clear and attainable strategic objectives.[4] After three long days the general resumed his tour.

The hearings droned on for several more weeks, and soon most people lost interest in them. The senators paraded dozens of administration officials through the verbal gauntlet, including General Bradley and Secretaries Marshall and Acheson, the latter two testifying for several days each. The hearing transcripts eventually filled 1,779 pages including supporting documents investigating MacArthur's actions, attitude, and strategic policies.[5]

Marshall testified that escalation in Korea and MacArthur's proposals would "risk involvement not only in an extension of the war with Red China, but in all-out war with the Soviet Union." Bradley made a clever statement that has resonated through history, saying that MacArthur's plan "would involve us in the wrong war, at the wrong time, at the wrong place, and with the wrong enemy." By this, he meant that fighting the Chinese in Korea with a total victory strategy could cause World War III. The hearings ended with no formal reports or opinions. There was no overall consensus that the president was justified or not in relieving MacArthur. It was a hung jury.[6]

• • •

After speaking before Congress in April 1951, Douglas, Jean, and Arthur IV settled into their civilian life, choosing New York City as their place of abode. Neither of them had ever lived in the great metropolitan American city before, but New York had all the cultural and social amenities that the general and his family would enjoy. They moved into Suite 37A, a penthouse, in the Waldorf Astoria Hotel, where they would remain until the general's death in 1964. He continued to draw his military salary of $18,000 in lieu of a retirement pension, because he was technically and legally on active duty as a general of the army (five-star general). He also was authorized a personal staff of eight members until Truman ordered a reduction to only three. Since he was still on active duty, he donned his uniform for official and public events, which was usually his khakis and the worn-for-wear service cap from his time as field marshal of the Philippines.[7]

That summer MacArthur became involved in a controversial event that demonstrated his loyalty to a close friend and his alma mater, the US Military Academy. He came to the rescue of Coach "Red" Blaik and the varsity football during a scandal that threatened not only the upcoming season but also the very football program itself. In May 1951 ninety-four cadets were accused of cheating and being part of a secret ring that had existed for years among the football team and associated roommates and team tutors. This was a well-organized cabal that had infiltrated honor committees and whose members saw to it that cases against fellow conspirators were dismissed. Sometimes cadets used intimidation and physical threats to discipline their secret group. This was not a matter of a few cadets cheating together, it was an organized ring of scores of cadets with leaders who managed this widespread effort. Eventually, thirty-eight members of the squad resigned or were dismissed, decimating the 1951 season and team.[8]

Coach Blaik protested the crushing consequence for his number-one nationally ranked team and the fact that his son, the star quarterback, was among those who had cheated. Blaik challenged the superintendent, Maj. Gen. Fred Irving, who had commanded a division under MacArthur in the Philippines, both personally and publicly. Blaik went on a rampage in the newspapers against the process and the loss of his entire starting team. He approached all the leaders in the army establishment, including Gen. Omar Bradley and Gen. Maxwell Taylor, and he even had an office call with President Truman, trying to save his team. The three reviews and investigations conducted by academy officers were proper, and there was no doubt of the fact these cadets had transgressed the Honor Code, newly codified in language in 1947 that "A cadet will neither lie, cheat or steal."[9]

MacArthur with former cadet Earl Blaik, class of 1920, head football coach and athletic director at West Point for many years. *Courtesy MacArthur Memorial.*

Jean MacArthur years later remembered the scandal and how it caused such concern to General MacArthur and that Coach Blaik "was so distressed." She recalled that "he called up and he wanted to see the General . . . so he came" to the penthouse in the Waldorf Towers. Jean MacArthur recorded that "the general was determined . . . [to] lend his moral support" to Coach Blaik, regardless of the outcome.[10]

This was prior to the public announcement of the scandal on August 3, which was just weeks before the season kicked off.[11] MacArthur's support was recorded in Blaik's 1974 autobiography *The Red Blaik Story*, based on an interview that summer with reporter Bob Considine. "There was no real need for the cribbing [cheating] scandal that wrecked West Point football. It could have been settled quickly, quietly, by a reprimand from the superintendent. That was all that would have been needed except in the case of perhaps two of the boys. And they could have been helped by a kick in the pants."[12]

The "kick in the pants" seemed to infer a minor punishment for a major infraction of the Honor Code by an organized cheating group. MacArthur's love of sports and loyalty to Blaik impaired his judgment. His public support was inappropriate; even if he was a private citizen, he was still one of the most senior officers in the defense establishment. It was a poor decision personally that tarnished his professional standing and reputation. Here, MacArthur was endangering his legacy, especially considering the fact that it was he who established the honor system in 1922 and had endorsed it ever since. He was caught in the middle between two of his great loves regarding West Point: honor and sports. By publicly announcing his backing of the football program—the only senior general officer, in active service or on the retired list, to do so—he undermined the authority of the academy officials and challenged the system that he created. But this was to no avail. The guilty cadets, footballers or not, were dismissed and separated from the academy.

When they first settled in New York City, the MacArthurs attended home games at West Point, but Douglas eventually relied on Blaik to travel to New York City on Sundays to inform MacArthur about the game played the day before, upcoming games, and the latest developments. Accompanying Blaik were star players and coaches, such as Felix "Doc" Blanchard, then a US Air Force lieutenant serving as assistant coach for Blaik at West Point. (The US Air Force Academy did not exist until 1955.) They brought game films and showed them to MacArthur and Jean in their home.[13]

Coach Blaik retired as both coach and athletic director in 1959 and later published his autobiography, *The Red Blaik Story*, wherein Blaik praised MacArthur thoroughly. In 1986 Blaik received the Presidential Medal of Freedom from President Ronald Reagan.

Another love of MacArthur's was his class of 1903 and the fellow members of the Long Gray Line of his era. He received literally hundreds of letters and communications from these graduates during his life. As these men aged, their memories turned back to their youth. Some of these letters were merely notices that a classmate had died, or was ill, or news that a friend's wife had passed on, or grandchildren were attending West Point. Though he only had three army staff members, MacArthur did his best to answer each letter he received from friends, classmates, and fellow citizens. But he and his small inner circle could not reply to the thousands of birthday cards he received each year and for holiday seasons.[14]

Dorsey Rodney, a classmate, wrote Douglas in April 1952, addressing him as "MacArthur" only. Dorsey extended a welcome to MacArthur, who was coming on May 15 to speak to the Michigan state legislature. Douglas replied to Dorsey, a retired dean of the Business and Public Service at Michigan State College, saying, "As time goes on I find my affections centered more and more upon the boys who formed the Class of 1903 at West Point."[15]

In another letter in 1954 to a former cadet, MacArthur reminisced about his time as superintendent, "But to me they will always remain 'my boys' just as I hope that in each of their hearts may linger some memory of the 'Old Supe' who took such pride and gratification in mustering them into the military service."[16] In a reply to retired Maj. Gen. Leon Kromer, who graduated in 1899 (the year MacArthur arrived as a new plebe), he emphasized the connection between sports at the Military Academy and winning on the battlefield. He wrote in June 1957, "Both games, football and baseball changed greatly since our days, but the essence of each—the will for victory—will never change."[17]

Perhaps his most frequent and loyal supporter from the class of 1903 was George Cocheu, his former roommate. Cocheu retired in 1938 after thirty-years of service and was reactivated during World War II, retiring again in 1945 as a colonel. George died just two years after Douglas, in 1966.[18] George Cocheu was perhaps representative of the class of 1903, serving well and devoting most of his life to the army, but he did not achieve the level of rank and responsibility as his roommate. Douglas remained on active duty through age seventy-one and achieved general rank at age thirty-eight, rising eventually to general of the army. MacArthur was the exception for his class and most classes. Few graduates have achieved what he did.

• • •

As MacArthur aged, his visits to West Point dropped off, though he was still relatively healthy. Soon a tradition developed when cadets from the academy would visit him in his suite at the Waldorf Astoria on his birthday on January 26. They would bring gifts and memorabilia from ball games or other tokens. MacArthur and Jean were delighted to host the cadets and relished their time together. In 1955 there was an attempt to convince Arthur IV, then age seventeen, to apply for a nomination to West Point. But the young man was determined not to follow after his father's career and wanted to attend another college. This nomination was not forced on young Arthur but was probably a disappointment to his proud father.[19]

Knowing that his time was ending, MacArthur and Jean made a last trip to the Philippines in 1961. They met friends, old war veterans, and government leaders, and visited historic sites as well as battlefields on Leyte and Luzon. They also made a brief layover in Japan but had no formal activities. It was his last major trip aboard.[20] MacArthur always saw the island archipelago nation as a type of second home, having lived there for a dozen years of his life. Yet, his spiritual home remained the US Military Academy. Jean recorded this comment in an oral history interview: "I think of all the places in the world maybe the General loved West Point best." She said that MacArthur always referred to the academy as "The Point."[21]

As General MacArthur reached eighty years old, he was faced with how to preserve his legacy and all the thousands of letters, documents, mementos, and other cultural gems he and Jean had on hand. Several options were available to him, and various officials approached him. West Point was one location he was considering, along with the Smithsonian Institution, and the city of Little Rock, Arkansas, where he was born. He also knew he had to decide where he and Jean would be interned. Again, West Point was a prominent choice, but his parents were buried at Arlington National Cemetery. But he had no deep personal connection with Arlington or other locations. As MacArthur had not been president of the United States, no federal government archive and library would be authorized especially for him. He would have to seek private means or use his own resources to preserve his legacy and contributions.[22] As will be addressed in the epilogue, Douglas and Jean made an arrangement with the city of Norfolk, Virginia, for their remains and for his personal and public papers. These decisions were put in abeyance, as he did with his medical care.

MacArthur reviewing the Corps of Cadets on parade. Courtesy MacArthur Memorial.

In the 1960s MacArthur's health began to slide downward, especially after his trip to the Philippines and Japan, but he kept up a public schedule. He had fewer speaking engagements but was seen more and more as a senior statesman in the vein of George Washington or Thomas Jefferson in their retirement. Even though age and infirmities began to take their toll, he continued to meet with senior leaders, visiting Washington, DC, and the Capitol. He had two meetings with a great admirer, President John F. Kennedy, in 1961 to discuss the escalating war in Southeast Asia. The first was in April, soon after the Bay of Pigs debacle in Cuba. In their second meeting that July, MacArthur "implored the President to avoid a U.S. military build-up in Vietnam.... Kennedy came out of the meeting somewhat stunned."[23]

• • •

In 1956 the class of 1931 for its twenty-fifth anniversary offered an idea to the West Point Association of Graduates and to academy officials for an annual award to be presented to the individual "whose service and accomplishments in the national interest exemplify personal devotion to the ideals expressed in the West Point motto: Duty, Honor, Country." The award was named after Sylvanus Thayer, the Father of the US Military Academy, and rightfully so. In 1958, after the review process, the first recipient was Dr. Ernest Lawrence, a Nobel Prize–winning scientist and a founder of the Lawrence Livermore National Laboratory. The 1961 recipient was Dwight Eisenhower, who had just left office as president that January, the first of three West Point graduates to receive this distinguished award.[24]

In early 1962, General MacArthur learned that he had been selected by the Sylvanus Thayer Award committee to be the recipient to be presented the award in May. Unfortunately, during this time MacArthur had some serious health problems that nearly affected this event. For some weeks Jean and he had been planning to visit West Point to receive a new West Point blanket and an Army robe with the letterman "A" presented by the football team. But his condition would not allow it. Jean explained that originally there were to be two trips, but the two events were combined on the day of the Thayer Award banquet on May 12, 1962. According to Jean, "the General was pretty wobbly."[25]

MacArthur was deeply touched to receive this relatively new but significant honor, as he related in his opening remarks: "No human being could fail to be deeply moved by such a tribute as this. Coming from a profession I have served so long, and a people I have loved so well, it fills me with an emotion I cannot express."[26]

As the presentation day approached MacArthur received an interesting request from a cadet of the class of 1962, the senior or first class. Cadet Terrance C. McCarthy from Washington State wrote on May 4 a request that, if fulfilled, would make him a hero to the Corps of Cadets of some 2,500 young men. Cadet McCarthy requested a long-held action that all the cadets of all class years knew about and prayed for—amnesty. That is, amnesty from the drudgery of "punishment tours" or walking in the "area," the courtyard in the central barracks area. There cadets marched under arms to walk off demerits accumulated for minor infractions. Upon receiving a request from a "head of state" of a foreign nation, the superintendent might grant amnesty to the entire corps, a rare but greatly prized facet of the cadet experience. Cadet McCarthy wrote, "Sir, as we eagerly await your coming on 12 May, there is a select group

Receiving the Sylvanus Thayer Award in 1962 from Lt. Gen. Leslie Groves, president of the Association of Graduates, before delivering his famous "Duty, Honor, Country" speech. *Courtesy MacArthur Memorial.*

of us, namely, those members of the infamous, 'area squad.' ... As you know, amnesty is an old tradition at West Point, the granting of which is generally reserved for heads of state."[27]

McCarthy then recited how in 1959, just three years earlier, Gen. Garrison Davidson, the departing superintendent, had granted amnesty to the corps. McCarthy's youthful enthusiasm was admirable, especially with his final plea in rather poetic terms: "From the Punishment Squad I send you one thought, one sole idea, written in perspiration from the shimmering concrete lanes of Central Area, to the cold, dark walls of confinement, there is no substitute for amnesty."[28]

MacArthur's response was not what McCarthy expected and probably dampened the young man's hope. He replied on May 7, opening the missive using only the cadet's surname. "Dear McCarthy" was a rather unusual greeting. The letter was short: "I have just received your note of May 4th and completely understand the situation. Of course you know that I have no authority in the matter but I will use my persuasive powers as best I may to influence those who do have the authority."[29]

The authority General MacArthur referred to was the superintendent in 1962, Maj. Gen. William Childs Westmoreland, who graduated from the academy in 1936 and had been, like MacArthur, the First Captain of the Corps. Westmoreland had a remarkable war record in Europe as an artillery officer in North Africa, Sicily, and France. After the war he served in the infantry and commanded airborne units, including the 101st Airborne Division prior to accepting the West Point post. Later, he would become the commander of the Military Assistance Command, Vietnam (MACV) and then army chief of staff. Only the superintendent could grant amnesty for these minor infractions for the entire corps.[30]

• • •

The momentous day came. MacArthur anticipated that this would be the last time that he would walk the grounds and parade field on the historic Plain surrounded by the gray granite barracks and academic halls. These he first saw in 1899, some sixty-three years earlier. He and Jean had made numerous trips to West Point over time, some announced, and some not. Now was the last time he would see the home he loved and nearly worshiped.

Frail, old, and wobbly in body but not in mind, MacArthur would deliver the greatest speech in West Point history, and one of the greatest speeches in American history, the famous "Duty, Honor, Country." MacArthur first stood on the Plain and watched the corps march on the parade field. There were thirty thousand spectators at the parade observing this historic event, which included dozens of senior officers. He then climbed aboard an army jeep with Westmoreland and conduct the review, one of many he presided over during his career.[31]

MacArthur (in dark suit) and Gen. William Westmoreland, superintendent, reviewing the Corps of Cadets in 1962. *Courtesy USMA Archives.*

Then the official party entered the cadet mess hall, through the entrance of the three-winged building where some 2,500 cadets stood at attention as they arrived. Maj. Gen. Westmoreland and Lt. Gen. Leslie Groves, retired, the president of the Association of Graduates, escorted the guest of honor to the open mess. Accompanying them were Jean MacArthur and Kitsy Westmoreland, wife of General Westmoreland. The ladies were seated on the balcony above the main floor along with other dignitaries.[32]

The serving First Captain of the Corps, Cadet James Ellis, an enterprising young man, learned the day before ceremony that there was no plan to record MacArthur's remarks. Cadet Ellis arranged with a fellow cadet to record the ceremony using a state-of-the-art recording device of 1962, a reel-to-reel tape recorder. The recording was used later to document MacArthur's famous speech, and soon thereafter, copies were made and so was history.[33] James Ellis went on to become a lieutenant general with combat time in Vietnam.

There was also a shorthand version of the speech. General Westmoreland wrote a letter of appreciation to Mrs. Mary P. Riedel, the personal secretary of the superintendent, in which he thanked her for her painstaking "effort in recording in shorthand, then transcribing General MacArthur's acceptance speech." These two formats have preserved the general's remarks for all time.[34]

On the raised dais were MacArthur and other dignitaries, who were briefly introduced by Westmoreland, including General Groves, who was himself an interesting historical character. Groves graduated third in his class of November 1918 and served as an engineer officer. He was the project manager who finished the construction of the Pentagon in 1943, and then was the director of the Manhattan Project that developed the atomic bomb.[35]

Groves outlined MacArthur's accomplishments and enormous achievements during his career, saying: "Throughout more than a half century of active Army duty, Douglas MacArthur advanced his country's welfare by his outstanding military leadership, both in war and peace." Groves then presented the Sylvanus Thayer Award to him. After a huge applause by the corps and visitors, General MacArthur delivered perhaps the greatest and most eloquent speech of his life. He began: "As I was leaving the hotel this morning, a doorman asked me, 'Where are you bound for, General?' and when I replied, 'West Point.' He remarked, 'Beautiful place, have you ever been there before?'"

The story is true according to Jean MacArthur, who witnessed the exchange. The doorman was Bill Mann, a common face among the Waldorf employees, who knew the MacArthurs well and whom Jean MacArthur remembered decades later.[36]

"Duty—Honor—Country." MacArthur tapped the lectern as he spoke these words, as recorded on the reel-to-reel.

> Those three hallowed words reverently dictate what you ought to be, what you can be, what you will be. They are your rallying points: to build courage when courage seems to fail; to regain faith when there seems to be little cause for faith; to create hope when hope becomes forlorn. Unhappily, I possess neither that eloquence of diction, that poetry of imagination, nor that brilliance of metaphor to tell you all that they mean. The unbelievers will say they are but words, but a slogan, but a flamboyant phrase.... You now face a new world—a world of change.

The thrust into outer space of the satellite, spheres and missiles marked the beginning of another epoch in the long story of mankind—the chapter of the space age . . .

You are the leaven which binds together the entire fabric of our national system of defense. From your ranks come the great captains who hold the nation's destiny in their hands the moment the war tocsin sounds. The Long Gray Line has never failed us. Were you to do so, a million ghosts in olive drab, in brown khaki, in blue and gray, would rise from their white crosses thundering those magic words—Duty—Honor—Country.

This does not mean that you are war mongers. On the contrary, the soldier, above all other people, prays for peace, for he must suffer and bear the deepest wounds and scars of war. But always in our ears ring the ominous words of Plato that wisest of all philosophers, "Only the dead have seen the end of war" . . .

The shadows are lengthening for me. The twilight is here. My days of old have vanished tone and tint; they have gone glimmering through the dreams of things that were. Their memory is one of wondrous beauty, watered by tears, and coaxed and caressed by the smiles of yesterday. I listen vainly for the witching melody of faint bugles blowing reveille, of far drums beating the long roll. In my dreams I hear again the crash of guns, the rattle of musketry, the strange, mournful mutter of the battlefield.

But in the evening of my memory, always I come back to West Point.

Always there echoes and re-echoes Duty—Honor—Country.

Then came a benediction more than a farewell. His voice choked and waivered. Douglas MacArthur was saying good-bye to his home—forever. "Today marks my final roll call with you, but I want you to know that when I cross the river my last conscious thoughts will be-of The Corps, and The Corps, and The Corps. I bid you farewell."[37]

After a few moments the hall ripped into a roar of applause. MacArthur turned around and looked up to the balcony, now known as the "Poop Deck," and blew a kiss to Jean.[38]

Superintendent Westmoreland stood before the microphone and announced an official order. As recorded by journalist Robert Considine, Westmoreland informed the corps that he had approved amnesty, declaring:

"I so decree!" The cadets raised a cheer and roar that raised the roof.[39] Cadet Terrance McCarthy had obtained his wish.

MacArthur's last grand day was not quite over. After the ceremony and hundreds of handshakes and comments, he and Jean observed the annual spring football scrimmage and final day of practice. After the first half, they left for New York City, never to see West Point again.[40]

Lt. Col. M. A. Laitman, retired, and a member of the class of 1939, wrote to the general two days later: "I have never heard anyone who even approached the eloquent definition of West Point as exemplified in its motto, 'Duty, Honor, Country' as you did in your thrilling message. Your message, like your career, will serve as a stirring inspiration to the members of the Long Gray Line present to future."[41]

MacArthur's response to Laitman was brief but poignant: "It was a rare privilege to receive the Sylvanus Thayer Award and I enjoyed so much meeting many old graduates at that time." His signature block during his last years was simple and unpretentious: "Douglas MacArthur."[42]

Though many articles and news stories were published about the speech at the time, the coverage was most accurately recorded in the Association of Graduates magazine, *Assembly*, in the summer 1962 issue. "General MacArthur delivered the inspiring address which will occupy forever a prominent niche in the history of West Point," which it certainly has.[43] Chairman of the Senate Armed Services Committee, Senator John Stennis of Mississippi, thought MacArthur's remarks were so inspiring that he entered the entire speech into the *Congressional Record*, saying, "It will surely go down in history as one of the best, clearest and truest expositions of the proper role of the military man in non-military matters."[44]

An interesting letter written by a cadet to his parents the next day, May 13, 1962, can be found in the MacArthur Memorial Archives. There is no identifying information, who he was, what class he was a member of, other than the signature of "Spot." After his greeting, he wrote, "Yesterday, I heard an address to the Corps by the greatest living American—Douglas MacArthur." He continued, "The General made his final speech to a packed Washington Hall in which were four 4-star general officers. . . . When finally he concluded—the greatest speech I have ever heard . . . the entire corps and every one of the officers there, lept to their feet and shook the Mess Hall with tribute."[45]

As the years went by, MacArthur's "Duty, Honor, Country" address became legend. Copies of the speech were made, pamphlets and brochures printed; there were even fifty special copies printed by the office of the superintendent and later signed by MacArthur. These copies have been special gifts presented by the later superintendents to special guests or dignitaries. Many Americans came to believe that the US Military Academy's motto "Duty, Honor, Country" was created or first employed by MacArthur in May 1962. As was noted earlier, the coat of arms and motto were developed in 1898, a year before Douglas arrived at the academy. Many visitors to West Point ask where the "famous Duty, Honor, Country speech was delivered."[46]

Douglas MacArthur could not have planned a better send-off and grand finale of his relationship with the United States Military Academy than his last visit for the Sylvanus Thayer Award ceremony. Always a man of destiny, especially his own, he saw the great and special significance of his visit and

Cadets often made both official and social calls on MacArthur at his residence in New York City. *Courtesy MacArthur Memorial.*

speech—to speak to the assembled Corps of Cadets for the last time and say his farewell. He planned accordingly. Regardless of his hopes and dreams of a legacy, his entire life and career reached its zenith that day in the cadet mess hall. The next two years would witness his slow slide toward immortality.

Interestingly enough, MacArthur's autobiography, *Reminiscences*, published in 1964, ended with his visit and speech at West Point.

• • •

Douglas MacArthur's association with West Point did not end in May 1962 with his famous speech. Cadets and officers traveled to New York City on his birthday to present tokens and laudatory comments and for other occasions. He greeted them with great warmth and relished their youth and exuberance. MacArthur continued to follow the accomplishments of the sports teams, especially football and baseball. One of the cadets who made a pilgrimage to the Waldorf was Cadet John P. Otjen, class of 1964. On January 26 of that year, Cadet Otjen was a senior and soon to graduate, and he met the ailing general for his last birthday celebration. Later, during MacArthur's funeral procession in Washington, DC, Cadet Otjen carried the general's star flag. In 1979 then Lieutenant Colonel Otjen represented his family and the army at the MacArthur statue dedication in downtown Milwaukee. Otjen had a second West Point connection with MacArthur: Congressman Theobald Otjen of Milwaukee, Wisconsin, appointed young Douglas to the academy in 1899. The congressman was Cadet Otjen's great uncle.[47]

MacArthur's health had been deteriorating for the past few years. He had a tumor removed from his prostate in March 1960, and his declining health and appearance were obvious to friends and visitors. A physician remarked that "General MacArthur was a victim of medical [self] neglect," and that he was "utterly obsessed and convinced that he should not seek any medical care whatsoever."[48]

Like U.S. Grant nearly a hundred years earlier, as his health failed him, he commenced writing his memoirs, *Reminiscences*. He often postponed medical treatment in order to dedicate time to his research and writing. He was also spending valuable time preparing his papers, documents, and artifacts for preservation. Finally, in March 1964 Douglas flew with Jean and his advisor, Courtney Whitney, to Washington, DC. In the course of the next three weeks,

Days before his passing in 1964, General MacArthur met President Lyndon B. Johnson in Walter Reed Army General Hospital. He died wearing his West Point letterman's robe. *Courtesy MacArthur Memorial.*

MacArthur had his gall bladder and spleen removed at Walter Reed Army Medical Center on Georgia Avenue.[49]

MacArthur convalesced in Ward 8, in the original general hospital building built in 1909. Ward 8 was the Distinguished Visitor area where Eisenhower had stayed during two stays as president in the 1950s. In this suite on the fourth floor just days before his death, MacArthur met with President Lyndon B. Johnson. There is a historic photograph of MacArthur in his West Point robe with its letterman "A," slumped in an easy chair, frail, old, and dying. Across from him was Lyndon Johnson, younger, robust, and posing for the camera. On April 3, 1964, General MacArthur slid into a coma; he died two days later in this room that would later memorialize his former military secretary and chief of staff, Dwight D. Eisenhower, who also died in the same room in 1969.[50]

The old soldier had faded away wearing his West Point robe.

• • •

Within hours of his death, the general's remains were enroute to New York City. Two days later in the old 7th New York Regiment Armory, his casket was opened to the public, with thousands coming to pay their respects. The next day, April 8, a horse-drawn caisson carried the flag-draped coffin on a procession to Pennsylvania Station. The marching West Point Band led the procession that was several blocks long, followed by a battalion of West Point cadets in gray, matching the gloomy, gray April day. The remainder of the column contained other military service detachments, with senior officers from all the branches following behind.[51]

Learning of the general's death on Sunday, April 5, West Point honored the great soldier and general. During a rainy afternoon the next day, the entire Corps of Cadets, 2,500 strong, formed on the parade field on the Plain of West Point and observed a brief tribute to one of the greatest and most distinguished members of the Long Gray Line. West Point honored General

MacArthur's funeral procession, Norfolk, Virginia, April 11, 1964. *Courtesy USMA Archives.*

MacArthur with a salvo of artillery echoing across the Hudson River and Valley. It bore a striking resemblance to the time that young Douglas experienced as a cadet, when he heard the volleys of smooth-bore Civil War pieces. Superintendent Maj. Gen. James Lampert, class of 1936, remarked, "The gallant battle which he waged in his last days symbolized to all of us the very principles to which he dedicated his living."[52]

Traveling by rail to Washington, DC, the funeral party arrived at Union Station on April 8, where the casket lay in-state in the Capitol rotunda until the next day. During the procession to Capitol Hill, some 100,000 people gathered as the caisson and casket passed with Cadet John P. Otjen bearing the red, five-star flag aloft. Then General MacArthur made his last trip on earth to Norfolk for his funeral and interment.[53]

Some 150,000 people assembled in downtown Norfolk on April 11, 1964, for the funeral service, after which thousands filed past the general's remains in the newly prepared MacArthur Memorial rotunda. Sadly, General MacArthur had not seen the new memorial that was designed and prepared for his and Jean's remains, nor the library archives and museum occupying the remainder of the old courthouse.[54]

• • •

In the final analysis, Douglas MacArthur is remembered for many brilliant successes and achievements, and some alarming shortcomings and failures. One of his great achievements was his years as superintendent of the US Military Academy and the many enduring reforms he made. MacArthur's record as superintendent for three years has been reviewed and highlighted in the pages herein. As vast and far-reaching as his reforms and successes were, he was not alone. Before his tenure there were others, earlier superintendents, who made important contributions to West Point, such as Richard Delafield and Albert Mills—and, of course, Sylvanus Thayer. Others who followed in his wake also made remarkable improvements and significant reforms that greatly enhanced the Corps of Cadets and the academy. Two of these exceptional superintendents were Garrison Davidson, 1956 to 1960, and Andrew Goodpaster, 1977 to 1981.[55]

Lieutenant General Davidson, academy class of 1927, made many improvements in admissions, allowing elective courses and planning for a significant renovation in buildings and facilities. There was perhaps no superintendent who worked so smoothly with the Academic Board and gained their support and loyalty. Together, "Gar" Davidson and the faculty made positive and important reforms and changes, one of which was a major review of the curriculum and academic program with surveys and input from cadets, as well as staff and faculty. He also required doctorate degrees for permanent professors and achieved much academically with the assistance of the dean's office.[56] He planned and oversaw some changes in infrastructure such as converting the Riding Hall into Thayer Hall, the major academic building on campus.[57] Davidson had taught and coached at West Point earlier in his career, so he was well prepared to serve—besides having thirty years of US Army experience. He, like MacArthur, sought to remove many of the traditions and conditions that supported paternalism.[58]

In 1976 two significant events occurred at the academy: women were admitted to the corps; and a major cheating scandal involving more than a hundred cadets occurred. The army leadership needed the right officer to serve as superintendent with the vision, wisdom, and diplomacy to serve at this critical time. Gen. Andrew Goodpaster, academy class of 1939, had retired as a full general and commander of NATO but was recalled in 1977, accepting the reduced rank of lieutenant general. Goodpaster accepted the call and served with great distinction to improve his beloved West Point.

Goodpaster had a major source to assist him, two studies and investigations, the first known today as the Borman Report, and then the West Point Study Group. These reports laid out dozens of recommendations covering the full scope of the academy, including admissions, academics, the honor system, improving faculty relations and instruction, and especially governance. Goodpaster executed many of these recommendations and points with wisdom, diplomacy, and firm leadership at a time when the academy was at one of its lowest points in its history. Following the examples of other American colleges, Goodpaster oversaw the establishment of committees and boards to manage, assess, and govern policies and programs. He also revitalized academic processes and procedures. The major focus was to conduct a thorough review and then improve the honor system.[59] This process helped move the academy away from the attrition model to a developmental concept, which took decades to do.

These two superintendents made valuable reforms and changes to resolve the problems and improve West Point. The one aspect they did not face that MacArthur did was the great turmoil that the academy had experienced to the early graduations during the Great War. After Sylvanus Thayer, these three superintendents are among the most effective leaders the US Military Academy has had.

Epilogue

★ ★ ★ ★ ★

MacArthur and Memory at the Academy

One could argue that there are three memorials or shrines dedicated to, or that focus on, the life and legacy of General of the Army Douglas MacArthur. First is the MacArthur Memorial in Norfolk, Virginia; next is the MacArthur Corridor in the Pentagon, across the Potomac River from Washington, DC; finally, West Point itself. Some may disagree with this last claim, but if one considers the following points and facts, the assertion is more palpable. As this book has shown, even before MacArthur's death his connection to the US Military Academy was remarkably strong.

The memorial devices and real property or institutional features honoring Douglas MacArthur, nationally and internationally, number in the hundreds. There are cities named after him in the Philippines, and dozens of American public schools of all levels carry his name. Scores of physical structures or areas, such as roads, bridges, parks, plazas, stadiums, town squares, and public highways in America and overseas honor him. There are institutions, colleges and other educational entities, and academic and even leadership awards, military and civil, bearing his name. An airport on Long Island, New York, and a tunnel on the south side of the Golden Gate Bridge in San Francisco are named for him. There is the Douglas MacArthur Museum in Brisbane, Australia. The list of memorials and statuary number in the hundreds in the Philippines, Taiwan, Australia, South Korea, Indonesia, and New Guinea.[1]

The US Army every year presents an award to junior officers, the General Douglas MacArthur Leadership Award, established in 1987, governed by Army Regulation 600–89. The regulation states that "the intent of the General Douglas MacArthur Leadership Award is to recognize leadership contributions of officers in a field Army environment during the calendar year of consideration." A total of twenty-eight awards are presented each year to deserving company grade (captains, lieutenants, and warrant officers) in the army.[2]

The very day that MacArthur died, on April 5, 1964, the memorial process and history moved into a new realm that had been long underway. Most people keep souvenirs, keepsakes, mementos, and other tangible artifacts of their lives. MacArthur, as a life-long student of history and a voracious reader of political and military histories, knew what he had to do. For several years of his retirement he was approached by various archives, repositories, and institutions about his papers and private collection. Eventually, he elected to donate most of his public, professional, and even private possessions to the city of Norfolk, Virginia.

Why?

In 1960 officials from Norfolk approached MacArthur about establishing a memorial and archives in his name. His mother, Mary Pickney Harding MacArthur, was born and raised in Norfolk on the south side of the eastern branch of the Elizabeth River in the Berkley area. In November 1951 Douglas attended a dedication ceremony at the old Riveredge estate of the Hardy family. The site was dedicated as the Mary Hardy MacArthur Memorial Park, making clear the fact that the MacArthurs had a connection to Norfolk. In 1960 a new city hall building was under construction in Norfolk, and the old 1850 city hall, then later a courthouse, was available for a memorial. MacArthur accepted the Norfolk offer with one condition: that he and Jean be buried there. City officials agreed that the memorial would be their burial site also. A ceremonial opening was scheduled for the end of May 1964, but the general died a month earlier.[3]

The dedication of the MacArthur Memorial occurred as scheduled. Most of Douglas MacArthur's artifacts and papers are housed there. Jean died in 2000 at the age of 102 and was interred next to her husband of twenty-seven years in the rotunda. Eventually, a library and archive, then a modern visitors center with a theater, were built on the city block, later called MacArthur Square. Across the street is a modern shopping mall called the MacArthur Center with its emblem of five stars.[4]

In September 1981 a corridor in the Pentagon received an official new name. Presiding over the ceremony was the new president of the United States, Ronald Reagan, in his first year. Joining him was Secretary of Defense Casper Weinberger, and a special guest: Jean MacArthur. Corridor 4 on the first floor, E-ring, became known as the General Douglas MacArthur Corridor—the only corridor memorializing a person in the large, spacious executive building of America's military might. The MacArthur Corridor is a shrine of information and history, telling MacArthur's storied career with images and text covering his fifty years of service. The 1981 dedication was held outside in the bright September sun, where eighty-three-year-old Jean was the guest of honor. Secretary Weinberger provided a few remarks and explained that he served under General MacArthur in the 41st Infantry Division in the Pacific, then later served on his staff as an intelligence officer. President Reagan gave a stirring dedicatory speech citing many of MacArthur's accomplishments and ending with a reference to the famous "Duty, Honor, Country" speech of 1962 before the Corps of Cadets, which he called one of the great speeches in American history. Paraphrasing in a unique and clever way, Reagan ended by saying, "Our thoughts will turn to the General, and the General, and the General." In the forty years since, the MacArthur Corridor has seen hundreds of thousands of people, Americans and others, military and civilians, pass by its exhibits and displays.[5]

The third and last shrine honoring General MacArthur is, of course, the US Military Academy. No other graduate or person associated with the academy has so many artifacts, statuary devices, plaques, and real property that memorialize him on the post. Two other individuals have two major structures named after them: Sylvanus Thayer and Dwight Eisenhower, whereas MacArthur only has one major building, MacArthur Barracks, the largest cadet barracks. However, in the campus area of West Point, called the Central

Area, it is impossible to escape the association, achievements, contributions, and even the very spirit of MacArthur that is ubiquitous. In the West Point Museum there is the pen he used to sign the Japanese surrender instrument in 1945, ending the war in the Pacific. As part of the museum collection, but on display in the new 2008 library, is MacArthur's class ring of 1903. (Eisenhower and Omar Bradley's rings are there also.) In the library collection are scores of microfiche rolls, copies from the MacArthur Memorial in Norfolk containing thousands of documents and papers.

Across from the library is Honor Plaza, a memorial celebrating the Honor Code and system at the academy that he established in 1922 as superintendent. An inscription of a quote from the general is engraved there. In the courtyard of Taylor Hall, the headquarters building, there are two bronze plaques, replicas of the markers on the deck of the USS *Missouri* that memorialize the surrender of the Japanese in September 1945. On the larger vertical tablet is MacArthur's name and title as Supreme Commander of Allied Powers in the Pacific. There are three locations where all the portraits of the superintendents are listed or displayed. Two are in Taylor Hall, photographic copies in the superintendent's office—the same office that MacArthur used during his tenure; the third set of photos is displayed in the superintendent's conference room down the hallway.

The academy also is home to three paintings of General MacArthur. In Washington Hall, the cadet mess, hangs his image as a young general in World War I with his swagger stick under arm and cocky grin. In Grant Hall, the former reception hall for guests and families, and now a small cafeteria, hang portraits of all the five-star generals of the army: George Marshall, the only non–West Point graduate; Henry "Hap" Arnold, class of 1907; Dwight Eisenhower and Omar Bradley, both of the class of 1915; and Douglas MacArthur, class of 1903. In the Thayer Award Room in Taylor Hall hangs his portrait as a recipient of the Sylvanus Thayer Award, right next to Dwight Eisenhower's image.

In Cullum (Memorial) Hall there are large bronze plaques for all the superintendents who have passed away. Among them is the plaque dedicated to General MacArthur. These plaques have biographical information regarding awards, decorations, and positions held during their careers. MacArthur is the only superintendent to reach General of the Army rank.[6]

Plaque at West Point declaring MacArthur's legacy and devotion to the athletic program. Attached on the east wall of Arvin Cadet Physical Development Center (gymnasium). *Author's collection.*

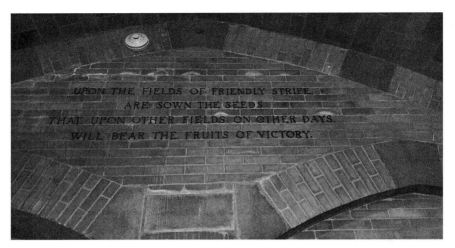

MacArthur's famous quote "Upon the fields of friendly strife..." in the old entrance of the academy's 1910 original gymnasium. *Author's collection.*

Outside the Arvin Cadet Physical Development Center—the cadet gymnasium—a plaque mounted near the entrance is devoted to MacArthur's contribution to sports and athletics. Displayed inside is the famous quote about physical fitness and combat: "Upon the fields of friendly strife are sown the seeds that upon other fields, on other days, will bear the fruits of victory."

MacArthur Barracks is perhaps the most prominent memorial to the general, constructed in 1965 to 1969. It has several devices dedicated to MacArthur. Above each sally port are engravings of battles and campaigns that he led from the Philippines to Korea. Above one of the entrances, up high, is an engraving depicting his famous service cap with the oak leaves on the band and the brim, and the five stars of his rank. At the northeast corner, where "MAC Long" and "MAC Short," as the cadets call them, meet, is a bronze plaque honoring his Medal of Honor with its citation from 1942.

Exactly opposite the plaque and wall is MacArthur Plaza. There are several statues on the historic Plain of West Point, but none are as large and as impressive as that of Douglas MacArthur. The large granite plaza has a small retaining wall with a dozen engravings of his famous and historic quotes made during his career and life. Centered in the plaza is a massive statue by famed sculptor Walker Hancock, who was one historical figures in the film *Monument Men* a recent Hollywood release. This piece is a duplicate of the statue of

Medal of Honor citation plaque regarding MacArthur's gallant leadership in the Philippines, mounted on the northeast corner of MacArthur Barracks. *Author's collection.*

the general at the MacArthur Memorial on the square in Norfolk. MacArthur Barracks and the statue were both dedicated in 1969 with Jean MacArthur in attendance. Every year members and veterans of the 42nd Rainbow Division lay a wreath at the statue. One of the most important memorials or contributions that MacArthur provided to the cadets of West Point was the large mural in the mess hall.

Statue and plaza honoring Gen. Douglas MacArthur's service and legacy, featuring a dozen quotes from his "Duty, Honor, Country" speech. The MacArthur Plaza, dedicated in 1969, is the largest such memorial at West Point. MacArthur Barracks, the largest barracks on campus, is in the background. *Author's collection*

General MacArthur's Sylvanus Thayer Award speech, as mentioned, soon became one of the most celebrated speeches in American history. No other speech, graduation, Thayer Award, or other occasion at West Point has caught the imagination of Americans as has MacArthur's "Duty, Honor, Country" address. So much so, that in 1987, during the twenty-fifth anniversary of the speech, a special commemoration was ordered by the superintendent, Lt. Gen. David R. Palmer, class of 1956. He directed an operations order be issued to plan and support a May 12, 1987, ceremony to take place on the historic Plain. The planning was thorough, and the ceremony included a dais erected exactly in front of the MacArthur Memorial and statue. One of the guests of honor was Mrs. Jean MacArthur, who was eighty-nine years old at the time. No other speech or speaker has been so honored at the academy.[7]

In recent years, MacArthur's great speech of 1962 still resonated at West Point. In 2022 during the sixtieth anniversary, academy officials held two separate commemorations in April. First, on April 14 during the weekly Spirit Night dinner, the Corps of Cadets leaders arranged a special commemoration of General MacArthur's famous "Duty, Honor, Country" speech with a slide show and broadcast of segments of the speech and tables filled with the general's artifacts. Then a week later, the US Military Academy Band held special concert in the Cadet Chapel (built in 1910).[8]

• • •

Each year a thousand cadets graduate from the US Military Academy, and a month later, more than a thousand arrive to start their forty-seven months at West Point. Except for the barracks name and the portraits in the mess hall, it is doubtful that many of the cadets are aware of and understand how much Gen. Douglas MacArthur is memorialized at the academy. The most quoted lines that cadets must memorize are from his "Duty, Honor, Country" speech. His address established the motto as a household saying; his life helped make it renowned. One can honestly say that West Point is also a memorial to Douglas MacArthur.

The US Military Academy represents many things and has endured into its third century. Along with West Point, the memory and legacy of Douglas MacArthur is also moving into its third century.

NOTES

Preface

1. William Addleman Ganoe, *MacArthur: Close-up, Much Then and Some Now* (New York: Vantage Press, 1962), 167.

Introduction

1. Douglas MacArthur, *Reminiscences: General of the Army Douglas MacArthur* (New York: McGraw-Hill, 1964), 142.
2. Geoffrey Perret, *Old Soldiers Never Die: The Life of Douglas MacArthur* (New York: Random House, 1996), 176.
3. D. Clayton James, *The Years of MacArthur, Vol. 1, 1880–1941* (Boston: Houghton Mifflin, 1970), 263.
4. Adam Badeau, *Grant in Peace: From Appomattox to Mount McGregor* (Hartford, CT: S. S. Scranton, 1887), 401.
5. MacArthur, *Reminiscences*, 426.
6. Malcolm MacArthur died in 1883 at age five; he was the second child of the MacArthur family.

Chapter 1. The School above the Hudson

1. Russell Shorto, *The Island at the Center of the World: The Epic Story of Dutch Manhattan and the Forgotten Colony that Shaped America* (New York: Vintage, 2005), 30–33.
2. Shorto, *The Island at the Center of the World*, 33.
3. Shorto, *The Island at the Center of the World*, 76–78.
4. Theodore Crackel, *West Point: A Bicentennial History* (Lawrence: University Press of Kansas, 2002), 7.

5. "From George Washington to William Heath," March 21, 1781, *Founders Online*, National Archives.
6. Crackel, *The Illustrated History of West Point* (West Point, NY: Association of Graduates, 1991), 11–12.
7. Dave Richard Palmer, *The River and the Rock: The History of Fortress West Point, 1775–1783* (New York: Greenwood, 1969), 140.
8. Palmer, *The River and the Rock*, 154–69.
9. Arnold also had married Margret Shippen, twenty years younger and a Loyalist, who only helped stoke his anger. See James Kirby Martin, *Benedict Arnold: Revolutionary Hero (An American Warrior Reconsidered)* (New York: New York University Press, 1997).
10. Crackel, *West Point: A Bicentennial History*, 21–3.
11. Richard W. Stewart, ed., *American Military History, Vol. I: Forging a Nation, 1775–1917* (Washington, DC: US Army Center of Military History, 2004), 109.
12. Crackel, *West Point: A Bicentennial History*, 37.
13. Stewart, *American Military History, Vol. I*, 116.
14. Theodore Crackel, *Mr. Jefferson's Army: The Political and Social Reform of the Military Establishment, 1801–1809* (New York: New York University Press, 1987); Seventh Congress of United States, "An Act fixing the Military Peace Establishment of the United States," March 16, 1802.
15. *Acts of Congress of the 7th Congress, March 16, 1802*, 137, cited in *The Public Statutes at Large of the United States of America, from the Organization of the Government in 1789, to March 3, 1845*, vol. 2 (Boston: Charles C. Little and James Brown, 1845).
16. Stephen Ambrose, *Duty, Honor, Country: A History of West Point* (Baltimore: Johns Hopkins University Press, 1999), 34–5.
17. Crackel, *West Point: A Bicentennial History*, 85.
18. Crackel, *West Point: A Bicentennial History*, 86–8; the Texas city of Fort Worth was named for William Worth.
19. Crackel, *The Illustrated History of West Point*, 103–105.
20. Crackel, *West Point: A Bicentennial History*, 115.
21. John S. D. Eisenhower, *Agent of Destiny: The Life and Times of General Winfield Scott* (Norman: University of Oklahoma Press, 1997), 303; C. W. Larned, "The Memorial Hall at West Point," *The Junior Munsey* 8, no. 4 (July 1900), 513–23, 516–17.
22. 37th Cong., 3d sess. (1863), *Congressional Globe*, 325.
23. Crackel, *West Point: A Bicentennial History*, 134–35.
24. Charles Larned, "West Point and Our Military Future," *Metropolitan Magazine* 22, no. 2 (May 1905): 151–52.
25. See Crackel, *West Point: A Bicentennial History*, p. 159.
26. The author having served for many years as the command historian at the US Military Academy has been asked this question hundreds of times.

27. "The Booz Case Inquiry: Military Board Hears Testimony at Bristol and Philadelphia," *New York Times*, December 18, 1900; copy on file.
28. Crackel, *The Illustrated History of West Point*, 163–64.

Chapter 2. A Military Family

1. Kenneth Ray Young, *The General's General: The Life and Times of Arthur MacArthur* (Boulder, CO: Westview Press, 1994), 18–19.
2. Letter, Arthur MacArthur to President Abraham Lincoln, May 13, 1862, Office of the Adjutant General, RG 94, NARA; cited in D. Clayton James, *The Years of MacArthur, Vol. 1, 1880–1941* (Boston: Houghton Mifflin, 1970), 12–13.
3. Young, *The General's General*, 19.
4. James, *The Years of MacArthur, Vol.1, 1880–1941*, 8–9.
5. MacArthur, *Reminiscences*, 4.
6. Ibid., 5.
7. See Young, *The General's General*, 1994.
8. Mark M. Boatner III, *The Civil War Dictionary* (New York: David McKay, 1987 [1959]), 498.
9. Young, *The General's General*, 71–73.
10. Charles B. Flood, *Grant and Sherman: The Friendship that Won the Civil War* (New York: Farrar, Straus & Giroux, 2005), 218–19.
11. Young, *The General's General*, 75.
12. Ibid., 77.
13. James, *The Years of MacArthur, Vol.1 1880–1941*, 15.
14. William Manchester, *American Caesar: Douglas MacArthur, 1880–1964* (New York: Little and Brown, 1978), 16.
15. Francis B. Heitman, *Historical Register and Dictionary of the United States Army from Its Organization, September 29, 1789 to March 2, 1903*, 2 vols. (Washington, DC: Government Printing Office, 1903; reprinted, Urbana: University of Illinois Press, 1965), 652.
16. E. B. Quiner, *Military History of Wisconsin* (Chicago: Wisconsin Historical Society, 1866), 729, available at http://content.wisconsinhistory.org/cdm/compoundobject/collection/quiner/id/16582, accessed August 20, 2018.
17. Heitman, *Historical Register*, 652.
18. MacArthur, *Reminiscences*, 10.
19. Allan R. Millett and Peter Maslowski, *For the Common Defense: A Military History of the United States of America*, rev. ed. (New York: Free Press, 1994), 248.
20. James, *The Years of MacArthur, Vol. 1, 1880–1941*, 19, 28.
21. Ibid., 23–24.
22. MacArthur, *Reminiscences*, 14.
23. Ibid., 15.
24. Ibid., 14.

25. Major G. H. Burton to Asst. Adjutant General, Dept. of Missouri, Sept. 22, 1885, National Archives, RG 94; James, *The Years of MacArthur, Vol. 1, 1880–1941*, 26.
26. US Army Center of Military History, https://history.army.mil/moh/civilwar_mr.html#MacARTHUR, accessed July 2018.
27. Dwight S. Mears, *The Medal of Honor: The Evolution of America's Highest Military Decoration* (Lawrence: University of Kansas Press, 2018), 29–30; Robert Manning, ed., *Above and Beyond: A History of the Medal of Honor from the Civil War on Vietnam* (Boston: Boston Publishing Co., 1985), 122.
28. MacArthur, *Reminiscences*, 16–17.
29. Ibid., 17.
30. James, *The Years of MacArthur, Vol. 1, 1880–1941*, 59–60.
31. MacArthur, *Reminiscences*, 6, 17.
32. See Ivan Musicant, *Empire by Default: The Spanish-American War and the Dawn of the American Century* (New York: Henry Holt, 1998).
33. Brian M. Linn, *The Philippine War: 1899–1902* (Lawrence: University of Kansas Press, 2000), 213–14.
34. James, *The Years of MacArthur, Vol. 1, 1880–1941*, 37–38.
35. MacArthur, *Reminiscences*, 25.
36. Ibid., 19.
37. Ibid., 18.
38. James, *The Years of MacArthur, Vol. 1, 1880–1941*, 62, 65.
39. Perrett, *Old Soldiers Never Die*, 23.
40. James, *The Years of MacArthur, Vol. 1, 1880–1941*, 62–63.
41. Both Billy Mitchell and Douglas MacArthur would be awarded a Congressional Gold Medal.
42. Arthur Herman, *Douglas MacArthur: American Warrior* (New York: Random House, 2017), 31.
43. MacArthur, *Reminiscences*, 18.
44. Ibid., 18.
45. Frazier Hunt, *The Untold Story of Douglas MacArthur* (New York: Devin-Adair, 1954), 18.

Chapter 3. Facing the Beast

1. James, *The Years of MacArthur, Vol. 1, 1880–1941*, 69.
2. Hugh L. Scott, *Some Memories of a Soldier* (New York: Century, 1928), 421.
3. *Annual Report of the Superintendent, 1899*, USMA Library Archives.
4. Colonel Mills received the Medal of Honor after the 1902 Centennial Ceremony.
5. *Annual Report of the Superintendent of the United States Military Academy, 1899*, (Washington, DC: Government Printing Office), 13.

6. Lance Betros, *Carved from Granite: West Point since 1902* (College Station: Texas A&M Press, 2012), 35–36.
7. Robie Lange, *Historic Structures Survey, United States Military Academy, West Point, NY, Historic American Buildings Survey*, 4 vols. (Washington, DC: National Park Service, 1984), 2:25.
8. Lange, *Historic Structures Survey*, 2:20, 22.
9. Crackel, *The Illustrated History of West Point*, 175–79.
10. *Annual Report of the Board of Visitors*, 1901.
11. Crackel, *The Illustrated History of West Point*, 106.
12. MacArthur, *Reminiscences*, 25.
13. *Annual Report of the Superintendent of the United States Military Academy, 1901* (Washington, DC: Government Printing Office, 1901), 5.
14. Crackel, *The Illustrated History of West Point*, 162.
15. Hunt, *The Untold Story of Douglas MacArthur*, 19.
16. Robert E. Wood, "An Upperclassman's View," *Assembly* 23 (Spring 1964): 4.
17. Philip W. Leon, *Bullies and Cowards: The West Point Hazing Scandal, 1898–1901* (Westport, CT: Greenwood, 2000), 77.
18. George Cocheu, Remarks at University of Tennessee dedication of bust for General Douglas MacArthur, October 1943, MacArthur Archives, RG 10, Box 4, file 14; capitalization original.
19. Wood, "An Upperclassman's View," 4.
20. Betros, *Carved from Granite*, 22.
21. *Report of the Special Committee on the Investigation of Hazing at the United States Military Academy* (Washington, DC: Government Printing Office, 1901), IV, 1146.
22. Cited in Herman, *Douglas MacArthur: American Warrior*, 48.
23. *Report of the Special Committee on the Investigation of Hazing*, 924.
24. James, *The Years of MacArthur, Vol. 1, 1880–1941*, 69.
25. Wood, "An Upperclassman's View," 4.
26. Leon, *Bullies and Cowards*, 84.
27. Hunt, *The Untold Story of Douglas MacArthur*, 19–20.
28. US Congress, *Report of the Special Committee on the Investigation of Hazing at the United States Military Academy*, 56th Cong., 2d sess., 3 vols. (Washington, DC: Government Printing Office, 1901).
29. Leon, *Bullies and Cowards*, 82.
30. *Report of the Special Committee on the Investigation of Hazing*, 1939.
31. Leon, *Bullies and Cowards*, 44.
32. Ibid., 42.
33. *Annual Report of the Superintendent of the United States Military Academy, 1901*, (Washington, DC: Government Printing Office), 5.
34. *Report of the Special Committee*, IV, 1939.

35. *Report of the Special Committee*, IV, 1252.
36. *Report of the Special Committee*, IV, 1981.
37. MacArthur, *Reminiscences*, 25–26.
38. *Report of the Special Committee*, IV, 1770.
39. Michael Doubler, *I Am the Guard: A History of the Army National Guard, 1636–2000* (Washington, DC: Government Printing Office, 2001), 143–44.
40. Kevin Keller, "Shameless, Villainous, and Wicked: A Keller Family History," *Appendix* 2, no. 4 (October 2014).
41. *Report of the Special Committee on the Investigation of Hazing*, title page cover.
42. Leon, *Bullies and Cowards*, 44.
43. James, *The Years of MacArthur, Vol. 1, 1880–1941*, 35.
44. *Report of the Special Committee on the Investigation of Hazing*.
45. *Report of the Special Committee on the Investigation of Hazing*, IV, 916, 1714.
46. MacArthur, *Reminiscences*, 25.
47. See Hunt, *The Untold Story of Douglas MacArthur*; William Manchester, *American Caesar: Douglas MacArthur, 1880–1964* (New York: Little, Brown, 1978); Perret, *Old Soldiers Never Die*; and Herman, *Douglas MacArthur: American Warrior*, who did not address MacArthur's tormentors and whether he gave up any names before the Inquiry.
48. *Report of the Special Committee*, IV, 1714.
49. *Report of the Special Committee*, IV, 1714.
50. Leon, *Bullies and Cowards*, 21 and 83. Lieutenant Zell died during the campaign against Mexican raiders in 1916, and Shannon died in the Great War in France in 1918; see also *Register of Graduates and Former Cadets*, Association of Graduates, 2010 edition, 4156.
51. *Report of the Special Committee*, III, 829.
52. *Annual Report of the Superintendent of the United States Military Academy, 1901*, 6.
53. *Annual Report of the Superintendent of the United States Military Academy, 1901*, 5–6.
54. *Annual Report of the Superintendent of the United States Military Academy, 1901*, 7.
55. Leon, *Bullies and Cowards*, 137–39.
56. Ibid., *Bullies and Cowards*, 140–41.
57. MacArthur, *Reminiscences*, 25.

Chapter 4. The Corps

1. Arthur P. S. Hyde, "Douglas MacArthur," *Assembly* 1, no. 3 (October 1942): 3.
2. James, *The Years of MacArthur, Vol. 1, 1880–1941*, 72.
3. Hyde, "Douglas MacArthur."
4. Lange, *Historic Structures Survey United States Military Academy, West Point, NY*, 2:15–16.
5. Hyde, "Douglas MacArthur," 3.

6. Ibid.
7. George W. Cocheu, "Cadet Days, 1899–1903," *Assembly* 23, no. 1 (Spring 1964): 6–7.
8. James, *The Years of MacArthur, Vol. 1, 1880–1941*, 82.
9. Marty Maher, *Bringing up the Brass: My 55 Years at West Point* (Quechee: Vermont Heritage Press, 2002), 73.
10. MacArthur, *Reminiscences*, 27.
11. Ibid.
12. Bess B. Follansbee, Typescript of Journal, 9–10 February 1903, MacArthur Archives and Memorial, RG 10 Box 143, File 9.
13. Follansbee, Typescript of Journal, page 1.
14. David J. Yerba, "Colonel Herman J. Koehler: The Father of Physical Education" (unpublished master's thesis, Long Island University, 1998), 13.
15. Yerba, "Colonel Herman J. Koehler," 1.
16. Ibid., 11.
17. Maher, *Bringing up the Brass*, 65.
18. Ibid., 70.
19. Mike Huber and Jack Picciuto, "The First Army-Navy Baseball Game," *Baseball: A Journal of the Early Game* 1, no. 1 (Spring 2007): 96–102.
20. Doug Dean, Rick McPeak, and Scotty Autin, "How Army's Mascot Came to Be," *West Point* 10, no. 1 (Winter 2020): 62–64.
21. Manchester, *American Caesar*, 56.
22. Huber and Picciuto, "The First Army-Navy Baseball Game," 97.
23. *Register of Graduates and Former Cadets*, 2002 edition, 4–84.
24. MacArthur, *Reminiscences*, 26; Aguinaldo was the Filipino insurgent leader against the Americans.
25. *Annual Report of Army Officers Athletic Association* for the year 1901; tragically Edward Zell took his own life in 1916 during the Mexican Punitive Expedition at age thirty-five; *Register of Graduates and Former Cadets*, 2002 edition, 4–90.
26. *Annual Report of Army Officers Athletic Association* for the year 1901.
27. MacArthur, *Reminiscences*, 27.
28. *Annual Report of Army Officers Athletic Association* for the year 1901; Huber and Picciuto, "The First Army-Navy Baseball Game," 98.
29. James, *The Years of MacArthur, Vol. 1, 1880–1941*, 79.
30. Hyde, "Douglas MacArthur," 3.
31. Herman, *Douglas MacArthur: American Warrior*, 52.
32. James, *The Years of MacArthur, Vol. 1, 1880–1941*, 74–75.
33. "Douglas MacArthur, Class of 1903" printout summary, USMA Register 1901–1903 archive; James, *The Years of MacArthur, Vol. 1, 1880–1941*, 74.
34. James, *The Years of MacArthur, Vol. 1, 1880–1941*, 74.
35. Ibid., 74.

36. MacArthur, *Reminiscences*, 27.
37. James, *The Years of MacArthur, Vol. 1, 1880–1941*, 77.
38. Ibid.
39. "Douglas MacArthur, Class of 1903" printout summary, USMA Register 1901–1903 archive.
40. Hyde, "Douglas MacArthur."
41. Ibid.
42. "Douglas MacArthur, Class of 1903" printout summary, USMA Register 1901–1903 archive.
43. Honors Register, September 1, 1949, Official Records of the US Military Academy, USMA Archives.
44. George S. Pappas, "More to the Point: The West Point Centennial in 1902," *Register of Graduates and Former Cadets, Bicentennial 2002 Edition* (Association of Graduates), 1:44.
45. *Annual Report of the Superintendent, 1902*, 57.
46. Calvin P. Titus, "A Day in the Life of a Company Bugler," *Register of Graduates and Former Cadets, Bicentennial 2002 Edition* (Association of Graduates), 1:64.
47. Crackel, *West Point: A Bicentennial History*, 166.
48. Titus, "A Day in the Life a Company Bugler," 1:65.
49. Robert Manning, *Above and Beyond: A History of the Medal of Honor from the Civil War on Vietnam* (Boston: Boston Publishing, 1985).
50. Robert J. Nichols, "West Point's First Captains," *Assembly* 28, no. 4 (Winter 1970).
51. Nichols, "West Point's First Captains."
52. Hunt, *The Untold Story of Douglas MacArthur*, 27.
53. *Register of Graduates and Former Cadets*, 2002 edition.
54. Wood, "An Upperclassman's View," 5.
55. Hunt, *The Untold Story of Douglas MacArthur*, 50.
56. *Register of Graduates and Former Cadets*, 2002 edition, 4:89–90.
57. MacArthur, *Reminiscences*, 28.
58. Cocheu, "Cadet Days, 1899–1903," 7.

Chapter 5. Classmates, Connections, and Careers

1. *Register of Graduates and Former Cadets*, 2002 edition, 6:5.
2. Ibid., 4:89–90.
3. Headquarters, Corps of Engineers, Subject, Stations and Duties, Washington, July 1, 1903; MacArthur Archives, RG 15, Box 15, File 16.
4. *Annual Report of the Superintendent*, 1899, 7.
5. James, *The Years of MacArthur, Vol. 1, 1880–1941*, 88.
6. Linn, *The Philippine War: 1899–1902*, 326–28.
7. MacArthur, *Reminiscences*, 29.

8. Ibid.
9. Carol Petillo, *Douglas MacArthur: The Philippine Year* (Bloomington: Indiana University Press, 1981), 25.
10. MacArthur, *Reminiscences*, 30–32.
11. Millett and Maslowski, *For the Common Defense*, 272–76.
12. MacArthur, *Reminiscences*, 30.
13. Ibid., 31.
14. Ibid., 31–32.
15. Perret, *Old Soldiers Never Die*, 54.
16. White House to W. H. Taft, Department of War, December 8, 1908, MacArthur Memorial Archive, RG 15, Box 15, File 16.
17. James, *The Years of MacArthur, Vol. 1, 1880–1941*, 96.
18. Young, *The General's General*, 1994.
19. W. Judson to the Adjutant General, July 17, 1908, MacArthur Memorial Archive, RG 15, Box 15, File 16.
20. James, *The Years of MacArthur, Vol. 1, 1880–1941*, 99–100.
21. Ibid., 649–50.
22. Chief of Engineers to Adjutant General, April 1, 1908, RG 15, Box 15, File 16.
23. MacArthur, *Reminiscences*, 34.
24. *Annual Report of the Superintendent*, 1901, 19.
25. James, *The Years of MacArthur, Vol. 1, 1880–1941*, 104–05.
26. *Annual of the Superintendent*, 1900, 42–43.
27. MacArthur, *Reminiscences*, 34.
28. Ibid., 35–36.
29. Ibid., 39.
30. John S. D. Eisenhower, *Intervention: The United States and the Mexican Revolution, 1913–17*, (New York: W. W. Norton, 1993), 79–108.
31. Eisenhower, *Intervention: The United States and the Mexican Revolution*, 109–124.
32. Manchester, *American Caesar*, 75.
33. James, *The Years of MacArthur, Vol. 1, 1880–1941*, 118–19.
34. MacArthur, *Reminiscences*, 42.
35. Ibid.
36. Ibid.
37. James, *The Years of MacArthur, Vol. 1, 1880–1941*, 121.
38. Funston to the Adjutant General, January 13, 1915, Adjutant General Correspondence, RG 94, NARA.
39. James, *The Years of MacArthur, Vol. 1, 1880–1941*, 125.
40. Ibid., 126.
41. Hunt, *The Untold Story of Douglas MacArthur*, 58–59.

Chapter 6. Fighting in France

1. Scott to the Adjutant General, March 23, 1916, Adjutant General Correspondence, RG 94, NARA cited in James, *The Years of MacArthur, Vol. 1, 1880–1941*, 131.
2. Ibid.
3. MacArthur, *Reminiscences*, 44.
4. James, *The Years of MacArthur, Vol. 1, 1880–1941*, 131.
5. Hugh S. Johnson, obituary, *Assembly* 2, no. 1 (April 1943): 10–12.
6. Michael D. Doubler, *I Am the Guard: A History of the Army National Guard, 1636–2000* (Washington, DC: Government Printing Office 2001), 173–74.
7. MacArthur, *Reminiscences*, 46.
8. Henry J. Reilly, *Americans All: The Rainbow in War* (Columbus, OH: F. J. Heer, 1936), 28–30.
9. C.D.H. "Briant H. Wells," obituary, *Assembly* (January 1951): 50–52; the initials are the unknown author.
10. MacArthur, *Reminiscences*, 46–47.
11. James, *The Years of MacArthur, Vol. 1, 1880–1941*, 140.
12. "Order of Battle of the United States Land Forces in the World War, American Expeditionary Forces: Divisions" (1931; repr., Washington, DC: Office Chief of Military History, 1988), 272.
13. Cooke, *The Rainbow Division in the Great War*, 22–23.
14. MacArthur, *Reminiscences*, 53.
15. Hunt, *The Untold Story of Douglas MacArthur*, 71.
16. Perret, *Old Soldiers Never Die*, 86.
17. MacArthur helped established both the Silver Star and the Purple Heart in 1932; the process was, if Pershing concurred with the board, then the Medal of Honor endorsement would go to the president.
18. Manchester, *American Caesar*, 86–88.
19. James, *The Years of MacArthur, Vol. 1, 1880–1941*, 156.
20. Manchester, *American Caesar*, 88.
21. Ibid., 86.
22. MacArthur, *Reminiscences*, 54.
23. *New York Times*, March 16, 1918; James, *The Years of MacArthur, Vol. 1, 1880–1941*, 157.
24. See Edward M. Coffman, *The War to End All Wars: The American Military Experience in World War I* (Lexington: University Press of Kentucky, 1998).
25. MacArthur, *Reminiscences*, 47.
26. Hunt, *The Untold Story of Douglas MacArthur*, 74.
27. Ibid., 75.
28. Cited in James, *The Years of MacArthur, Vol. 1, 1880–1941*, 169–71; letters are found in the John J. Pershing Papers, Library of Congress.

29. James, *The Years of MacArthur, Vol. 1, 1880–1941*, 170.
30. Ibid., 171–72.
31. Cooke, *The Rainbow Division in the Great War*, 130.
32. John Mosier, *The Myth of the Great War: A New Military History of World War I* (New York: Perennial, 2002), 7.
33. John Keegan, *The First World War* (New York: Alfred A. Knopf, 1998), 409–11.
34. Manchester, *American Caesar*, 102.
35. John S. D. Eisenhower, *Yanks: The Epic Story of the American Army in World War I* (New York: Free Press, 2001), 198.
36. Cooke, *The Rainbow Division in the Great War*, 164.
37. MacArthur, *Reminiscences*, 66.
38. US Senate, Report No. 2116, 87th Cong., September 21, 1962, 10–11; Bowman and Caubarreaux, *The Decorations, Awards, and Honors of General of the Army Douglas MacArthur* (self-published, CreateSpace, 2012), 33.
39. MacArthur, *Reminiscences*, 66.
40. James, *The Years of MacArthur, Vol. 1, 1880–1941*, 219.
41. Reilly, *Americans All: The Rainbow in War*, 677–78.
42. Ibid., 678.
43. Cooke, *The Rainbow Division in the Great War*, 173.
44. Reilly, *Americans All: The Rainbow in War*, 678.
45. MacArthur, *Reminiscences*, 67.
46. *United States Army in the World War 1917–1919, Military Operations of the American Expeditionary Forces* (Washington, DC: Historical Division Department of the Army, 1948), 281; this is the same George Marshall who became chief of staff during World War II, and secretary of state and defense after the war.
47. John Keegan, *The First World War* (New York: Alfred A. Knopf, 1998), 423–24.
48. MacArthur, *Reminiscences*, 71, note.
49. Herman, *Douglas MacArthur: American Warrior*, 143.
50. Hunt, *The Untold Story of Douglas MacArthur*, 96.
51. MacArthur, *Reminiscences*, 67.
52. Bowman and Caubarreaux, *The Decorations, Awards and Honors of General of the Army Douglas MacArthur*.

Chapter 7. Chaos on the Hudson

1. Millett and Maslowski, *For the Common Defense*, 349–50.
2. Jacob L. Devers, "The Mark of the Man in USMA," *Assembly* 23, no. 1 (Spring 1964): 17.
3. Stewart, *American Military History, Vol. II*, 22.
4. Ambrose, *Duty, Honor, Country*, 252–53.
5. George Washington Cullum, *Biographical Register of the Officers and Graduates of the United States Military Academy*, 3d ed. (Boston : Houghton, Mifflin, 1891), 128.

6. James, *The Years of MacArthur, Vol. 1, 1880–1941*, 262; Betros, *Carved from Granite*, 119.
7. Ganoe, *MacArthur: Close-up*, 14–15.
8. Ibid., 15.
9. Ibid., 13.
10. *Register of Graduates and Former Cadets*, 2010 edition, 5772.
11. MacArthur, *Reminiscence*s, 80.
12. James, *The Years of MacArthur, Vol. 1, 1880–1941*, 263.
13. Ganoe, *MacArthur: Close-up*, 20.
14. *Annual Report of the Superintendent 1919*, 5, 63.
15. *Annual Report of the Superintendent 1919*, 4–5.
16. Ambrose, *Duty, Honor, Country*, 256.
17. Lewis Sorley, *Honor Bright: History and Origins of the West Point Honor Code and System* (West Point, NY: Association of Graduates, 2009), 39.
18. *Annual Report of the Superintendent 1919*, 28.
19. Ganoe, *MacArthur: Close-up*, 13.
20. Ibid.
21. *Annual Report of the Superintendent 1919*, 3.
22. *Howitzer*, 1921, 75.
23. Ibid., 76–77.
24. Ganoe, *MacArthur: Close-up*, 88–89.
25. Ibid., 120–21.
26. Gary D. Langford, "1919: MacArthur's Vision of West Point's Future Warriors" (MA thesis, USMA History Department, 1991), 8.
27. Robert M. Danford, "USMA's 31st Superintendent," *Assembly* 22, no. 1 (Spring 1964): 14.
28. Ganoe, *MacArthur: Close-up*, 54.
29. John H. Beasley, "The USMA Honor System: A Due Process Hybrid" (Charlottesville: Judge Advocate General's School, 1983), 5.
30. Earl "Red" Blaik, "A Cadet under MacArthur," *Assembly* 23, no. 1 (Spring 1964): 8.
31. Betros, *Carved from Granite*, 111.
32. *New York Times*, May 21, 1919.
33. James, *The Years of MacArthur, Vol. 1, 1880–1941*, 271.
34. *New York Times*, May 9, 1920.
35. *Annual Report of the Superintendent 1919*, 42–45.
36. Ambrose, *Duty, Honor, Country*, 262.

Chapter 8. King of West Point

1. Jean Edward Smith, *Eisenhower in War and Peace* (New York: Random House, 2013), 59.
2. Smith, *Eisenhower in War and Peace*, 60.

3. *Register of Graduates and Former Cadets*, Bicentennial Edition, 2002.
4. MacArthur, *Reminiscences*, 77.
5. James, *The Years of MacArthur, Vol. 1, 1880–1941*, 261.
6. Benjamin Runkle, *Generals in the Making: How Marshall, Eisenhower, Patton, and Their Peers Became the Commanders who Won World War II* (Guilford, CT: Stackpole Books, 2019), 34.
7. Letter, MacArthur to Weller, May 13, 1919, MacArthur Memorial Archives, RG 5, Box 5, File 3.
8. Letter, MacArthur to Weller, May 13, 1919, MacArthur Memorial Archives, RG 5, Box 5, File 3.
9. *Annual Report of the Superintendent, 1920*, 3.
10. Lange, *Historic Structures Survey United States Military Academy, West Point, NY*, vol. 2, 30.
11. Lange, *Historic Structures Survey United States Military Academy, West Point, NY*, vol. 2, 26–29.
12. Ganoe, *MacArthur: Close-up*, 23; Ganoe was a temporary lieutenant colonel in the National Army during the war, but then reverted to his permanent rank of major; he is listed as a major in the *Annual Report of Superintendent, 1919*.
13. Ganoe, *MacArthur: Close-up*, 21, 23.
14. *Register of Graduates and Former Cadets*, 2010 edition, 4–90.
15. Ganoe, *MacArthur: Close-up*, 20.
16. Ibid., 24–25.
17. Ibid.
18. Ibid., 23–24.
19. Ibid., 25.
20. Ibid., 26.
21. See Donald E. Alberts, *Brandy Station to Manila Bay: A Biography of General Wesley Merritt* (Austin, TX: Presidial Press, 1980).
22. Ganoe, *MacArthur: Close-up*, 23.
23. Ibid., 26–27.
24. Ibid.
25. Blaik, "A Cadet under MacArthur," 8.
26. Betros, *Carved from Granite*, 31.
27. Ibid., 13.
28. Crackel, *The Illustrated History of West Point*, 92, 99; Betros, *Carved from Granite*, 7.
29. Betros, *Carved from Granite*, 12.
30. Crackel, *The Illustrated History of West Point*, 214.
31. Betros, *Carved from Granite*, 32.
32. James, *The Years of MacArthur, Vol. 1, 1880–1941*, 266.
33. Ibid., 267–68.
34. Ganoe, *MacArthur: Close-up*, 88–89.

35. Ibid., 88.
36. Ganoe, *The History of the United States Army*, first published in 1924, again in 1942, and finally in 1964.
37. Ganoe, *MacArthur: Close-up*, 10.
38. Roger H. Nye, "The United States Military Academy in an Era of Educational Reform, 1900–1925" (PhD diss., Columbia University, 1968), 325, n42.
39. Ganoe, *MacArthur: Close-up*, foreword.
40. Crackel, *The Illustrated History of West Point*, 213.
41. MacArthur, *Reminiscences*, 82.
42. Crackel, *The Illustrated History of West Point*, 213.
43. *Annual Report of the Superintendent, 1920,* 5.
44. *Annual Report of the Superintendent, 1920,* 44.
45. James, *The Years of MacArthur, Vol. 1, 1880–1941,* 270–71.
46. Robert M. Danford, "USMA's 31st Superintendent," *Assembly* 23, no. 1 (Spring 1964): 13.
47. James, *The Years of MacArthur, Vol. 1, 1880–1941,* 266.
48. Danford, "USMA's 31st Superintendent."
49. James, *The Years of MacArthur, Vol. 1, 1880–1941,* 268.
50. *Annual Report of the Superintendent,* 1920, 5.
51. *Annual Report of the Superintendent,* 1920, 3.
52. *Annual Report of the Superintendent,* 1920, 3.
53. *Annual Report of the Superintendent,* 1920, 4.
54. "Historical Record of the Authorized Strength of the U.S. Corps of Cadets," Factsheet, USMA History Office.
55. Ganoe, *MacArthur: Close-up*, 65–66; Bowman and Caubarreaux, *The Decorations, Awards and Honors of General of the Army Douglas MacArthur*, 58.
56. Ganoe, *MacArthur: Close-up*, 68.
57. Ibid.
58. Ibid., 69–71.
59. Ambrose, *Duty, Honor, Country*, 66.
60. Ganoe, *MacArthur: Close-up*, 72.
61. Letter, Joseph M. O'Donnell to Maj. Gen. Charles G. Stevenson, August 11, 1966, USMA Archives.
62. *New York Times*, December 12, 192; James, *The Years of MacArthur, Vol. 1, 1880–1941*, 274.
63. Lange, *Historic Structures Survey United States Military Academy, West Point, NY*, vol. 2.
64. Dr. A. G. Wilde to D. MacArthur, January 26, 1947, MacArthur Memorial Archives, RG 10; James, *The Years of MacArthur, Vol. 1, 1880–1941*, 265–66; Crackel, *The Illustrated History of West Point*, 125.
65. Manchester, *American Caesar*, 120.

66. Ibid., 121.
67. James, *The Years of MacArthur, Vol. 1, 1880–1941*, 291.

Chapter 9. Reforming the Monastery

1. Betros, *Carved from Granite*, 45.
2. *New York Times*, May 21, 1919; MacArthur, *Reminiscences*, 81.
3. MacArthur, *Reminiscences*, 81.
4. Betros, *Carved from Granite*, 27.
5. T. Bentley Mott, "West Point: A Criticisim," *Harpers,* March 1934.
6. MacArthur, *Reminiscences*, 81.
7. *Annual Report of the Superintendent, 1920,* 3.
8. MacArthur, *Reminiscences*, 80.
9. Ganoe, *MacArthur: Close-up*, 113.
10. *Annual Report of the Superintendent, 1920,* 4.
11. MacArthur, *Reminiscences*, 79; *Annual Report of the Superintendent, 1920,* 4.
12. *Annual Report of the Superintendent, 1922,* 7–8.
13. Danford, "USMA's 31st Superintendent," 14.
14. The old Central Barracks had meeting halls above the sally ports named after prominent academy officials or graduates. Ganoe, *MacArthur: Close-up*, 123.
15. James, *The Years of MacArthur, Vol. 1, 1880–1941*, 279.
16. Ganoe, *MacArthur: Close-up*, 122.
17. MacArthur, *Reminiscences*, 81.
18. Ganoe, *MacArthur: Close-up*, 124.
19. Ibid., 114, 122.
20. Runkle, *Generals in the Making*, 57.
21. Blaik, "A Cadet under MacArthur," 9.
22. *Register of Graduates and Former Cadets*, 2010; Leonidas Warren Payne, *Survey of Texas Literature* (New York: Randy McNally, 1928), available at https://tshaonline.org/handbook/online/articles/fbi17.
23. Ganoe, *MacArthur: Close-up*, 104–105.
24. *USMA Regulations, 1920,* 42.
25. Devers, "The Mark of the Man on USMA," 17.
26. *Annual Report of the Superintendent, 1921,* 8.
27. Danford, "USMA's 31st Superintendent," 14.
28. Ganoe, *MacArthur: Close-up*, 110.
29. Sorley, *Honor Bright*, 43.
30. Ganoe, *MacArthur: Close-up*, 111–12.
31. Maxwell D. Taylor, *Swords and Ploughshares* (New York: W. W. Norton, 1972), 26.
32. USMA, Class of 1920, *Traditions and Customs of the Corps*.
33. MacArthur, *Reminiscences*, 81.
34. Thom Yates, "MacArthur in Sports," *Esquire,* August 1942, 27.

35. Ganoe, *MacArthur: Close-up*, 76.
36. Betros, *Carved from Granite*, 172.
37. Maher, *Bringing up the Brass*, 64.
38. Earl Blaik, *The Red Blaik Story* (New Rochelle, NY: Arlington House 1974), 36.
39. There are several historical summaries in the USMA History Office files debating whether MacArthur coined the line.
40. Sydney Forman, *The Educational Objectives of the U.S. Military Academy* (West Point, NY: USMA Publications, 1946), 28,
41. Betros, *Carved from Granite*, 168.
42. Ibid., 171.
43. Ganoe, *MacArthur: Close-up*, 86.
44. Ibid., 83.
45. Letter, MacArthur to Ralph Cannon, April 18, 1939, USMA History Office files; MacArthur Folder.
46. *Annual Report of the Superintendent, 1922*, 11.
47. Ganoe, *MacArthur: Close-up*, 78–79.
48. Ibid., 76.
49. Crackel, *The Illustrated History of West Point*, 213.
50. James, *The Years of MacArthur, Vol. 1, 1880–1941*, 273.
51. Crackel, *West Point: A Bicentennial History*, 191.
52. Ibid., 189.
53. Ibid., 191.
54. James, *The Years of MacArthur, Vol. 1, 1880–1941*, 271.
55. *Annual Report of the Superintendent, 1920*, 20.
56. MacArthur memorandum, March 22, 1921, "Aerodynamics Course (1918–1925)," Permanent Records, USMA Archives.
57. Devers, "The Mark of the Man on USMA," 17.
58. *Annual Report of the Superintendent, 1921*, 4.
59. Ganoe, *MacArthur: Close-up*, 91.
60. Ibid., 128.
61. Devers, "The Mark of the Man in USMA," 19.
62. Ganoe, *MacArthur: Close-up*, 30.
63. Betros, *Carved from Granite*, 219.
64. Ganoe, *MacArthur: Close-up*, 30.
65. James, *The Years of MacArthur, Vol. 1, 1880–1941*, 279.
66. *Annual Report of Superintendent, 1920*, 3.
67. Ganoe, *MacArthur: Close-up*, 120.
68. Ibid, 121.
69. Crackel, *West Point: A Bicentennial History*, 193.
70. Ganoe, *MacArthur: Close-up*, 151–53.
71. *Howitzer*, USMA, 1922, 353.

72. Ganoe, *MacArthur: Close-up*, 151.
73. *Annual Report of the Superintendent, 1921*, 19–20.
74. *Annual Report of the Superintendent, 1921*, 17–20.
75. *Annual Report of the Superintendent, 1921*, 17–20.
76. James, *The Years of MacArthur, Vol. 1, 1880–1941*, 319–20. Quekemeyer was assigned to be commandant of cadets in 1926 but died before he could take office.
77. MacArthur, *Reminiscences*, 83; James, *The Years of MacArthur, Vol. 1, 1880–1941*, 291–92.
78. *Register of Graduates and Former Cadets*, 2010.
79. Nye, "The United States Military Academy in an Era of Educational Reform, 1900–1925," 330–31.
80. Crackel, *Illustrated History of West Point*, 205.
81. Runkle, *Generals in the Making*, 59.
82. *Annual Report of the Superintendent, 1923*, 6.
83. *Annual Report of the Superintendent, 1923*, 7.
84. Betros, *Carved from Granite*, 246.
85. James, *The Years of MacArthur, Vol. 1, 1880–1941*, 291.
86. Douglas MacArthur 201 File, MacArthur Memorial Archive.
87. Ambrose, *Duty, Honor, Country*, 283.
88. MacArthur to Louise Brooks, November 10, 1921, RG 10, MacArthur Memorial Archive.
89. Herman, *Douglas MacArthur: American Warrior*, 177.

Chapter 10. Mentoring the Long Gray Line in Peace

1. MacArthur, *Reminiscences*, 84.
2. Hunt, *The Untold Story of Douglas MacArthur*, 116.
3. MacArthur, *Reminiscences*, 84.
4. Hunt, *The Untold Story of Douglas MacArthur*, 114.
5. James, *The Years of MacArthur, Vol. 1, 1880–1941*, 298–99.
6. Ibid., 295.
7. Manchester, *American Caesar*, 133.
8. Ibid., 38.
9. James, *The Years of MacArthur, Vol. 1, 1880–1941*, 304–305.
10. Petillo, *Douglas MacArthur: The Philippine Years*, 135.
11. MacArthur, *Reminiscences*, 84.
12. Letter, Adjutant General's Office, War Department, July 17, 1925; copy in MacArthur 201 File, Military Records Administration, St. Louis, Missouri.
13. Peg Brickley, "Wealth and Folly and More," *Philadelphia Business Journal*, January 10, 2000.
14. James, *The Years of MacArthur, Vol. 1, 1880–1941*, 306–17.
15. Ibid., 64.

16. Millett and Maslowski, *For the Common Defense*, 388–90.
17. MacArthur, *Reminiscences*, 85; James, *The Years of MacArthur, Vol. 1, 1880–1941*, 306–307.
18. Isaac D. Levine, *Mitchell: Pioneer of Air Power* (New York: World Publishing, 1943), chs. 12 and 13.
19. Herman, *Douglas MacArthur: American Warrior*, 188–89.
20. Levine, *Mitchell: Pioneer of Air Power*, chs. 12 and 13.
21. MacArthur, *Reminiscences*, 84–85.
22. Petillo, *Douglas MacArthur: The Philippine Years*, 140.
23. MacArthur, *Reminiscences*, 86.
24. Manchester, *American Caesar*, 140.
25. *The Olympic*, October 1927, p. 53; copy on file.
26. MacArthur, *Reminiscences*, 86.
27. West Point Olympians, fact sheet; copy on file.
28. James, *The Years of MacArthur, Vol. 1, 1880–1941*, 672.
29. Hunt, *The Untold Story of Douglas MacArthur*, 121.
30. MacArthur, *Reminiscences*, 83.
31. Ibid., 88.
32. John Costello, *The Pacific War: 1941–1945* (New York: Harper Perennial, 2009), 40.
33. Perrett, *Old Soldiers Never Die*, 140.
34. Johnson Hagood, "Down the Big Road," 457–58, Hagood Papers, US Army Military History Institute.
35. MacArthur, *Reminiscences*, 88.
36. Manchester, *American Caesar*, 143.
37. MacArthur, *Reminiscences*, 89.
38. *Register of Graduates and Former Cadets*, Association of Graduates, 2010, 4–86.
39. MacArthur, *Reminiscences*, 88–89.
40. MacArthur, *Reminiscences*, 89.
41. James, *The Years of MacArthur, Vol. 1, 1880–1941*, 344.
42. Herbert Hoover, *The Memoirs of Herbert Hoover*, 3 vols. (New York: Macmillan, 1951–52), 2: 339.
43. James, *The Years of MacArthur, Vol. 1, 1880–1941*, 344.
44. Ibid., 347.

Chapter 11. Chief of Staff

1. David M. Kennedy, *Freedom from Fear: The American People in the Depression and War, 1929–1945* (Oxford: Oxford University Press, 1999), 38, 58–59.
2. Perrett, *Old Soldiers Never Die*, 144.
3. MacArthur, *Reminiscences*, 90.
4. James, *The Years of MacArthur, Vol. 1, 1880–1941*, 347.
5. Smith, *Eisenhower in War and Peace*, 95, 105.

6. James, *The Years of MacArthur, Vol. 1, 1880–1941*, 358.
7. MacArthur to Bertrand D. Snell, May 9, 1932, Adjutant General Records, 1932; cited in James, *The Years of MacArthur, Vol. 1, 1880–1941*, 360.
8. Fred L. Borch, "The Purple Heart—The Story of America's Oldest Military Decoration and Some Soldier Recipients," *On Point: The Journal of Army History* 21, no. 3 (Winter 2016).
9. MacArthur, *Reminiscences*, 102.
10. Fred L. Borch, "Army Silver Stars for World Wars I and II, and Korea: A Study of Official Naming," *Journal of the Order and Medals Society of American* (July/August 2014).
11. MacArthur, *Reminiscences*, 92.
12. Perrett, *Old Soldiers Never Die*, 154.
13. Herman, *Douglas MacArthur: American Warrior*, 224.
14. *Register of Cadets and Former Graduates*, Association of Graduates, 2015 edition; James, *The Years of MacArthur, Vol. 1, 1880–1941*, 388–89, 391, 398.
15. Roger Daniels, *The Bonus March: An Episode of the Great Depression* (Westport, CT: Greenwood, 1971), 40.
16. MacArthur, *Reminiscences*, 93.
17. Daniels, *The Bonus March*, 121; James, *The Years of MacArthur, Vol. 1, 1880–1941*, 383–4; *Washington Star*, June 19, 1932.
18. Daniels, *The Bonus March*, 141.
19. Ibid., 153; some accounts have a baby dying from the use of tear gas.
20. Report from the Chief of Staff, United States Army, to the Secretary of War on the Employment of Federal Troops in Civil Disturbance in the District of Columbia, July 28–30, 1932, cited in Daniels, *The Bonus March*, 296.
21. Mark Perry, *The Most Dangerous Man in America: The Making of Douglas MacArthur* (New York: Basic Books, 2014), xv.
22. Perry L. Miles, *Fallen Leaves: Memories of an Old Soldier* (Berkeley, CA: Wuerth, 1961), 307; also cited in Perrett, *Old Soldiers Never Die*, 158.
23. Daniels, *The Bonus March*, 149–50; MacArthur, *Reminiscences*, 97.
24. Manchester, *American Caesar*, 152; Daniels, *The Bonus March*, 168–69; Herman, *Douglas MacArthur: American Warrior*, 220–21.
25. James, *The Years of MacArthur, Vol. 1, 1880–1941*, 406.
26. *Washington Daily News*, July 29, 1932.
27. Smith, *Eisenhower in War and Peace*, 115.
28. Perrett, *Old Soldiers Never Die*, 161.
29. The entire Report of the Chief of Staff, dated August 15, 1932, is cited in Daniels, *The Bonus March*, 291–97; a few sources declared a child died indirectly from tear gas effects. See Herman, *Douglas MacArthur: American Warrior*, 220.
30. Hunt, *The Untold Story of Douglas MacArthur*, 147.
31. Mark Perry, *The Most Dangerous Man in America*, xi.

32. Manchester, *American Caesar*, 156.
33. James, *The Years of MacArthur, Vol. 1, 1880–1941*, 412–13.
34. "New York Passenger and Crew Lists, 1909–1957," database of FamilySearch, citing National Archives microfilm, T175.
35. Manchester, *American Caesar*, 145.
36. Petillo, *Douglas MacArthur: The Philippine Years*, 164–66.
37. Ibid., 270, n115.
38. Isidra Reyes, "The Colorful Life and Tragic End of the Pinay Showgirl who Stole MacArthur's Heart," https://news.abs-cbn.com/ancx/culture/spotlight/08/11/19/the-colorful-life-and-tragic-end-of-the-pinay-showgirl-who-stole-macarthurs-heart, accessed September 28, 2020.
39. Perry, *The Most Dangerous Man in America*, 25.
40. *Register of Graduates and Former Cadets*, 2010.
41. Ibid.
42. "Biographical Register of the Officers and Graduates of the U.S. Military Academy at West Point, N.Y., from Its Establishment, in 1802" (Supplement, vol. 9, 1940–1950).
43. "Address USMA Graduates," *Army and Navy Journal*, June 17, 1933, 830.
44. "Address USMA Graduates," *Army and Navy Journal*, June 17, 1933, 830.
45. "MacArthur Warns against Economy," *New York Times*, June 14, 1933.
46. "Address USMA Graduates," *Army and Navy Journal*, June 17, 1933, 830.
47. "MacArthur Warns against Economy," *New York Times*, June 14, 1933.
48. Rick Atkinson, *Day of Battle: The War in Sicily and Italy, 1943–44* (New York: Henry Holt, 2007), 585–86.
49. Devers, "The Mark of the Man on USMA," 17.
50. Letter, MacArthur to P. Egner, May 5, 1934; copy USMA History Office.
51. Betros, *Carved from Granite*, 181.
52. Herman, *Douglas MacArthur: American Warrior*, 227.
53. James, *The Years of MacArthur, Vol. 1, 1880–1941*, 418.
54. *New York Times*, May 10, 1932; also James, *The Years of MacArthur, Vol. 1, 1880–1941*, 360.
55. Herman, *Douglas MacArthur: American Warrior*, 230.
56. Ibid., 230.
57. MacArthur, *Reminiscences*, 100.
58. Ibid., 101.
59. Ibid.
60. Ibid.
61. James, *The Years of MacArthur, Vol. 1, 1880–1941*, 446.
62. Perret, *Old Soldiers Never Die*, 186.
63. Sorley, *Honor Bright*, 16.
64. *Annual Report of the Secretary of War*, 1935, Part I, 47–49.

65. Perret, *Old Soldiers Never Die*, 177.
66. Lange, *Historic Structures Survey United States Military Academy, West Point, NY*, 2:33.
67. T. L. Johnson, "The Washington Hall Mural," *Assembly* 2, no. 4 (January 1944): 1.
68. Johnson, "The Washington Hall Mural."
69. James, *The Years of MacArthur, Vol. 1, 1880–1941*, 452.

Chapter 12. The Field Marshal Prepares for War

1. Petillo, *Douglas MacArthur: The Philippine Years*, 173, 175.
2. James, *The Years of MacArthur, Vol. 1, 1880–1941*, 494–96.
3. MacArthur to O'Laughlin, December 9, 1935, John Callin O'Laughlin Papers, Library of Congress; Petillo, *Douglas MacArthur: The Philippine Years*, 177.
4. James, *The Years of MacArthur, Vol. 1, 1880–1941*, 480.
5. Petillo, *Douglas MacArthur: The Philippine Years*, 153.
6. James, *The Years of MacArthur, Vol. 1, 1880–1941*, 484.
7. Perrett, *Old Soldiers Never Die*, 271.
8. James, *The Years of MacArthur, Vol. 1, 1880–1941*, 553–56.
9. Perrett, *Old Soldiers Never Die*, 225.
10. *Register of Cadets and Former Graduates*, Association of Graduates, 2015 edition.
11. Manchester, *American Caesar*, 32, 132.
12. Jose G. Syjuco, *Military Education in the Philippines* (Quezon City, Philippines: New Day, 1977) 16.
13. Clarence E. Endy Jr., "The Gentlemen from the Philippines, *Assembly* 40, no. 4 (December 1981), 20.
14. Commonwealth Act, No. 1, January 11, 1936; copy on file.
15. Endy, "The Gentlemen from the Philippines," 42.
16. Pastor Martelino, obituary, *Assembly* 5, no. 3 (October 1946).
17. James, *The Years of MacArthur, Vol. 1, 1880–1941*, 506.
18. MacArthur to Maj. Gen. William D. Connor, September 15, 1936, Eisenhower Library.
19. Smith, *Eisenhower in War and Peace*, 133.
20. James, *The Years of MacArthur, Vol. 1, 1880–1941*, 530.
21. Ibid., 511.
22. Jean MacArthur, Oral History, RG 13, Box 15, Folder 29, MacArthur Memorial Library, 10.
23. Jean MacArthur, Oral History, RG, Box 15, Folder 29, MacArthur Memorial Library, 10.
24. Ibid.
25. MacArthur, *Reminiscences*, 106.
26. Ibid., 107.
27. Smith, *Eisenhower in War and Peace*, 129–30.

28. James, *The Years of MacArthur, Vol. 1, 1880–1941*, 565–66.
29. Betros, *Carved from Granite*, 181; Davidson had a record of thirty-five wins and eleven losses over four years.
30. James S. Edson, *The Black Knights of West Point*, vol. 1 (New York: Bradbury, Sayles O'Neil, 1954), 175–76.
31. Perrett, *Old Soldiers Never Die*, 210.
32. MacArthur to William H. Wood, July 27, 1939, RG 1, MacArthur Memorial Archive; cited in James, *The Years of MacArthur, Vol. 1, 1880–1941*, 558.
33. James, *The Years of MacArthur, Vol. 1, 1880–1941*, 558–59.
34. Perrett, *Old Soldiers Never Die*, 242.
35. James, *The Years of MacArthur, Vol. 1, 1880–1941*, 535–36.
36. MacArthur to Quezon, October 12, 1940, RG 1, MacArthur Memorial Archives.
37. Smith, *Eisenhower in War and Peace*, 146.
38. Dwight D. Eisenhower, *At Ease: Stories I Tell to Friends* (Garden City, NY: Simon & Schuster, 1967), 229–30.
39. John S. D. Eisenhower, *General Ike: A Personal Reminiscence* (New York: Free Press, 2003), 28.
40. Perrett, *Old Soldiers Never Die*, 215.
41. Smith, *Eisenhower in War and Peace*, 149.
42. Ibid., 149.
43. MacArthur, *Reminiscences*, 113.
44. James, *The Years of MacArthur, Vol. 1, 1880–1941*, 563–64.
45. Ibid., 567.
46. Louis Morton, *Germany First: The Concept of Allied Strategy in World War II* (Washington, DC: US Army Center of Military History, 1960; reprinted 2000), 45.
47. James, *The Years of MacArthur, Vol. 1, 1880–1941*, 552.
48. Ibid., 585–86.
49. Marshall to MacArthur, June 20, 1941; cited in James, *The Years of MacArthur, Vol. 1, 1880–1941*, 586.
50. John H. Bradley, *The Second World War: Asia and the Pacific* (West Point, NY: USMA, 1984), 5.
51. Radio message, Marshall to MacArthur, July 26, 1941, Office Chief of Staff 18136–35; see also Louis Morton, *The Fall of the Philippines* (Washington, DC: US Army Center of Military History, 1953; reprinted 1993), 19.
52. James, *The Years of MacArthur, Vol. 1, 1880–1941*, 615.
53. Morton, *The Fall of the Philippines*, 65.
54. John Gordon, *Fighting for MacArthur: The Navy and Marine Corps' Desperate Defense of the Philippines* (Annapolis, MD: Naval Institute Press, 2011), 15.
55. Walter R. Borneman, *MacArthur at War: World War II in the Pacific* (New York: Little, Brown, 2016), 64; James, *The Years of MacArthur, Vol. 1, 1880–1941*, 611.
56. Herman, *Douglas MacArthur: American Warrior*, 309.

57. Costello, *The Pacific War, 1941–1945*, 61–65.
58. MacArthur, *Reminiscences*, 114.

Chapter 13. More War and Victory

1. Costello, *The Pacific War: 1941–1945*, ch. 6.
2. Manchester, *American Caesar*, 208–210.
3. James, *The Years of MacArthur, Vol. 2, 1941–1945*, 14–15.
4. Manchester, *American Caesar*, 203.
5. Bradley, *The Second World War: Asia and the Pacific*, 74.
6. Manchester, *American Caesar*, 203.
7. MacArthur, *Reminiscences*, 120.
8. Herman, *Douglas MacArthur: American Warrior*, 321–22.
9. *Register of Graduates and Cadets of the USMA*, Association of Graduates, 2015 edition; Capt. Robert M. Losey, class of 1929, was with the American embassy delegation in Norway when he was killed on April 21, 1940, during a German bombing raid. He is the first American and first West Point graduate in US service to die in World War II.
10. Bradley, *The Second World War: Asia and the Pacific*, 74.
11. MacArthur, *Reminiscences*, 111–12; Borneman, *MacArthur at War*, 99.
12. Bradley, *The Second World War: Asia and the Pacific*, 81.
13. James, *The Years of MacArthur, Vol. 1, 1880–1941*, 605; Morton, *The Fall of the Philippines*, 474.
14. Bradley, *The Second World War: Asia and the Pacific*, 81–82.
15. Costello, *The Pacific War: 1941–1945*, 177.
16. Ibid., 203.
17. Herman, *Douglas MacArthur: American Warrior*, 345.
18. Ibid., 346.
19. D. Clayton James, *The Years of MacArthur, Vol. 2, 1941–1945* (Boston: Houghton Mifflin, 1975), 84.
20. Herman, *Douglas MacArthur: American Warrior*, 345.
21. James, *The Years of MacArthur, Vol. 2, 1941–1945*, 73.
22. Herman, *Douglas MacArthur: American Warrior*, 348.
23. MacArthur, *Reminiscences*, 131.
24. Bradley, *The Second World War: Asia and the Pacific*, 65–72.
25. James, *The Years of MacArthur, Vol. 2, 1941–1945*, 98.
26. MacArthur, *Reminiscences*, 141.
27. Ibid., 142.
28. Keith Barlow, ed., *Bunker's War: The World War II Diary of Col. Paul D. Bunker* (Novato, CA: Presidio Press, 1996), 94.
29. Barlow, *Bunker's War*, 115.
30. Ibid., 304.

31. Bradley, *The Second World War: Asia and the Pacific*, 84–85.
32. MacArthur, *Reminiscences*, 146.
33. Ibid., 145.
34. James, *The Years of MacArthur, Vol. 2, 1941–1945*, 111.
35. Memo, G. Marshall to F. D. Roosevelt, August 22, 1944, George Marshall Library, Lexington, VA.
36. Marshall to MacArthur, July 31, 1942, MacArthur to Marshall, August 1, 1942, RG 4, Box 15, File 14, WD 169, MacArthur Memorial Archives.
37. James, *The Years of MacArthur, Vol. 2, 1941–1945*, 150–51, 848 n61.
38. Bradley, *The Second World War: Asia and the Pacific*, 103.
39. Hyde to MacArthur, April 13, 1942, RG 10, Box 2, File 9, MacArthur Memorial Archives.
40. Cocheu to MacArthur, May 7, 1942, RG 10, Box 4, File 8, MacArthur Memorial Archives.
41. MacArthur, *Reminiscences*, 154; James, *The Years of MacArthur, Vol. 2, 1941–1945*, 137–38.
42. Radio message, MacArthur to USMA, May 30, 1942, RG 10, Box 4, MacArthur Memorial Archives.
43. Cocheu to MacArthur, October 25, 1943, RG 10, MacArthur Memorial Archives.
44. MacArthur to Fellers, June 18, 1943, RG 5, MacArthur Memorial Archives.
45. Perret, *Old Soldiers Never Die*, 301.
46. James, *The Years of MacArthur, Vol. 2, 1941–1945*, 117–19.
47. Ibid., 112.
48. MacArthur, *Reminiscences*, 152.
49. Borneman, *MacArthur at War*, 211, 214.
50. Harry A. Gailey, *MacArthur's Victory: The War in New Guinea, 1943–44* (New York: Presidio Press, 2004), 3–6.
51. Herman, *Douglas MacArthur: American Warrior*, 435.
52. James, *The Years of MacArthur, Vol. 2, 1941–1945*, 199–201.
53. MacArthur, *Reminiscences*, 162–65; Bradley, *The Second World War: Asia and the Pacific*, 134–39.
54. Perret, *Old Soldiers Never Die*, 337–38.
55. Ibid., 311.
56. Betros, *Carved from Granite*, 186.
57. Crackel, *The Illustrated History of West Point*, 236.
58. Ibid., 246.
59. Blaik to MacArthur, letter, January 1, 1945, RG 10, Box 4, File 55, MacArthur Memorial Archives.
60. Perret, *Old Soldiers Never Die*, 323.
61. Bradley, *The Second World War: Asia and the Pacific*, 138.

62. John Miller, Jr., *Cartwheel: The Reduction of Rabaul* (Washington, DC: Office of the Chief of Military History, 1959), 312.
63. Gailey, *MacArthur's Victory*, 132.
64. Miller, *Cartwheel*, 29.
65. Bradley, *The Second World War: Asia and the Pacific*, 144.
66. Gailey, *MacArthur's Victory*, 176–79, 191–95.
67. Perret, *Old Soldiers Never Die*, 406.
68. MacArthur, *Reminiscences*, 198.
69. Perret, *Old Soldiers Never Die*, 422.
70. *Register of Graduates and Cadets of the USMA*, Association of Graduates, 2015 edition.
71. MacArthur, *Reminiscences*, 217; President Manuel Quezon had died in August 1944.
72. Cocheu to MacArthur, February 4, 1945, RG 10, MacArthur Memorial Archives.
73. Bradley, *The Second World War: Asia and the Pacific*, 192–94.
74. James, *The Years of MacArthur, Vol. 2, 1941–1945*, 590–91.
75. Robert R. Smith, *Triumph in the Philippines* (Washington, DC: US Army Center of Military History, 1961; reprinted 1991), 341–50.
76. MacArthur, *Reminiscences*, 247.
77. James, *The Years of MacArthur, Vol. 2, 1941–1945*, 775–76.
78. Ronald H. Spector *Eagle Against the Sun: The American War with Japan* (New York: Free Press, 1985, paperback edition, 2020), 555.
79. James, *The Years of MacArthur, Vol. 2, 1941–1945*, 775.
80. Costello, *The Pacific War: 1941–1945*, 581–84.
81. MacArthur, *Reminiscences*, 265.

Chapter 14. American Shogun

1. James, *The Years of MacArthur, Vol. 2, 1941–1945*, 785–86.
2. Costello, *The Pacific War: 1941–1945*, 594–95.
3. Perret, *Old Soldiers Never Die*, 467–68.
4. Rick Atkinson, *The Guns at Last Light: The War in Western Europe, 1944–45* (New York: Henry Holt, 2013), 620–28.
5. MacArthur, *Reminiscences*, 272.
6. Ibid., 271–72.
7. Ibid., 275.
8. Perret, *Old Soldiers Never Die*, 478–79.
9. MacArthur, *Reminiscences*, 275.
10. Arthur Herman, *Douglas MacArthur: American Warrior*, xv.
11. D. Clayton James, *The Years of MacArthur: Triumph & Disaster, Volume 3, 1945–1964* (Boston: Houghton Mifflin, 1985), 689–90.
12. James, *The Years of MacArthur, Vol. 2, 1941–1945*, 779.
13. James, *The Years of MacArthur, Vol. 3, 1945–1964*, 105.

14. MacArthur to Eisenhower, January 25, 1946, in *Foreign Relations of the United States*, 1946, VIII, Department of State, 395–97.
15. James, *The Years of MacArthur, Vol. 3, 1945–1964*, 98–101.
16. James M. Scott, *Rampage: MacArthur, Yamashita, and the Battle of Manila* (New York: W. W. Norton, 2018), 500–504.
17. Official message, CinC SWA to Superintendent USMA, September 5, 1945, USMA Archives.
18. James, *The Years of MacArthur, Vol. 3, 1945–1964*, 102–3.
19. MacArthur, *Reminiscences*, 318.
20. James, *The Years of MacArthur, Vol. 3, 1945–1964*, 58–59.
21. Ibid., 62–63.
22. Perret, *Old Soldiers Never Die*, 505–6.
23. MacArthur, *Reminiscences*, 300.
24. James, *The Years of MacArthur, Vol. 3, 1945–1964*, 121–25.
25. Department of State, *The Constitution of Japan, Effective May 3, 1947* (Washington, DC, 1947), 1–13.
26. MacArthur, *Reminiscences*, 301.
27. James, *The Years of MacArthur, Vol. 3, 1945–1964*, 148.
28. MacArthur, *Reminiscences*, 302.
29. Ibid., 292.
30. Forrest C. Pogue, *George C. Marshall: Statesman 1945–1959* (New York: Viking, 1987), 232–33.
31. James, *The Years of MacArthur, Vol. 3, 1945–1964*, 228.
32. Ibid., 377–84.
33. MacArthur to Blaik, radio message, December 2, 1945, RG 10, MacArthur Memorial Archives.
34. James, *The Years of MacArthur, Vol. 3, 1945–1964*, 364.
35. MacArthur to Blaik, radio message, November 27, 1949, RG 10, MacArthur Memorial Archives.
36. Letter, Fenton to MacArthur, May 16, 1947, RG 10, MacArthur Memorial Archives.
37. Letter, Fenton to MacArthur, May 16, 1947, RG 10, MacArthur Memorial Archives.
38. Letter, MacArthur to Chauncey Fenton, May 25, 1947, USMA Archives.
39. Betros, *Carved from Granite*, 84–85.
40. Letter, MacArthur to Earl Blaik, August 8, 1949, USMA Archives.
41. Letter, MacArthur to Earl Blaik, May 19, 1950, USMA Archives.
42. *Register of Graduates and Cadets of the USMA*, Association of Graduates, 2015 edition.
43. Cocheu to MacArthur, June 5, 1947, RG 10, MacArthur Memorial Archives.

Chapter 15. The Fall

1. MacArthur, *Reminiscences*, 327.
2. James F. Schnabel, *Policy and Direction: The First Year, United States Army in the Korean War* (Washington, DC: Office of the Chief of Military History, 1972), 47–49, 69.
3. Burton I. Kaufman, *The Korean War: Challenges in Crisis, Credibility, and Command* (New York: McGraw-Hill, 1986), 5.
4. Bryan R. Gibby, *The Will to Win: American Military Advisors in Korea 1946–1953* (Tuscaloosa: University of Alabama Press, 2012), 53.
5. Schnabel, *Policy and Direction*, 51–52.
6. Kaufman, *The Korean War: Challenges in Crisis*, 32.
7. Bryan R. Gibby, *Korean Showdown: National Policy and Military Strategy in a Limited War 1951–1952* (Tuscaloosa: University of Alabama Press, 2021), 13–15.
8. Schnabel, *Policy and Direction*, 73–74.
9. MacArthur, *Reminiscences*, 332–35.
10. Schnabel, *Policy and Direction*, 101–102.
11. Walton H. Walker obituary, *Assembly* 13, no. 1 (April 1954).
12. Schnabel, *Policy and Direction*, 140–42.
13. MacArthur, *Reminiscences*, 346.
14. Perret, *Old Soldiers Never Die*, 546.
15. Ibid., 548.
16. Stanley Weintraub, *MacArthur's War: Korea and the Undoing of an American Hero* (New York: Free Press, 2000), 131.
17. Herman, *Douglas MacArthur: American Warrior*, 737.
18. Schnabel, *Policy and Direction*, 193.
19. James, *The Years of MacArthur, Vol. 3, 1945–1964*, 488; MacArthur, *Reminiscences*, 358.
20. Schnabel, *Policy and Direction*, 178, 200.
21. Ibid., 210–12.
22. James, *The Years of MacArthur, Vol. 3, 1945–1964*, 193–94, 452–55.
23. Harry S. Truman, *Memoirs*, vol. 2 (Garden City, NY: Doubleday, 1955–56), 404, 405.
24. Perret, *Old Soldiers Never Die*, 536.
25. Herman, *Douglas MacArthur: American Warrior*, 757–58.
26. James, *The Years of MacArthur, Vol. 3, 1945–1964*, 507–8.
27. Ibid., 515.
28. MacArthur, *Reminiscences*, 363.
29. Schnabel, *Policy and Direction*, 178, 216–19.
30. MacArthur, *Reminiscences*, 366.

31. James, *The Years of MacArthur, Vol. 3, 1945–1964*, 534.
32. Ibid., 535.
33. Kaufman, *The Korean War: Challenges in Crisis*, 116–17.
34. MacArthur, *Reminiscences*, 369.
35. Ibid., 365.
36. MacArthur, *Reminiscences*, 370.
37. James, *The Years of MacArthur, Vol. 3, 1945–1964*, 543.
38. Ibid., 537.
39. James, *The Years of MacArthur, Vol. 3, 1945–1964*, 541.
40. Truman, *Memoirs*, 2: 537, 539.
41. James, *The Years of MacArthur, Vol. 3, 1945–1964*, 542.
42. MacArthur, *Reminiscences*, 378.
43. Walker obituary, *Assembly*.
44. US Military Academy, *Howitzer*, 1921, 14.
45. James, *The Years of MacArthur, Vol. 3, 1945–1964*, 545.
46. Perret, *Old Soldiers Never Die*, 565.
47. Gibby, *Korean Showdown*, 28.
48. James, *The Years of MacArthur, Vol. 3, 1945–1964*, 577.
49. MacArthur, *Reminiscences*, 388.
50. James, *The Years of MacArthur, Vol. 3, 1945–1964*, 587–88.
51. Perret, *Old Soldiers Never Die*, 567.
52. MacArthur, *Reminiscences*, 386.
53. Truman, *Memoirs*, 346–47.
54. James, *The Years of MacArthur, Vol. 3, 1945–1964*, 589.
55. *Military Situation in the Far East* (the MacArthur Hearings), 2 vols. Washington, DC: US Senate, 1951), 3546.
56. MacArthur, *Reminiscences*, 395.
57. Ibid.
58. James, *The Years of MacArthur, Vol. 3, 1945–1964*, 612.
59. Ibid., 602.
60. *Representative Speeches of General of the Army Douglas MacArthur*, Senate 88th Cong., 2d sess., no. 95, April 29, 1964 (Washington, DC: US Government Printing Office, 1964), 18–19.
61. Ibid., 19.
62. Ibid., 19–20.
63. James, *The Years of MacArthur, Vol. 3, 1945–1964*, 630.
64. James, *The Years of MacArthur: Vol. 1, 1880 to 1941*, 575–76.

Chapter 16. Home at Last

1. James, *The Years of MacArthur, Vol. 3, 1945–1964*, 671–72.
2. Ibid., 617.

3. Ibid., 619–20.
4. Schnabel, *Policy and Direction*, 392.
5. James, *The Years of MacArthur, Vol. 3, 1945–1964*, 623.
6. Ibid., 632–33.
7. Ibid., 618, 641–42.
8. Betros, *Carved from Granite*, 273.
9. The original Honor Code statement was published in 1947 by superintendent Major General Taylor in a pamphlet. Later, the line was changed to, "A Cadet will not lie, cheat or steal, nor tolerant those who do."
10. Papers of Jean MacArthur: Oral Histories Series 7, MacArthur Memorial Archives, Box 15, Folder 29, 11–12.
11. USMA News Release, "Breach of the West Point Code of Honor," August 3, 1951, USMA History Office.
12. Blaik, *The Red Blaik Story*, 279.
13. Papers of Jean MacArthur, Box 15, Folder 29, 12.
14. James, *The Years of MacArthur, Vol. 3, 1945–1964*, 658.
15. Letter, MacArthur to Rodney Dorsey, April 12, 1952, RG 10, Box 100, File 21, MacArthur Memorial Archives.
16. Letter, MacArthur to Eleazar Parmly II, May 10, 1954, RG 10, Box 120, File 14, MacArthur Memorial Archives.
17. Letter, MacArthur to Leon Kromer, June 17, 1957, RG 10, Box 134, File 6, MacArthur Memorial Archives.
18. *Register of Graduates and Former Cadets*, 2010 edition.
19. James, *The Years of MacArthur, Vol. 3, 1945–1964*, 659–60.
20. Ibid., 677–78.
21. Papers of Jean MacArthur, Box 15, Folder 29, 29.
22. James, *The Years of MacArthur, Vol. 3, 1945–1964*, 675–76.
23. Ibid., 681.
24. West Point Association of Graduates Sylvanus Thayer Award brochure, 2014; "Sylvanus Thayer Award presented to General MacArthur," *Assembly* 21, no. 2 (September 1962), 12–13.
25. Papers of Jean MacArthur, Box 15, Folder 29, 13.
26. *Representative Speeches of General of the Army Douglas MacArthur*.
27. Letter, McCarthy to MacArthur, May 4, 1962, RG 10, Box 157, MacArthur Memorial Archives.
28. Letter, McCarthy to MacArthur, May 4, 1962, RG 10, Box 157, File 6, MacArthur Memorial Archives.
29. Letter, MacArthur to McCarthy, May 7, 1962, RG 10, Box 157, File 6, MacArthur Memorial Archives.
30. *Register of Graduates and Former Cadets*, 2010 edition.
31. "Sylvanus Thayer Award presented to General MacArthur"; see note 24 above.

32. Papers of Jean MacArthur, Box 15, Folder 29, File 13.
33. Email, Lt. Gen. James Ellis (retired) to the author, April 26, 2021.
34. Letter, William Westmoreland to Mary P. Riedel, May 15, 1962, USMA Archives.
35. Leslie Groves obituary, *Assembly* 32, no. 1 (June 1973):116–18.
36. Papers of Jean MacArthur, Box 15, Folder 29, File 18.
37. *Representative Speeches of General of the Army Douglas MacArthur*, 100–103.
38. Jean MacArthur, Box 15, Folder 29, File 13; "Sylvanus Thayer Award presented to General MacArthur."
39. Robert Considine, Press Statement, May 14, 1962, RG 10, Box 157, Folder 6, MacArthur Memorial Archives.
40. "Sylvanus Thayer Award presented to General MacArthur."
41. Letter, Laitman to MacArthur, May 14, 1962, RG 10, Box 157, MacArthur Memorial Archives.
42. Letter, MacArthur to Laitman, May 14, 1962, RG 10, Box 157, MacArthur Memorial Archives.
43. "Sylvanus Thayer Award presented to General MacArthur."
44. James, *The Years of MacArthur, Vol. 3, 1945–1964*, 680–81.
45. Letter, "Spot" to Mom and Dad, May 13, 1962, RG 10, Box 157, MacArthur Memorial. Archives.
46. The USMA command historian has been asked this question literally hundreds of times between 2009–2022 while conducting tours.
47. "West Point Cadets to Bring MacArthur Birthday Salute," *Minneapolis Morning Tribune*, January 25, 1964; "MacArthur Memorial Week," June 3–7, 2014, Milwaukee, Wisconsin, 33.
48. James, *The Years of MacArthur, Vol. 3, 1945–1964*, 686.
49. Ibid., 687.
50. Office of the Surgeon General, *Walter Reed Army Medical Center: Centennial, A Pictorial History, 1909–2009* (Washington, DC: Office of the Surgeon General, 2009, 149; James, *The Years of MacArthur, Vol. 3, 1945–1964*, 687.
51. Manchester, *American Caesar*, 704.
52. Ibid., 705.
53. James, *The Years of MacArthur, Vol. 3, 1945–1964*, 689; Manchester, *American Caesar*, 706.
54. "The MacArthur Memorial" (Lawrenceburg, IN: Creative Company, 2012).
55. See Sorely, *Honor Bright*, ch. 5.
56. *Annual Report of the Superintendent, 1957*, 7.
57. Robie Lange, *Historic Structures Survey United States Military Academy, West Point, NY*, 3:101.
58. "Final Report of the Special Commission of the Chief of Staff on the Honor Code and Honor System at USMA," May 1989.
59. The full name of the Commission Report is laborious; the informal name is the Borman Report, 1976; *Annual Report of the Superintendent, 1977*.

Epilogue

1. There probably is not an exact list of devices and property that exists; see list of places named for Douglas MacArthur—Wikipedia, accessed April 25, 2021.
2. AR 600–89, *General Douglas MacArthur Leadership Award Program*, August 22, 2017, 2.
3. "The MacArthur Memorial."
4. Ibid.
5. *Assembly* 40, no. 4 December 1981): 16–17.
6. According to Army Regulation 1–33, only deceased individuals are memorialized.
7. USMA Operations Order, 87–11, HQ US Military Academy; copy on file in USMA History Office.
8. USMA Annual Command History, Academic Year 2021–2022, 14.

BIBLIOGRAPHY

Government and Public Records

Annual Report of Army Officers Athletic Association. USMA Archives.

Annual Report of the Superintendent of the United States Military Academy. USMA Library Archives.

Cullum, George Washington. *Biographical Register of the Officers and Graduates of the United States Military Academy*, 3d ed. Boston: Houghton Mifflin, 1891.

Department of State. *The Constitution of Japan, Effective May 3, 1947.* Washington, DC, 1947.

——— *Foreign Relations of the United States, 1946, VIII.* Washington, DC, 1946.

Final Report of the Special Commission of the Chief of Staff on the Honor Code and Honor System at USMA, 1989.

Hagood, Johnson. Memoir. Hagood Papers. US Army Military History Institute, Carlisle Barracks, PA.

Lange, Robie. *Historic Structures Survey United States Military Academy, West Point, NY, Historic American Buildings Survey.* 4 vols. Washington, DC: National Park Service, 1984.

Letter, Arthur MacArthur to President Abraham Lincoln, May 13, 1862. Office of the Adjutant General, Record Group 94, NARA.

Military Situation in the Far East (The MacArthur Hearings). 2 vols. Washington, DC: US Senate, 1951.

Order of Battle of the United States Land Forces in the World War, American Expeditionary Forces: Divisions. Washington, DC : Office Chief of Military History, 1931 (reprint of 1988).

Office of the Surgeon General. *Walter Reed Army Medical Center: Centennial, A Pictorial History, 1909–2009.* Washington, DC, 2009.

Papers of Jean MacArthur. Oral Histories Series VII. Record Group 13, MacArthur Memorial Archives, Norfolk, VA.

Proceedings of a Board of Officers, Convened Pursuant to Letter Orders, HQ USCC, West Point, NY, 28 May 1951, USMA Archives.

The Public Statutes at Large of the United States of America, from the Organization of the Government in 1789, to March 3, 1845, vol. 2. Boston: Charles C. Little and James Brown, 1845.

Report from the Chief of Staff United States Army, to the Secretary of War on the Employment of Federal Troops in the Civil Disturbance in the District of Columbia July 28–30, 1932. Record Group 319, Army Staff, NARA.

Report of the Special Committee on the Investigation of Hazing at the United States Military Academy. Washington, DC: Government Printing Office, 1901.

Representative Speeches of General of the Army Douglas MacArthur. Senate, 88th Cong., 2d Sess., No. 95, April 29, 1964. Washington, DC: Government Printing Office, 1964.

United States Army in the World War 1917–1919, Military Operations of the American Expeditionary Forces. 17 vols. Vols. 4–9. Washington, DC: Historical Division, Department of the Army, 1948.

USMA Annual Command History, Academic Year 2021–2022. USMA Library Archives.

The War of the Rebellion: A Compilation of the Official Records of the Union and Confederate Armies. 128 vols. Washington, DC, 1880–1901.

Newspapers and Other Media

"Event Program, June 3–7, 2014." MacArthur Memorial Week. Milwaukee, WI.

Howitzer, US Military Academy, 1921, 1922.

"The MacArthur Memorial." Lawrenceburg, IN: Creative Company, 2012.

Register of Graduates and Former Cadets, Association of Graduates, 2002 and 2010 editions.

The World Tomorrow. New York: Fellowship Press, 1918–1934.

Books

Alberts, Don E. *Brandy Station to Manila Bay: A Biography of General Wesley Merritt.* Austin, TX: Presidial Press, 1980.

Ambrose, Stephen. *Duty, Honor, Country: A History of West Point.* Baltimore: Johns Hopkins University Press, 1999.

Atkinson, Rick. *Day of Battle: The War in Sicily and Italy, 1943–44.* New York: Henry Holt, 2007.

———. *The Guns at Last Light: The War in Western Europe, 1944–45.* New York: Henry Holt, 2013.

Badeau, Adam. *Grant in Peace: From Appomattox to Mount McGregor.* Hartford, CT: S. S. Scranton, 1887.

Barlow, Keith, ed. *Bunker's War: The World War II Diary of Col. Paul D. Bunker*. Novato, CA: Presidio Press, 1996.

Betros, Lance. *Carved from Granite: West Point since 1902*. College Station: Texas A&M Press, 2012.

Blaik, Earl. *The Red Blaik Story*. New Rochelle, NY: Arlington House, 1974.

Boatner, Mark M. III. *The Civil War Dictionary*. New York: David McKay, 1987 [1959].

Borneman, Walter R. *MacArthur at War: World War II in the Pacific*. New York: Little, Brown, 2016.

Bowman, Joseph P., and Eric R. Caubarreaux. *The Decorations, Awards and Honors of General of the Army Douglas MacArthur: The U.S. Military's Most Decorated Serviceman*. Self-published, CreateSpace, 2012.

Bradley, John H. *The Second World War: Asia and the Pacific*. West Point Military History Series. West Point, NY: USMA, 1984.

Coakley, Robert W. *The Role of Federal Military Forces in Domestic Disorders, 1789–1878*. Washington, DC: Center of Military History, 1988.

Coffman, Edward M. *The Hilt of the Sword: The Career of Peyton C. March*. University of Wisconsin Press: 1966.

———. *The War to End All Wars: The American Military Experience in World War I*. Lexington: University Press of Kentucky, 1998.

Cooke, James L. *The Rainbow Division in the Great War*. Westport, CT: Praeger, 1994.

Costello, John. *The Pacific War: 1941–1945*. New York: Harper Perennial, 2009.

Crackel, Theodore. *The Illustrated History of West Point*. West Point, NY: Association of Graduates, 1991.

———. *Mr. Jefferson's Army: The Political and Social Reform of the Military Establishment, 1801–1809*. New York: New York University Press 1987.

———. *West Point: A Bicentennial History*. Lawrence: University Press of Kansas, 2002.

Daniels, Roger. *The Bonus March: An Episode of the Great Depression*. Westport, CT: Greenwood, 1971.

Doubler, Michael D. *I Am the Guard: A History of the Army National Guard, 1636–2000*. Washington, DC: Government Printing Office, 2001.

Edson, James S. *The Black Knights of West Point*, vol. 1. New York: Bradbury, Sayles O'Neil, 1954.

Eichelberger, Robert L. *Our Jungle Road to Tokyo*. New York: Viking, 1950.

Eisenhower, Dwight D. *At Ease: Stories I Tell to Friends*. Garden City, NY: Simon & Schuster, 1967.

Eisenhower, John S. D. *Agent of Destiny: The Life and Times of General Winfield Scott*. Norman: University of Oklahoma Press, 1997.

———. *General Ike: A Personal Reminiscence*. New York: Free Press, 2003.

———. *Intervention: The United States and the Mexican Revolution, 1913–17*. New York: W. W. Norton, 1993.

———. *Strictly Personal*. New York: Doubleday, 1974.

———. *Yanks: The Epic Story of the American Army in World War I*. New York: Free Press, 2001.

Fleek, Sherman L. *Place the Headstones where They Belong: Thomas Neibaur, WWI Soldier*. Logan: Utah State University Press, 2008.

Flood, Charles B. *Grant and Sherman: The Friendship that Won the Civil War*. New York: Farrar, Straus & Giroux, 2005.

Forman, Sydney. *The Educational Objectives of the U.S. Military Academy*. West Point, NY: USMA Publications, 1946.

Gailey, Harry A. *MacArthur's Victory: The War in New Guinea, 1943–44*. New York: Presidio Press, 2004.

Ganoe, William Addleman. *MacArthur: Close-up, Much Then and Some Now*. New York: Vantage Press, 1962.

Gibby, Bryan R. *Korean Showdown: National Policy and Military Strategy in a Limited War 1951–1952*. Tuscaloosa: University of Alabama Press, 2021.

———. *The Will to Win: American Military Advisors in Korea 1946–1953*. Tuscaloosa: University of Alabama Press, 2012.

Gordon, John. *Fighting for MacArthur: The Navy and Marine Corps' Desperate Defense of the Philippines*. Annapolis, MD: Naval Institute Press, 2011.

Grant, John, James Lynch, and Ronald Bailey. *West Point: The First 200 Years*. Guilford, CT: Globe Pequot Press, 1996.

Heitman, Francis B. *Historical Register and Dictionary of the United States Army from Its Organization, September 29, 1789 to March 2, 1903*. 2 vols. Washington, DC: Government Printing Office, 1903; reprinted, Urbana: University of Illinois Press, 1965.

Herman, Arthur. *Douglas MacArthur: American Warrior*. New York: Random House, 2017.

Hoover, Herbert. *The Memoirs of Herbert Hoover*. 3 vols. New York: Macmillan, 1951–52.

Hunt, Frazier. *The Untold Story of Douglas MacArthur*. New York: Devin-Adair, 1954.

James, D. Clayton. *The Years of MacArthur, Vol. 1, 1880–1941*. Boston: Houghton Mifflin, 1970.

———. *The Years of MacArthur, Vol. 2, 1941–1945*. Boston: Houghton Mifflin, 1975.

———. *The Years of MacArthur: Triumph & Disaster, Vol. 3, 1945–1964*. Boston: Houghton Mifflin, 1985.

Kaufman, Burton I. *The Korean War: Challenges in Crisis, Credibility, and Command*. New York: McGraw-Hill, 1986.

Keegan, John. *The First World War*. New York: Alfred A. Knopf, 1998.

———. *The Second World War*. New York: Viking, 1989.

Kennedy, David M. *Freedom from Fear: The American People in the Depression and War, 1929–1945*. Oxford: Oxford University Press, 1999.

Leon, Philip W. *Bullies and Cowards: The West Point Hazing Scandal, 1898–1901.* Westport, CT: Greenwood, 2000.
Levine, Isaac D. *Mitchell: Pioneer of Air Power.* New York: World Publishing, 1943.
Linn, Brian M. *The Philippine War: 1899–1902.* Lawrence: University of Kansas Press, 2000.
MacArthur, Douglas. *Reminiscences: General of the Army Douglas MacArthur.* New York: McGraw-Hill, 1964.
McPherson, James M. *Battle Cry of Freedom: The Civil War Era.* New York: Oxford University Press, 1988.
Maher, Marty. *Bringing up the Brass: My 55 Years at West Point.* Quechee: Vermont Heritage Press, 2002.
Manchester, William. *American Caesar: Douglas MacArthur, 1880–1964.* New York: Little, Brown, 1978.
Manning, Robert. *Above and Beyond: A History of the Medal of Honor from the Civil War on Vietnam.* Boston: Boston Publishing, 1985.
Martin, James Kirby. *Benedict Arnold: Revolutionary Hero (An American Warrior Reconsidered).* New York: New York University Press, 1997.
Matloff, Maurice. *Strategic Planning for Coalition Warfare, 1943–1944.* Washington DC: Center of Military History, 1990 [1959].
Mears, Dwight S. *The Medal of Honor: The Evolution of America's Highest Military Decoration.* Lawrence: University of Kansas Press, 2018.
Miller, John Jr. *Cartwheel: The Reduction of Rabaul.* Washington, DC: Office of the Chief of Military History, 1959.
Millett, Allan R., and Peter Maslowski. *For the Common Defense: A Military History of the United States of America*, rev. ed. New York: Free Press, 1994.
Miles, Perry L. *Fallen Leaves: Memories of an Old Soldier.* Berkeley, CA: Wuerth, 1961.
Morton, Louis. *The Fall of the Philippines.* Washington, DC: US Army Center of Military History, 1953; reprinted 1993.
———. *Germany First: The Concept of Allied Strategy in World War II.* Washington, DC: US Army Center of Military History, 1960; reprinted 2000.
Musicant, Ivan. *Empire by Default: The Spanish-American War and the Dawn of the American Century.* New York: Henry Holt, 1998.
Palmer, Dave Richard. *The River and the Rock: The History of Fortress West Point, 1775–1783.* New York: Greenwood, 1969.
Perrett, Geoffrey. *Old Soldiers Never Die: The Life of Douglas MacArthur.* New York: Random House, 1996.
Perry, Mark. *The Most Dangerous Man in America: The Making of Douglas MacArthur.* New York: Basic Books, 2014.
Petillo, Carol. *Douglas MacArthur: The Philippine Years.* Bloomington: Indiana University Press, 1981.

Pogue, Forrest C. *George C. Marshall: Statesman 1945–1959.* New York: Viking, 1987.
Quiner, E. B. *Military History of Wisconsin.* Chicago: Wisconsin Historical Society, 1866.
Reilly, Henry J. *Americans All: The Rainbow in War.* Columbus, OH: F. J. Heer Printing, 1936.
Ridgway, Matthew B., with Harold H. Martin. *Soldier: The Memoirs of Matthew B. Ridgway.* New York: Harper, 1956.
Rogers, Clifford J., Ty Seidule, and Steve R. Waddell, eds. *The West Point History of World War II,* vol. 2. New York: Simon & Schuster, 2016.
Runkle, Benjamin. *Generals in the Making: How Marshall, Eisenhower, Patton, and Their Peers Became the Commanders who Won World War II.* Guilford, CT: Stackpole Books, 2019.
Schnabel, James F. *Policy and Direction: The First Year. United States Army in the Korean War.* Washington, DC: Office of the Chief of Military History, 1972.
Scott, Hugh L. *Some Memories of a Soldier.* New York: Century, 1928.
Scott, James M. *Rampage: MacArthur, Yamashita, and the Battle of Manila.* New York: W. W. Norton, 2018.
Shorto, Russell. *The Island at the Center of the World: The Epic Story of Dutch Manhattan and the Forgotten Colony that Shaped America.* New York: Vintage, 2005.
Smith, Jean Edward. *Eisenhower in War and Peace.* New York: Random House, 2013.
Smith, Robert R. *Triumph in the Philippines.* Washington, DC: US Army Center of Military History, 1961; reprinted 1991.
Sorley, Lewis. *Honor Bright: History and Origins of the West Point Honor Code and System.* West Point, NY: Association of Graduates, 2009.
Spector, Ronald H. *Eagle Against the Sun: The American War with Japan.* New York: Free Press, 1985; paperback edition, 2020.
Stewart, Richard W. ed. *American Military History, Vol. I: The United States Army and the Forging of a Nation, 1775–1917.* Washington, DC: US Army Center of Military History, 2004.
———. *American Military History, Vol. II: The United States Army in a Global Era, 1917–2003.* Washington, DC: US Army Center of Military History, 2004.
Syjuco, Jose G. *Military Education in the Philippines.* Quezon City, Philippines: New Day, 1977.
Taylor, Maxwell D. *Swords and Ploughshares.* New York: W. W. Norton, 1972.
Truman, Harry S. *Memoirs.* 2 vols. Garden City, NY: Doubleday, 1955–56.
Wallace, Chris. *Countdown 1945.* New York: Avid Reader Press, 2020.
Weintraub, Stanley. *MacArthur's War: Korea and the Undoing of an American Hero.* New York: Free Press, 2000.
Wukovitz, John F. *Eisenhower.* New York: Palgrave Macmillan, 2006.
Young, Kenneth Ray. *The General's General: The Life and Times of Arthur MacArthur.* Boulder, CO: Westview Press, 1994.

Journals and Pamphlets

Blaik, Earl "Red." "A Cadet under MacArthur." *Assembly* 23, no. 1 (Spring 1964).
Borch, Fred L. "Army Silver Stars for World Wars I and II, and Korea: A Study of Official Naming." *Journal of the Order and Medals Society of America* (July/August 2014).
———. "The Purple Heart—The Story of America's Oldest Military Decoration and Some Soldier Recipients." *On Point: The Journal of Army History* 21, no. 3 (Winter 2016).
Cocheu, George W. "Cadet Days, 1899–1903." *Assembly* 23, no. 1 (Spring 1964).
Danford, Robert M. "USMA's 31st Superintendent." *Assembly* 23, no. 1 (Spring 1964).
Dean, Doug, Rick McPeak, and Scotty Autin. "How Army's Mascot Came to Be." *West Point* 10, no. 1 (Winter 2020).
Devers, Jacob L. "Mark of the Man on USMA." *Assembly* 1, no. 3 (Spring 1947).
Endy, Clarence E. Jr. "The Gentlemen from the Philippines." *Assembly* 40, no. 4 (December 1981).
Hyde, Arthur P. S. "Douglas MacArthur." *Assembly* 1, no. 3 (Spring 1947).
Huber, Mike, and Jack Picciuto. "The First Army-Navy Baseball Game." *Baseball: A Journal of the Early Game* 1, no. 1 (Spring 2007): 96–102.
Johnson, T. L. "The Washington Hall Mural." *Assembly* 2, no. 4 (January 1944).
Larned, Charles. "The Memorial Hall at West Point," *The Junior Munsey* 8, no. 4 (July 1900): 513–23.
———. "West Point and Our Military Future." *Metropolitan Magazine* 22, no. 2 (May 1905): 130–54.
Miller, Roger G. "A 'Pretty Damn Able Commander': Lewis Hyde Brereton, Part I." *Air Power History* 47, no. 4 (December 2000).
Nichols, Robert J. "West Point's First Captains." *Assembly* 28, no. 4 (Winter 1970).
Pappas, George S. "More to the Point: The West Point Centennial in 1902." *Register of Graduates and Former Cadets, Bicentennial 2002 Edition*. West Point, NY: Association of Graduates, 2002.
Wood, Robert E. "An Upperclassman's View." *Assembly* 23, no. 1 (Spring 1964): 4.
Yates, Thom. "MacArthur in Sports." *Esquire*, August 1942.

Unpublished Materials

Beasley, John H. "The USMA Honor System: A Due Process Hybrid." Charlottesville, VA: Judge Advocate General's School, 1983.
Langford, Gary D. "1919: MacArthur's Vision of West Point's Future Warriors." US Military Academy History Department, HI 600 Paper.
Nye, Roger H. "The United States Military Academy in an Era of Educational Reform, 1900–1925." PhD diss., Columbia University, 1968.
Yerba, David J. "Colonel Herman J. Koehler: The Father of Physical Education." master's thesis, Long Island University, 1998.

INDEX

Note: Page numbers in italics refer to illustrations. Page numbers followed by *n* indicate material in notes.

Academic Board: Davidson's relationship with, 293; establishment and furtherance of, 16, 124; as guardian of tradition, 112; logo and motto approved by, 19–20; MacArthur's conflict with, 115, 120, 124–30, 150, 157; members of (1919), 126; Mills's conflict with, 37–40; mission statement approved by, 131; governance by, 18–19, 39–40, 124–25; reform-minded members of, 128–30
academics at West Point: bachelor's degrees for, 192; class rankings in, 62–63; criticism of, 113–14, 140, 152; curriculum of 1920, *129*; Davidson's reforms and, 293; Goodpaster's reforms and, 293; MacArthur's cadet record, 5–6, 46, 61–66, 95; MacArthur's challenge of exam rules, 63–64; MacArthur's superintendency and, 115, 125–30, 151–54; recitation emphasis in, 63; recommended curriculum (1920), *129*; Thayer and, 15–16; World War I and, 105, 109–10, 112–14, 119

Acheson, Dean, 256, 274
admission process, for West Point, 16–17, 32–35, 109–10
Alamo Force, 228
Albert I (king of Belgium), 132–37
Alexander, Roger G., 126
allowances, for cadets, 138, 141, 143–44
Almond, Edward "Ned," 246, 249, 259, *260*
Ambrose, Stephen, 107–108, 114, 162
American Caesar (Manchester), vii
American Expeditionary Force (AEF), 90. *See also* World War I
American Revolution, 10–12
amnesty for cadets, in MacArthur's name, 281–83, 286–87
Anderson, Robert, 16
Army Athletic Association, 193
army chief of staff: Eisenhower as, 243–44; Hine as, 166; MacArthur's father not selected as, 80; Marshall as, 205, 207–208; Pershing as, 161–62, 165–66; Summerall as, 91, 173–74, 175

army chief of staff, MacArthur as, 172–93; unusual appointment process for, 172–74; Bonus March incident and, 178–83, *179*; Civilian Conservation Corps and, ix–x, 188–89; FDR and, 176–77, 188–91, *190*; funding challenges facing, 175, 176–77, 189–91; initial objectives of, 175–76; inspiration by, 177–78; opposition to, 174; personal doubts about becoming, 172; personal staff of, 176; Purple Heart award reestablished by, 177–78, 314*n*17; relationship with West Point, 185–87, 191–93; Silver Star devised by, 178, 314*n*17

Army-Navy football game, 59, 151, 203, 210, 226, 249–50

Arnold, Benedict, 12, 306*n*9

Arnold, Henry "Hap," 233

Asian tour, MacArthur as aide to father on, 77–79

Association of Graduates (AOG), 66–67, 111–12, 250, 280–81, *282*, 284, 287

athletes, MacArthur's favoritism toward, 151, 160

athletics. *See* physical fitness and athletics

atomic bombs, 234–37

Australia: Douglas MacArthur Museum in, 296; MacArthur a hero in, 219–20, 221; MacArthur revered in, x–xii, 254; MacArthur's evacuation to, 1–2, 163, 218–19; as World War II base of operations, 215–16, 219–28

aviation course, at West Point, 152–53

bachelor's degrees, at West Point, 192

Badeau, Adam, 5

Baker, Newton, 88–89, 91, 117, 127

Baker, Scott, 185

Baltimore (Maryland), MacArthur assignment in, 166–70

Barbey, Daniel, 224

Bare, Walter E., 99–100

Barry, J. B. A., 49–50

baseball, 59–61, *60*, 66, 93

Bataan Death March, 187, 219, 245

"Bataan Gang," 206, 209, 214, 218, 224, 249

Bataan Peninsula: Bataan aircraft, *235*, 257; defense of, 214–15, 217–18, 220, 222, 232 (1942); MacArthur's survey of, 164–65, 171

Baum, James L., 159

"Beast Barracks," 20, 36, 40–41, 156

Beauregard, P. G. T., 121

Beazley, Kim, xii

Belcher, Aurelia, 22

Berry, Sydney, 108

Betros, Lance, 42, 112–13, 124, 139, 140

Biddle, John, 104

Bird, Stephen M., 145

"Black Book," 51

Blaik, Earl "Red": cheating scandal involving, 232, 275–77; as football coach, 123, 203–204, 225–26, 232, 249–50, 275–77; and future of West Point, 252; on MacArthur's superintendency, 123–24, 144–45, 147, 149, 150; relationship with MacArthur, 210, 225–26, 249–50, 275–77, *276*; retirement of, 277; on West Point during WWI, 112

Blake, Edmund M., 53, 69

Blamey, Sir Thomas, 224

Blanchard, Felix "Doc," 226, 277

Bliss, Tasker, 87

"Blue Book," 40, 51, 143

Board of Visitors, 16, 40, 125, 128

Bonneville, Benjamin, 16
Bonus March, 178–83, *179*
Booz, Oscar L., 20, 44–51
Borch, Fred, 177
Borman Report, 293, 334*n*59
Boswell, Walter O., 49–50
boxing contests, 50
Boyd, Carl, 185
Bradley, Omar, viii, 159–60, 249, 261, 274, 275, 298
Brady, James ("Diamond Jim Brady"), 56
Bragg, Braxton, 24–25
Brereton, Lewis, 212–14, 215
Bringing up the Brass (Maher), 55–56
Brooke, John R., 45–50
Brooks, Louise Cromwell, 138, 158–59. *See also* MacArthur, Louise Brooks
Brown, Edward Aloysius, 172–73
Brown, Robert A., 91, 97
Bulkeley, John, 218
Bunker, Paul, 1–2, 72, 74–75, 218–19
Bureau of Information, 88
Burgoyne, John, 12

cadet demerits, "bellyaches," 111, 155
Cadet Mess Hall, 158, *192*, 192–93, 298, 301
Carrithers, Truman W., 185
Carter, Clifton C., 126, 153
Carved from Granite (Betros), 124
Casey, Hugh "Pat," 206
Centennial Commemoration, 5, 66–68
Central Barracks, 39, 54, 66, *104*, 319*n*14
Chaffee, Adna R., Jr., 177
Chamberlain, Harry D., 169
Chase, William, 233
cheating scandals, 232, 275–77, 293
Chiang Kai-shek, 261
chief of staff, army. *See* army chief of staff

China: interests in Korea, 255–56; MacArthur's warning about, 274; military intervention in Korean War, 260–66
Churchill, Winston, vii, 216, 237
Citation Stars (Siver Star Medal), 102, 178
Civilian Conservation Corps, ix–x, 188–89
Civil War: service of Arthur MacArthur, Jr., in, 21–26; West Point and, 17–18
classmates. *See* West Point classmates
class rings, 298
class system, at West Point, 68, 105–108
Clay, Lucius, 204
Cleveland, Grover, 33, 59
Clinton, Henry, 11
Coast Artillery Corps, 74–75
Cocheu, George W.: career of, 164, 222, 278; hazing hearings testimony of, 46; support from and enduring relationship with, 164, 221–22, 233, 252–53, 278; as West Point classmate and roommate, 42, 46, 55, 64, 72, 221–22
Collins, J. Lawton, 264–65
Communists: Bonus March attributed to, 178–83; MacArthur's warnings about, 273–74
Company Sports, 151
Congress, MacArthur's address to, 267–70
Congressional Record, statements recorded, 287
Congreve, Charles, 10
Connor, Fox, 92
Connor, William D., 186, 193, 200, 201
Considine, Robert, 277, 286–87
Constitution, Japanese, 247–48
Cooke, George, 16

Cooper, Isabel Rosario "Dimples," 183–84
Cordier, Constant, 84, 86
Corps of Artillerists and Engineers, 13–14
Corps of Engineers: academy established under, 14; cadet preparation for, *173*; elite status of, 73; MacArthur's assignment to, 73–75; MacArthur's career slump in, 79–81; MacArthur's career turnaround in, 81–83; MacArthur's opportunity to lead, 172–73; MacArthur as young officer in Philippines, 72, 74, 75–76
Corps Squad Sports, 149–51
Corregidor (Philippines), 1–2, 72, 163, 215, 217–19
Costello, John, 211
Côte de Châtillon assault, in WWI, 98–100, 102
court martial, of Mitchell, 167–68
Crackel, Theodore, 125, 152, 159
Craig, Malin, 68–69
Cram, Goodhue, and Ferguson (architectural firm), 58, 118
Cray, Quinn, 185
Creasy, Sir Edward, 193
Crosby, Herbert B., 180–81
Cullum, George Washington, 73, 137
Cullum (Memorial) Hall, 39, 56–57, 158, 298
Cunningham, Frederick, 43–44
Curtin, John, xii, 219, 223

Danford, Robert M.: and discipline system, 111, 155–56; as commandant with MacArthur, 126–30, 143; and hazing reforms, 146–47; as member of Academic Board, 126, 128–30; and West Point military training, 155–57; and West Point visitors, 134–35

Darby, William O., 187
Davidson, Garrison, 188, 203, 282, 292–94, 326*n*29
Davis, Glenn, 226
Davis, Jefferson, 16
Delafield, Richard, 292
Dern, George H., 186, *190*, 191, 195, 196
Devall, James W., 49–50
Devers, Jacob L., 103, 146, 154, 187, 225
Dick, Charles, 46–47
discipline process, at West Point, 111, 155–56, 281
dismissal, by Truman, viii, 266–71, *268*; congressional address after, 267–70; life after, 273–90; personal staff after, 275; popularity and national tour after, 273–74; Senate hearings after, 274
disobeying orders, MacArthur on, 93
Distinguished Service medal, *101*, 102
Doak, Sloan, 169
Dockery, Albert B., 49–51
DOG (Disgruntled Old Graduate), 112, 144, 156–57
Donitz, Karl, 239
Doolittle, James R., 21
Doubleday, Abner, 58
double envelopment, 100
draft, for World War I, 88–89
Driggs, Edmund, 47, 50–51
drill instructors, 40–41, 69
"Dude, The," 93
"Dugout Doug," viii, 217
"Duty, Honor, Country" motto, 6, 19–20, 162, 271–72, 281, 288
"Duty, Honor, Country" speech, 3, 7–8, 19–20, 283–89, 297, *302*, 302–303

eagling, 43–44, 48
Echols, Charles P., 126
Economic Rehabilitation of Occupied Areas, 248–49

Index

Edgerton, Wright P., 63–64
Edward (Prince of Wales), *133*, 133–34
Egner, Philip, 187–88
Eichelberger, Robert, 203–204, 225, 231, 249
Eisenhower, Dwight D. "Ike": as army chief of staff, 243–44; Bonus March incident and, 179, 181–82; Connor as mentor to, 92; frustration with MacArthur, 199–200; German surrender accepted by, 239; "Germany First" strategy of, 216; health and death of, 290; indictment of emperor urged by, 243–44; MacArthur as chief of staff and, 176; MacArthur's efficiency report on, 205; Marshall as mentor to, 205; memorialized at West Point, 134, 297, 298; Ord's death and, 202; peacetime reduction in rank, 116; Philippine service of, 196–97, *197*, 199–200, 202, 204–206; praise for CCC, 189; promotion to General of the Army (five stars), 233; promotion to lieutenant colonel, 199; rift with MacArthur, 204–206; as Supreme Commander Allied Forces in Europe, 205; Thayer Award recipient, 281; West Point classmates of, 249
Eisenhower, John S. D., 205
Eisenhower, Mamie, 202
Eliot, Charles W., 113–14, 152
Ellis, James, 284
Engineer School (Washington, DC), 79–80

Faircloth, Jean, 194–95, 201. *See also* MacArthur, Jean Faircloth
Far East Command: Korean War, 254–72; MacArthur as military governor of Japan, 241–53

Farrell, Thomas, 234–35
Fellers, Bonner, 200–201, 222, 247
Fenton, Chauncey L., 250–52
Fiebeger, Gustav J., 37, 63, 81, 125, 126, 130, *153*
Fifteen Decisive Battles of the World (Creasy), 193
First Captain(s) at West Point, 5–6, 61, 68–72, 94, 95, 283
First Division, at West Point, 54
Flagler, Clement A., 82, 101–102
"Flirtation Walk," 56, 158
Foch, Ferdinand, 135, *136*
Follansbee, Bess B., 56
football team: Army–Navy football game, 59, 151, 203, 210, 226, 249–50; Blaik as coach of, 123, 203–204, 225–26, 249–50; cheating scandal involving, 232, 275–77; "Game of the Century," 226; MacArthur as fan of, 59, 61, 188, 202–203, 210, 225–26, 249–50; MacArthur as manager of, 57, 61, 71; MacArthur's superintendency and, 144, 151, 158, 160; MacArthur's support as army chief of staff, 188; practice during MacArthur's final visit, 287; World War II and, 210, 225–26
Force, Juliana, 193
Ford, John, 58
Fort Leavenworth, 27–29, 79, 81–83
Fort Mason, 74
42nd Rainbow Division. *See* Rainbow Division, in WWI
Foulois, Benjamin, 2
Founders Day remarks, 251–53
France, and West Point, 134–35, *136*
freedom of cadets, 140–44, 159, 160
French, Walter E., 160
Funston, Frederick, 84, 86

"Gaijin Shogun," 246
Gallagher, Walter V., 185
"Game of the Century," 226
Ganoe, William, *106*; rank of, 317*n*12; at West Point during WWI, 105–107; at West Point under MacArthur, 118–23, 125–27, 132–34, 151, 154
General Douglas MacArthur Leadership Award, 296
Germany, in World War II: aggression and invasions by, 205, 206–209; Eisenhower as leader of forces against, 205
"Germany First" strategy, 216
Gerow, Leonard, 212
Gettysburg Battlefield, cadet visit to, *70*
Glassford, Pelham D., 179–81
Goethals, George Washington, 73, 82
Goodpaster, Andrew, 292–94
governance, West Point, 124–30
graduation from West Point: forty-fifth anniversary of MacArthur's class, 252–53; MacArthur as speaker at (1933), 185–87; MacArthur's (class of 1903), 70–72, *71*; wartime classes and, 69, 103, 105–108, 225
graduation furlough, 74–75
Granger, Gordon, 23
Grant, Frederick Dent, 36
Grant, Ida Honoré, 36
Grant, Ulysses S., 5, 17–18, 22–25, 197, 289
Grant, Ulysses S., III: Bonus March incident and, 179, 180; in Corps of Engineers, 72; as West Point classmate, 36, 43, 46, 65, 70
Great Depression: Bonus March incident during, 178–83, *179*; Civilian Conservation Corps during, ix–x, 188–89; funding challenges during, 175, 177, 189–91; West Point mural painted during, *192*, 192–93
Groves, Leslie, *282*, 284, 285
Guild, George R., 185

Hagood, Johnson, 171
Hains, Peter C., 169
Hamilton, Alexander, 13
Hancock, Walker, 300–301
Harbord, James G., 91–92
Harding, Edwin Forest, 224, 226
Harding, Warren G., 135
Hardy, Mary Pickney, 27. *See also* MacArthur, Mary Pickney "Pinky"
Hardy, Thomas, 27
Harriman, Averell, 261
Harris, Charles Dashiell, 106
Harris, Peter C., 105–106
Hart, Thomas C., 209–10, 215
hazing: "Beast Barracks" and, 20, 36, 40–41, 156; code of silence and, 44, 48–49; culture of, 18; death blamed on, 19–20, 44–51; definition of, 145; investigations and hearings, 20, 44–52; MacArthur's cadet experiences with, 5–6, 18, 20, 36–37, 40–51, 145; MacArthur's collapse during, 43–44, 49; MacArthur's naming of tormentors, 48–50; MacArthur's opinion of, 52; MacArthur's superintendency and, 136, 139, 144–47, 156, 159–60; MacArthur's testimony about, 20, 44, 46–50; suicide attributed to, 145; Summer Encampment and, 40–44; supporters of, 18, 42–43; targets of, 18, 41–42; World War I disruptions and, 112
Hein, Otto L., 39, 44, 46, 51
Herman, Arthur, 62, 102, 162, 168, 178, 242

Index

Hindenburg Line, 98
Hine, Frank, 166
Hines, Charles, 126
Hirohito (emperor of Japan), 238–39, 243–44, *244*, 246, 247–48
Holt, Lucius H., 110, 126, 128, 152
Homma, Masaharu, 214, 218, 244–45
Honors Plaza, 298
honor system, 136, 146–47, 275–77, 333*n*9
Hooker, Joseph, 17–18, 24
Hoover, Herbert, 174, 177–83
hospital, at West Point, 114, 158
Howze, Robert Lee, 168
Hudson, Henry, 9–10
Huff, Sydney, 218, 249, 267
Hurley, Patrick, 174, 178, 180–82
Hyde, Arthur, 53–54, 61–62, 65, 221

Ickes, Harold, 188
Inchon (Korea) landing, 258–60, *260*
Influence of Sea Power upon History 1660–1783, The (Mahan), 78
influenza epidemic (1918), 114
intramural sports, 150–51
Irvine, Charles, 59
Irving, Frederick A., 230–32, 275

Jackson, Andrew, US president, 16
James, D. Clayton, 3, 55, 64, 125, 193, 203, 242, 262, 271
Japan: atomic bombs dropped on, 234–37; fall of Philippines to, 211–19; invasion plans for, 234; liberation of Philippines from, 163, 222, 228–34; MacArthur revered in, x–xi, 254; MacArthur's arrival in, 237, *238*; MacArthur's final visit to, 279; MacArthur's visit in 1905, 77–79; occupation of French Indochina, 208–209; Pearl Harbor attack, 210–11; Philippine attack (December 1941), 210–14; Philippine defense preparations and, 171–72, 195–96, 198, 204, 207–10, *207*; Plan Orange for, 165, 171, 198, 207, 209, 215; postwar (*see* Japan, MacArthur as military governor of); surrender of, 236–41, *242*, 298; US trade restrictions against, 209. *See also specific World War II operations*
Japan, MacArthur as military governor of, 79, 241–53; connections with West Point, 249–53; Constitution overseen by, 247–48; crowning achievement of, 247; economic aid and rebuilding of, 248–49; Emperor Hirohito spared by, 243–44, *244*; family life of, 249; as greatest professional accomplishment, 241–42; Lincoln as model for, 239; offices and residence of, 246; personal staff of, 246, 249
Jefferson, Thomas, 13–14, 280
Johnson, Harold K., 187
Johnson, Hugh S., 89, 95–96
Johnson, Lyndon B., 290, *290*
Johnson, Nelson T., 219
Johnson, Thomas Lofton, 192–93
Jomini, Antoine Henri, 18
Judson, William, 80–81

Kelly, Colin P., Jr., 214
Kennedy, John F., 280
Kenney, George, 221, 224
Kesselschlact, 100
Kim Il-Sung, 256
King, Ernest, 222, 228–29
Kinkaid, Thomas C., 224
Knoxville (Tennessee), MacArthur honored in, 222

Koehler, Herman J., 37, 58, 126, 148–49; *Theory and Practice of Athletics at the Military Academy*, 149
Korean War, 254–72; historical context for, 254–56; Inchon landing and victory in, 258–60, *260*; MacArthur as UN commander-in-chief in, 257, *258*; MacArthur's conflict with Truman over, viii, 254, 263–74; as MacArthur's downfall, 254, 255; MacArthur's reception upon return to US, 267–70, 273–74; MacArthur's relief during, viii, 266–71, *268*; MacArthur's request to be relieved in, 263; 38th parallel in, 256–57, 259–60, 265; UN invasion of north, 259–62; Wake Island conference during, 260–62
Kosciusko, Tadeusz, 11
Kriemhilde Stellung, 98–100
Krueger, Walter, 228, 233
Kuhn, Joseph E., 82

LaFollette, Robert M., Jr., 221
LaGuardia, Fiorella, 168
Laitman, M. A., 287
Lampert, James, 292
Laurson, Emil "Dotty," 56, 72, 185
Lawrence, Ernest, 281
Lawrie, Lee, 120
leadership award, named for MacArthur, 296
Leahy, William D., 184, 228–29
Leary, Herbert, 224
Lee, Robert E., 16, 62, 66, 121
Lenni Lenape, 9–10
Leopold (prince of Belgium), 133
letterman, MacArthur as, 57, 59, 61
letterman's robe: pride in and cherishing of, 61, 196, 250, 281; supply of, 250, 281; worn at death, 290, *290*; worn during Inchon landing, 259
letterman's sweater, worn in WWI, 93, 196
Leyte Island (Philippines): iconic image of MacArthur on, 230, *232*; strategy for, 228–30, *229*; US invasion of, 230–33
Lim, Vicente, 198–99
Lincoln, Abraham, 21–22, 23, 239
Lindbergh, Charles, 273
Long, Huey, 183
Long Gray Line, 7, 23, 58, 162–63, 185, 277, 286–87, 291
Long Gray Line, The (film), 58
Longstreet, James, 17–18
Losey, Robert M. (first American soldier killed in World War II), 327*n*9
Ludendorff offensives (World War I), 94, 97
Luzon (Philippines), US retaking of, 233–34

MacArthur (Ganoe), 127
MacArthur, Arthur, III, 8, 27–30, *28*
MacArthur, Arthur, III, (brother) 8, 27–30, *28*, 137, 138, 165
MacArthur, Arthur, IV, (son) 246, 249, 279
MacArthur, Arthur, Jr. (father): as "boy colonel," 23; Civil War service of, xiii, 8, 21–26; commander of Department of Pacific, 74, 77–79; death of, 83; Douglas as aide during Asian tour by, 77–79; family background of, 22; and family military tradition, 8, 35; family's residency in Milwaukee, 31, 33–35; feud with Robert Taft, 32, 80; marriage and children of, 27, *28*;

Medal of Honor awarded to, xiii, 8, 29–30, 68, 219–20; military career of, 21–32 (*see also specific assignments*); Mitchell family and, 34, 167; Philippine service of, 31–32, 47, 75; post-Civil War service of, 26–32; promotions and rank attained by, 22, 80; retirement of, 80; return from Philippines, 70; son's oath administered by, 72; West Point appointment sought for, 21–22; West Point superintendents and, 121–22

MacArthur, Arthur, Sr. (grandfather), 21–22, 30

MacArthur, Douglas: academic examinations, 63–64; aging and health of, 279–80, 283, 289–90; appointment to West Point, 32–35; as army chief of staff and West Point, 185–87, 191–93; Asian tour as aide to General MacArthur (father), 77–79; author's changing view of, vii–xiii; birth of, 27; burial site of, 279, 292; cadet record of, 5–6, 46, 61–66, 95; childhood of, 27–29; congressional address after dismissal by Truman, 267–70; corps of engineers assignment, 73–75; criticism of, vii–viii, x, xiii, 94; death of, 290; death of brother, 165; death of father, 83; death of mother, 195; defying authority, 266–72; demerits, 62, 65, 111, 155, 281; destined for greatness, xii–xiii; dismissal by Truman, viii, 266–71, *268*; divorce of, 170; as enigma, 2; family background of, 22, 27, *28*; first wife of, 138, 158–59, 166–68, 170; funeral of, 289, *291*, 291–92; later life, 273–90; memorials to, ix, *xi*, 199, 289, 295–303, *299–302*; libel lawsuit, against Pearson, 183–84; national popularity after dismissal, 273–74; post-dismissal life of, 273–89; reciprocal influence between West Point and, 2–8; retirement from army, 201–202; reverence of foreign nations toward, x–xii, 254; second wife of, 194–95, 201 (*see also* MacArthur, Jean Faircloth); Senate hearings 1951, 274; showmanship of, 93; as young man (circa 1905), *28*. *See also specific topics*

MacArthur, Jean Faircloth (second wife): academy robes ordered by, 250; burial site of, 279, 297; death of, 297; early relationship with MacArthur, 194–95, 201; final West Point visit with husband, 281, 283, 284, 285, 287; on football team scandal, 276; on husband's devotion to West Point, 279; life in Japan, 246, 249; love and support from, 201; newlywed visit to West Point, 201; news of MacArthur's dismissal reaching, 267; pen from surrender given to, 241; post-dismissal tour and, 273; presence at ceremonies honoring husband, 297, 301, 302; wedding of, 201; in World War II, *235*

MacArthur, Louise Brooks (first wife): conflict with mother-in-law, 168; courtship and marriage of, 138, 158–59; dissatisfaction with Philippines, 165, 166; divorce of, 170; marital relationship of, 166–68; Mitchell's trial attended by, 168; Pershing's relationship with, 158, 161–62

MacArthur, Malcolm, 27

MacArthur, Mary Hendry McCalla (wife of brother Arthur), *28*, 168

MacArthur, Mary Pickney "Pinky" (mother): conflict with daughter-in-law, 168; death of, 195; husband's military career and, 27–32; illness of, 165, 194–95; journey for funeral of, 200–201; marriage and children of, 27, *28*; "mother for son" letters of, 95–97, 165; muffler knitted by, 93; Norfolk connections of, 296; preparation of son for West Point, 34; residency in Milwaukee, 31, 33–35; son's cadet years and, 36, 52–55, 57, 70; son's military career and, 95–97, 135, 137–38, 165, 167, 175, 194–95; Southern background of, 27

MacArthur Barracks, ix, 118, 199, 297, 300–303, *301–302*

MacArthur Corridor, in Pentagon, 295, 297

MacArthur Day (1942), 221

MacArthur Memorial (Norfolk), 279, 295–97, 300–301

MacArthur Memorial Archives, Norfolk, Virginia, 287

MacArthur Plaza (West Point), 300–302

MacArthur Week Conference, x–xii

MacPherson, James B., 73

Mahan, Alfred Thayer, 78

Mahan, Dennis Hart, 78

Maher, Marty, 55–56, 58, 149

"makes" (room assignment), 53–54

malaria, 76–77

Malinta Tunnel, 215, 217

Manchester, William, vii, 59, 94, 137–38, 172

Manila (Philippines): declared open city December 1941, 215; US retaking of, 233–34

Mann, Bill, 285

Mann, William A., 89–90

Mao Zedong, 256, 260

March, Peyton, 35, 116–17, 139–41, 161

Marquat, William F., 206, 249

Marshall, George C.: as army chief of staff, 205, 207–208; Connor as mentor to, 92; Eisenhower as protégé of, 205; evacuation recommended by, 218; MacArthur recalled to active duty by, 209; Medal of Honor recommended by, 220; Philippines support from, 216; promotion to General of the Army (five stars), 233; Senate testimony (1951) of, 274; in triumvirate of generals, 205; West Point painting of, 298; in World War I, 100, 315*n*46

Marshall, Richard, 206, 246

Marshall Plan, 248

Martelino, Pastor, 199

Martin, Joseph, 266

Mary Hardy MacArthur Memorial Park, 296

master of the sword, 37, 57–58, 148–49

Mayo, Richard, 169

McCarthy, Terrance C., 281–83, 287

McClellan, George, 17–18, 73

McKinley, William, 33

Medal of Honor: to Albert Mills, 37, 67; to Arthur MacArthur (father), xiii, 8, 29–30, 68, 219–20; and Centennial Commemoration attendees, 66–68; denied to MacArthur (1914), 86–87, 102; to Douglas MacArthur (1942), 68, 219–20, 240, 300, *301*, 308*n*41; to Jonathan Wainwright, 220, 240; and second denial of (1919), 101–102; to Veracruz participants, 84; during World War II, 214, 218, 219–20, 240

memorials to MacArthur, ix, *xi*, 199, 289, 295–303, *299–302*
Menoher, Charles, 90, 94, 95, 97, 100–102
Merritt, Wesley, 31, 58, 121–22
Mexican–American War, 17–18
Mexico, Veracruz expedition in, *83–87*, *85*, 102
Michie, Peter Smith, 37, 42–43
Michie Stadium, 158
Miles, Nelson A., 45, 66–68
Miles, Perry, 179, 181
military governor of Japan. *See* Japan, MacArthur as military governor of
Military Power of the United States, The (Upton), 78
Mills, Albert, 37–40, 44–52, 55, 67, 70–72, 149, 292
Milwaukee (Wisconsin): MacArthur family in, 31, 33–35, 70; MacArthur's service in, 80–81; MacArthur statue in, *xi*, 289; MacArthur Week Conference in, x–xii
mission statement, of West Point, 130–32
Mitchell, John L., 34, 167
Mitchell, William "Billy," 34, 167–68, 308*n*41
monastery, West Point as, 6, 140–42
Moore, George F., 218
Moore, John, 10
Morin, John M., 128
Moseley, George Van Horn, 176
mural, in cadet mess hall, *192*, 192–93, 301
Murphy, Grayson, 90

National Collegiate Athletic Association (NCAA), 151, 154
National Defense Acts, 88–89, 103–104
National Guard: commissions granted in, 103–104; MacArthur's organizational plan for, 89–90; modern, establishment of, 88–89; Rainbow Division, in WWI, 89–102, *93*
New Guinea campaign, 223–28, *234*
New York City: parade in, 273; post-dismissal life in, 274–75, 279, *288*, 289
Nimitz, Chester, 164–65, 222, 228–29, *230*, 240–41
"Ninety-eighters," 92
Nininger, Alexander "Sandy," Jr., 214
Norfolk (Virginia): burial in, 279, 292; connection of MacArthur's mother to, 296; funeral procession in, *291*, 292; MacArthur Memorial in, 279, 295–97, 300–301
Nuremberg Tribunal, 246
Nye, Roger H., 127, 159

Olympic Games (1928), 168–70
Operation Cartwheel, 228, *229*
Operation Chromite, 258–59
Operation Downfall (invasion plan of Japan), 234
Ord, James B., 196–97, 199, 202
Ord, James G., 197
"Orioles," post war cadets (1919), 109–10
Osmeña, Sergio, 77, 165, 232
Otjen, John P., 289, 292
Otjen, Theobald, 34, 289

Pace, Frank, 267
Pace, John, 182
painting of West Point, *17*
paintings at West Point, *192*, 192–93, 298, 301
Palmer, David R., 302
Panama Canal, 73, 82–83
Parker, George, 215

Parker, Samuel M., 185
Parson, Samuel, 11
Parsons, Edwin B., 25, 26
Partridge, Alden, 15
Patterson, Charles H., 170–71
Patton, George S.: Bonus March incident and, 179, 181–82; Connor as mentor to, 92; MacArthur meeting (WWI), 97–98; peacetime reduction in rank, 116; Walker's service under, 257; West Point classmates of, 197, 224, 225; West Point record of, 98
Payne, Frederick, 176
Pearl Harbor, attack on, 210–11
Pearson, Drew, 183–84
Pentagon, MacArthur Corridor in, 295, 297
Percival, Arthur E. (British general), 240–41
Perrett, Geoffrey, 33, 175, 178, 259
Pershing, John J.: amalgamation opposed by, 94; as chief of staff, 165–66; evaluation of MacArthur, 162; First Captain bond with, 94, 95; hazing supported by, 43; MacArthur awarded Distinguished Service Medal by, *101*, 102; MacArthur reassigned from superintendency by, 161–62; MacArthur's feud with, 90, 91–92, 94–95, 174; MacArthur's Medal of Honor denied by, 101–102; MacArthur's promotion by, 95, 97; mandatory retirement of, 166; "mother for son" letters to, 95–97, 165; operations and offensives in World War I, 97–100; Pétain's West Point visit with, 141; as rival suitor for MacArthur's wife, 158, 161–62; West Point classmates and associates of, 47, 82, 116; West Point mural dedicated by, 193

Pétain, Henri-Phillipe, 141
Petillo, Carol Morris, 184
Philippine-American War (1899–1902), 31–32
Philippine Military Academy, 198–99
Philippines: cities named after MacArthur in, 295; commonwealth and independence of, 194–95; dissatisfaction of MacArthur's first wife with, 165, 166; insurrection against US (1899–1902), 31–32, 75; MacArthur considered as a home, 7, 31, 164, 279; MacArthur revered in, x–xi, 254; MacArthur's final trip to, 279; return to, as Call to Duty, 163; service of Arthur MacArthur, Jr., in, 31–32, 47, 75, 121–22; Spanish-American War and, 31
Philippines, MacArthur assignment in (1903–1904), 72, 74, 75–77; first combat experience, 76–77; illness (malaria), 76, 77
Philippines, MacArthur assignment in (1922–1925), 163–66; Bataan survey during, 164–65, 171; as commander of Manila District, 164; reassignment to after superintendency, 158–59, 161–62; promotion during, 166; relationships strengthened during, 165; West Point classmates and, 164–65
Philippines, MacArthur assignment in (1928–1930), 163, 170–72; as commander of Military Department, 170; defense preparations during, 171–72; lifestyle during, 170–71
Philippines, MacArthur as military advisor in (1935–1941), 163, 194–209; "Bataan Gang" and, 206, 209; defense preparations of, 195–96, 198, 207–10, *208*; Eisenhower's rift

with, 204–206; Eisenhower's service with, 196–97, *197*, 199–200, 204–206; lifestyle of, 196; military academy established by, 198–99; personal staff of, 196–98, 206; promotion in Filipino army (field marshal), 196, 200; reassignment from *vs.* retirement, 201–202; recall to active duty (1941), 209; salary and compensation for, 196, 200, US army general, 195–202, 209–10, Filipino field marshal, 202–209

Philippines, in World War II, 204–19; Bunker's capture and death in, 1–2, 72, 75, 218–19; Corregidor as last stronghold in, 215, 217–19; failures in defense of, 211–15; fall of, 211–19; FDR's vow to support, 216; first Japanese attack on (December 8, 1941), 210–14; "Germany First" strategy *vs.*, 216; "I have returned," 230, 232; "I shall return," 163, 219, 222; liberation campaign of, 163, 222, 228–34; MacArthur awarded Medal of Honor for leadership in, 68, 219–20, 240, 300, *301*; MacArthur haunted by surrender of, 219; MacArthur command of, 209–10; MacArthur's evacuation from, 1–2, 163, 218–19; MacArthur's pledge to liberate, 219, 222, 230, *232*; MacArthur's tactical failure, 214–15; MacArthur's relationship with troops in, *231*, 233–34; reinforcements expected for, 215–16; strategy for retaking, 228–30, *230*; war crimes tribunals in, 244–45

Philippine Scouts, 198, 209

physical fitness and athletics: athletics at West Point, 58–59; Koehler and, 58, 148–49; MacArthur as cadet and, 57–61; MacArthur as Olympic Committee president, 168–70; MacArthur as superintendent and, 115–16, 147–51, 168–69; MacArthur's dedication to, 57, 148, 169; MacArthur's as letterman, 57, 59, 61; MacArthur's support of West Point sports, 59, 61, 188, 202–203, 210, 225–26, 249–50, 289; plaque honoring MacArthur's contributions to, 300, *300*; World War II and, 225–26

Pickett, George, 17–18

Plan Orange, 165, 171, 198, 207, 209, 215

Plattsburg Movement, 104

Potsdam Conference, 237–39

Proctor, Redfield, 33

promotions: on basis of seniority, 73–74; General of the Army (WWII), 233

promotions, MacArthur's: to brigadier general, 95–97; to colonel, 90; in Filipino army (field marshal), 196, 200; to first lieutenant, 77; to General of the Army (five stars), 233; to lieutenant general, 209; to major, 88; to major general, 166; mother's entreaties for, 95–97, 165; peacetime retention of, 115–17; rapid advance *vs.* classmates' progress, 164–65

protocol, at West Point, 132–37

public affairs officer, MacArthur as, 88–90, 128

Puller, Lewis "Chesty," *258*

Purple Heart awards, 92, 102, 177–78, 314n17

Pusan Perimeter, 258–60

Quekemeyer, John G. "Quek" or "Harry," 158–59, 321n76

Quezon, Manuel L., 77, 165, 194, 196, 198–200, 204

Rainbow Division (42nd Division): continuing honors for MacArthur, 301; postwar inactivation of, 116; Reilly's history of, 99; role in MacArthur's wedding, 159; in WWI, 89–102, *93*
Read, George, 165
Reagan, Ronald, 277, 297
Rees, Thomas H., 82
Reilly, Henry, 99
Reminiscences (MacArthur memoirs), 289–90; on appointment as superintendent, 117; on arrival in Philippines (1922), 163; on death of mother, 195; on divorce, 170; ending of, 289; on family background, 22; on Flirtation Walk, 56; on hazing testimony, 48–49; incidents not addressed in, 81; on return to Philippines (1928), 170; on youth, 27
retirement, MacArthur's, 201–202
Reynolds, Frederick P., 126
Rhee, Syngman, 256
Richardson, Robert C., 164–65
Ridgway, Matthew, 264–65, 267, 271
riding crop, 93, *96*
Riedel, Mary P., 284
Roberts, William L., 256
Robinson, Wirt, 108, 126
Rodney, Dorsey, 278
Roosevelt, Franklin D.: Corregidor evacuation ordered by, 1, 163, 218; election of (1932), 183, 188; "Germany First" strategy of, 216; gratitude for MacArthur's service, 202; MacArthur as army chief of staff and, 176–77, 188–91, *190*; on MacArthur as dangerous man, 183; MacArthur as military advisor to Philippines and, 194–96; Medal of Honor awarded by, 219–20; plans to reduce officer corps, ix–x; promise to defend Filipino people, 216; strategy for Philippines approved by, 228–30, *230*; trade restrictions against Japan, 209; West Point changes by, 225
Roosevelt, Theodore, 67–68, 74, 79–80, *80*
Roosevelt, Theodore, Jr., 68
Root, Elihu, 45, 52, 66, 72
royal visitors, to West Point, 132–34, *133*

St. Mihiel operation, in WWI, 97–98
Schofield, John, 66–68, 121
"School of the Soldier," 40, 155
Scott, Hugh, 81, 86–87, 88
Scott, Winfield, 17
Selective Service Act of 1917, 89
Selfridge, Thomas E., 72, 153, 185–86
Senate hearings, after MacArthur's dismissal, 274
Sesquicentennial, of West Point (1952), 250–53
Severson, Charles, 55
Shakespeare, William, xii
Shannon, James A., 50, 72, 185, 310*n*50
Sheridan, Phillip, viii, 18, 23, 42
Sheridan, Phillip H., Jr., 42
Sherman, William T., viii, 18, 23–25
Shigemitsu, Mamoru, 241
silence, code of, 44, 48–49
Silver Star Medal, 178, 314*n*17
Simpson, William H., 225
"skin sheet," list of demerits, 111, 155
Sladen, Fred, 160–62, 166
Southwest Pacific Area (SWPA), 222–23
Soviet Union: declaration of war against Japan, 238; involvement in Korean War, 255–56, 260, 263; as post-WWII threat, 246, 248, 274
Spanish-American War, 31, 37, 39, 67

Spanish flu, 114
sports. *See* physical fitness and athletics
spread eagle, 43–44, 48
Stalin, Joseph, 256
status quo antebellum, 255
Stennis, John, 287
"Stick, The," 93
Stotesbury, Edward T., 166
Stratemeyer, George, 249
Strong, George V., 126
Summerall, Charles P.: as army chief of staff, 91, 173–74, 175; and Côte de Châtillon operation, 99; as First Captain at West Point, 68–69; and MacArthur's chief of staff appointment, 173–74; and MacArthur's Olympic leadership, 169–70; and Medal of Honor nomination, 101; transfer from Rainbow Division, 91
Summer Encampment, 40–44, 115, 136, 155–60, *156*
superintendents of West Point: Beauregard, 121; Biddle, 104; Connor, 186, 193, 200, 201; Davidson, 188, 282, 292–94; Delafield, 292; Eichelberger, 203–204, 225, 231; Goodpaster, 292–94; in invasion of Leyte, 231–32; Irving, 232, 275; legacies of, 292–94; MacArthur, 115–62 (*see also* West Point, MacArthur as superintendent of); Merritt, 121–22; Mills, 37–40, 44–52, 149, 292; portraits of, 121; quarters of, 118, 137–38; Schofield, 121; Sladen, 160–62; Thayer, ix, 15–16 (*see also* Thayer, Sylvanus); Tillman, 104–110, 119, 123–25, 148; Townsley, 104, 148; Wilby, 221
Supreme Commander Allied Powers (SCAP) in Japan, 236, 240–41, 246, 247, 267, 298

surrender of Japan, 236–41; ceremony, MacArthur as presiding officer for, 239–41, *242*; signing of, 241, *242*, 298; unconditional, demand for, 237–39
Sutherland, Richard K., 202, 204–206, 212, 218, 246
Syjuco, Jose G., 198
Sylvanus Thayer Award, 3, 280–89, *282*, 298, 302

tactical officers (TACs), at West Point, 110–11, 155–56
Taft, Howard W., 32, 80
Taylor, Maxwell D., 144, 147, 252–53, 275
Telford, Charles, 70–72, 74
Thayer, Sylvanus, ix, 15–16; Academic Board established by, 124; award named for, 3, 280–89, *282*, 298, 302; buildings planned/built during superintendency of, 36, 39, 137; class system established by, 68, 107; commandant under, 39; in Corps of Engineers, 73; European studies of, 134; Father of the Academy, ix, 16, 162, 281; influence and legacy of, 191; MacArthur compared with, ix, 114, 137, 139, 162; memorialized at West Point, 297; tactical officers under, 110–11
Thayer Hotel, 158
38th parallel, in Korea, 256–57, 259–60, 265
Thomas, George H., 17–18, 23–24, 26
Tillman, Samuel, 37, 104–10, 119, 123–25, 148
Titus, Calvin, 67–68
Tojo, Hideki, 245
Totten, Denis B., 159
Townsley, Clarence P., 104, 148

Traditions and Customs of the Corps (pamphlet), 147
Treat, Charles G., 39, 86–87
Treaty of Versailles, 100
Truman, Harry: Blaik's appeal to, 275; conflict with MacArthur, 254, 263–74; Korean War polices of, 259–67; MacArthur's denunciation of, 273–74; military restrictions imposed by, 263, 265; political concerns of, 261; removal of MacArthur, viii, 266–71, *268*; response to Soviet threat, 248; Wake Island conference with MacArthur, 260–62
Tydings-McDuffie Act of 1934, 194, 199

uniforms, at West Point, 15, 108–109
United Nations, and Korean War, 257
United States Army Forces in the Far East (USAFFE), 1941–1946, 209–36; Australia as base of operations, 215–16, 219–28; available forces in 1941, 209–10; "Bataan Gang" and, 206, 209, 218, 224; fall of Philippines, 211–19; first Japanese attacks on (December 1941), 210–14; liberation of Philippines, 228–34; MacArthur's promotion to command of, 209; New Guinea campaign, 223–28, *234*; Operation Cartwheel, 228, *229*
US Military Academy. *See* West Point
Upton, Emory, 78
USAFFE. *See* United States Army Forces in the Far East

Veracruz (Mexico) expedition, 83–87, *85*, 102
Veterans of Foreign Wars, MacArthur's letter to, 261
Vietnam War, 280, 283

Wainwright, Jonathan "Skinny," *208*, 215, 218, 220, 240–41
Wake Island conference, 260–62
Waldorf Astoria Hotel: MacArthur's residency in, 274–75; West Point visitors to, 279, *288*, 289
Walker, Sam Sims, 264
Walker, Walton Harris, 249, 257–59, 262, 264
war crime tribunals, 243–46, 247
War Department, MacArthur's assignment to (1913), 83
War Emergency Acts, 105
War of 1812, 15, 17
Washington, George, 11, 13, 177, 280
Washington (Cadet Mess) Hall, *192*, 192–93, 298, 301
Weinberger, Casper, 297
Weintraub, Stanley, 259
Weissmuller, Johnny, 169
Wells, Briant H., 90
Westmoreland, William C., 283–87, *284*
West Point (New York): American Revolution and, 10–12; colonial history of, 9–10; Indigenous people of, 9; post-Revolution fate of, 13–14
West Point (US Military Academy): admission process for, 16–17, 32–35, 109–10; building boom (1908–1913), 38–39, 118; cadet privileges at, 143, 160; cheating scandals at, 275–77, 293; Civil War and, 17–18; competition for new cadets, 110, 251–52; discipline at, 111, 155–56, 281; "Duty, Honor, Country" speech, 3, 7–8, 19–20, 283–89, 297, *302*, 302–303; early years of, 15–17; establishment of, 14–15; Filipino cadets at, 198–99; governance of, 124–30; graduates as officers, MacArthur's attitude toward, 5, 6,

206; hazing at (*see* hazing); higher standards for graduates of, 80; honor system of, 136, 146–47, 275–77, 333*n*9; Japanese surrender commemorated at, 241, 298; logo and motto of, 6, 19–20, 162, 271–72, 281, 288; MacArthur as army chief of staff and, 185–87, 191–93; MacArthur as graduation speaker at (1933), 185–87; MacArthur memorialized at, ix, 199, 295, 297–303, *299–302*; MacArthur's admission to, 32–35; in MacArthur's congressional address, 270; MacArthur's devotion to, viii–ix, xii, 3, 72, 193, 250–53, 279, 285; MacArthur's faithfulness to values of, 271–72; MacArthur's final visit to, *280*, 280–89, *282*, *284*; as MacArthur's home, ix, xii, 3, 7–8, 201, 279, 285; MacArthur's legacy at, ix, 2–3, 162, 292–94, 303; map of (1891), *41*; Mexican-American War and, 17–18; mission statement of, 130–32; as monastery, 6, 140–42; painting of, *17*; Patton's record at, 98; Pershing's record at, 54, 68–69; post-Civil War stagnation at, 18–19; post-World War II issues for, 250–53; size of Corps of Cadets, 131–32, 191; superintendents of (*see* superintendents of West Point); teaching offer for young MacArthur, 81; War of 1812 and, 15, 17; women admitted to, 293; World War I and, 103–14, 119; World War II and, 225–26; Yamashita's sword sent to, 245

West Point, MacArthur as cadet at, 3–7, *4*, 36–72, *38*; academic record of, 5–6, 46, 61–66, 95; baseball exploits of, 59–61, *60*, 66, 93; Centennial Commemoration and, 5, 66–68; collapse during extreme exercise, 43–44, 49; company assignment of, 53; competitiveness of, 65; descriptions of, 42, 54, 58, 69–70; father's fame and, 41–42, 59–60; flirtations and romances of, 56–57; football team duties of, 57, 61, *71*; graduation of, 70–72, *71*; hazing of, 5–6, 18, 36–37, 40–51, 145; hazing testimony of, 20, 44, 46–50; leadership by (First Captain), 5–6, 61, 68–72, 94, 95; pranks of, 55–57; mother's residence at, 36, 52–55, 57; physical fitness and athletics of, 56–61; plebe-year room assignment of, 53–54; superintendent/faculty and, 37–40; visit to Gettysburg, 70

West Point, MacArthur as superintendent of, 3, 115–62; Academic Board conflict with, 115, 120, 124–30, 150; academics during, 115, 125–30, *129*, 151–54; accomplishments of, 139; as apogee of relationship with West Point, 162; Blaik on, 123–24, 144–45, 147, 149, 150; as "boy superintendent," 130, 151; cadet athletic pledge established by, 150; cadet reactions to reforms by, 157; cadet suicides during tenure, 159; charge to revitalize academy, 116–17, 139, 161; classroom visits by, 151–52; concern about appointment, 118–20; daily schedule of, 137–38; demeanor of, 120, 121, *122*, 144; departure of, 158–59, 161–62; distinguished visitors to, 132–37, *133*, *136*; Filipino cadets during tenure, 199; first day of, 118, 120–24; first decision of, 120–21; Ganoe's book about, 127; Ganoe's resignation

West Point (cont.)
refused by, 122–23; governance under, 124–30; hazing reforms of, 136, 144–47, 156, 159–60; honor system established by, 136, 146–47; as "King of the Hudson," 117; legacy of, 292–94; MacArthur's assessment of tenure, 162; mission statement of, 130–32; mother's presence and role, 135, 137–38; new campus plan of, 158; outside educational influences sought by, 153–54; philosophy of, 117; physical fitness and athletics under, 115–16, 147–51, 168–69; problems inherited by, 103–14; quarters of, 118, 137–38; rank retained because of appointment as, 115–17; reaction to appointment, 117; reforms undertaken by, 6, 115–16, 135–37, 139–62; relationship with cadets, 144; reversal of reforms made by, 154, 159–62; thematic approach to tenure, 139–40; training for modern war under, 155–59; as visionary, 135–37, 157–59; World War I experiences and, 147–48

West Point Alumni Foundation, 250

West Point classmates: assignments after graduation, 73–75; fate of, 70–72, 185–86; graduation (1903), 70–72, 71; MacArthur's lasting relationships with, 4–7, 164–65, 170–71, 176; post-career correspondence with, 277–78; reminiscences of, 6–7; reunion of, 252–53. *See also specific individuals*

West Point Hotel, 36, 52, 55, 56, 70, 158

West Point Museum, 13, 120, 241, 298

West Point Study Group, 293

West Texas Military Academy, 30, 33, 62

Whistler, George Washington, 16

Whitney, Courtney, 247, 289

Wilby, Francis B., 221

Williams, Ferdinand, 185–86

Willoughby, Charles A., 206, 218, 249

Wilson, Woodrow, 45, 83–84, 88–89

Winslow, E. Eveleth, 79–80, 81

Wisconsin 24th Voluntary Infantry Regiment, 22–26, 34, 83

women, admission to West Point, 293

Wood, Leonard, 83, 84

Wood, Robert E., 42, 44, 69–70, 83, 90

Wood, William H., 203

"wooden willies," 43, 48

World War I, 88–102; army organization in, 89–90; draft for, 88–89; MacArthur's combat patrols in, 92–94; MacArthur's image and showmanship in, 93, *96*; MacArthur's promotion in, 95–97; MacArthur's reputation and honors after, *101*, 101–102; MacArthur wounded (gassed) in, 92, 93, 99, 166, 177; peacetime army after, 116; West Point during, 103–14, 119; West Point records on, 166. *See also specific operations and events*

World War II, 204–36; Japanese surrender in, 236–41, *242*, 298; MacArthur as SWPA commander in, 222–23; MacArthur's greatest error in, 214–15; MacArthur's losses (casualties) during, 226–27, *227*; MacArthur's relationship with troops in, *231*, 233–34; Pacific operational areas in, 222–23; US entry into, 210–11; US strategic priorities: European *vs.* Pacific, 207, 216; West Point connections and, 221–22; West

Point during, 225–26. *See also specific commands, events, and locations*
Worth, William, 16, 39
wound chevrons, 92, 102, 166, 178
Wright, Orville, 72, 153, 186

Yamashita, Tomoyuki, 244–45
"Yearlings," 41

Zell, Edward M., 50, 60, 72, 185–86, 310*n*50, 311*n*25